The Politics of Furniture

In many different parts of the world modern furniture elements have served as material expressions of power in the post-war era. They were often meant to express an international and in some respects apolitical modern language, but when placed in a sensitive setting or a meaningful architectural context, they were highly capable of negotiating or manipulating ideological messages. The agency of modern furniture was often less overt than that of political slogans or statements, but as the chapters in this book reveal, it had the potential of becoming a persuasive and malleable ally in very diverse politically charged arenas, including embassies, governmental ministries, showrooms, exhibitions, design schools, libraries, museums and even prisons.

This collection of chapters examines the consolidating as well as the disrupting force of modern furniture in the global context between 1945 and the mid-1970s. The volume shows that key to understanding this phenomenon is the study of the national as well as transnational systems through which it was launched, promoted and received. While some chapters squarely focus on individual furniture elements as vehicles communicating political and social meaning, others consider the role of furniture within potent sites that demand careful negotiation, whether between governments, cultures, or buyer and seller. In doing so, the book explicitly engages different scholarly fields: design history, history of interior architecture, architectural history, cultural history, diplomatic and political history, postcolonial studies, tourism studies, material culture studies, furniture history, and heritage and preservation studies.

Taken together, the narratives and case studies compiled in this volume offer a better understanding of the political agency of post-war modern furniture in its original historical context. At the same time, they will enrich current debates on reuse, relocation or reproduction of some of these elements.

Fredie Floré is an engineer-architect and Associate Professor in history of (interior) architecture at KU Leuven, Faculty of Architecture. She is a member of the research group Architecture Interiority Inhabitation (A2I). Her research focuses on the representational role of architecture, interiors and design in the post-war era.

Cammie McAtee is an independent curator and architectural historian based in Montréal. For many years, she was a curator at the Canadian Centre for Architecture. Her research focuses on post-war North American architecture and design.

The Politics of Furniture
Identity, Diplomacy and Persuasion
in Post-war Interiors

Edited by Fredie Floré and
Cammie McAtee

LONDON AND NEW YORK

First published 2017
by Routledge
2 Park Square, Milton Park, Abingdon, Oxon OX14 4RN

and by Routledge
711 Third Avenue, New York, NY 10017

First issued in paperback 2018

Routledge is an imprint of the Taylor & Francis Group, an informa business

© 2017 selection and editorial matter, Fredie Floré and Cammie McAtee; individual chapters, the contributors

The right of Fredie Floré and Cammie McAtee to be identified as the authors of the editorial material, and of the authors for their individual chapters, has been asserted in accordance with sections 77 and 78 of the Copyright, Designs and Patents Act 1988.

All rights reserved. No part of this book may be reprinted or reproduced or utilised in any form or by any electronic, mechanical, or other means, now known or hereafter invented, including photocopying and recording, or in any information storage or retrieval system, without permission in writing from the publishers.

Trademark notice: Product or corporate names may be trademarks or registered trademarks, and are used only for identification and explanation without intent to infringe.

British Library Cataloguing-in-Publication Data
A catalogue record for this book is available from the British Library

Library of Congress Cataloging-in-Publication Data
Names: Floré, Fredie, editor. | McAtee, Cammie D. (Cammie Dale), 1966– editor.
Title: The politics of furniture : identity, diplomacy and persuasion in post-war interiors / edited by Fredie Floré and Cammie McAtee.
Description: New York : Routledge, 2017. | Includes bibliographical references and index.
Identifiers: LCCN 2016030486 | ISBN 9781472453556 (hardback : alk. paper) | ISBN 9781315554389 (ebook)
Subjects: LCSH: Furniture—History—20th century. | Furniture—Styles—Social aspects. | Politics and culture.
Classification: LCC NK2395 .P65 2017 | DDC 749.09/04—dc23
LC record available at https://lccn.loc.gov/2016030486

ISBN 13: 978-1-138-34215-6 (pbk)
ISBN 13: 978-1-4724-5355-6 (hbk)

Typeset in Sabon
by Apex CoVantage, LLC

Contents

List of illustrations	vii
List of contributors	xiii
Acknowledgments	xvi

Introduction: the politics of furniture	1
FREDIE FLORÉ AND CAMMIE McATEE	

Furniture and identity politics	13

1 Nomadic furniture in the "heart of darkness": colonial and postcolonial trajectories of modern design artifacts to and from tropical Africa	15
JOHAN LAGAE	

2 Modernism on vacation: the politics of hotel furniture in the Spanish Caribbean	33
ERICA N. MORAWSKI	

3 When modernity confronts tradition: conflicting visions for post-war furniture design in Québec	47
MARTIN RACINE	

4 The interiors of the Belgian Royal Library: an expression of national identity with an international imprimatur	62
FREDIE FLORÉ AND HANNES PIETERS	

Spaces of persuasion	81

5 Exhibitions for modern living: lifestyle propaganda and the promotion of modern furniture and furnishings in the United States, 1930s–1950s	83
MARGARET MAILE PETTY	

vi *Contents*

6 Knolling Paris: from the "new look" to *Knoll au Louvre*   98
CAMMIE McATEE AND FREDIE FLORÉ

7 Corrections fairs and Japanese furniture made in prison   119
YASUKO SUGA

The diplomacy of furniture   133

8 National identity and modern furniture in Brasília's
Itamaraty Palace   135
LUCIANA SABOIA, ELANE RIBEIRO PEIXOTO
AND JOSÉ AIRTON COSTA JUNIOR

9 All-over inside-out: Eero Saarinen's United States
Embassy in London   152
CAMMIE McATEE

10 Designed diplomacy: furniture, furnishing and art in
Australian embassies for Washington, DC, and Paris   179
PHILIP GOAD

Index   199

Illustrations

Figures

0.1 Knoll International advertisement in *Zodiac* 1 (1956). Herbert Matter, graphic designer. Courtesy of Knoll, Inc.   3

1.1 Cover of *Habiter en Belgique et au Congo* (October 1955). Unknown photographer. Collection of the author.   16

1.2 *L'heure de l'apéritif au poste agricole de la Romée, en 1902.* Unknown photographer. HP.1957.34.164, Collection Royal Museum for Central Africa, Tervuren, 1902.   18

1.3 Model house for "white colonizers" presented at Expo 58, Brussels. Fonds Noterman © Archives d'Architecture Moderne, Brussels.   21

1.4 Commercial Fair of Kisangani/Stanleyville, 1955. Unknown photographer. *La Maison* 9 (1955). Courtesy of the Faculty Library of Engineering and Architecture, Ghent University.   22

1.5 Belgian Congo Pavilion, Paris World's Fair, 1937. Unknown photographer. *L'Ossature Métallique* 5 (1938). Courtesy of the Faculty Library of Engineering and Architecture, Ghent University.   22

1.6 Air terminus building, Kinshasa, ca. 1956. Unknown photographer. © Archives Laurens Paris.   25

1.7 Proposal for the interior of a guesthouse for the tropics, late 1940s. Fonds Henri-Jean Calsat, Université de Genève. Courtesy of University of Geneva.   26

1.8 Hôtel Relais, Brazzaville, ca. 1952. Fonds Henri-Jean Calsat, Université de Genève. Courtesy of University of Geneva.   26

2.1 Typical Caribe Hilton guestroom, ca. 1949. Unknown photographer. Courtesy of the Hospitality Industry Archives, Conrad Hilton College, University of Houston.   37

2.2 Havana Riviera lobby, ca. 1957. Rudi Rada, photographer. Courtesy of HistoryMiami.   40

2.3 Cubans burn furniture and gambling equipment from the Plaza Casino in Havana, January 1, 1959. Fernando Lezcano, photographer. Courtesy of Lezcano/AP.   43

3.1 Art Deco dressing table. Denis Farley, photographer. Collection of the Montréal Museum of Fine Arts; purchase Horley and Annie Townsend bequest.   51

3.2 Coffee Table. Christine Guest, photographer. Collection of the Montréal Museum of Fine Arts. Gift of the Maurice Corbeil Estate.   52

viii *Illustrations*

3.3 Triangular hammock-type seat. Michel Brault, photographer. Musée national des beaux-arts du Québec, Québec City, Fonds Julien Hébert. Courtesy of the Estates of Julien Hébert and Michel Brault. 54

3.4 Aluminum folding chair. Michel Brault, photographer. Musée national des beaux-arts du Québec, Québec City, Fonds Julien Hébert. Courtesy of the Estates of Julien Hébert and Michel Brault. 55

3.5 Aluminum Contour chaise longue. Michel Brault, photographer. Musée national des beaux-arts du Québec, Québec City, Fonds Julien Hébert. Courtesy of the Estates of Julien Hébert and Michel Brault. 56

3.6 Scandinavian-influenced chair assembly projects made at the École du meuble, 1951. Unknown photographer. Fonds de l'École du meuble, Archives du Cégep du Vieux Montréal. 57

4.1 The Royal Library on the Mont des Arts, ca. 1969. Pol De Prins, photographer. Sint-Lukasarchief, collection Centre d'Information de Bruxelles. 63

4.2 Precious works reading room of the Belgian Royal Library, ca. 1969. Pol De Prins, photographer. Sint-Lukasarchief, collection Centre d'Information de Bruxelles. 64

4.3 Winning competition entry for the urban layout of the new Mont des Arts area, 1946. © Archives d'Architecture Moderne, Bruxelles. 66

4.4 Perspective for the periodicals reading room, Royal Library, 1946. Algemeen Rijksarchief, Brussels, Bibliotheekfonds Albert I. 68

4.5 Periodicals reading room, Royal Library, ca. 1969. Roger Van Obberghen, photographer. Archive Stichting De Coene, collection Verzameling De Coene nv., Rijksarchief Kortrijk, no. 12. 69

4.6 Distribution center in the main reading room, ca. 1969. Unknown photographer. Photo collection of the Royal Library. 74

4.7 Main boardroom of the Royal Library, ca. 1969. Roger Van Obberghen, photographer. Photo collection of the Royal Library. 75

5.1 *Machine Art*, Museum of Modern Art, New York, March 5–April 29, 1934. Unknown photographer. The Museum of Modern Art Archives. Acc. IN34.5 © Photo SCALA, Florence. 85

5.2 Herman Miller showroom, Merchandise Mart, Chicago, 1939. Unknown photographer. Courtesy of the Herman Miller Archives. 88

5.3 Herman Miller showroom, 8806 Beverly Boulevard, Los Angeles, 1949. Unknown photographer. Courtesy of the Herman Miller Archives. 89

5.4 Knoll showroom, 601 Madison, New York City, 1948. Florence Knoll Bassett Papers, 1932–2000. Archives of American Art, Smithsonian Institution. 90

5.5 Eames room in *For Modern Living*, September 11–November 20, 1949. Alexander Girard and W.D. Laurie Jr., eds., *An Exhibition for Modern Living*, The Detroit Institute of the Arts, 1949. Unknown photographer. Courtesy of the Detroit Institute of Arts, USA/ Bridgeman Images. 93

6.1 *Knoll au Louvre*, January 13–March 13, 1972. Jacques Primois, photographer. Florence Knoll Bassett Papers, 1932–2000. Archives of American Art, Smithsonian Institution. 99

Illustrations ix

6.2 Section for *Knoll au Louvre*, October 1971. Massimo and Lella Vignelli papers, Vignelli Center for Design Studies, Rochester Institute of Technology, Rochester, NY. Courtesy of Knoll, Inc.   100

6.3 Knoll International France showroom, 13, rue de l'Abbaye, Paris, between 1951 and 1961. Unknown photographer. Courtesy of Knoll, Inc.   102

6.4 Knoll International France showroom, between 1951 and 1955. Jean Collas, photographer. *Maison & Jardin* (August 1955).   103

6.5 Knoll International France advertisement in *Aujourd'hui: Art et Architecture* (March/April 1955). Herbert Matter, graphic designer. Courtesy of Knoll, Inc.   108

6.6 Yves Vidal seated in a Womb chair on the terrace of York Castle, September 1963. Robert Freson, photographer. *LOOK* (January 28, 1964). © Robert Freson.   110

7.1 Prison-made aprons, 2007. *Keisei* (October 2007).   120

7.2 Butterfly stool. Mushashino Art University, Tokyo.   120

7.3 Living room in a B-2 type Dependent House. Unknown photographer. GHQ Design Branch Japanese Staff and Shoko-Sho Kogei Shidosho, ed., *Dependents Housing* (Tokyo: Gijutsu Shiryo Kanko-kai, 1948).   123

7.4 Drawing room unit furniture produced by Kofu Prison in the early 1990s. *Keisei* (October 1992).   125

7.5 Furniture sets displayed at a corrections fair, Tokyo, 1960. *Keisei* (September 1960).   126

7.6 Views of a corrections fair, Tokyo, 1977. *Keisei* (August 1977).   129

8.1 Exterior of Itamaraty Palace, 2015. José Airton Costa Jr., photographer. Collection of the Ministry of Foreign Affairs, Brazil.   136

8.2 Main floor of Itamaraty Palace, 2015. José Airton Costa Jr., photographer. Collection of the Ministry of Foreign Affairs, Brazil.   137

8.3 Second floor of Itamaraty Palace, 2015. José Airton Costa Jr., photographer. Collection of the Ministry of Foreign Affairs, Brazil.   137

8.4 Top floor of Itamaraty Palace, 2015. José Airton Costa Jr., photographer. Collection of the Ministry of Foreign Affairs, Brazil.   138

8.5 Three interconnected jacarandá and straw conversation chairs in Itamaraty Palace, 2015. José Airton Costa Jr. photographer. Collection of the Ministry of Foreign Affairs, Brazil.   141

8.6 Lina Bo Bardi seated in Bowl chair, 1953. Francisco Albuquerque, photographer. Instituto Moreira Salles. Reproduced courtesy of the Instituto Lina Bo and P.M. Bardi.   142

8.7 Dinner reception for Queen Elizabeth II of England in the banquet hall of Itamaraty Palace, 1968. Marcel Gautherot, photographer. Instituto Moreira Salles.   146

8.8 Bahia Room of Itamaraty Palace, 2015. José Airton Costa Jr., photographer. Collection of the Ministry of Foreign Affairs, Brazil.   148

9.1 US Embassy, London, ca. 1960. Balthazar Korab, photographer. Balthazar Korab Collection, Prints and Photographs Division, Library of Congress.   153

x *Illustrations*

9.2 View into Grosvenor Square from the main entrance, ca. 1960. Balthazar Korab, photographer. Balthazar Korab Collection, Prints and Photographs Division, Library of Congress.   154

9.3 Eero Saarinen, sketch for US Embassy, London, late 1955/early 1956. Balthazar Korab, photographer. Balthazar Korab Collection, Prints and Photographs Division, Library of Congress.   157

9.4 Model for the US Embassy, London, 1955–6. Balthazar Korab, photographer. Balthazar Korab Collection, Prints and Photographs Division, Library of Congress.   158

9.5 Model for the US Embassy, London, 1956–7. Balthazar Korab, photographer. Balthazar Korab Collection, Prints and Photographs Division, Library of Congress.   160

9.6 Eero and Aline Saarinen and Kevin Roche discussing façade patterns, ca. 1956. Balthazar Korab, photographer. Balthazar Korab Collection, Prints and Photographs Division, Library of Congress.   162

9.7 Bell tower of the MIT Chapel, Cambridge, Massachusetts, ca. 1955. Balthazar Korab, photographer. Balthazar Korab Collection, Prints and Photographs Division, Library of Congress.   165

9.8 Maquettes for lamps for the US Embassy, London, ca. 1957. Amanda Millet-Sorsa, photographer. © Estate of Theodore Roszak/Licensed by VAGA, New York, NY.   166

9.9 Early maquette for the eagle sculpture, US Embassy, London, ca. 1957. Amanda Millet-Sorsa, photographer. © Estate of Theodore Roszak/Licensed by VAGA, New York, NY.   167

9.10 US Information Services library, ca. 1960. Balthazar Korab, photographer. Balthazar Korab Collection, Prints and Photographs Division, Library of Congress.   168

9.11 US Information Services auditorium, ca. 1960. Balthazar Korab, photographer. Balthazar Korab Collection, Prints and Photographs Division, Library of Congress.   168

9.12 Typical office, ca. 1960. Balthazar Korab, photographer. Balthazar Korab Collection, Prints and Photographs Division, Library of Congress.   171

10.1 Entry foyer, Australian Chancery, Washington, DC, 1969. Australian News and Information Bureau, photographer. Image No. A1200, L82324 (Barcode 11664468), National Archives of Australia.   185

10.2 Opening exhibition, Australian Chancery, Washington, DC, 1969. Australian News and Information Bureau, photographer. Image No. A1200, L82239 (Barcode 11664394), National Archives of Australia.   186

10.3 Australian Embassy, Paris, France, 1978. Max Dupain, photographer. © Penelope Seidler. Eric Sierins Photography.   189

10.4 Salon of the Ambassador's apartment, Australian Embassy, Paris, 1978. Max Dupain, photographer. © Penelope Seidler. Eric Sierins Photography.   191

10.5 Ground-floor gallery, Australian Embassy, Paris, 1978. Max Dupain, photographer. David Moore Photography

Exhibition, photographs © Lisa Moore; interior photograph, Max Dupain, 1978. © Penelope Seidler. Eric Sierins Photography.   192

Color plates

1   Claude Pompidou in the private presidential dining room, Élysée Palace, Paris, December 1971. Patrice Habans, photographer. *Paris Match* (January 1, 1972). © Getty Image HABANS Patrice/ Contributor.
2   Brochure for the Caribe Hilton, 1949. Unknown graphic designer. Courtesy of the Hospitality Industry Archives, Conrad Hilton College, University of Houston.
3   Promotional brochure for the Havana Riviera, ca. 1957–8. Unknown photographer. Courtesy of HistoryMiami.
4   Philips chairs in the cafeteria of the Royal Library, 2009. Hannes Pieters, photographer.
5   *Sens de l'espace et couleur*, Grands Magasins du Printemps, Paris, February 1955. Jean Collas, photographer. Fonds Jean Collas, Les Arts Décoratifs, Paris.
6   *Sens de l'espace et couleur*, Grands Magasins du Printemps, Paris, February 1955. Jean Collas, photographer. Fonds Jean Collas, Centre de documentation, Les Arts Décoratifs, Paris.
7   Knoll International France advertisement in *L'Oeil* (March 1962). Claude Michaélidès, photographer. Courtesy of Knoll, Inc.
8   Knoll International brochure from the 1970s. Jacques Primois, photographer. Unimark International London, graphic designers. Massimo and Lella Vignelli papers, Vignelli Center for Design Studies, Rochester Institute of Technology, Rochester, NY. Courtesy of Knoll, Inc.
9   Advertisement for Knoll International France and Revillon frères. Unknown photographer. Centre de documentations, Les Arts Décoratifs, Paris. Courtesy of Knoll, Inc.
10 Top floor banquet hall of Itamaraty Palace, 2015. José Airton Costa Jr., photographer. Collection of the Ministry of Foreign Affairs, Brazil.
11 Portinari Room of Itamaraty Palace, 2015. José Airton Costa Jr., photographer. Collection of the Ministry of Foreign Affairs, Brazil.
12 Visa and passport services section, US Embassy, London, ca. 1960. Balthazar Korab, photographer. Balthazar Korab Collection, Prints and Photographs Division, Library of Congress.
13 Visa and passport services section, US Embassy, London, ca. 1960. Balthazar Korab, photographer. Balthazar Korab Collection, Prints and Photographs Division, Library of Congress.
14 Australian Pavilion, Expo 67, Montréal, 1967. Unknown photographer. Image No. AA1982/206, 28 (Barcode 7649625), National Archives of Australia.

xii *Illustrations*

15 Salon of the Ambassador's apartment, Australian Embassy, Paris, France, 1978. Max Dupain, photographer. © Penelope Seidler. Eric Sierins Photography.
16 Ground-floor gallery, Australian Embassy, Paris, 1978. Max Dupain, photographer. David Moore Photography Exhibition, photographs © Lisa Moore; interior photograph, Max Dupain, 1978. © Penelope Seidler. Eric Sierins Photography.

Contributors

José Airton Costa Junior is an architect and urban planner. He teaches architecture and interior design at the University Center of Brasília. He holds a master's degree in architecture and urbanism from the University of Brasília (2014). His research focuses on the interaction between modern and contemporary architecture and design. He is currently conducting research on industrial technological development – surface design production as a differential factor applied to the furniture industry (Scholarship in 2013, CNPq, the National Council for Scientific Research and Development).

Fredie Floré is an engineer-architect and Associate Professor in history of (interior) architecture at KU Leuven, Faculty of Architecture. She wrote a PhD on discourses on 'better living' in Belgium in the period 1945–58 (Ghent University, 2006; published in 2010 by Leuven University Press). Her current research focuses on the representational role of architecture, interiors and furniture design in the second half of the twentieth century. Her work has been published in academic journals and books, including *Writing Design* (2011) and *Atomic Dwelling* (2012). Floré is a board member of the International Conferences of Design History and Studies (ICDHS). Together with Hilde Heynen (KU Leuven), she established the research group Architecture Interiority Inhabitation (A2I) as part of the KU Leuven Department of Architecture.

Philip Goad is Redmond Barry Distinguished Professor and Chair of Architecture in the Faculty of Architecture, Building and Planning at the University of Melbourne. He has written and published widely on twentieth-century Australian architecture. Among his many publications, he is co-editor of *Modernism and Australia: Documents on Art, Design and Architecture 1917–1967* (2006); *Modern Times: The Untold Story of Modernism in Australia* (2008); and *The Encyclopedia of Australian Architecture* (2012). In 2014, he was co-curator of *Augmented Australia: Regenerating Lost Architecture, 1914–2014*, the Australian exhibit at the Venice International Architecture Biennale.

Johan Lagae is Full Professor in the Department of Architecture and Urban Planning at Ghent University. His research focuses on (post)colonial architecture and urbanism in Central Africa, colonial built heritage, colonial photography and the relation between architecture and bureaucracy. In addition to publishing widely on these topics in international journals and books, including *Journal of Architecture, Journal of Architectural Education* and *Stichproben*, he was actively involved in several

xiv *Contributors*

internationally acclaimed Congo-related exhibitions, among them *Memory of the Congo: The Colonial Era* (2005) and *Congo belge en images* (2010). In collaboration with Mercedes Volait (INHA, Paris), he initiated an international research network on the theme 'European Architecture Beyond Europe', which resulted in the establishment of the peer-reviewed journal *ABE*.

Cammie McAtee is an independent curator and architectural historian. For many years, she was a curator at the Canadian Centre for Architecture. She has published articles in *Harvard Design Magazine, Bauwelt, Casabella* and *Genesis*, and chapters in *Atomic Dwelling: Anxiety, Domesticity, and Postwar Architecture* (2012), *Josep Lluís Sert: The Architect of Urban Design, 1953–1969* (2008) and *Mies in America* (2001). Her research focuses on North American architectural culture and the work of such architects as Eero Saarinen, Philip Johnson and Louis Kahn. She is currently completing her dissertation at Harvard University on the question of form in post-war American architecture and preparing the exhibition and publication *Montréal's Geodesic Dreams* for the fiftieth anniversary of Expo 67.

Erica N. Morawski is currently a postdoctoral fellow and lecturer at Smith College in Northampton, Massachusetts. Her scholarly interests center around transnational histories of architecture and design in the Americas, with an emphasis on the intersection of design, foreign policy and tourism. Her research has been funded by the Society of Architectural Historians, the Graham Foundation for Advanced Studies in the Fine Arts and the Center for the Advanced Study in the Visual Arts at the National Gallery (Washington, DC).

Elane Ribeiro Peixoto is Professor in the Faculty of Architecture and Urbanism at the University of Brasília. She received her PhD from the University of São Paulo (2003). In 2001, she was a fellow at the Fondation Maison des sciences de l'homme (Paris). Peixoto's research focuses principally on twentieth-century and contemporary Brazilian architecture and urbanism, as well as issues of memory and heritage. In 2016 she was a researcher at the Istituto Universitario di Architettura di Venezia.

Margaret Maile Petty is Professor and Head of the School of Design in the Creative Industries Faculty at Queensland University of Technology (AU). Her research broadly investigates the discourse, production and consumption practices of the modern built environment, with a particular focus on artificial lighting and interiors. She has published in journals such as *JSAH, Journal of Design History, Home Cultures, Interiors* and *PLAT* and is co-editor of *Cities of Light: Two Hundred Years of Urban Illumination* (Routledge, 2015) with Sandy Isenstadt and Dietrich Neumann, as well as *Architectures of Display: Department Stores and Modern Retail* (Routledge, 2017) with Anca Lasc and Patricia Lara-Betancourt.

Hannes Pieters is a practicing engineer-architect. Until recently he collaborated on an FWO-funded research project on the architecture of socialist workers' assembly buildings (2011–14, Ghent University). Pieters has a particular interest in the architecture of the first half of the twentieth century and in the relations between building projects and their political, social and cultural context, their impact on and interaction with the city and the issue of (national) representation through architecture, urban planning and interior design. His master thesis (Ghent University) on the urban renewal project, the architecture and the interior design of the Royal Library of Belgium was published in 2012 (Academia Press) and was awarded several prizes.

Martin Racine is Graduate Program Director and Associate Professor in the Department of Design and Computation Arts at Concordia University in Montréal. He holds a PhD in design, specialized in design theory and history, and a master's degree in communication sciences, focusing on the field of visual semiotics. Interested in the history of modern design, Martin Racine has published a number of articles and book chapters on the emergence of the design field in Québec and Canada, and on Expo 67. He recently published a book on the pioneering designer Julien Hébert, *Julien Hébert, fondateur du design moderne au Québec* (Éditions du passage).

Luciana Saboia received her degree in architecture from the University of Brasília (UnB) in 1997 and completed her PhD at the Université Catholique de Louvain in 2009. She is Professor in the Department of Theory and History of Architecture and Urbanism at UnB, where she has conducted research and taught architectural theory and design studio since 2010. She coordinates the Urban Studies Laboratory – LabEUrbe – at PPG-FAU/UnB, the master program at the Faculty of Architecture and Urbanism and also participates as research associate at the Center for Aesthetics, Hermeneutics and Semiotics – NEHS research group at CNPq, the National Council for Scientific Research and Development. Her research focuses on issues of modernity, urban landscape, public space, modern heritage and design theory. Currently she is the vice-director of the Faculty of Architecture and Urbanism at UnB.

Yasuko Suga, PhD (RCA) and FRSA, is Associate Professor and teaches history at Tsuda College, Japan. She is the secretary of the Design History Workshop Japan. She has published books and articles on different aspects of nineteenth- and twentieth-century British and Japanese design in *Design Issues*, *Journal of Design History*, *Journal of William Morris Studies* and other journals and edited volumes. Her recent book was on *The Reimann School: a design diaspora* (Artmonsky Arts, 2014). Her research interests include William Morris and the Arts and Crafts movement, Japonisme, Modernism, cultural history of plants at home, transnational design, and craft and design and the prison industry.

Acknowledgments

First of all, we would like to thank the authors who contributed to this volume. Some of them entered the project as participants in one of the two conference sessions organized by the editors, the first on 'Postwar Architecture and the Diplomacy of Furniture' held at the 2013 annual meeting of the Society of Architectural Historians in Buffalo; the other, 'Promoting Modern Architecture in Canada 1945–1976', presented at the Universities Art Association of Canada conference in Banff in 2014. These events proved perfect vehicles for exploring the rich topic of politics in relation to post-war furniture import and export, mediation and appropriation and went far in defining the direction of the present volume. It was at the first of these conferences that we met Valerie Rose, then a commissioning editor at Ashgate, who suggested that we develop our ideas into a volume of essays. We are grateful for her enthusiasm and early guidance.

We also want to acknowledge the invaluable research help we have received from various institutions, private businesses and individuals. This project was launched by a shared fascination in the US-based furniture company Knoll, and as we worked on the book, we were fascinated by the recurrent references to the company in diverse contexts. Intrigued by the way Knoll coordinated and supervised a growing number of overseas subsidiaries and licensees, we decided to conduct additional primary research. If only a small amount of our research made it into the present volume, it most certainly informed our reading of the global situation. We are most grateful to David E. Bright, Senior Vice President of Communications of Knoll, Inc., for granting us access to the company's archives; Katie Okamoto, communications manager, for facilitating our work in every way; Todd Cooke for help with images; and Linda Kasper, curator of the Knoll Museum, for putting us in contact with the archives. We also warmly thank Jennifer Whitlock, archivist, and R. Roger Remington, director of the Vignelli Design Center, for generously supporting our explorations in the Massimo and Lella Vignelli archives at the Rochester Institute of Technology.

We were extremely fortunate to have the opportunity to present the book concept and our own chapters to two extremely knowledgeable audiences late in the project. In this regard, we would like to thank Harriet Atkinson, Verity Clarkson and participants in the 'Changing Visions of Diplomacy by Design' conference at Brighton University in 2015 for their responses to our project; and Penny Sparke, director of the Modern Interiors Research Centre at Kingston University, for inviting us to present at MIRC's January 2016 symposium. Our thinking was enriched by the lively discussion on design, interiors and politics at these two events.

Acknowledgments xvii

We would also like to express our gratitude to several design scholars who stimulated the project in a myriad of ways, among them Kjetil Fallan, Jørn Guldberg, Margaret Hodges, Robin Jones, Yuko Kikuchi, Marie-Christine Pitre, and Catharine Rossi. Ricardo Costa Agarez and Réjean Legault offered invaluable criticism on the introduction. Our editors at Routledge, Grace Harrison and Sadé Lee, production editor Philip Stirups (Taylor & Francis) and project manager Sheri Sipka (Apex CoVantage) brought the project to fruition. We also want to thank Louise Baird-Smith for understanding that a book on modern interiors and furniture needs color images and photographer Robert Freson for allowing us to use one of his beautiful images of York Castle for the cover.

Finally, we would like to thank Jef Vervoort and Réjean and Constance Legault for sustaining our work through their patience, curiosity, enthusiasm, feedback and, occasionally, by offering much-needed distraction. We are especially grateful to Robin Schuldenfrei, who unwittingly laid the groundwork for this project by introducing us to each other at the Association of Art Historians conference in Glasgow in 2010. It turned out to be a most memorable conference, not only because of the eruption of the Iceland volcano, but because it was the beginning of a most fruitful, enriching and pleasant transcontinental collaboration.

Introduction
The politics of furniture

Fredie Floré and Cammie McAtee

Not long after moving into the Élysée Palace in June 1969, the newly elected French president, Georges Pompidou, and his wife, Claude, began making adjustments to their new home. Both were well-known supporters of modern art and culture, and Claude Pompidou soon began personalizing their private apartments on the second floor to reflect their interests. In late 1971, she invited the popular Parisian weekly *Paris Match* for a rare glimpse into these very private spaces (see Plate 1).[1] While a few of the historical pieces of furniture remained from Charles and Yvonne de Gaulle's long tenure in the Élysée, Claude Pompidou had made substantial changes, pairing important historical pieces with modern ones that were just as significant to furthering the couple's vision of modern France. She brought in a pedestal dining table and chairs by Eero Saarinen (1954–7) and a pair of Ludwig Mies van der Rohe's Barcelona ottomans (1929), both manufactured in France by the American company Knoll International.[2] She matched a Louis XV desk with a Knoll pedestal chair in her own room. The Pompidous' intervention was a uniquely French take on the *cohabitation* of modernity and tradition.

But the will to modernize such an important site of Western power could not rely on American-designed furniture alone. Working through the Mobilier national, the national service responsible for the furnishing of official buildings, the Pompidous commissioned the dynamic young French designer Pierre Paulin to re-conceive the private reception rooms on the first floor of the palace (1969–72).[3] Designed in collaboration with the Mobilier national's recently established research arm, the Atelier de recherche et de création (est. 1964), and produced by the Manufactures des Gobelins, de Beauvais et de la Savonnerie (the same workshops that had been producing and maintaining official furniture for the French state since the seventeenth century), the dining room, smoking room, library and *salon aux tableaux* triumphantly announced that France was still a significant force of industry, craftsmanship and design. Yet the fact that the new furniture designs were, by Paulin's own admission, strongly influenced by Saarinen as well as other American designers, testifies to the long shadow cast by the internationalization of the Knoll model.

As this anecdote illustrates, in the post-war decades furniture produced by Knoll became a well-known and highly respected ingredient of the modern interior in many Western countries. Building on the company's visual presence in a variety of contemporary architectural, design, art, lifestyle and cultural magazines, the furniture brand, known for its clean lines and sculptural forms, as well as for the textures, patterns and bright colors of its textile line, quickly conquered a worldwide audience. Established by Hans Knoll in New York City in 1938, with a factory in East Greenville,

2 Fredie Floré and Cammie McAtee

Pennsylvania set up in 1941 to manufacture Knoll's products, the company's expansion nationwide began after Knoll partnered with designer Florence Schust in 1943. Florence Knoll, as she became known after their marriage in 1946, developed a distinct look for the brand, between the early 1940s and 1960 designing, in addition to furniture, the showrooms of Knoll Associates, Inc. in New York, Dallas, Chicago, San Francisco, Detroit, Atlanta, Boston, Washington, DC, Miami and Los Angeles.[4] At the same time, Hans Knoll pressed forward with international expansion, establishing Knoll International G.m.b.H. as a legal entity in 1951.[5] The success of Knoll's efforts was reflected in the speed with which he established outposts: by 1955 there were five Knoll International subsidiaries based in Paris, Stuttgart, Brussels, Toronto and Havana. By the end of the decade, the company had founded more subsidiaries, sold licenses and opened factories as well as showrooms in cities on every continent in the world, including Brisbane, São Paulo, Nicosia, London, Helsinki, Guatemala, New Delhi, Tehran, Milan, Mexico City, Amsterdam, Oslo, Madrid, Stockholm, Zurich, Caracas and Tangier.[6] Setting up training facilities for the sale and marketing as well as the manufacture of Knoll's furniture, Hans Knoll created a business model that gave him great control over the diffusion of Knoll products worldwide. The strength of this system was proven by the continuing success of the company after his sudden death in 1955. By the end of the decade, under Florence Knoll's direction, Knoll's "global conquest" was proudly demonstrated in full-page ads depicting a globe covered with many letter Ks, one for each American showroom, foreign subsidiary or licensee (see Figure 0.1).

This brief sketch of the "Knoll phenomenon," as the company's fast rise to prominence in the 1950s and 1960s might be termed, serves as a starting point for considering the approach to the history of post-war modern furniture taken in this book. The success of Knoll was clearly balanced between excellent design and manufacture, and innovative and shrewd business acumen. Although this project does not concentrate solely on Knoll, it grew out of a shared fascination with the introduction, dissemination and mediation of Knoll furniture worldwide. Of course the company is a familiar subject, the focus of several books, articles and exhibition catalogs.[7] These publications mainly discuss Knoll's development in the United States, and in many respects this is as it should be. The literature sheds light on the company's origins and cultural context and illustrates the importance of politics as a key factor in its success. A significant part of Hans Knoll's achievements came through the close connections he developed within the US government in addition to those within private industry. His company directly profited from the European reconstruction program and the Cold War politics that underlay it.[8] However, there are still important questions to ask about Knoll's worldwide expansion. How exactly were Knoll products and their political connotations mediated and perceived outside the United States? Only very few fragmented cases have been studied in detail, such as the link between Knoll and the Swedish department store Nordiska Kompaniet as discussed by Susan Ward in the recent *Knoll Textiles* volume, the unauthorized local reproduction of Knoll furniture in Sri Lanka as examined by Robin Jones in his work on architect Geoffrey Bawa, the introduction and reception of Knoll furniture in Belgium as researched by Fredie Floré, and the licensed manufacture of Knoll furniture in England in the 1960s by Rosamond Allwood.[9]

Similar questions can and should be asked for other furniture brands. For example, how and to what extent did Herman Miller – Knoll's closest US competitor – contribute to the political representation of the United States in the Cold War era?[10] How did

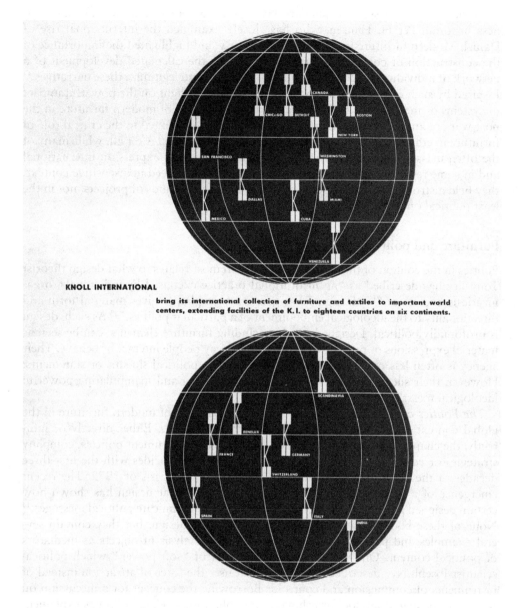

Figure 0.1 Knoll International advertisement in *Zodiac* 1 (1956). Herbert Matter, graphic designer. Courtesy of Knoll, Inc.

local furniture producers in different parts of the world respond to the increasing presence through importation from the United States and other countries? Which roles did furniture elements perform when positioned in highly charged interiors of national representation in the post-war decades?

There is also much research to do on the systems through which these products were launched, promoted and received in different countries. As rich as the literature on post-war furniture is, many studies have taken the perspective of individual designers

4 Fredie Floré and Cammie McAtee

or brands. Nevertheless, some scholars have opened up other avenues, including business historian Per H. Hansen, who has closely examined the international rise of Danish Modern furniture in the twentieth century and highlighted the importance of the construction of consumer narratives as well as the calculated development of a network of individuals and organizations to promote and legitimize these narratives.[11] Inspired by such examples, this volume intends to shed light on the powerful impact of systems or mechanisms that facilitated the distribution of modern furniture in the post-war era and more particularly on the way they contributed to the critical role of furniture in crafting political messages in very diverse arenas. After all, while many of the often mass-produced furniture elements were meant to express an international and in some respects apolitical modern language, when placed in a sensitive context, they held a strong potential to serve as allies for different kinds of projects, not in the least political ones.

Furniture and political agency

Politics in the context of this volume first and foremost relates to what design theorist Tony Fry has described as "an institutional practice exercised by individuals, organizations and states."[12] "Design," Fry goes on to explain, "gives material form and directionality to the ideological embodiment of a particular politics."[13] As such, design is profoundly political. Designed goods, including furniture elements, can be seen as material expressions of power, which inform the way people interact or behave. Their agency is often less overt than that of, for example, political slogans or statements. However, their silent presence is capable of negotiating and manipulating powerful ideological messages.

The Politics of Furniture examines the political agency of modern furniture in the global context primarily between 1945 and the late 1970s. Either directly or indirectly, the chapters in this book focus on or deal with government policies, company strategies or educational programs. The period largely coincides with the first three decades of the Cold War and ends with the Second Oil Crisis of 1979. The recent emergence of a substantial body of literature on Cold War design has shown how certain designed goods were conceived or staged to communicate political messages.[14] None of these books exclusively focuses on furniture design, but they contain several examples and provide useful concepts for the analysis of objects as mediators of political content. One of these concepts is that of "soft power," which political scientist Joseph Nye described as a power that uses the force of attraction instead of instruments of compulsion and control.[15] Borrowing the concept for a discussion on post-war housing, domestic furnishings and appliances, Greg Castillo has explained: "unlike hard power, which is concentrated in the hands of those at the source, soft power is dispersed and malleable. The allure of effective soft power lies in its capacity for requisition and reuse by foreign recipients to advance their own interests, but in ways that ultimately benefit the donor nation."[16] This observation is particularly relevant in relation to American and Russian propaganda of consumer goods as most tellingly illustrated by the well-known 1959 "kitchen debate" between US Vice President Richard M. Nixon and Soviet Premier Nikita S. Khrushchev. This "act of diplomatic high drama," as Ruth Oldenziel and Karin Zachmann described it, took place against the backdrop of a lemon-yellow General Electric kitchen on display and as such highlighted the political connotations of this setting.[17]

In the Cold War era, soft power strategies were widely applied and also involved furniture companies, as Castillo's book *Cold War on the Home Front*, Jane Loeffler's study of post-war American embassies and Gay McDonald's articles on several travelling exhibitions organized by New York's Museum of Modern Art (MoMA) illustrate.[18] While in the 1950s, many European modernist circles strongly disapproved of American streamline styling – in particular Raymond Loewy's work – because of its so-called superficiality and all too explicit focus on increasing sales, the more functionalist-inspired objects that MoMA promoted with the encouragement and support of the American government were mostly embraced without reservation.[19] Knoll and Herman Miller furniture were key components of the positively appreciated range of American products. For example, the catalog of the *50 Years of American Art* exhibition curated by MoMA in 1955 and hosted by the Musée National d'Art Moderne in Paris, featured among others, chairs by Charles and Ray Eames, Eero Saarinen and Harry Bertoia, the first produced by Herman Miller, the latter two by Knoll.

Soft power, however, was not only a tool of the superpowers that emerged from the Second World War. Many middle-power countries applied or otherwise experienced similar strategies. To develop a better understanding of the role of furniture as a mediator of political messages, this volume takes a global perspective. As such it connects with recent scholarly directions in design and architectural history, and in history in general, which underline the importance of transnational and global dynamics for the interpretation of nationally or locally produced phenomena or artifacts.[20] Through a series of case studies drawn from widely ranging contexts – countries in North and South America, the Caribbean, Europe, Africa, Asia and Australia – this book showcases examples of design and architectural history analyses that deal with a transnational and global arena. Export, licensed reproductions and local design productions responding to increased foreign import are key mechanisms addressed in this volume. A thorough understanding of these mechanisms is crucial for the interpretation of the politics of furniture in the Cold War era as well as in other time periods. For example, in her article on late nineteenth-century British and Australian furniture design, Tracey Avery has shown that a close reading of import and production patterns can offer revealing insights in the way formally related goods produced different meanings in colonizing and colonized societies.[21] Fashion historian Alexandra Palmer's work on the transatlantic trade of haute couture fashion, especially on how such fashion houses as Christian Dior negotiated the problem of copying, may also open some new avenues in thinking about how "high design" in furniture was protected as well as produced and marketed.[22]

The Politics of Furniture discusses both well- and lesser-known post-war furniture elements within a range of contexts. While some of the chapters may contribute to the "cultural biographies" of some pieces of modern furniture, this volume first and foremost intends to provide fresh insights on their agency within different political climates and societies.[23] The actor-network theory by Bruno Latour and others has been credited for emphasizing the importance of objects in the analysis of social relations.[24] As Latour has argued, objects as well as humans have agency and can take part in dynamic networks based on the accumulation and execution of power.[25] Studying the actions and interactions of both humans and nonhumans, he claims, is essential to understanding social connections.[26] While several scholars criticize the way Latour seeks to give nonhumans a voice, his insights have stimulated new and interesting perspectives

6 *Fredie Floré and Cammie McAtee*

on design studies. As Kjetil Fallan has also observed: "Historians have often tended to get seduced by the agency of the so-called great human actors, losing sight of the other inhabitants – human as well as non-human – of the actor network. . . . Latour's insistence on the agency of nonhumans can function as a corrective."[27]

In this volume, the focus is on furniture as one of many interrelated actors negotiating power relations, including furniture brands, manufacturers, designers, governmental bodies, institutional representatives, architects, design schools, hotel chains, consumers, prison institutions and libraries. All chapters deal with processes of mediation. As design historian Grace Lees-Maffei has summarized, "to study mediation is to study the phenomena which exist between production and consumption, as being fundamentally important in inscribing meanings for objects."[28] Some authors focus on individual furniture elements as agents in the communication of political and social meaning and on the worldwide diffusion and circulation of their images in brochures, articles, catalogs or books. Other authors consider the role of furniture within potent sites that demand careful negotiation, whether between governments, cultures or buyers and sellers. In all cases, the mediation of meaning often relates to the context of an interior, defined here as the inside of a building or an urban environment. In this volume, a range of different interiors is discussed, including the inside spaces of hotels, houses, commercial venues, schools, museums, embassies, exhibition halls, government buildings and prisons.

While the ideas just explored in this section underlie the overall premise of this volume, the individual contributions by design and architectural historians bring a variety of perspectives from such fields as diplomatic and political history, colonial and postcolonial studies, tourism studies, material culture studies, furniture history and heritage and preservation studies.

Identity, persuasion and diplomacy

This volume's first part, "Furniture and Identity Politics," focuses on the role of furniture in the negotiation of and between different national, corporate or cultural identities. The chapters examine a series of highly charged contexts. Johan Lagae opens the section with a discussion of the role furniture played in crafting the modern identities of the Belgian Congo and French Equatorial Africa. He shows how the introduction of modern furniture in tropical Africa was closely linked to the politically inspired efforts to launch a consumer culture in these colonized areas. Through tracing the postcolonial life of some of these objects, he at the same time demonstrates a striking continuity of colonial attitudes and practices to the present day. Indeed, parallel with the scholarly rediscovery of "tropical modernism" in Africa from the mid-1990s onward, design furniture produced for the former colonies – including work by Jean Prouvé and Charlotte Perriand – developed into highly valued commodities. Erica Morawski's chapter analyzes two responses to the hegemony of American politics and values in the space of the resort hotel in Puerto Rico and Cuba. It underscores how modern furniture and hotel design, informed and manipulated by various agents, including local governments, private operators, guests and the local population, promoted or contested contemporaneous debates on national identity, US–insular relations and the politics of tourism. Concluding with a brief examination of the contemporary status of midcentury modern hotels in the Spanish Caribbean, Morawski points to the ways their histories have been reshaped over time to support new

Introduction 7

political strategies. Martin Racine's chapter explores how design schools in Québec served as powerful stages for engaged negotiations involving furniture design and cultural identity. It considers the battle for modern design education in Québec during the decades leading up to the 1960s Quiet Revolution, a key era in the emancipation of Québec society and its quest for a distinctive identity. Focusing on the work of two key educators, Jean-Marie Gauvreau and Julien Hébert, Racine unfolds a highly charged discussion involving different readings of traditional-style furniture, handicraft techniques, materiality and industrial production. The section closes with a chapter on the modern interiors of the Belgian Royal Library by Fredie Floré and Hannes Pieters. Designed and constructed during a critical moment of self-definition in the country's history, the entire building project reflects a long and complex process of national representation. The interior design and furnishings of the library represent the final stage in this process and, as the authors argue, manifestly articulate the institute's ambition to be a modern enterprise within an increasingly globalizing context.

"Spaces of Persuasion" considers the role of modern furniture in the promotion of a positive image of an institution, a company or a country through exhibitions and showrooms and the fluid ground between them. The first chapter, by Margaret Maile Petty, addresses the promotion and reception of modern furniture within the United States. It shows how exhibitions curated for both retail and cultural contexts facilitated the codification of the American "way of life" for domestic consumption and contributed to the imaging of US furniture and ideology for international exportation. Crucial in this process, Petty argues, was the emergence of a new distribution model: the independent manufacturer-operated furniture showroom. Herman Miller and Knoll were pioneers in developing these showrooms, which together with well-known exhibitions as MoMA's *Good Design* shows aimed at persuading the public as well as the American industry to go modern. The essay "Knolling Paris: From the 'New Look' to *Knoll au Louvre*" focuses on the introduction of Knoll in Paris and suggests that the axis of influence between the United States and other parts of the world was not necessarily unidirectional. McAtee and Floré explain how Knoll in the post-war decades conquered the French cultural elite through the use of, among others, showrooms, strategic advertising in art, architecture and culture journals and exhibitions in the Printemps department store and at the Musée des Arts Décoratifs in Paris. While at first the content of these mediations was strongly based on the corporate image designed by Florence Knoll, later on a French version of the "Knoll look" can be discerned, which, the authors argue, consequently infiltrated American interior design practices. The final chapter in this section, by Yasuko Suga, examines a rather different space of persuasion: Japanese "corrections fairs," annual exhibitions organized by the Ministry of Law intended to introduce the products of prison industry to the general public. Suga analyzes the furniture shown at these fairs and explains how the production of even this remote segment of the national industry was influenced by US examples. Prison workshops quietly facilitated the development of locally inspired responses to Western import and other processes of modernization. The results were successfully mediated by the corrections fairs, which as such stimulated the relations between prisons and society.

The final part, "The Diplomacy of Furniture," examines the way in which modern furniture and furnishings answered the explicit diplomatic mission of highly symbolic official buildings like embassies and ministries of foreign affairs. It considers the role furniture played in a series of highly charged representational spaces of power

8 *Fredie Floré and Cammie McAtee*

and authority. Luciana Saboia, Elane Ribeiro Peixoto and Airton Costa Jr. focus on Brasília's Itamaraty Palace, designed by Oscar Niemeyer to house the Ministry of Foreign Affairs. The building, the authors explain, was populated with mixtures of colonial, imperial and modernist furniture in varying degrees throughout the years, and as such reflected changing interpretations – in particular during the military regime – of how to construct and project a synthetic image of the country's identity. The chapter highlights conflicting opinions in this debate, not the least that of the diplomat in charge who managed the interior design assignments. Cammie McAtee reconsiders Eero Saarinen's highly controversial project for the US Embassy in London. Arguing that the embassy's exterior image and the interior public areas were intended to work hand in hand in conveying a progressive image of the United States, McAtee considers the container and the contained, revealing the embassy to be a sophisticated work of architectural state- as well as stagecraft. As she shows, Saarinen, as a cultural Cold Warrior, deployed modern art as well as design in a play to win over the British public. The thematic section closes with a chapter on another case of design diplomacy: the furniture, furnishings and art in the Australian embassies for Washington, DC, and Paris. Through these two cases Philip Goad studies the shifting approach to Australia's cultural diplomacy. While the interiors of the chancery in Washington, DC, marked the nation's complicity in Cold War politics and the importance of trade alliances, the Paris embassy, Goad argues, must first and foremost be read as a statement of independence.

Post-war interiors in transition

Some of the interiors discussed in this volume are carefully orchestrated scenographies designed by an architectural office, an interior designer or a furnishing company in response to the commissioner's (political) beliefs, needs or wishes. However, as several scholars have explained, in the end all inhabited interiors are highly ephemeral constructs.[29] From the moment they are in use, their meanings and those of their constituting elements rapidly evolve under influence of changing cultural, political or economic contexts. Often it doesn't take long before inhabitants add, remove or replace objects, including furniture, and as such infuse the interior with new narratives. Finally strategies of redevelopment can also quickly lead to an interior's (partial) physical disappearance even if it has landmark status, as the recent and much-debated example of the fate of the original furniture in Philip Johnson's Four Seasons Restaurant (1959) in the Seagram Building in New York illustrates.[30] Several post-war interiors discussed in this volume have undergone profound changes since their conception and initial installation, a process some of the authors explicitly address.

However, as Edward Hollis has argued, interiors seldom completely vanish.[31] To make this point, he considered the example of the Rome apartment of Italian writer Mario Praz, which became the subject of Praz's 1958 autobiography, *La Casa Della Vita*.[32] Although Praz left the apartment in 1969 and moved his personal possessions to another place, his "house of life" left traces of its own. It did so in the architecture that once enclosed it, through the objects that once filled it and in the book that recorded its constellation and meanings.[33] Many of the interiors discussed in this volume were highly charged and unique contexts characterized by a careful selection of furniture elements, which themselves were mostly mass-produced or intended to be mass-produced. Some of these furniture elements, if not destroyed, now lead a different life than the one they were originally made for. They have been removed from the interiors they were located in and have been rearranged possibly many times over. Similarly to the objects in the Praz apartment, they hold the potential to remind us of the politically charged interiors they once inhabited. However, the narratives they relate need to be recorded or discussed. If not, in the context of an ever-growing market of interior furnishings, they risk becoming simply items of vintage design.

Notes

1 "Profession: Présidente. Domicile: Elysée. Nom: Claude Pompidou," *Paris Match*, no. 1182, January 1, 1972, 28–32. The photographs were taken by Patrice Habans.
2 Jean Coural, *Le Palais de l'Élysée: Histoire et décor* (Paris: Délégation à l'action artistique de la Ville de Paris, 1994), 133–4.
3 Paulin's various designs for the Élysée Palace have recently been exhibited in the retrospective Pierre Paulin, Centre Pompidou, May 11–August 22, 2016. See the accompanying publication, Cloé Pitiot, ed., *Pierre Paulin* (Paris: Centre Pompidou, 2016), as well as *Pierre Paulin: le design au pouvoir: Collections du Mobilier national* (Paris: Réunion des musées nationaux, 2008).
4 New York (1948 and 1951), Dallas (1950), Chicago (1953 and an undated earlier one, likely a temporary exhibition at the Merchandise Mart), San Francisco (1954), Detroit (1947 and an undated later one, likely the Knoll section in the *For Modern Living* exhibition held at the Detroit Institute of Arts in 1949), Atlanta (1950), Boston (1950), Washington, DC (1957), Miami (1959) and Los Angeles (1960).
5 According to an undated document in the Knoll Archives, "Knoll International Limited was incorporated under the State laws of Delaware in March 1951 to import, export, and license abroad the manufacture and sale of furniture and textiles which are the exclusive designs of Knoll Associates, Inc." "Knoll International Limited," October 1957, typescript, 2; "Knoll in the News" file, 1957, Knoll, Inc. archives, New York.
6 Memo to Knoll International affiliated Companies and Friends from A. W. Boyd, n.d. [late 1955], Knoll, Inc. archives.
7 Key reference works on Knoll include: Christine Rae, "Knoll: Portrait of a Corporation," *Graphis* 26, no. 1948 (1970/71): 154–62, 188, 193–4; Eric Larrabee and Massimo Vignelli, *Knoll Design* (New York: H. N. Abrams, 1981); Brian Lutz, *Knoll: A Modernist Universe* (New York: Rizzoli, 2010); Earl Martin, ed., *Knoll Textiles: Nineteenhundredfortyfive–Twothousandandten* (New Haven/London: Yale University Press, 2011). There have also been several significant interviews with and articles on Florence Knoll Bassett: Paul Makovsky, "Shu U," *Metropolis Magazine* 20, no. 11 (July 2001): 89–97, 122; Bobbye Tigerman, "'I Am Not a Decorator': Florence Knoll, The Knoll Planning Unit and the Making of the Modern Office," *Journal of Design History* 20, no. 1 (2007): 61–74.
8 These connections are mentioned, for example, in Larrabee and Vignelli, *Knoll Design*, 176; and by Lutz, *Knoll*, 61. On Knoll and the Marshall Plan, see also Greg Castillo, *Cold War on the Home Front: The Soft Power of Midcentury Design* (Minneapolis: University of Minnesota Press, 2010), 62–4.
9 Susan Ward, "Making Knoll Textiles: Integrated Fabrics for Modern Interiors, 1945–65," in *Knoll Textiles*, 102–77; Robin Jones, "'Thinking' the Domestic Interior in Postcolonial South Asia: The Home of Geoffrey Bawa in Sri Lanka, 1960 to 1998," *Interiors* 3 (2012): 203–26; Fredie Floré, "Architect-Designed Interiors for a Culturally Progressive Upper-Middle Class: The Implicit Political Presence of Knoll International in Belgium," in *Atomic Dwelling: Anxiety, Domesticity, and Postwar Architecture*, ed. Robin Schuldenfrei (Abingdon: Routledge, 2012), 169–85. The manufacture of Knoll furniture in England in the 1960s has been considered in Rosamond Allwood's study of the British furniture firm of D. Meredew Ltd: "Meredew of Letchworth: A Brief History," *Furniture History* 33 (1997): 305–10.
10 Key reference works on Herman Miller and some of the company's key designers include: Ralph Caplan, *The Design of Herman Miller* (New York: Whitney Library of Design, 1976); Stanley Abercrombie, *George Nelson: The Design of Modern Design* (Cambridge,

MA: MIT Press, 1994); Phyllis Ross, "Merchandising the Modern: Gilbert Rohde at Herman Miller," *Journal of Design History* 17, no. 4 (2004): 359–76; John R. Berry, *Herman Miller: The Purpose of Design* (New York: Rizzoli, 2004); and the exhibition catalog *George Nelson – Architect, Writer, Designer, Teacher* (Weil am Rhein: Vitra Design Museum, 2008). Some scholars have adopted a thematic approach to Herman Miller's production. See, for, example, Kristina Wilson, "Like a 'Girl in a Bikini Suit' and Other Stories: The Herman Miller Furniture Company, Gender and Race at Mid-Century," *Journal of Design History* 28, no. 2 (2015): 161–81; Jeffrey L. Cruikshank and Malcolm Clark, *Herman Miller, Inc.: Buildings and Beliefs* (Washington, DC: American Institute of Architects Press, 1995). Herman Miller's expansion into France in the late 1950s is briefly discussed by Karine Lacquemant, "Créateurs et éditeurs: Mobilier International," in *Mobi Boom: L'Explosion du design en France. 1945–1975*, ed. Dominique Forest (Paris: Les Arts Décoratifs, 2010), 282.

11 Per H. Hansen, "Networks, Narratives, and New Markets: The Rise and Decline of Danish Modern Furniture Design, 1930–1970," *The Business History Review* 80, no. 3 (2006): 449–83. Studies on the mediation and international distribution of Danish design should also be mentioned here. See, for instance, Kevin Davies, "Markets, Marketing and Design: The Danish Furniture Industry, c. 1947–65," *Scandinavian Journal of Design History* 9 (1999): 56–73.

12 Tony Fry, *Design as Politics* (Oxford/New York: Berg, 2011), 5–6.

13 Fry, *Design as Politics*, 6.

14 These publications include: Mart Kalm and Ingrid Ruudi, ed., *Constructed Happiness: Domestic Environment in the Cold War Era* (Tallinn: Eesti Kunstiakadeemia, 2005); Paul Betts, *The Authority of Everyday Objects: A Cultural History of West German Industrial Design* (Berkeley: University of California Press, 2007); David Crowley and Jane Pavitt, ed., *Cold War Modern: Design 1945–1970* (London: V&A, 2008); Ruth Oldenziel and Karin Zachmann, ed., *Cold War Kitchen: Americanization, Technology and European Users* (Cambridge, MA: MIT Press, 2009); and Castillo's *Cold War on the Home Front*.

15 Joseph S. Nye, *Soft Power: The Means to Success in World Politics* (New York: PublicAffairs, 2004).

16 Castillo, *Cold War on the Home Front*, xii.

17 Oldenziel and Zachmann, "Kitchens as Technology and Politics: An Introduction," in *Cold War Kitchen*, 1.

18 Castillo, *Cold War on the Home Front*, 61–4; Jane C. Loeffler, *The Architecture of Diplomacy: Building America's Embassies*, rev. 2nd ed. (New York: Princeton, 2011 [1998]); Gay McDonald, "Selling the American Dream: MoMA, Industrial Design and Post-war France," *Journal of Design History* 17, no. 4 (2004): 397–412; McDonald, "The 'Advance' of American Postwar Design in Europe: MoMA and the *Design for Use, USA* Exhibition 1951–1953," *Design Issues* 24, no. 2 (2008): 15–27; and McDonald, "The Modern American Home as Soft Power: Finland, MoMA and the 'American Home 1953' Exhibition," *Journal of Design History* 23, no. 4 (2010): 387–408.

19 On the post-war reception of American streamline styling in West Germany, see, for example, Betts, *The Authority of Everyday Objects*, 10, 87–9. On the post-war perception of American material culture in France, see McDonald's "Selling the American Dream." In recent years, more scholars have studied the reception in Europe of American industrial design in the post-war era. See, for instance, Kjetil Fallan, "Love and Hate in Industrial Design: Europe's Design Professionals and America in the 1950s," in *The Making of European Consumption: Facing the American Challenge*, ed. Per Lundin and Thomas Kaiserfeld (Basingstoke: Palgrave Macmillan, 2015), 134–56.

20 See, for instance, Grace Lees-Maffei, "Local/Regional/National/Global: Introduction," in *The Design History Reader*, ed. Grace Lees-Maffei and Rebecca Houze (Oxford/New York: Berg, 2010), 467–9; Glenn Adamson, Giorgio Riello and Sarah Teasley, ed., *Global Design History* (New York: Routledge, 2011); Akira Iriye, *Global and Transnational History: The Past, Present and Future* (Basingstoke: Palgrave MacMillan, 2013).

21 Tracey Avery, "Furniture Design and Colonialism: Negotiating Relationships between Britain and Australia, 1880–1901," *Home Cultures* 4, no. 1 (2007): 69–92; a shorter version of this article is also published in *The Design History Reader*, 478–84.

22 Alexandra Palmer, *Couture & Commerce: The Transatlantic Fashion Trade in the 1950s* (Vancouver: University of British Columbia Press, 2001).

23 Igor Kopytoff, "The Cultural Biography of Things: Commoditization as Process," in *The Social Life of Things: Commodities in Cultural Perspective*, ed. Arjun Appadurai (Cambridge: Cambridge University Press, 1986), 64–91.

24 Bruno Latour, *Reassembling the Social: An Introduction to Actor-Network-Theory* (Oxford: Oxford University Press, 2005); and Kjetil Fallan, *Design History: Understanding Theory and Method* (Oxford/New York: Berg, 2010), 66. Other key contributors to the actor-network theory are Michel Callon and John Law.

25 See Latour, *Reassembling the Social*, 71–2.

26 Latour, *Reassembling the Social*, 74–5.

27 Fallan, *Design History: Understanding Theory and Method*, 76.

28 Grace Lees-Maffei, "Mediation: Introduction," in *The Design History Reader*, 427.

29 For instance, Edward Hollis tellingly describes the interiors as "temporary arrangements: the meeting places of building, lining, furnishing and occupation." Hollis, "*The House of Life* and the Memory Palace: Some Thoughts on the Historiography of Interiors," *Interiors* 1, no. 1–2 (2010): 105–17.

30 See, for instance, Jennifer Nalewicki, "Wright to Auction Furnishings from the Four Seasons Restaurant in NYC," accessed May 24, 2016, www.interiordesign.net/articles/118 47-wright-to-auction-furnishings-from-the-four-seasons-restaurant-in-nyc/; Vanessa Quirk, "'It makes me sick:' Belmont Freeman on the Four Seasons," accessed May 25, 2016, www. metropolismag.com/Point-of-View/May-2016/It-Makes-Me-Sick-Belmont-Freeman-on-the-Four-Seasons/.

31 Hollis, "*The House of Life* and the Memory Palace," 105–17 (114).

32 Mario Praz, *La Casa Della Vita* (Milan: Arnoldo Mondadori Editore, 1958).

33 Hollis, "*The House of Life* and the Memory Palace," 114.

Furniture and identity politics

1 Nomadic furniture in the "heart of darkness"

Colonial and postcolonial trajectories of modern design artifacts to and from tropical Africa

Johan Lagae

In 1954, the editors of the *Bulletin de l'Union des Femmes Coloniales*, the main periodical targeting a female audience in the former Belgian colony (today the Democratic Republic of the Congo), invited Belgian architect Charles Van Nueten to write a contribution on the design of the colonizer's house. Apart from discussing what he considered the most apt architectural conception in the tropics, Van Nueten also explicitly paid attention to the amenities, which in his opinion were necessary to provide comfort for the white body in a "climate of concern." In that respect, he made a plea to use "simple and light furniture, of the Swedish type, meaning a furniture that facilitates the frequent cleaning needed to keep out all kinds of insects, cockroaches, flies, etc."[1] The statement is in line with the strong functionalist tenets that underscore Van Nueten's whole oeuvre.[2] Yet, promoting the use of lightweight furniture in the tropics was a widely shared idea, as is demonstrated by illustrations in Maxwell Fry and Jane Drew's 1956 seminal book *Tropical Architecture in the Humid Zone* as well as articles on architecture in the tropics in leading professional journals of the time.[3]

One of the most recurrent pieces of furniture discernible in photographs of 1950s interiors in such sources is the so-called Butterfly or BKF chair, designed in 1939 by Jorge Ferrari Hardoy along with Antonio Bonet and Juan Kurchan.[4] Possessing the kind of functional qualities Van Nueten called for, the BKF chair exemplifies the post-war obsession with "lightness" that, as Lesley Jackson has argued, "was considered an essential quality of all types of 'Contemporary furniture.'"[5] Appearing on an international scale in the interior as part of a larger discourse promoting "modern living" that also emerged in Belgium during the post-war years, the introduction of the BKF chair in tropical Africa testifies to the attempt to bring the everyday life of white colonial society to "metropolitan" standards of comfort.[6]

Yet, as I will argue in this chapter, the appearance of 1950s modern design furniture in tropical Africa also needs to be linked to political economy governing this part of the world during the immediate post-war years, a moment in time when Central Africa became seen as a potential locale for the large-scale introduction of consumer culture. In such a context, furniture manufacturers in Europe and the United States were seeking to expand their markets, deliberately playing on strategies of promoting "modern living" in the tropics via lifestyle periodicals or commercial fairs (see Figure 1.1). Having its roots in the exploitative logic of the late nineteenth-century "Scramble for Africa," this post-war economy became strongly influenced by the shifting geopolitical tensions of the Cold War. As a result, flows of commodities no longer exclusively

Figure 1.1 Cover of the Kinshasa-based magazine *Habiter en Belgique et au Congo* depicting "good design" furniture promoted at the time both in Belgium and in the Belgian colony. Unknown photographer. *Habiter en Belgique et au Congo* 5 (October 1955). Collection of the author.

followed trajectories from the *métropole* to the colony, but gradually developed along more complex, transnational routes. It was this particular, albeit short-lived context that led to the introduction of modern furniture in Central Africa.

In recent years, this particular legacy of modern design has been – partially – rediscovered and documented. In some cases, it even has been the subject of a reverse trajectory, being returned to the "home country" often to be sold on the global market as precious vintage furniture "saved" from the "heart of darkness." In a sense, this furniture then has become "nomadic," detached from its African context, even though its origin is intrinsically linked to it in profound ways. By following the trajectories to and from Central Africa of some of these artifacts of modern furniture design, I aim to contribute to recent scholarship on global design history that "addresses the political implications of design's imbrication in global networks."[7] Indeed, in a late colonial context, modern furniture in tropical Africa becomes a "difficult object," the study of which requires investigating specific forms of interconnectivity and asymmetrical power relationships embedded in cultural production in this part of the world, both in the past and today.

Accommodating the reclining body in the hot-humid tropics

One of the most recurrent tropes in the post-war discourse on architecture in Central Africa reads that living in the tropics equals, by definition, living in the outdoors. If there had been an effort during the interwar years to interiorize family life in the Belgian Congo, then architects in post-war Central Africa viewed the tropics as the ideal setting to realize the kind of "Befreites Wohnen" ["Living Liberated"] advocated some three decades earlier by members of the modern movement in Europe.[8] Even the interior itself had to be fully opened by means of what Fry and Drew termed "breathing walls" in order to create a natural cross-ventilation crucial to secure physiological comfort for the white colonizer's body. This new style of building, labeled "tropical modernism" in current historiography, was explicitly legitimized on the ground of its climate responsiveness.[9]

In this respect, tropical modernist architects revived some of the design principles inherent to early colonial buildings, in particular the so-called tropical bungalow with its all-round veranda. During the late nineteenth century, doctors promoted this particular typology as the most suitable housing solution in the tropics. As a crucial instrument of environmental control, offering protection against sun and rain, the all-round veranda formed a key component of the bungalow typology, and it resurfaced in various shapes and forms in 1950s modern architecture for the tropics. The Maison tropique à portique, developed by Jean Prouvé in 1949, closely followed this original bungalow typology.[10] Charles Van Nueten even claimed that apartment buildings in Congo had to be conceived as a series of bungalows, stacked one on top of the other.[11] But even less radical architectural designs for the tropics relied on the use of a veranda or, in a more limited form, a loggia, as such outdoor rooms formed the space of colonial sociability par excellence. It was here that one relaxed after a long day's work, or chatted with family and friends. In colonial parlance, in the Belgian Congo the veranda was often referred to as the "whisky-barza," a phrase that reinforces the leisurely image of colonial life, which, of course, forms a rather distorted representation of everyday reality.[12]

Such a popularizing perception of colonial life colored the 1950s discourse on furniture for the tropics. In their book *Tropical Architecture in the Humid Zone*, Fry and Drew stressed on one hand the importance of using functional and climate responsive furniture. Included illustrations all displayed a preference for "open design" artifacts that did not hamper the free circulation of air, a lesson the architects had learned from the vernacular tradition. Furniture was to be made out of durable materials with finishes that "should be cool, clean and easy to keep up" and because of the "open-air character of living . . . surfaces which are used externally in the West [are] more suited to internal use in the tropics." But on the other hand their text also echoed the popular focus on the leisurely dimension of life, when they explicitly stressed the need in the tropics for seats allowing a reclining position, such as a chaise longue, "with a low table near at hand for drinks and other uses."[13]

There is a striking parallel here with some images dating from the early decades of Belgian colonization of Central Africa, such as the photograph titled *L'heure de l'apéritif au poste agricole de la Romée, en 1902* [*Happy hour at the agricultural outpost of Romée, 1902*], which depicts a number of white pioneers having a drink in front of a building that, somewhat ironically, is labeled *Villa beau-séjour* (see Figure 1.2). The static nature of the building, firmly grounded and skillfully constructed out of – most probably locally produced – brick, contrasts sharply with the "carry-on" furniture that was the only option in remote areas not yet unlocked by roads or railways – and Romée was just such a site. A late nineteenth-century article described "the indispensable chair" for the white colonizer in the Congo exactly as the model we see in the photograph: "a foldable chair composed out of three frames and a strong canvas. It is well known in Belgium for being used on the beach or while camping in the open."[14] The article emphasized "its solidity, the ease of repair, [and] its lightness making it particularly suitable to be transported," qualities characteristic of what in the literature is commonly labeled "campaign furniture," used by the military since the mid-nineteenth century. The simple foldable chair indeed was as much

Figure 1.2 L'heure de l'apéritif au poste agricole de la Romée, en 1902. Unknown photographer. HP.1957.34.164, Collection Royal Museum for Central Africa, Tervuren, 1902.

a "tool of empire" as were guns, adapted clothing or medication protecting against tropical diseases of all kinds.[15] These qualities were exactly in tune with the functionalist tenets underlying architects' pleas of the 1950s to introduce modern furniture in tropical Africa. The origin of the BKF chair in fact can be traced back to examples of campaign furniture, such as the late nineteenth-century foldable Paragon chair the British army used, or the so-called Tripolina chair employed in the 1930s by the Italians during their military ventures in Libya. But what also links the furniture of these two different eras beyond a mere obsession with mobility and functionality is a preference for a particular sitting position: that of the reclining, relaxing body.

Expanding markets

In 1982, Joseph Rykwert formulated an acerbic critique of the BKF chair that forms a forceful reminder not to take for granted the functionalist discourse of 1950s architects. In his opinion, the BKF chair completely lacks sitting comfort, which led him to conclude that "buyers who choose the chair cannot do so on rational grounds" and that they are "guided in their choice by promptings quite different from the dictates of reason."[16] Reconstructing what made this chair a design icon provides us with some hints of what these "promptings" underlying its worldwide success might have been. Originally designed for an apartment building in Buenos Aires by three former employees of Le Corbusier's office, the BKF chair quickly gained an international reputation after being noticed in 1940 by Edgar Kaufmann Jr., then design director of the Museum of Modern Art in New York. Commercialized by Knoll from 1947 onward, the BKF chair was also heavily promoted by André Bloc, editor in chief of *L'Architecture d'Aujourd'hui*, who was instrumental in having it produced from 1951 onward by the French firm Airborne under the label AA.[17] Its popularity occurred precisely at a moment in time when furniture designers and manufacturers were seeking to expand their markets, confronting designers with the challenge of how to make more efficient – and thus lucrative – the export of what was still an expensive and bulky commodity to transport.[18] In that respect, foldable or easy to demount and (re-)assemble artifacts, often resulting from new and ingenious construction methods, offered promising prospects for reaching new markets.

During the immediate post-war years, Central Africa presented itself as such a potentially lucrative market. The Belgian Congo in particular witnessed important economic development, with Europeans arriving in growing numbers. From the late 1940s onward, housing shortages for white colonizers posed a major challenge in most major urban centers in Congo, triggering Brussels-based building firms and real estate agents to develop activities in various Congolese cities. Kinshasa in particular became known as "la ville champigonne" ["the mushrooming city"], as its skyline gradually was reshaped by multistory constructions along its main boulevards.[19] For the average Belgian family, moving to the Congo often implied a certain upward social mobility, making modern housing amenities a rather common aspect of a colonial lifestyle. Apartment buildings were equipped with up-to-date bathrooms, the Cubex kitchen started to make its entry in the Congo and Philips launched publicity campaigns to promote its household utensils to a colonial clientele.[20]

Furniture manufacturers were rather slow to make their move on the colonial scene, however. Already in 1950 Maurice Delétang critiqued what he defined in more general terms as the "ostrich policy" of Belgian design firms who avoided the risk of

20   *Johan Lagae*

being innovative. As a result "Belgian products were less and less in demand abroad and foreign products more and more in demand in Belgium."[21] Delétang cited the demountable furniture conceived for colonial export by Belgian designer Anatole Vanden Berghe as an exception to this rule and praised in particular a living and dining room ensemble that, due to its ingenious construction, could be shipped in a volume of only one and a half m³. Delétang also expressed his appreciation for those rare colonial firms choosing to rely exclusively on Belgian products to furnish their offices and housing accommodations of their agents, as they had well understood that "their interest is related, directly or indirectly, to the economic well-being of the *métropole* and that it is their task to help their countries of origin."

Yet furniture produced by foreign manufacturers that became popular in Belgium at the time also quickly entered the Central African market. Swedish-produced Dux furniture, which was distributed in Belgium by the Dutch-based firm Artifort and was well received in design circles, for instance, quickly made its way to the Belgian colony, as the enterprise opened a furniture factory in Kinshasa already in the early 1950s, quickly becoming a key player on the market.[22] In 1954, the De Coene firm obtained the license to sell Knoll furniture such as the BKF chair or artifacts designed by Harry Bertoia and Arne Jacobsen in the Benelux and the Belgian Congo.[23] The popularity of such modern furniture among colonizers in Congo was in tune with a more general emergence of an American way of life in post-war Congo and its capital city, Kinshasa, in particular, a phenomenon that late colonial propaganda stressed by presenting photographs of big boulevards filled with American cars or shop windows filled with the most up-to-date consumer goods.[24] In a Cold War context of shifting geopolitical tensions, the coverage of the prosperous economic situation in Congo in popular American magazines such as *Life* or *Reader's Digest*, however, points at a US interest in the Belgian colony that was not only economic but also political in nature.[25]

The post-war era also witnessed a continuity of the economic logic underscoring the early colonization of sub-Saharan Africa, which since the late nineteenth century was based on the extraction of raw materials that were subsequently processed in the home country to finally be exported again as finished products to the overseas territories for metropolitan benefit. Publicity pages of 1950s issues of *L'Architecture d'Aujourd'hui* make abundantly clear that firms situated all over the French nation, from building companies to producers of concrete building components, roof sheets or even paint, benefited from the building boom in tropical Africa. The workshop of Jean Prouvé forms a case in point. Indeed, the origin of the specific furniture that he developed for tropical Africa, such as the Fauteuil Colonial FC 10 (1949) or the Tropique versions of the Chaise Cafétéria n°300 (1950), as well as his prototype Maison tropique à portique (1949–50), is intrinsically linked to the interests of the French colonial authorities and the economic agenda of the firm Aluminium française that sought to expand its market to the overseas territories.[26]

Promoting "modern living" in the tropics

Expanding markets also requires informing one's target audience, as Jean Prouvé understood well. Advertisements for Prouvé furniture "conceived especially for tropical regions" were included in issues of leading professional magazines such as *L'Architecture d'Aujourd'hui*,[27] while the first prototype of the Maison tropique, before being shipped to Niamey (Niger), was presented on the banks of the River Seine in

Paris during the exhibition *l'Equipement de l'Union française*, held in October 1949.[28] Such public presentations had, of course, a long pedigree in late nineteenth-century national and international fairs, and world's and commercial fairs remained strategic instruments to promote commodities produced for the overseas market until the late colonial era. The Brussels World's Fair of 1958, for instance, included a large presentation of household amenities for export to Congo while in the garden of its colonial section a colonial model house was on show that, according to one of its designers, was largely inspired by Prouvé's Maison tropique (see Figure 1.3).[29]

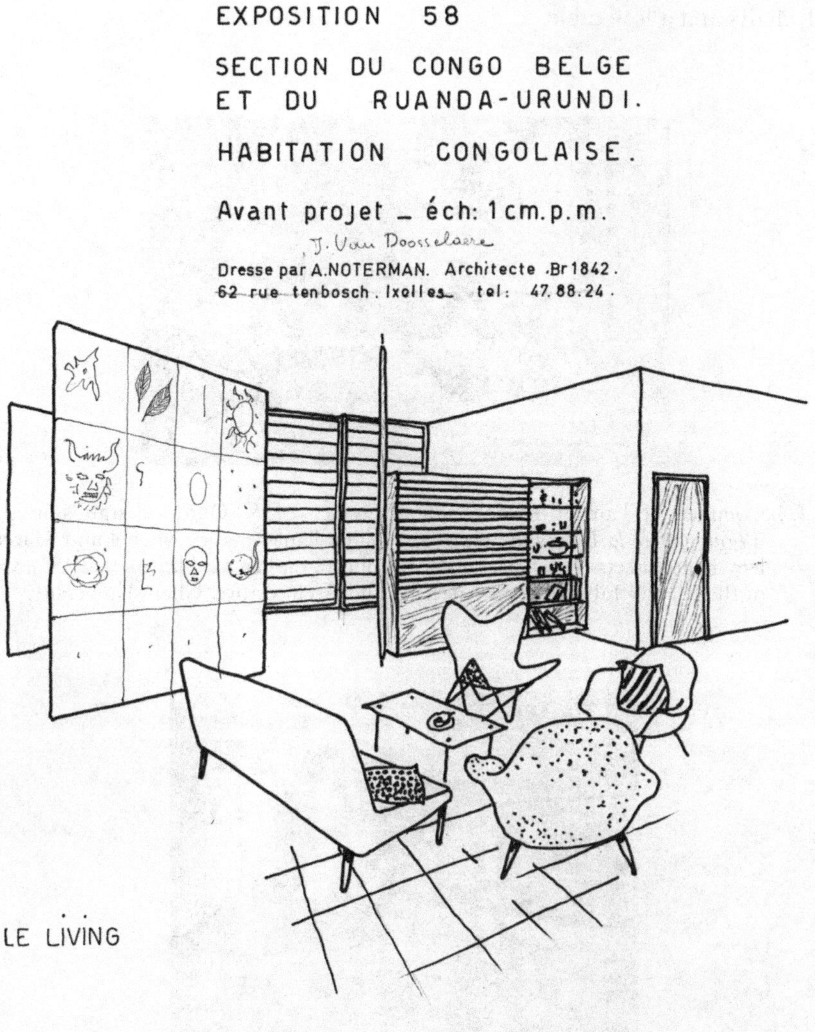

Figure 1.3 Model house for "white colonizers" presented at Expo 58 in Brussels: preliminary sketch of the interior with a BKF chair, among other furniture pieces. André Noterman and Jean Van Doosselaere, architects (1957–8). Fonds Noterman © Archives d'Architecture Moderne, Brussels.

22 *Johan Lagae*

Such commercial fairs were also organized in the colony itself, as was the case, for instance, in 1955 in the city of Kisangani (see Figures 1.4 and 1.5). It was the only such fair to be mediated in the Belgian architectural press, as its scenography was authored by the prominent Belgian modernist architect Paul-Amaury Michel in collaboration with the lesser known, locally based designer Marcel Molleman.[30] The various pavilions were set in a beautiful natural setting treated à la Roberto Burle Marx. Some were inspired by the free forms of Brazilian modernism while the elegant tubular structures of the main official pavilion, the so-called Honorary Salon of Belgium, echoed the woven structures of traditional artifacts. The latter housed the stand of the tourist office situated adjacent to the one of the Ministry of Economic Affairs, which was shaped as the veranda of a modern colonial home, including an ensemble of BKF chairs and a low table.

Figure 1.4 Commercial Fair of Kisangani/Stanleyville, 1955. Outdoor stands in the *Hall d'honneur de la Belgique*, with BKF chairs. Paul-Amaury Michel and Marcel Molleman, architects (1954–5). Unknown photographer. *La Maison* 9 (1955). Courtesy of the Faculty Library of Engineering and Architecture, Ghent University.

Figure 1.5 Belgian Congo Pavilion, Paris World's Fair, 1937: living room of a model house for a "white colonizer," with furniture by René Donckers. Fernand Petit, architect (1937). Unknown photographer. *L'Ossature Métallique* 5 (1938). Courtesy of the Faculty Library of Engineering and Architecture, Ghent University.

This presentation echoed the official representation of the Belgian Congo at the 1937 Paris World's Fair, which was the first colonial section to break with the exotic displays of the Belgian colony at earlier events.[31] Designed by architect Fernand Petit as an elegant tropical bungalow, part of the interior display was conceived as a model home for the colonies, complete with contemporary tubular furniture that had made its appearance in the home country only a decade before (see Figure 1.5). Contemporary observers explicitly praised its functionalist design, authored by architect René Donckers, but also stressed the joyful character of the furniture that resulted from the possibility of completing the tubular structures with colorful canvases. This would even allow the introduction of a touch of *couleur locale* in one's interior by using cloth with African patterns and prints.[32] The 1937 colonial section thus conveyed an important new message. It suggested that the ideal home of a white colonizer in Congo "no longer was exclusively European" and that opting for a functional, modern interior instead should go hand in hand with an attention to include local artifacts, as the modern colonizer "loved to live amongst decorative artefacts in which the lyric sentiment of the black race was embodied."[33]

Not merely importing a Western-style interior, but rather making an effort at creating an environment responding to the local culture was a message that also pervaded the pages of the *Bulletin de l'Union des Femmes Coloniales*. This popularizing magazine targeted the growing community of colonial spouses in the Belgian Congo and discussed various aspects of colonial life, ranging from fashion to garden design, local art, aspects of local history and even living costs. Since its foundation in 1926, the magazine had opened it pages to contributions on the colonial house and already during the interwar years had promoted the use of modern furniture on several occasions.[34] This attention grew in the immediate post-war years. Modernist architects and designers such as Charles Van Nueten, Eric Lemesre or the Wery Brothers were given the opportunity to present their ideas on the colonial house and its interior,[35] while the magazine also featured contributions presenting contemporary furniture design that was marketed in Belgium at the time, such as that produced by the firm Pas Toe.[36] Such advice coincided with what the association advocated in a small guidebook directed to women leaving for the Congo titled *La femme au Congo. Conseils aux partantes,* published in 1956: "In Europe, and in the Nordic countries in particular, demountable furniture of a very practical kind is produced which is particularly suited for use in tropical regions and that is easily transportable. Such artefacts allow [you] to complement a banal interior by adding a personal touch."[37]

The Union des Femmes Coloniales (UFC) held an ambivalent position on the topic, however, as its periodical also functioned as a forum where colonial housewives articulated opinions and experiences, which sometimes opposed those held by architects and designers. A survey on the housing accommodation and its interior arrangement, organized by the UFC during the interwar years, for instance, makes clear that most colonial spouses did not favor lightweight metal furniture. Many confessed making use of wooden furniture produced by locally based carpenters or missionary workshops.[38] Pages of practical advice on house and garden decoration that were published in the post-war era similarly revealed a strong preference for an interior that can best be described as "petit bourgeois," giving attention to creating a cozy setting via upholstery, bibelots brought from the home country and so on. The upward social mobility that often resulted from a move to the Congo did not necessarily go hand in hand with a shift in taste. As most white colonizers only came to the Congo on short-term contracts

24   *Johan Lagae*

and as housing accommodation was generally provided by the employer, the context of domesticity also differed significantly from that in the home country. The colonial interior in fact functioned not only as a shelter for the tropical climate, as modernist architects wanted their clients to believe, but, more importantly, became an instrument via which these clients negotiated their "condition of temporary displacement."[39] Creating a "comme chez soi," often by mimicking the interior of one's home in Belgium, was the task of the colonial spouse who, as Pierre Halen has suggested, acted as a true "link with the metropole."[40] While suitable on functionalist grounds, mobile and lightweight modern furniture failed to respond to the psychological need for suppressing feelings of uprootedness. Permitting easy travel from one appointed housing accommodation to another, such "nomadic furniture" countered rather than reinforced a sense of belonging, which helps explain the public's reluctance to embrace it.

Corporate patronage

Modern furniture was thus less prominently present in tropical Africa than images in architectural periodicals or handbooks of the time suggest. Some substantial ensembles of it were, nevertheless, commissioned in specific cases. There are some indications that the upmarket segment of apartment buildings in post-war urban centers in the Belgian colony provided a specific niche for those firms seeking to export modern furniture. Offices and residential accommodations of institutions like the Banque du Congo belge as well as breweries in Congo that were realized in various urban centers formed another.[41] But the most prominent players in this respect probably were the national airline companies in both Congo-Kinshasa and Congo-Brazzaville, which provided the logistic backbone of the booming economy that turned Central Africa into a major center of international trade from the early 1950s onward. By using contemporary design to furnish their offices and the housing accommodation of their staff, they reinforced their corporate identities, presenting themselves as innovative and globally oriented enterprises fully embracing modernity.

The Belgian airline company Sabena explicitly promoted Kinshasa as central node in a continental traffic network, very much like it presented Brussels as the "crossroads of Europe." At the request of its director general, Gilbert Périer, a real "captain of industry" as well as a friend of the arts, architect Claude Laurens started to work for the company in 1951, designing, among others, a project for the Hôtel Aviamar. Situated in the city center of Kinshasa, and with a quick and efficient connection to the airport, the complex first and foremost targeted a clientele of businessmen, in a vein similar to the international Hilton hotels that were to emerge worldwide soon afterward. Early sketches of the hotel rooms already suggest the use of modern furniture and the waiting area of the air terminus building, the only part of the complex actually to be built, featured Dux fauteuils (see Figure 1.6). Laurens also designed two high-rise residential towers for housing the Sabena staff, a job that included a large-scale commission of furniture he had designed for previous projects.[42] Working for the top segment of the colonial real estate market, Laurens also was one of the first architects to equip his apartment projects with Cubex kitchens.

On the other side of the Congo River in French-ruled Congo-Brazzaville, Air France also started to build new infrastructures as a result of its expanding activities. In 1949, it commissioned French architect Henri-Jean Calsat to design the Hôtel Relais to house its transit passengers. The ensemble, which was well received in contemporary media, was conceived as a series of seven freestanding bungalow-like pavilions, composed out

Figure 1.6 Air terminus building, Kinshasa: interior with Dux fauteuils distributed by the Dutch firm Artifort, ca. 1956. Claude Laurens, architect (1954–5). Unknown photographer. © Archives Laurens Paris.

of prefabricated metal components completed with walls constructed by local labor.[43] Raoul Guys, a designer from Paris whose work has received little attention so far, was responsible for the interior furnishing. Under the name Oro, Guys had already developed a set of lightweight furniture he marketed specifically for furnishing colonial dwellings, promoting them on the basis of the same kinds of arguments used to market "campaign furniture" at the end of the late nineteenth century: "durable materials; robustness combined with lightness allowing safe, efficient and cheap transport; simple construction methods and flexibility in order to respond to the change of use."[44] The elegant tubular structure of most of the furniture in the series was directly inspired by the BKF chair, with which Guys was very familiar.[45] In sketches for the interior of a guesthouse for overseas territories that Guys presented in a promotional brochure, the latter appears next to his own designs (see Figure 1.7). The most eye-catching piece in the series was the so-called Fauteuil confort rotin, in which the tubular structure was replaced by a set of bent wooden elements tied together, as if the BKF chair had "gone native." It featured prominently in preliminary sketches for the Hôtel Relais in Brazzaville, where it was actually used in large numbers (see Figure 1.8).[46]

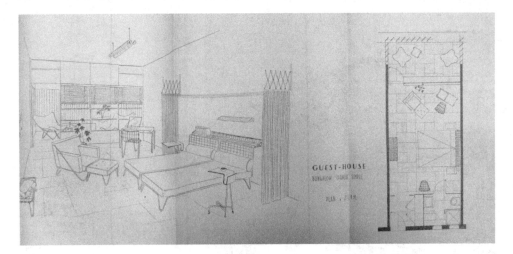

Figure 1.7 Proposal for the interior of a room in a guesthouse for the tropics, late 1940s. Raoul Guys, interior designer. Fonds Henri-Jean Calsat, Université de Genève. Courtesy of University of Geneva.

Figure 1.8 Hôtel Relais, Brazzaville, with interior furnishings by Raoul Guys, ca. 1952. Henri-Jean Calsat, architect (1949–50). Unknown photographer. Fonds Henri-Jean Calsat, Université de Genève. Courtesy of University of Geneva.

André Bloc, highly favored Guys' furniture and was instrumental in linking him with the most famous French designers of the time, Charlotte Perriand and Jean Prouvé.[47] Via the Airborne firm, Guys got involved with them for the commission of the interior furnishings of the Cité Universitaire Antony near Paris,[48] and some sources suggest that he had already been involved in producing what is no doubt the most substantial – and probably best known – ensemble of Perriand and Prouvé furniture in sub-Saharan Africa: the interior arrangements of the Air France building in Brazzaville, built to house the airline staff.[49] Locally known as "l'Unité d'Habitation Air-France," this landmark complex accommodating sixty-three housing units in an elongated five-level volume was constructed between 1950 and 1952 by a team of architects headed by J. Hébrard and J. Lefebvre. It counts as a prominent example of "tropical modernism" in Africa.[50] Prouvé's contribution extended beyond the mere production of the furniture, as he also manufactured metal building components that were crucial in the architectonic appearance of the building, in particular the adjustable aluminum *brise-soleil*. For the interior arrangements Perriand adapted some of her earlier furniture designs specifically to the local climate, making use of tropical wood and metal sheeting and providing a solution to ventilate cupboards in order to respond to the hot humid conditions. As such, her approach ties in with Fry and Drew's plea to base the design of furniture in the tropics on lessons taken from vernacular examples, thus reminding us that modern furniture in the tropics is not necessarily a mere object of import, but often is the result of varying degrees of adaption and transformation, producing a "local dialect" of what some would perhaps call too easily "global design."[51]

"Hey! Wanna sell that chair?"

Over the past decades, architectural historians have gradually become interested in the legacy of post-war architecture in Africa, a continent that for a very long time was overlooked in survey books.[52] This has also resulted in the rediscovery of the presence of modern furniture in this region, a phenomenon design historians and aficionados ignored until recently. Between 1994 and 1995, for instance, the first substantial research on the architectural legacy in Brazzaville was conducted, the resulting publication presenting, among other things, the surviving two prototypes of Prouvé's Maison tropique as well as the Air France building, mentioning explicitly its – at the time still almost intact – interior furnishing by Perriand and Prouvé.[53]

The modest publication appeared exactly at a time when 1950s design was becoming a highly sought after luxury commodity. The mid-1990s indeed were the era of an emerging *Prouvémania*, with original 1950s design artifacts produced by the French designer being sold at exorbitant prices at international auctions. Parisian gallery owners had succeeded in acquiring a considerable bulk of Prouvé and Perriand furniture as a result of the refurbishment of the interior of large-scale projects in France, such as the Maison de Brésil and the Maison de Turquie of Paris's Cité Universitaire. Via lavishly illustrated books, they not only documented this legacy, but also created a market for it.[54] Not surprisingly, the rediscovery of the particular legacy of 1950s furniture in tropical Africa that had completely remained "off the radar" immediately attracted their interest. In this context, Eric Touchaleaume, the owner of Galérie 54, a Paris-based gallery specializing in twentieth-century architecture and design, stands out. Described in 2008 by the *Guardian* as "the Indiana Jones of furniture collecting,"

28   *Johan Lagae*

Touchaleaume was instrumental in retrieving the three existing prototypes of Jean Prouvé's Maison tropique from Niamey and Brazzaville, as well as the furniture of the Air France building, introducing individual pieces on the Western market to his great profit.[55] More recently, he mounted a similar operation regarding the furniture that Pierre Jeanneret and Le Corbusier had designed for Chandigarh.[56]

While such practices are not uncommon with regard to twentieth-century design surviving in Europe, they become more messy in the context of postcolonial Central Africa, which bears a long history of asymmetrical power relations. The endeavors of Touchaleaume, who bluntly legitimized his operations as an act of "salvaging" heritage from the "heart of darkness,"[57] have created controversy, triggering harsh critiques in diverse media on what some considered no less than a perverse form of looting. Under the title "Hey! Wanna sell that chair?" an individual blogger unmasked the perverse mechanisms at work in the retrieval of the Brazzaville furniture,[58] while this questionable approach to objects that belong to a "shared heritage" has already been the subject of scholarly articles.[59] Subtle, yet profound forms of critique have also been articulated through artistic projects that resituate Prouvé's work in a larger African/colonial history, a context that Prouvé aficionados often deliberately downplay.[60] Angela Ferreira's entry for the Portuguese section of the 2007 Venice Biennale, for instance, poses very unsettling questions on the fate of the three prototypes of Prouvé's Maison tropique, through revisiting and documenting the sites in Niamey and Brazzaville after their retrieval.[61] As a counteract to what they considered the "disguised postcolonialism" of the earlier reappropriation of the originals by Touchaleaume and the like, the Danish artists' collective Superflex stressed the African nature of Prouvé's work in 2012 by commissioning local furniture makers in Brazzaville to execute a series of reproductions of his famous Cafétéria chair on the basis of a set of drawings they produced after an original chair from the collection of the Musée d'Art Moderne in St-Etienne.[62] Through the Superflex project, this particular design icon gains a complex, even subversive "geography." Originally conceived as a tool for creating comfort for the white man who travels, explores and exploits a colonial territory, and subsequently "returned to sender" decades later as a design commodity for satisfying the luxury appetite of an elite in the former colonial "center," the Cafétéria chair is finally brought back to postcolonial Brazzaville through an act of having it recopied by African carpenters. As such, the Superflex project forms a crucial reminder of the fact that "global design" cannot be understood as an abstract category, and that any meaningful discussion of it requires following the often sinuous and unexpected trajectories of particular artifacts through time and space.

Acknowledgements

The author wishes to thank Bernard Toulier and Tristan Gilloux, for sharing their knowledge on the architectural heritage in Brazzaville and providing information on their 1994–5 fieldwork; Angela Ferreira for sharing ideas on her Prouvé project; Fredie Floré for suggesting sources on specific aspects of design history; Moniek Bucquoye, for her prospective research in the Artifort archives; and Luc Bucquoye for his account of the Dux factory in Congo. I would also like to thank Bernadette Odoni-Cremer for her support when I consulted the archives of Henri-Jean Calsat in Geneva (research financed through the COST-action IS0904); and the Laurens family for having opened their archives to me in the mid-1990s. Finally, my gratitude also goes to all my students at the Department of Architecture and Urban Planning of Ghent University, who in the context of seminars organized over the past decade participated in research on specific topics related to the narrative presented here.

Notes

1 Charles Van Nueten, "Comment construirons-nous notre maison au Congo?" *Bulletin de l'Union des Femmes Coloniales* 4 (1954): 18–20.
2 Liane Liesens, "Charles Van Nueten," in *Dictionnaire de l'Architecture en Belgique de 1830 à nos jours*, ed. Anne Van Loo (Antwerp: Mercator Fonds, 2003), 580–1.
3 Maxwell Fry and Jane Drew, *Tropical Architecture in the Humid Zone* (New York: Reinhold Publishing Corporation, 1956), 105, 109–23.
4 Fernando Alvarez and Jordi Roig, ed., *Bonet Castellana* (Barcelona: Universitat Politècnica de Catalunya, 1999), 51–5.
5 Lesley Jackson, *Contemporary: Architecture and Interiors of the 1950s* (London: Phaidon Press, 1994), 147.
6 Fredie Floré, *Lessons in Modern Living* (Ghent: WZW Editions and Productions, 2004). I am using the word "metropolitan" in this text in its colonial sense to refer to the *métropole* or home country.
7 Glenn Adamson, Giorgio Riello and Sarah Teasley, ed., *Global Design History* (Abingdon: Routledge, 2011), 2. I'm borrowing the term "difficult objects" from the introduction to this edited volume.
8 See Johan Lagae, "In Search of a 'comme chez soi.' The Ideal Colonial House in Congo (1885–1960)," in *Itinéraires croisés de la modernité au Congo Belge (1920–1950)*, ed. Jean-Luc Vellut (Tervuren/Paris: CEDAF/L'Harmattan, 2001), 239–82.
9 See in this respect the work of Hannah Leroux for the anglophone sphere and Tristan Gilloux for the francophone sphere.
10 There is a substantial literature on Jean Prouvé's work and his projects in Africa. The third volume of the *Oeuvre complète* edited by Peter Sulzer, treating the period 1944–55 (Basel: Birkhaüser, 2005) remains an essential reference. For a recent publication on the Maison tropique, see Olivier Cinqualbre, ed., *Jean Prouvé: The Tropical House* (Paris: Editions du Centre Pompidou, 2009).
11 Van Nueten, "Comment construirons-nous notre maison au Congo?"
12 As several scholars have noted, boredom in fact constitutes a crucial characteristic of colonial life. See, for instance, Jeffrey A. Auberbach, "Imperial Boredom," *Common Knowledge* 2 (2005): 283–305.
13 Fry and Drew, *Tropical Architecture*, 105.
14 Anonymous, "Le Mobilier du blanc au Congo," *La Belgique Coloniale* 4 (1896): 43–4.
15 Daniel R. Headrick, *The Tools of Empire: Technology and European Imperialism in the Nineteenth Century* (New York: Oxford University Press, 1981).
16 Joseph Rykwert, "The Sitting Position: A Question of Method," in *The Necessity of Artifice*, ed. Joseph Rykwert (London: Academy Editions, 1982), 27.
17 Alvarez and Roig, *Bonet Castellana*, 51–5. Brian Lutz, *Knoll: A Modernist Universe* (New York: Rizzoli, 2010), 109. For a brief history of the firm Airborne, see Dominique Forrest, ed., *Mobi Boom: L'Explosion du design en France 1945–1975* (Paris: Les Arts Décoratifs, 2010), 269. For a more substantial discussion, see Pierre Deligne, *Airborne: Le Design Made in France (1945–1975)* (Paris: Galerie Les Modernistes, 2012).
18 Jackson, *Contemporary*, 152–7.
19 Bernard Toulier, Johan Lagae and Marc Gemoets, ed., *Kinshasa: Architecture et paysage urbains* (Paris: Editions Somogy, 2010), 78–85.
20 On the Cubex kitchen, see Arthur Ruëgg, "De Koninck's Contribution to the 'New Dwelling,'" in *Louis Herman De Koninck: Architect of Modern Times*, ed. Caroline Mierop and Anne van Loo (Brussels: Archives d'Architecture Moderne, 1998), 187–215.
21 Maurice Delétang, "Meubles belges démontables et combinables pour la colonie," *La Maison* 10 (1952): 330–2.

30   Johan Lagae

22 Especially the Dux fauteuil became a popular piece of furniture, both in Belgium and in Congo; see N. H., "Zetels bekijken en er in zitten," *Ruimte* 6 (1954): 39. Dux was founded in 1926 and was first known because of the very comfortable beds it produced; see www.dux.com/About-DUX/. During the post-war years, it also started to produce modern furniture. Information on the founding of a Dux furniture factory in Kinshasa was kindly provided by Luc Bucquoye in an interview with the author (May 25, 2015). On Artifort, see Forrest, *Mobi Boom*, 270; Ewald Jamin, Loes Schwenke and Sje Weijnen, *Artifort* (Rotterdam: 010 Publishers, 1990). One of Artifort's most successful products was the so-called Congo-chair designed by Theo Ruth. Its name refers to the fact that its designer took inspiration from a traditional African seat for the constructive principle of the chair.

23 Frank Herman and Terenja Van Dijck, ed., *De Kortrijkse Kunstwerkstede Gebroeders De Coene* (Kortrijk: Uitgeverij Groeninghe, 2006), 146.

24 We still lack substantial research on the post-war economy in Congo and the introduction of a consumer culture in which the American interest is clearly analyzed. Economic historian Guy Vanthemsche, however, claims that Congo never presented a mass market for consumer goods produced by Belgian industry, arguing that the main economic actors were situated in the mining industry, the sector of international transport or the production of metal. See Guy Vanthemsche, *La Belgique et le Congo: Nouvelle Histoire de la Belgique*, vol. 4 (Brussels: Editions Complexe, 2007), 197.

25 *The Belgian Congo Appraised: A Selection of Articles on the Belgian Congo Recently Published in the American Daily and Weekly Press*, Belgian Government Information Center, New York, undated [probably 1953]. On Congo as a playground in Cold War politics, especially after independence, see John Kent, *America, the UN and Decolonisation: Cold War Conflict in Congo* (Abingdon: Routledge, 2010).

26 Although the literature on Prouvé is extensive, the colonial context of his Africa work is most often neglected in discussions. The best analysis in this respect is Tristan Gilloux, "The Maison 'Tropique.' A Modernist Icon or the Ultimate Colonial Bungalow?" *Fabrications* 2 (2008): 6–25.

27 See, for instance, publicity for the "Ateliers Jean Prouvé (agent exclusive: Steph Simon, Paris): tous meubles d'habitat et de bureaux / meubles en alliage léger et démontables spécialement conçus pour les pays tropicaux," *L'Architecture d'Aujourd'hui* 35 (1951): LXXIX.

28 The presentation was also mediated in the same year via the *Revue de l'Aluminium* 161 (1949): 419–21.

29 See Johan Lagae, "Modern Living in the Congo: The 1958 Colonial Housing Exhibit and Postwar Domestic Practices in the Belgian Congo," *Journal of Architecture* 4 (2004): 477–94.

30 Pierre-Louis Flouquet, "Urbanisme et architecture à la foire de Stanleyville," *La Maison* 9 (1955): 272–4.

31 Johan Lagae, "Displaying Authenticity and Progress: Architectural Representation of the Belgian Congo at International Exhibitions in the 1930s," *Third Text* 50 (2000): 21–32.

32 Anonymous, "Le Pavillon du Congo belge à l'Exposition de Paris. Architecte: F. Petit," *l'Ossature métallique* 5 (1938): 221; G.-D. Périer, "L'art congolais à Paris," June 12, 1937, newspaper clipping; Afrika Archives, Brussels, file O.C. 476.

33 Gaston-Denys Périer, "Le Pavillon du Congo," *Les Beaux-Arts* 251 (1937): 63.

34 In the interwar period, advice on the interior arrangement of the colonial house was often inspired by articles in Belgian architecture and design periodicals such as *Clarté*. A 1937 issue featured furniture designed by R. M. Schindler. For a general assessment of the debate on colonial house that occurred in the pages of the *Bulletin*, see Lagae, "In Search of a 'comme chez soi.'"

35 *Bulletin de l'UFC*, April 1954, 18–20; *Bulletin de l'UFC*, July 1954, 16–18; *Bulletin de l'UFC*, October 1954, 14.

36 *Bulletin de l'UFC*, July 1952, 35; *Bulletin de l'UFC*, October 1953, 27.

37 *La femme au Congo: Conseils aux partantes* (Brussels: Union des Femmes Coloniales, 1956), 59. Traces of a similar discourse can be found in the pages of *Habiter en Belgique et au Congo*, a Kinshasa-based magazine, of which only six issues appeared in 1954–5.

38 See, for instance, responses to the survey in the *Bulletin de l'UFC*, January 1926, 4–5; *Bulletin de l'UFC*, March–April 1929, 11–12; *Bulletin de l'UFC*, September–October 1931, 10.

Nomadic furniture in tropical Africa 31

39 I'm borrowing this notion from Hilde Heynen and André Loeckx, "Scenes of Ambivalence: Concluding Remarks on Architectural Patterns of Displacement," *Journal of Architectural Education* 2 (1998): 100.

40 Pierre Halen, *Le petit belge a vu grand: Une littérature coloniale* (Brussels: Ed. Labor, 1993), 296–302, 344–8.

41 Preliminary research in the part of the archives of the Belgian construction firm Blaton that deals with its African activities confirms this, as we were able to locate in various files photographs and publicity folders depicting pieces of modern furniture used in colonial interiors. The Blaton archive is currently held at the Archives d'Architecture Moderne in Brussels. Luc Bucquoye pointed out that until the early 1970s, banks and breweries were almost the exclusive clients of the Dux furniture factory in Kinshasa.

42 Johan Lagae and Denise Laurens, *Claude Laurens: Architecture. Projets et Réalisations* (Ghent: Department of Architecture and Urban Planning, 2001).

43 Documentation on the project is to be found in the archives of Henri-Jean Calsat, University of Geneva. For a contemporary critique see, "Le relais-hôtel de l'Aéroport de Maya-Maya à Brazzaville," unidentified clipping, October 1950; Archives Henri-Jean Calsat, Geneva.

44 Raoul Guys (Paris), publicity brochure, Archives Henri-Jean Calsat, Geneva.

45 In fact, André Bloc had first presented the BKF chair to Guys, who started to manufacture it for the French market, but soon Airborne would take over its production, making an agreement with Guys to work together.

46 Guy's Oro ensemble was used in all transit points of the Air France network in tropical Africa, counting for twenty-four sites that included the important Hôtel N'Gor in Dakar, Senegal. Deligne, *Airborne*, 36–7.

47 Raoul Guys' link with André Bloc is mentioned in Pierre Deligne, *Airborne*, as well as on www.1stdibs.com/furniture/seating/lounge-chairs/important-raoul-guys-antony-lounge-chairscite-university-paris-1954/id-f_780053, where his involvement in the Air France building in Brazzaville is also mentioned.

48 See, for instance, Marianne Brabant and Dominique Forrest, "La période glorieuse des collectivités," in Forrest, *Mobi Boom*, 156–83.

49 The fact that Charlotte Perriand's husband was director of Air France helps explain in part why they received this as well as other commissions for the airline company. See Brabant and Forrest, "La période glorieuse des collectivités," 178. For Perriand and Prouvé's work for the Air France building in Brazzaville, see also Mary McLeod, ed., *Charlotte Perriand: An Art of Living* (New York: Harry N. Abrams Publishers, 2003), 138–40.

50 The building featured in "Brazzaville, immeuble d'habitation pour Air France," *L'Architecture d'Aujourd'hui* 46 (1953): 100–1, as well as in Fry and Drew, *Tropical Architecture*, 156–8.

51 I am borrowing the notion of "local dialect" from Maxwell Fry, who described "tropical modernism" as a "local dialect of internationalism." Fry, "West Africa," *Architectural Review* 761 (1960): 8.

52 For a recent, broad survey of post-war architecture in Africa, see Benno Albrecht, ed., *Africa: Big Chance, Big Change* (Bologna: Editrice Compositori, 2014).

53 Bernard Toulier, *Brazzaville-la-Verte: Congo* (Brazzaville: Centre Culturel Français, 1996). At the time of the mission led by Toulier, the Hôtel Relais by Calsat was already substantially transformed, with only one pavilion still standing and the interior completely refurbished. Information kindly provided by Bernard Touler and Tristan Gilloux.

54 For an example of such a publication, see Laurence Bergerot and Patrick Seguin, ed., *Jean Prouvé: Galerie Patrick Seguin – Sonnabend Gallery New York*, vol. 2 (Paris: Galerie Patrick Seguin, 2007).

55 Steve Rose, "House Hunting," *Guardian*, February 7, 2008. See also Eric Touchaleaume, ed., *Jean Prouvé # Les maison tropicales/Tropical Houses* (Paris: Galerie 54, 2006).

56 Eric Touchaleaume and Gerald Moreau, ed., *Le Corbusier – Pierre Jeanneret: The Indian Adventure. Design – Art – Architecture* (Paris: Editions Eric Touchaleaume, 2010).

57 In the publication on both his African and Indian operations, Touchaleaume presents his initiative explicitly in terms of an adventure, profiling himself as the explorer in search of design treasures, negotiating with Africans unaware of the value of the artifacts he is looking for.

58 Mondo Blogo, "Hey! Wanna Sell that Chair?" http://mondo-blogo.blogspot.be/2011/01/hey-wanna-sell-that-chair.html. The Air France building features in several other websites

32 *Johan Lagae*

that address its afterlife. See, for instance, some reviews of a show of photographs on the building by Philippe Guionie, presented in Brazzaville in 2013, www.jeuneafrique.com/article/ja2726p085.xml0.

59 "Shared heritage" is the rather problematic notion ICOMOS advanced to discuss built heritage in former colonized territories.

60 It is telling in this respect that Robert Rubin, who bought one of the prototypes of the Maison tropique, deliberately chose to restore it to "its moment of greatest promise: its pre-African configuration"; see Robert Rubin, "Jean Prouvé's Tropical House (Brazzaville, 1951): Preservation, Presentation, Reception," in *Jean Prouvé: The Tropical House*, ed. Olivier Cinqualbre, 115–32.

61 Jürgen Bock, ed., *Angela Ferreira: Maison tropicale* (Lisboa: Ministério da Cultura, 2007). African filmmaker Mantha Diawara shot a documentary of Angela Ferreira's visit to the former sites of the three prototypes of the Maison tropique. For a similar critical perspective on the fate of the Chandigarh furniture designed by Le Corbusier and Pierre Jeanneret, see Amie Siegel's 2013 film *Provenance*, http://amiesiegel.net/project/provenance.

62 David McLean, "Prouvé Made in Africa," 2012, www.superflex.net/tools/prouve_made_in_africa as well as Patrick Charpenel and Daniel McLean, ed., *Superflex: The Corrupt Show and the Speculative Machine* (Mexico City: Fundacion/Colleccion Jumex, 2013).

2 Modernism on vacation
The politics of hotel furniture in the Spanish Caribbean

Erica N. Morawski

In 1949, an article about the largest peacetime air shipment to date was published in newspapers throughout the United States.[1] This record-breaking transport included more than 3,000 chairs, 600 beds, 654 tables and 335 floor lamps sent to furnish the Caribe Hilton in San Juan, Puerto Rico from Chicago's Marshall Fields. While US business and industry were congratulating themselves for achieving this feat, the Puerto Rican popular press was extolling the Caribe Hilton project as the symbol of a redefined, modern Puerto Rico. That both the United States and Puerto Rico claimed the hotel as their own success points to the important role the Caribe Hilton played in shaping and projecting cultural identity and international relations, especially given the complex relationship between the United States and Puerto Rico, an unincorporated territory of the United States.[2] Based on goals of promoting democratic capitalist development in Latin American countries, the US government allowed Puerto Rico to project itself as a more independent nation than it really was. This policy was in contrast to the way US businesses involved in Cuba in the 1950s played an influential role in shaping the perception of this autonomous country as little more than a playground for US tourists. This was especially apparent in the case of hotel and casino building, a controversy that served as fuel for Fidel Castro's 1959 revolution. Using San Juan's Caribe Hilton (1949) and Cuba's Havana Riviera (1957) as representative case studies, this essay examines the pivotal part modern hotel interiors played in the promotion of various and often conflicting cultural nationalistic agendas in the post-war Spanish Caribbean.

Part of the power that vacation hotels wield stems from the fact that they are not generally seen as important civic structures, such as government buildings, which rank higher in a traditional hierarchy of building types. Moreover, part of the purpose of vacation hotels is to simply provide fun, leisure and other experiences that break from serious or everyday life. While their cocktail lounges and recreational pools project superficiality, this understudied type of design warrants more attention because hotels are, in fact, powerful agents of soft power, a concept political scientist Joseph Nye developed that entails the shaping of preferences and actions through attraction and persuasion, rather than through force or giving money. As architectural historian Greg Castillo described in relation to design, "rather than coercing, soft power entices, enlisting support through intangibles like culture, values, belief systems, and perceived moral authority."[3] Grounded in this framework and augmented by historian Dennis Merrill's use of soft power in his scholarship on tourism in Latin America, this chapter posits that as places where design and tourism intersect, these hotels were

34   *Erica N. Morawski*

especially potent agents of soft power and their interiors suggested complex notions of identity on the islands.[4] This analysis argues that modern design did not simply symbolize an imposition of powerful Western centers onto less powerful peripheral areas, but rather represents a complex web of adaptation, influence, negotiation and rejection.

Thanks to advancements in air travel combined with increased prosperity and vacation time after World War II, US citizens started to travel as never before, and San Juan and Havana were favored for being foreign yet close destinations.[5] Increased promotion of these two cities as post-war vacation destinations encouraged their popularity. Not only did these two cities have established tourism industries on which bigger programs could be built, but the US government was also eager to promote and support Latin American countries that favored democratic capitalism as a means of fighting the threat of communism.

Caribe Hilton: symbol of modernization

Although the United States has consistently excluded Puerto Rico from the nation while simultaneously denying its autonomy, the period under study here is marked by Puerto Rico's first popularly elected government and a growing sense of increased self-governance. Based on the power of the island's government, Puerto Rico functions as its own state, as defined as an organized political community under a government, albeit in complex and limited ways due to the ultimate control of the United States. However, Puerto Rico is quite commonly recognized as a nation, in the sense that nations can be defined as ethnic or cultural groups, and thus is also considered part of Latin America.

The Puerto Rican government devised the Caribe Hilton project as the symbol of Operation Bootstrap, the island's program of modernization. In the 1940s, the ruling Partido Popular Democrático (PPD) had endeavoured to establish industrial development and economic independence through government-owned and -operated factories. This unsuccessful initiative was followed by a decisive shift in the second half of the decade toward abandoning political independence in favor of cultivating economic growth through the development of US factories on the island. Although this change in policy positioned Puerto Rico as increasingly dependent on the United States, the local government cultivated a public image of Operation Bootstrap as representing the island's independence and self-sufficiency.[6]

Striving for American-style modernization through industry, program leaders recognized that along with luring foreign industry to Puerto Rico, the island could also benefit from a controlled increase in tourism.[7] As its first step, the government proposed a hotel project, which was to be financed and owned by the Puerto Rican government, but operated by a US company that would relinquish two-thirds of the profits back to the Puerto Rican government. In 1947, the Puerto Rican government approached Conrad Hilton, who had a reputation for running top-notch establishments, and he embraced the opportunity.[8] The complexity of the ownership and operational details of the Caribe Hilton contributed to the hotel's multiple identities. The Puerto Rican government conceived of it as a symbol of democracy and increased autonomy, and Hilton viewed the business venture with an attitude of paternalism shaped by anticommunist, capitalist values. As architectural historian Annabel Wharton showed, the Caribe Hilton established the business model that Hilton International Hotels would subsequently follow and was extremely important for Hilton's later success.[9] What has not been recognized, and is the focus of a larger research project I have undertaken, is the Puerto Rican government's authoritative role, rather than Hilton's, in defining the project's terms and design, which Hilton subsequently appropriated as the model for successive hotel projects around the globe.

In its attitude toward the hotel's design, the Puerto Rican government insisted that the architecture should represent nothing less than a statement to the world of the emergence of a redefined, modern Puerto Rico. Of the five firms the Puerto Rican government invited to participate in the competition for the commission, two were located in Florida and submitted Spanish Revival designs, which were indicative of the then-prevalent opinion of the style's appropriateness for Hispanic areas, including Florida. While Hilton preferred one of the Spanish Revival designs, the Puerto Rico Industrial Development Company (PRIDCO), the government entity led by Teodoro Moscoso that was organizing the project, selected a proposal by the local firm Toro, Ferrer and Torregrosa, which was dedicated to an aesthetic and approach inspired by the International Style.[10]

As construction of the hotel was nearing completion in the fall of 1949 for its December opening, *New York Times* art and architecture critic Aline B. Louchheim commented on the "bold new design" for this Caribbean hotel by poetically describing its design, especially in relation to the geography:

> Situated on a small peninsula, the hotel is a dazzling white concrete building, ten stories high. The determination to give each guest room its own private, shielded terrace and a full view of the multi-toned blue-green sea has resulted in an architectural expression which gives the narrow, rectangular building its special characteristics. For the walls of the eight floors of guest rooms are cantilevered out about five feet at a twenty-five-degree angle, with the concrete floor slabs hung between these vertical members.[11]

Throughout her review of the architecture, Louchheim underscored how the modern design of the hotel highlights the natural surroundings, and how the interior has a "pleasing mood" marked by "happy variety" through the use of "bamboo screens, travertine shielding walls, Brazilian burl woods, handsome Puerto Rican tiles [and] subtly colored walls and bright fabrics" (see Plate 2). Reviews in many other newspapers were consistent with Louchheim's positive reading of the hotel's design, ensuring an overall favorable vision of the hotel throughout the United States.

The Puerto Rican government's selection of modern architecture was bound to a larger campaign to shift away from identification with the past. Even though US tourists may have found Spanish Revival designs romantically appealing, the Puerto Rican government wanted to focus less on recreating traditional forms in favor of using climate and modernity as defining features that would help the island achieve first world status. The US government supported this campaign, as Puerto Rico was being used to showcase the Point Four Program, a US-sponsored program that promoted development through industrialization and capitalism.

"Tropical modernism" in Puerto Rican architecture

For US tourists, the experience of San Juan was largely defined through notions of tropicality, and while the Caribe Hilton's design stressed this, it complicated traditional notions of the tropics. A fundamental concept in establishing a place as foreign or exotic, tropical (or tropicality) refers to discursive representations of the tropics, which were the result of European, and later North American, ideas that have existed since the age of exploration in the late fifteenth century and are synonymous with the backward, the primitive and the primordial.[12] Art historian Krista Thompson has defined tropicality as "the complex visual systems through which the islands were imagined for tourist consumption and the social and political implications of these representations on actual physical space on the islands and their inhabitants."[13] Tropicality was visually captured through the picturesque, and its ability to be contained and manipulated allayed any fears that this foreign vocabulary was dangerous.

Though the concepts of tropicality and modernity were traditionally at odds with one another, much of the design in the Caribe Hilton redefined these notions by marrying the two. The design suggested that modernism and tropicality could be blended harmoniously in a manner that paralleled the concurrent trend in promoting a Puerto Rican identity as defined by tropicality and modernity. The focus on tropicality as a source of national identity helped avoid more contentious issues, such as the Spanish colonial past and the influence of the United States.

The use of pilotis, large glass walls, the absence of doors and other modern design elements in some of the public areas created an open plan that highlighted the outdoor environment and dissolved any sense of interior and exterior separation. This effect was perhaps most successfully achieved in a pool that flowed easily between the interior and exterior underneath a divider (see Plate 2). Located near the grand staircase, this water element was carefully placed so that all visitors would come in contact with it. Stepping stones and a handrail invited guests to interact with the nature in the hotel. An article from *Interiors + Industrial Design* noted that the pool's authenticity was maintained by keeping it "scrupulously muddy and disreputable, in conformance with the outdoor world it represents," so that the guests could experience the tropical world without having to go outside.[14] In effect, the architecture not only framed views of the tropical nature that was outdoors, but also brought it indoors, signaling modern design as an effective tool in taming nature for the guests' enjoyment.

Lobbies, bars and restaurants were the public face of the hotel and featured in promotional materials and articles that defined the Caribe Hotel as an innovative form of "tropical modernism." While the consistent reference to the hotel as "tropical modernism" does reveal the architects' attention to climate, this term was also employed as a way to promote difference or otherness. Promotional materials assuaged any fears that this otherness was too extreme through representations of the interior decoration of the lobby, which was defined by comfortable modern furniture and carefully incorporated elements of nature. One brochure for the hotel included a drawing showing Eero Saarinen's recent Womb chair (1946–8) placed next to the little indoor-outdoor pond (see Plate 2). Countering narratives that modern life had alienated man from nature, images of the Caribe Hilton's interiors projected a utopic vision that demonstrated how humankind had reconciled nature and modern life.

Modern living through modern design

As these descriptions demonstrate, the Caribe Hilton was a showcase for modern design. While interior decoration in Miami and Las Vegas hotels privileged stylistic themes, such as Louis XVI or Chinese, the Caribe Hilton took modern living as its theme, in conjunction with notions of the tropical, to promote a redefined Puerto Rican identity. For the majority of US tourists, their stay in the Caribe guestrooms was their first experience of living with modern design, which inverted the formality of the historical styles with which most of them lived. Puerto Rico seemed to be a place where life was easier, thanks to the informality and conveniences of modern design.

This message was conveyed in almost every aspect of the individual guestrooms, where convertible furniture with a modern aesthetic in flexible spaces functioned as living areas during the day and bedrooms at night (see Figure 2.1). Beds served as couches during the day and desks could transform into vanities. Modern design was incorporated in less visible ways as well. In order to attract US tourists and proclaim the technological sophistication of the island, the Puerto Rican government insisted on air-conditioned guestrooms. The first hotel to do so in the world,

Figure 2.1 Typical Caribe Hilton guestroom with Jens Risom chairs in foreground and telephone/radio console next to bed on right, ca. 1949. Toro, Ferrer and Torregrosa, architects (1947–9). Unknown photographer. Courtesy of the Hospitality Industry Archives, Conrad Hilton College, University of Houston.

38 *Erica N. Morawski*

the Caribe Hilton ensured each guest could control his or her comfort with the push of a button.[15]

The modern design of the guestrooms was accented with elements meant to impart a local flavor to the space. Chairs designed by Jens Risom boasted modern forms and had cushions covered with fabric with strong geometric patterns and bright colors, which US tourists most likely associated with local folk traditions.[16] The chair was representative of a global trend in modern design toward simplicity and functionality with an aesthetic that projected sophistication and refinement. By incorporating this fabric into his design, Risom demonstrated that traditional elements and progressive design were not mutually exclusive.

But perhaps no other aspect of the guestrooms exhibited the adept fusion of notions of the modern and the tropical better than the bedside console. The console housed modern devices, a telephone and radio, and had speakers covered with a rough, locally produced fabric meant to impart a local flavor to the piece. The incorporation of details that were understood as local within modern designs or technologies challenged the established notion of tropicality as primordial or timeless, instead pointing to the constructedness of tropicality as something that could be shaped and applied as desired.

Puerto Rican furniture design

Though most of the furniture was imported from the United States, chairs and benches by ARKLU were prominently displayed in the public spaces of the hotel (see Plate 2). ARKLU was a local furniture company founded by German émigré architect Henry Klumb and Stephen Arneson, both former Taliesin Fellows, in 1944. Initially drawn to Puerto Rico to run the Committee on the Design of Public Works, Klumb and Arneson were driven by social consciousness to adapt the architectural concepts of European and US modernism to the particularities of Puerto Rican culture in order to contribute to the development of the island.[17] Their modern furniture referenced global trends, but their use of local materials and techniques, coupled with their desire to blur the lines between interior and exterior, was uniquely Puerto Rican.

The incorporation of ARKLU furniture in the hotel helped the company gain international recognition. Advertisements described the furniture line as: "designed with striking simplicity, these pieces reflect the timeless beauty of simple, uncomplicated living."[18] Archival records indicate that ARKLU received a number of commissions as a result of the strong impression the furniture left on people who stayed at the hotel. Unfortunately, due to insufficient raw materials and labor, the company was unable to fill many of these orders and folded in 1948. However, the failure of ARKLU does not diminish the importance of its role in promoting modern Puerto Rican design, which advanced the government's goal of an island identity based on modernity and tropicality. ARKLU furniture underscored the important distinction between simplistic and simplicity. Rejecting notions that to be tropical was to be simplistic or unsophisticated, ARKLU furniture suggested that the tropical could be a valuable tool to guide the design world toward simplicity and functionality.

The Caribe Hilton was a success, financially and in terms of its design. *Architectural Forum* exclaimed in 1950, "This is the kind of hotel which should be built in Florida and California, but never has been," noting that the "highly refined, inventive form" of the Caribe Hilton ultimately signaled "the island's awakened ambition" because it broke from building resorts "in some pompous colonial style, charm-conditioned by a posh decorator, or in a kind of bleak Miami Beach *moderne*."[19] Through the modern design of the Caribe Hilton, the Puerto Rican government had succeeded in projecting a new island identity. This type of modern hotel created by the Puerto Rican government was quickly replicated around the globe as Hilton and other hospitality companies built new structures inspired by the Caribe Hilton's design.

The Havana Riviera: modernism on the Malecón

Though equally attentive to promoting modern identity through modern tourism design, the tourism industry in post-war Cuba followed a different path than that of Puerto Rico. The post-war period was marked by President Fulgencio Batista's efforts to modernize the country and to improve the economy through increased tourism. Unlike Puerto Rico's official Operation Bootstrap, the program in Cuba was largely fueled by rampant corruption within the Batista government, which was quasi-institutionalized through government-sanctioned organizations created for the purpose of funneling and laundering money from US businessmen and mobsters.[20] The ease of building under the authoritarian government allowed rules and regulations to be skirted and projects to be fast-tracked, and no fewer than a dozen major hotels were constructed in Havana in the 1950s.

By the 1950s, Cuba had fully embraced modern architecture, and the "tropical modernism" of the Caribe Hilton was now the favored model of building in the Caribbean. One of the most significant hotel projects was the 1957 Havana Riviera, which represented the political, social and cultural realities of Cuba in the 1950s, including the overwhelming force of American tourism in Havana. The Havana Riviera has often been derided as Miami kitsch because the architect was not Cuban and infamous US mobster Meyer Lansky initiated the project. The analysis here presents a new appraisal of the hotel as a significant example of modern Cuban design. The interiors, in particular, show how modern design could assimilate local practices to present a Cuban identity that was at once modern and traditional.

Even though Lansky's decision to commission Miami's Polevitzky, Johnson & Associates was probably based on the firm's agreement to build the hotel in under six months, the resulting architecture displays Russian émigré architect Igor Polevitzky's skill at designing modern architecture that respected the climate and the natural and manmade environment that surrounded it.[21] Polevitzky's tendency was not to design the spectacular, overdone type of hotel popular in Miami. For the Havana design, Polevitzky developed a twenty-one-story structure in a Y-shape with the base of the Y facing the ocean. The position of the building's curved façades in relation to the ocean suggests the smooth motion of ocean breezes across their surfaces. The two shorter wings on one end increased the typical number of rooms, in particular the number of end rooms with balconies that opened to the outdoors. The innovative structural shape was also a creative way to maximize space on the relatively small plot Polevitzky was given on the highly desirable Malecón, Havana's seaside thoroughfare that extends out from the historic center.

While the architecture was certainly impressive, indeed like the Caribe Hilton it was described as "ultra-modern," it was the interior decoration of the public areas

Figure 2.2 Havana Riviera lobby, ca. 1957. Polevitzky, Johnson & Associates, architects (1956–7). Rudi Rada, photographer. Courtesy of HistoryMiami.

that impressed upon visitors the richness of modern Cuban art and design (see Figure 2.2). With such an emphasis on Cuban materials, furniture and artwork in the main public areas, it seems quite striking that Alvin Parvin, of the Parvin-Dohrman Company of Los Angeles, was credited for designing all of the hotel's furniture. While the Parvin-Dohrman Company was officially credited for the interior design, it is most likely that a Cuban design firm was associated with the project. Such associations were common practice when foreign architects or designers took on projects in Cuba, and these Cuban firms undoubtedly enhanced projects through their knowledge of local conditions and regulations, and their relationships with local entities. For example, a vast amount of the Havana Riviera's furniture was made in Cuba, including the lobby furniture, and this was probably the result of the local design firm's relationship with Cuban furniture manufacturers.[22]

In general, Cuban society embraced modern design. As historian Louis Pérez documents, during this period of post-war affluence, Cuban culture was focused on a notion of modernity inspired by the United States – one defined by "a condition of material progress based on consumption, convenience, and comfort."[23] Cubans had ready access to a wide array of US goods, including modern furniture – a Knoll showroom and a shop that carried Herman Miller furniture operated within the city limits before the hotel was constructed.[24] This is all the more notable when compared to

Miami, another major Caribbean city, which did not have a modern design store until the Arango Design Store opened in 1959.[25] Post-war affluence and the resulting boom in residential building meant that many middle- and upper-class Cubans were looking to match their furniture to their new modern homes and there was an overall high literacy in terms of design in Havana in this period. Like architecture, interiors were a way for Cubans to proclaim their modernity and their participation in a global world of design and commerce. But at the same time, despite the heavy reliance on US imports, there was also keen interest within the architecture and design community in promoting local design. The Cuban design journal *Espacio* indicates that there were at least two furniture design studios in Havana in the 1950s, and *Espacio* and the architecture journal *Arquitectura* fostered a dialogue between Cuban architecture and furniture design in this period.

The furniture in the main lobby was typical of modern design in Cuba. Long, low-slung couches and tables filled the area with simple, angular forms complemented by organically shaped, abstract marble sculptures. Tropical vegetation was incorporated into the space, though neatly contained in rectangular planters built into the center of stone benches. While an open plan defined the main floor, the arrangement of the cubic furniture clearly demarcated the lobby lounge area.

Cubanidad in interior design

The lobby unequivocally presented Cuba and its people as equally engaged with heritage and modernity. References to global trends in design and art, combined with assertions of a unique Cuban identity through materials, style and subject matter, expressed Havana's cosmopolitanism as a defining feature of Cuban identity. The lounges, bars and restaurants encouraged guests to linger in spaces that presented the notion of *cubanidad*, or Cuban-ness, within the most luxurious and up-to-date in resort hotel amenities. Architectural historian Eduardo Luis Rodríguez has tied *cubanidad*, a theme that drove Cuban cultural production for much of the twentieth century, in architecture and design in the 1950s to *lo cubano*, which was a modernist approach to design that was adapted to the local climate as a means of conveying something authentically Cuban without having to resort to copying historicist forms.[26]

The interior included a profusion of Cuban artworks engaged with themes of heritage and culture, ranging from images of carnival to more abstract depictions of Cuba's syncretic faiths. Rolando López Dirube's *La Religión del Palo* (1957) was the most prominently displayed artwork in the hotel (see Plate 3).[27] This large-scale, dynamic, highly abstracted sculpture hung from the center of the spiral staircase located toward the back of the lobby area, centrally placed near the reception desk. The title refers to Palo, also known as Palo Monte or Las Reglas de Congo, a religion that developed in Cuba mostly among slaves that came from the Congo Basin. Basic tenets of the faith revolve around natural or earth powers and the spirits of ancestors, and significant ideas are conveyed through a visual system of symbols. Undoubtedly, US guests could not have fully grasped the meaning of this piece, but one wonders what this work, which contained symbols associated with Palo, may have meant to the Cubans who were practitioners of or familiar with this religion.

The spiral staircase within which the sculpture was located emphasized openness and voids. Referencing the grand staircases of the great hotels of the past, the design also revealed the antiquated-ness of the concept of the grand staircase by rendering the staircase as nothing more than a sculpture. In effect, the staircase and sculpture created one unified artwork, as it is impossible to tell if the staircase was intended to complement the sculpture or vice versa.[28]

Though perhaps not as obvious as the artworks by Cuban artists, other design elements of the lobby proclaimed the Cuban-ness of the hotel. As one entered through the front door, the lobby walls stretched in front, alternating between panels of decorative concrete grilles and Cuban marble panels. The use of marble presents a striking contrast to other approaches to materials in hotel design. The designers of the Havana Riviera did not adopt the popular tactic of relying on the cache of iconic luxury materials imported from faraway locations to express luxury in a hotel. Instead, they worked to connect notions of luxury to Cuba itself by displaying Cuban marble in the same fashion as precious Italian marble. The majority of the marble is one of the sandy-colored, moderately veined varieties found on the island, while accents in other colors reveal the rich variety in Cuban marble. The combination of materials, furniture and artworks projected a notion of *cubanidad* defined by a celebration of cultural heritage and the promotion of cosmopolitanism.

Popular publications in the United States acknowledged the innovative architecture of the Havana Riviera, which they tied to a growing internationalism in the city.[29] However, despite newspaper headlines like "Cuba's Newest Hotel Brings Tropical Beauty Indoors," it was the gambling and other illicit activities offered by the Havana Riviera – "a self-contained orbit for the pleasure seeker" – that the articles highlighted.[30] Indeed, the image of the hotel was shaped by the dominant conception of Cuba as the playground of the United States. The tourism and hotels developed under the Batista dictatorship catapulted gambling, prostitution, drinking and drug use to new levels in the country.[31]

For the purposes of revolutionary ideology, Fidel Castro actively engaged with hotels as symbols of the corrupt government and business practices that created them and as physical manifestations of the type of tourism they housed, which were both tied to the evils of US imperialism. Upon news of the revolutionaries' de facto victory and Batista's hasty escape from the island on December 31, 1958, Cubans in Havana began rioting against what they saw as symbols of Cuba's problems, which included many of the slot machines, gaming tables and other furniture that they seized from hotels and casinos and destroyed in the streets (see Figure 2.3). A few days later, Castro reclaimed these sites of US imperialism for the Cuban people, setting up temporary headquarters in the Havana Hilton and hosting a press conference in the Copa Room of the Havana Riviera. Castro's occupation and use of these hotels strategically symbolized the retaking of Cuba for the Cuban people, and promised Cuban agency in defining tourism. Through its incorporation into the ideological rhetoric and myth making of the revolution, the Riviera was labeled imperialist, imported Miami design, circumscribing its presence in the history of modern architecture, and the notion of the interior design as a confident statement of Cuban identity was erased from discourse.

Modernism on vacation 43

Figure 2.3 Cubans burning furniture and gambling equipment from the Plaza Casino in Havana after Fidel Castro takes power on January 1, 1959. Fernando Lezcano, photographer. Courtesy of Lezcano/AP.

Shifting identities

More than fifty years after the overthrow of Batista, the revolutionary government in Cuba has reappraised the potential of hotels such as the Havana Riviera to support economic development. Catering to tourists' desires to see a city and its architecture that is erroneously described as "frozen in time," the Cuban government has pledged to restore some post–World War II architecture in addition to its commitment to preserving colonial architecture. Most recently, the 1957 Hotel Capri was renovated with a design that celebrates the golden age of mafia bosses in Havana. The passage of time, along with the current government's emphasis on sensationalizing the history of US mobsters in Cuba while downplaying or ignoring the cultural vibrancy of Cuban identity under Batista, has helped render this period ideologically nonthreatening as the government endeavors to balance a continued commitment to socialism with a program of increasing international tourism. In general, these hotels are commonly considered imported Miami design and part of a vilified past that will never happen again. Therefore, the way in which they can be valued as significant Cuban design, especially through examples such as the Havana Riviera's interiors, is not part of the contemporary conversation because it conflicts with the general practice of viewing

44   *Erica N. Morawski*

the 1950s negatively, ranging from a void of cultural significance to damaging to the Cuban cultural legacy.

In San Juan, La Concha Hotel, a Toro-Ferrer hotel built after the Caribe Hilton, was recently renovated not to its original form, but re-themed to meet contemporary notions of and interest in midcentury design. This came on the heels of a controversial proposal to demolish the hotel in order to build a multiuse tourist complex in the Spanish Revival style. As architect John Hertz has argued, this contentious redevelopment revolved around debates over style, which promoted either modernist or historical styles to proclaim party politics regarding continued territory status or statehood status, respectively.[32]

While the identities of these hotels have been reevaluated and renegotiated over time, what we need to remember is that at the time of their construction, they presented modern design as something familiar, accessible and, above all, desirable. In many ways, modern design represented the strong ties, voluntary or not, of these islands to the economy and culture of the United States, and the struggle of these two islands to propose and realize their own national identity, which was not always at odds with US attributes. The significance of the modern furniture of these two hotels lies within the furniture design and its implementation within competing, and at times conflicting, discursive agendas. This is evidenced by the numerous agents – US and local governments, owners and operators, guests and workers – involved in the creation and life of these hotels who realized the power of hotels in projecting identity and shaping cross-cultural encounters and opinions.

Acknowledgements

Many thanks to Cammie McAtee and Fredie Floré for including an earlier version of this chapter in their panel on post-war furniture at the Society of Architectural Historians annual conference in 2013 and for subsequent insightful comments that have contributed greatly to its improvement. Additional thanks are due to Bob Bruegmann for overseeing the larger dissertation project from which this essay was born. Research for this project was supported by grants and fellowships from the Graham Foundation for Advanced Studies in the Fine Arts, the Society of Architectural Historians and the University of Illinois at Chicago.

Notes

1 Proliferation of articles discussed in "Caribe Hilton – World's First Hotel to be 'Moved By Air!,'" *Hotel Bulletin*, February 1950: 43.
2 Puerto Rico's ambiguous status vis-à-vis the United States was perhaps best defined in *Downes v. Bidwell*, a 1901 court case concerned with whether oranges coming into New York from Puerto Rico would be subject to import duties. The ruling stated that, as an unincorporated territory of the United States, Puerto Rico was not part of it, yet not *not* part of it, and Puerto Rico has since been considered an international entity in many senses. On the relationship between Puerto Rico and the United States, see César J. Ayala and Rafael Bernabe, *Puerto Rico in the American Century: A History since 1898* (Chapel Hill: University of North Carolina Press, 2007); and Pedro A. Cabán, *Constructing a Colonial People: Puerto Rico and the United States, 1898–1932* (Boulder, CO: Westview Press, 1999).
3 Greg Castillo, *Cold War on the Home Front: The Soft Power of Midcentury Design* (Minneapolis: University of Minnesota Press, 2010), xi.

Modernism on vacation 45

4 Dennis Merrill, *Negotiating Paradise: U.S. Tourism and Empire in Twentieth Century Latin America* (Chapel Hill: University of North Carolina Press, 2009).
5 Merrill, *Negotiating Paradise*, 105.
6 On Operation Bootstrap, see Ayala and Bernabe, *Puerto Rico in the American Century*, and A. W. Maldonado, *Teodoro Moscoso and Puerto Rico's Operation Bootstrap* (Gainesville: University Press of Florida, 1997).
7 For a history of the relationship between Operation Bootstrap and the Office of Tourism, see Merrill, *Negotiating Paradise*.
8 Correspondence between the Puerto Rican government and Conrad Hilton located at the Hospitality Industry Archives, Conrad N. Hilton College, University of Houston illustrates Hilton's enthusiastic engagement with the hotel project.
9 Wharton's discussion of the Caribe Hilton is brief as her focus is on the international Hiltons located closer to the Iron Curtain. Annabel Jane Wharton, *Building the Cold War: Hilton International Hotels and Modern Architecture* (Chicago: University of Chicago Press, 2001).
10 For documentation of the design competition, see Maldonado, *Teodoro Moscoso*, 124. Born and raised in Puerto Rico, Osvaldo Toro and Miguel Ferrer received their architectural training at Columbia University and Cornell University, respectively, and Luis Torregrosa studied structural engineering in the United States. Until the University of Puerto Rico established a School of Architecture in 1966, Puerto Ricans had to leave the island to study architecture.
11 Aline B. Louchheim, "Bold New Design for San Juan Hotel," *New York Times*, October 23, 1949.
12 David Arnold, "'Illusory Riches': Representations of the Tropical World, 1840–1950," *Singapore Journal of Tropical Geography* 21, no. 1 (2000): 7.
13 Krista A. Thompson, *An Eye for the Tropics: Tourism, Photography, and Framing the Caribbean Picturesque* (Durham, NC: Duke University Press, 2006), 5.
14 "The Caribe Hilton: An Object Lesson in What You Can Do with $7,000,000," *Interiors + Industrial Design* 109, no. 9 (April 1950): 77.
15 "1950 Hotel Accommodations at the Crossroads of the Nation," *Hotel Monthly* 58, no. 683 (February 1950): 39.
16 Although Danish-born furniture designer Jens Risom had worked closely with Hans Knoll in the early 1940s, Risom began working independently when he formed Jens Risom Design in 1946. The chairs in the Caribe Hilton are an example of Jens Risom Design's contract furniture designs.
17 On Klumb's career in Puerto Rico, see Enrique Vivoni Farage, ed., *Klumb: Una arquitectura de impronta social [Klumb: An Architecture of Social Concern]* (San Juan: La Editorial, Universidad de Puerto Rico, 2006).
18 Advertisement located in Archivo de Arquitectura y Construcción, University of Puerto Rico, Rio Piedras, Puerto Rico.
19 "Spectacular Luxury in the Caribbean: The Caribe Hilton Hotel at San Juan, Puerto Rico," *Architectural Forum* 92, no. 3 (March 1950): 97.
20 Batista required all projects to run through certain government banks and finance companies, ensuring a steep profit for Cuba. Batista freely appropriated money from state organizations as he saw fit. Rosalie Schwartz, *Pleasure Island: Tourism and Temptation in Cuba* (Lincoln: University of Nebraska Press, 1997), 151–4.
21 On Igor Polevitzky, see Allan T. Shulman, "Igor Polevitzky's Architectural Vision for a Modern Miami," *Journal of Decorative and Propaganda Arts* 23 (1998): 334–59; and Allan T. Shulman, ed., *Miami Modern Metropolis: Paradise and Paradox in Midcentury Architecture and Planning* (Miami Beach: Bass Museum of Art, 2009).
22 Architect Daniel Bejerano, who was responsible for overseeing the most historically accurate restoration of the hotel to date in 1996, claims the original furniture of the hotel was made in Cuba. I subscribe to his findings, as he knows how to accurately and fruitfully navigate the somewhat unorthodox avenues of scholarly information in Cuba. Daniel Bejerano, interview by author, February 2011.
23 Louis A. Pérez, *On Becoming Cuban: Identity, Nationality, and Culture* (Chapel Hill: University of North Carolina Press, 1999), 347.

46 Erica N. Morawski

24 American goods flooded the marketplace in Cuba. By 1947, the United States was supplying Cuba with 84 percent of its imports, and this percentage increased in the 1950s. Likewise, the United States supported the Cuban economy by absorbing 92 percent of its exports. See Ronald Fernandez, *Cruising the Caribbean: U.S. Influence and Intervention in the Twentieth Century* (Monroe, ME: Common Courage Press, 1994), 270.

25 On the Arango Design Store, see Anthony J. Abbate, "Arango Design: Progressive Style and Latin Influence," in *Miami Modern Metropolis*, 396–401.

26 Eduardo Luis Rodríguez, *The Havana Guide: Modern Architecture 1925–1965* (New York: Princeton Architectural Press, 2000).

27 López Dirube also designed the large relief mural in the entrance hallway to the International Salon. This work is discussed further, as well as its engagement with the Abakuá religion, in Erica Morawski, "Designing Destinations: Hotel Architecture, Urbanism, and American Tourism in Puerto Rico and Cuba" (PhD diss., University of Illinois at Chicago, 2014).

28 The staircase and sculpture and the interiors in general call to mind the popularity of *integración plástica* in Latin America since the 1920s. Conceived around the goal of accomplishing a harmonious relationship between architecture and art in constructed projects, *integración plástica* was certainly present in Cuban creativity in this period. However, because the concept of *integración plástica* was often framed by anticapitalist ideology in many Latin American countries, I would contend that interest in cohesive design in hotels in North and South America was propelled more by the long-established and valued hotel design practice of creating attractive, harmonious interiors that would entice visitors. While many post-war modern hotels were paying particular attention to the mix of art and design, including the Caribe Hilton and hotels by Morris Lapidus and Edward Durrell Stone, for example, this was nothing particularly new in terms of hotel design.

29 "Havana Riviera to Open Dec. 10," *Boston Globe*, December 1, 1957, B22.

30 "Cuba's Newest Hotel Brings Tropical Beauty Indoors," *Boston Globe*, December 8, 1957, B36.

31 On the devolution of tourism in the 1950s, see Schwartz, *Pleasure Island*, 167–203. Cuba was firmly established as a tourist destination of boozing and escapism in the 1920s, when US travelers flocked to Cuba to escape Prohibition.

32 John B. Hertz, "Authenticity, Colonialism, and the Struggle with Modernity," *Journal of Architectural Education* 55, no. 4 (May 2002): 220–7.

3 When modernity confronts tradition
Conflicting visions for post-war furniture design in Québec

Martin Racine

The province of Québec represents an exceptional case in North America, as it has inherited the French culture while attempting to resist the influences of the English ascendance. Even today, traces of the French regime can be found in the architecture of the first settlers' houses and in ancient furniture collections, as well as in the monumental buildings (hospitals, religious congregations, churches) built in the eighteenth century. This legacy still represents the unique character of the old districts of the two major cities in the province, Québec City and Montréal. The French heritage has not only been noticeable in the shaping of the territory and the built environment, but, most importantly, in the preservation of the French language, culture, and traditions and the Catholic religion. From the nineteenth to the mid-twentieth century, although the British community contributed to transform the development of the urban landscapes, as well as the development of the industrial and economic sectors, the intellectual and political elites of Québec have tended to express their interest in the preservation of cultural bonds with France, facilitated by the common language, and in part to resist the cultural pressure of the British and later Anglo-Canadians and Americans.

In the post-war period, the identity of Québec was characterized by conservative values. From 1944 to 1959, the province was led by Prime Minister Maurice Duplessis, an era that became later known as "La grande noirceur" ("The Great Darkness") as he prioritized traditional principles, imposed rigid conservative policies, and, being a convinced anticommunist, stubbornly opposed trade unions. With the active support of the Roman Catholic Church, his government championed rural areas over urban development, which led to the control of the economic and industrial development by American and English Canadian companies, a frustrating situation for the French Canadian labor force who worked in hard conditions and felt alienated in its own province. Moreover, many artists, feminist groups, and intellectuals who dreamed of a more liberal and modern society considered Duplessis's policies anachronistic in the post-war era and felt oppressed in such an archaic political environment. In a period of demographic growth, both the government and the clergy discouraged younger generations from questioning the legitimacy of their values, a situation that impeded social progress.

Duplessis's death in 1959 inaugurated an important decade for Québec and a major shift in its social construct. Identified as the "Quiet Revolution," it was a new era for the province, a period in which the clergy lost its hegemony on political and social structures while a new generation of politicians deeply transformed the society, reforming the education system, improving health care services, and creating

48 Martin Racine

innovative urban infrastructures. Montréal became a modern city, with a new metro, its first skyscrapers, and an ambitious project, welcoming the world for Expo 67. In parallel to this sociocultural change, the quest for a distinctive identity less influenced by France grew stronger in Québec and found its expression in numerous cultural manifestations including literature, cinema, theatre, and song writing. In parallel, a sovereigntist political movement became increasingly important, reflecting a desire to affirm an independent national identity. As a demonstration of this evolution, the French-speaking population started to identify itself as "Québécois," abandoning the term "French Canadian" in use since Confederation.

The evolution of the political landscape in Québec through the twentieth century led to a number of debates in the economic, social, and artistic spheres, which impacted the field of education. An excursion into the world of furniture design education between 1935 and 1965 will illustrate Québec society's emancipation and show the tensions that existed between two key figures, Jean-Marie Gauvreau (1903–70) and Julien Hébert (1917–94), who both influenced education in furniture design and shaped the character of local furniture production. The question at stake for both of them was how to reconcile the richness of the traditional style expressed in handicraft furniture production with the desire to value a modern identity in contemporary creations.

Jean-Marie Gauvreau and the École du meuble

Following the creation of the Écoles des Beaux-Arts (Schools of Fine Arts) in Québec City and Montréal in 1922, the government became more and more concerned by the need for encouraging local furniture production and reviving the languishing heritage of Québec craftsmanship. Before the Great War, the trades had been neglected and the local production of furniture was limited. The government's ambition was to train craftsmen in a field remunerative for its practitioners, and to fulfill the demand for contemporary furniture and interior decoration.[1] Toward the objective of developing local furniture production, a government initiative led to the creation of a furniture school, the École du meuble, in Montréal in 1935. Jean-Marie Gauvreau would prove a perfect ally for this project. As the school's director for more than thirty years, Gauvreau, through his vision for the development of furniture design, was influential in the expansion of local production. An advocate of handmade quality over standardized production, Gauvreau was deeply committed to developing a distinct national style in Québec and dedicated his entire career to fulfilling the ambitious goal of promoting his vision for the development of local crafts.

After completing his studies in Montréal at the École Technique and the École des Hautes études commerciales (Business School) in 1924, Gauvreau received a provincial grant to study cabinetmaking and interior design at Paris's famous École Boulle.[2] Paris during *les années folles* was the capital of the arts, and attracted artists from every part of the world. Gauvreau, who arrived the year after the close of the famous *Exposition international des arts décoratifs et industriels modernes* of 1925, would have had no doubt that he was in the center of the world of art and design. For him, Art Deco represented the most important and innovative movement for furniture design, cabinetmaking, and architecture of the twentieth century.

During his three years in Paris, Gauvreau developed close relations with professors Léon-Émile Bouchet and André Frechet, both highly regarded masters in cabinetmaking. In addition to mastering the crafts of furniture and interior design, Gauvreau also studied the economic structure and organization of labor behind furniture production at the Faubourg Saint-Antoine, where hundreds of highly skilled cabinetmakers and craftsmen worked at the center of Paris's craft-based manufacturing sector. Gauvreau also discovered the system of promotion and distribution of furniture creations in *grands magasins* such as the Galeries Lafayette and Le Bon Marché. He clearly understood the political and economic strategies for furniture and luxury goods in France, and the importance of great exhibitions to support the prestige of a national style. A visit to New York in 1927 confirmed Gauvreau's conviction that Art Deco was the style of the times.[3]

In 1929, upon his return to Montréal, Gauvreau published a book, *Nos intérieurs de demain* (*Interiors of Tomorrow*). In it, he describes what he had learned during his years at the École Boulle and presents his vision for the development of a unique furniture design strategy in Québec, emphasizing the importance of defining an autonomous French Canadian identity and style. He praises Art Deco, and promotes craftsmanship as a means to strengthen national identity:

> The International Exposition of Decorative Arts of 1925 is a landmark in the history of furniture; it has now gained a worldwide influence and it is transforming profoundly the aesthetic of decorative arts. . . . We, French Canadians, should take profit from our relations with French designers, and avoid the influence of our neighbors. . . . Let us adopt furniture that truly responds to our needs and that symbolizes our national character.[4]

Upon his return to Montréal and following the publication of his book, Gauvreau was hired to teach cabinetmaking at the École Technique, and two years later became chair of his department. Thanks to his leadership role and despite being only thirty-two years old, he was appointed director of the newly founded École du meuble in 1935, and played a key role in defining the school's curriculum, which he largely based on the model of the École Boulle.

The importance of wood

One of Gauvreau's first strategies toward affirming an autonomous French Canadian identity and style was to identify the best species of wood found in Québec for cabinetmaking. The province was an important wood producer, and it seemed evident that this local resource had to be valorized, recognized as unique, and fully exploited. At the invitation of Frechet, Gauvreau returned to Paris in 1930 to lecture on the richness of Québec forests. He focused on the subtle qualities of more than twenty local wood species, including maple, elm, ash, walnut, oak, pine, and birch. He even encouraged French decorators to import wood from Québec. As art historian Gloria Lesser summarizes: "Gauvreau's ideology was born out of the potential far-reaching economic and artistic consequences of indigenous wood furniture. In its form and content, wood symbolized the integrity and continuity of the national and provincial heritage."[5] Throughout his career, Gauvreau published numerous books and articles promoting the use of local woods and denouncing the lack of a system of production, especially in the sphere of wood. He instead proposed the coordination of major provincial institutions, to develop a common program to encourage the establishment

50 *Martin Racine*

and development of small industries dedicated to the exploitation of wood for every conceivable use, an objective that would lead to independence for future generations of local entrepreneurs. He even called on housewives to participate in this effort: "It is you, madams and mademoiselles, who will have a great role to play in the decoration of our future interiors. If you judge, one day, that it is 'chic' to have furniture from here, built with our own local woods, by our local artists, you will have filled your national duty."[6]

The École du meuble replicated several of the École Boulle's courses, introducing students to diverse specialties, including carpentry, wood carving, and paperhanging. It also had a metal section that included lathe-work, bronze decorations, chiseling and engraving in steel, precious stones, and plated metal. In the 1940s, a glass and ceramics section and textile design were added to complement cabinetmaking. The objectives of the program were to train cabinetmakers and home decorators capable of designing all the furniture, lighting, wallpaper, and details of each room in the house, from the powder room and the master bedroom to the living room and dining room. As these examples suggest, the program essentially focused on the domestic sphere, but also addressed the interior decoration of hotels and public buildings. The strategy for Gauvreau and for the school's graduates was to address themselves to the upper-middle-class market and possibly export furniture throughout Canada and the United States. After all, in Gauvreau's mind, the École du meuble had many assets that could help his students achieve this ambitious objective: it benefited from the French tradition of culture and good taste, and belonged to that Latin culture where historical and artistic values were privileged. In a time of economic crisis, it seemed a winning strategy for Québec manufacturers to offer competitive prices for high-end furniture in order to replace European imports. At the same time, despite his economic and cultural ambition for exporting throughout North America, Gauvreau knew that the local market was rather limited and that his students should also design simpler products addressed to the budgets of a broader clientele.

But this realistic perspective did not include mass production. Gauvreau valorized craftsmanship above all else, and, opposing industrial design applied to mass manufacturing, turned his back on the ideas that emerged from the Bauhaus, including the exploration of metal tubing for furniture fabrication. In the post-war period, the German design school, founded in 1919, had gained a strong reputation and the dissemination of its ideas was more and more important in North America, especially when the most prominent faculty members fled the Nazi regime, which had shut down the school in 1933, and emigrated to the United States.[7] Gauvreau rejected the Bauhaus model entirely, staying true to Art Deco aesthetics and the French tradition of cabinetmaking. Given Gauvreau's position, it is all the more remarkable that the École du meuble is famous for its connection to painter Paul-Émile Borduas, who was fired from his teaching position after the 1948 release of *Le Refus Global*, a manifesto considered to have launched the Quiet Revolution.

Furniture production at the École du meuble

As a cabinetmaker and educator, Gauvreau seldom advocated decoration except when it could be sensitively applied, allowing forms and materials to express their nature unadorned. In this regard, the École du meuble's cabinetry production reflects an indigenous aesthetic that embodied local craftsmanship and traditional materials.

Figure 3.1 Art Deco dressing table. Jean-Marie Gauvreau, designer (ca. 1928–30). Denis Farley, photographer. Collection of the Montréal Museum of Fine Arts; purchase Horley and Annie Townsend bequest.

Hence, a Québec Art Deco style was made in native woods, which took into account international trends, and which also integrated a number of elements found in the French regime. In the late 1920s, Gauvreau created a line of furniture clearly inspired by Léon-Émile Bouchet's Art Deco pieces presented at the *Salon des artistes décorateurs* exposition in 1928 (see Figure 3.1).

The cabinetry curriculum relied on programs of both craft and art. Training in carpentry began with learning the basic joints such as mortise-and-tenon, dovetail, and tongue-and-groove, and only after extended practice construction of model joining in rougher woods was a student allowed to work in the more expensive veneers. The second-year project focused on the creation of small occasional tables of standard dimensions, made to individual taste, with the marquetry custom designed by the student but approved by the professor. Students would then design and build more complex furniture, tables with drawers, tray-top tables, lamps, chandeliers, and upholstered chairs. Alphonse Saint-Jacques (1911–96), who graduated from the École du meuble in 1934, was trained by Gauvreau as technical director of the carpentry and cabinetry workshops. His work exemplifies the style of furniture developed at the school in the 1930s.

The school was located in downtown Montréal in a former academic institution, the Académie Marchand, a building designed in the Beaux-Arts style. The distinct character of the École du meuble was expressed in an extension designed in 1941 by

Figure 3.2 Coffee Table. Marcel Parizeau, architect and designer (1937–40). Christine Guest, photographer. Collection of the Montréal Museum of Fine Arts. Gift of the Maurice Corbeil Estate.

Marcel Parizeau, an architect who taught interior design at the school. In Parizeau's architectural work, one can recognize the influence of Robert Mallet-Stevens and René Herbst, especially in the use of glass blocks, and of purist cubic geometrical shapes with rounded corners found in his residences. Parizeau's interiors reveal the trend of pure geometrical shapes and simplification of the Art Deco style that was still dominant in the 1940s. He used similar volumes and planes to create elegant furniture without any added ornament, and explored details with rounded edges and contrasting materials such as glass and wood (see Figure 3.2). The furniture expressed a great deal of refinement and attention to details in its construction.

Although it evolved slightly throughout the decades, the school's furniture creation and production essentially remained loyal to its Art Deco origins. In the 1950s, the Scandinavian influence grew stronger among its faculty and students, but the idea of modern design was never integrated in the curriculum.

Julien Hébert – design as modern craft

In his memoirs Julien Hébert wrote in 1970:

> Jean-Marie Gauvreau died a few weeks ago. In many ways he achieved many great things, and he was a brave man that I liked quite a lot. Despite his many qualities and ideas, he made one major error, initiating his educational project on false premises. When he founded the École du meuble thirty-five years ago he ought to have put the emphasis on industrial furniture production instead of following the path of French craft traditions. He should have developed the crafts as a point of departure for small industrial fabrication rather than promoting handmade furniture. Gauvreau could not know. He had done his studies in France in a time when this country resonated as a symbol of "quality" in the minds of French Canadians.[8]

Hébert continues by expressing his disappointment vis-à-vis the missed opportunity to create a school of design of international reputation, instead of an arts and crafts institute. He underlines the fact that, by ignoring the potential of modern design, Gauvreau had prevented Québec from playing a significant cultural and economic role in furniture manufacturing. Hébert felt that through his position as director, Gauvreau could have favored the conditions to see design emerge as a major discipline in the province:

> What would have happened if, by chance, Gauvreau had spent a few months in Scandinavia? His philosophy would have been different and his actions would have had extraordinary repercussions on the industry in Québec. The craftspeople of yesterday would today be industrial furniture producers, their modest enterprises would today be important companies, and the young generations would be ready to take the succession. It is always easy to reinterpret history, but it is certainly a case that demonstrates the importance of an initial inspiration, of a valid initial vision. Gauvreau understood this at the end of his life, and all the conversations that we had together confirm this conclusion.[9]

These comments perfectly illustrate the opposing visions between Gauvreau and Hébert concerning the crafts and industrial design. For Hébert, contrasting these two fields was not the solution. He considered design a form of modern craft, a continuity of traditional know-how.

Born in 1917, Hébert studied sculpture at the École des Beaux-Arts de Montréal from 1936 to 1941.[10] Graduates would typically find work with religious institutions, in projects related to the construction of churches, sculpting and painting religious scenes and ornaments for the interior decoration. Though talented, Hébert wasn't truly interested in this avenue, and he was even less tempted to become an independent sculptor, creating works only accessible to the upper class. In asking himself what he could do as a sculptor, he was actually questioning the role of art in society. This led to studies in philosophy at the Université de Montréal, where he obtained his degree in 1944. Hébert then returned to sculpture and, interested in teaching, found a part-time position teaching art history at the École des Beaux-Arts. But in the late 1940s, many students began to criticize the school for its outdated program, cut off as it was from the modern art currents emerging in Europe. Moreover, many artists of that period, including Hébert, felt that they didn't have freedom to express themselves within the rigid and conservative Duplessis regime in Québec, a province still dominated by the clergy and Catholic authority.

Seeking a more stimulating environment, in 1946, Hébert, like Gauvreau and many other Québec artists before him, went to Paris, where he did a fifteen-month internship under the supervision of Russian sculptor Ossip Zadkine at the Académie de la Grande Chaumière. Impressed by Zadkine's cubist approach, Hébert became more familiar with the interrelation and interaction of art with architecture and design. He also traveled throughout Europe and became interested in the Bauhaus and fascinated by artists such as Klee and Kandinsky, who embraced architecture and modern design as an integrated artistic and social project. Upon his return to Montréal in 1948, Hébert felt so enthusiastic about his discoveries in Europe that he decided to move things along in his own country. He resumed his position at the École des Beaux-Arts, and shared his European experiences with his students. He still wished to work as a sculptor, but focused his efforts on participating in competition for site-specific projects. Hébert later would say in an interview: "I became a designer, probably because I studied both sculpture and philosophy. Sculpture is related to the form, the sensual, the touch. Philosophy is the mind, the reflection. Hence, moving to design was a logical step."[11]

The birth of design in Canada

In the post-war era, the federal government wished to facilitate the conversion of wartime industry into the manufacture of consumer goods. With this objective in mind, the first design competition in Canada, "Design for Normal Living Requirements," was held in 1951 and was organized under the initiative of Donald Buchanan, head of the Industrial Design Division of the National Gallery in Ottawa. Buchanan was inspired by the design exhibitions and competitions organized by Elliot Noyes at the Museum of Modern Art in New York.[12] He had great esteem for Noyes's initiatives, such as the organic furniture competition held in the 1940s, where the talents of designers such as Charles Eames and Eero Saarinen were revealed. Buchanan wished to create similar success stories in Canada, and hoped to see Canadian manufacturers employ modernist designers for improving the quality of their production.[13] In this sense, Buchanan expressed a completely different vision of furniture design in comparison to Gauvreau's attachment to craft traditions. Working at the federal level, Buchanan obviously had a different national agenda. He recognized the potential of design for the development of Canadian industry, while Gauvreau's objectives were to develop furniture with a distinct Québec Art Deco style, favoring handmade quality over industrial production.

The competition clearly promoted modernist criteria and valorized technical innovation in the use of new materials for furniture, such as aluminum and plywood, rather than focusing on decorative aesthetics and ornamentation. Overall, few Canadian designers submitted entries, a disappointment for the organizers of the competition. None came from the École du meuble. Although Hébert had no experience in design, excited by this new challenge, he submitted a hammock-type seat formed from intertwined bent aluminum tubes. The suspended canvas seat held the entire structure (see Figure 3.3). The piece was functional, comfortable, and easy to mass-produce,

Figure 3.3 Triangular hammock-type seat. Julien Hébert, designer (1951). Michel Brault, photographer. Musée national des beaux-arts du Québec, Québec City, Fonds Julien Hébert. Courtesy of the Estates of Julien Hébert and Michel Brault.

Figure 3.4 Aluminum folding chair. Julien Hébert, designer (1953). Michel Brault, photographer. Musée national des beaux-arts du Québec, Québec City, Fonds Julien Hébert. Courtesy of the Estates of Julien Hébert and Michel Brault.

qualities recognized by the jury chaired by Serge Chermayeff, director of Chicago's Institute of Design, which also included Toronto-based architect John B. Parkin. Another participant from Québec, Norman Slater, submitted a design for a metallic lamp. Hébert was one of few participants who met the objectives of the competition, which was attracting the interest of manufacturers.

This competition project marked the start of Hébert's design career. After seeing his aluminum chair in a newspaper article, Sigmund Werner, an Austrian manufacturer who had immigrated to Montréal to escape the Nazis, hired Hébert to design a line of aluminum furniture.[14] Werner had been a manufacturer of aluminum ski poles, but after several poor snow seasons and therefore slow sales, he was looking to diversify his production. Hébert designed a complete line of garden furniture, including folding aluminum lawn chairs with nylon webbing, which were a huge commercial success when introduced in 1953. This type of foldable outdoor furniture met a need of Canadian consumers in Québec; they were convenient, comfortable, lightweight, low cost, and easily maintained (see Figure 3.4). Within a few years, the chairs, now known by the company name Sun-Lite, rapidly became quintessential lawn furniture across the country. What would become a modern summer vernacular artifact was copied by many manufacturers looking to compete for this growing market in the economic and demographic boom of the 1950s.

While working for Werner, Hébert discovered his passion for design, a field through which he could express his creativity while satisfying his social consciousness. Design appeared to him as a revelation, an answer to the existential questions he had in relation to the social meaning and dimension of art in society. In this sense, he shared a similar vision with design pioneers of the Bauhaus. In 1953, inspired by the tubular steel furniture of Ludwig Mies van der Rohe, Le Corbusier, and Marcel Breuer, Hébert designed for Sun-Lite a chaise longue with an aluminum structure (see Figure 3.5). It

Figure 3.5 Aluminum Contour chaise longue. Julien Hébert, designer (1953). Michel Brault, photographer. Musée national des beaux-arts du Québec, Québec City, Fonds Julien Hébert. Courtesy of the Estates of Julien Hébert and Michel Brault.

consisted of two bent tubular forms resting on a triangular base that also functioned as an armrest. The outdoor chaise was stable in two positions: balanced on its base or lowered with its foot on the ground. Nylon or canvas covers were available in red, green, royal blue, and gold.

The National Industrial Design Council selected the Contour chaise longue to represent Canada at the Triennale di Milano in 1954. It also appeared that same year in the prestigious *Domus* magazine.[15] It was one of the first Canadian products to receive international praise. The chaise longue is the perfect synthesis of Hébert's design philosophy: inexpensive, practical, and well adapted to both the demands of production and of suburban lifestyle trends. It also has very pure structural lines and is elegantly proportioned.

From then on, Hébert put all of his energy into developing design as a professional field. Unlike the fine arts, reserved for the elite, Hébert considered design a form of art for the masses – and this vision definitely contrasted with Gauvreau's perspective. Hébert emphasized "utilitarian forms," and wished that more artists would become interested in design to improve the aesthetics and functionality of everyday objects. Every aspect of design interested him: objects, furniture, graphic, and interior design. He developed a global vision for his profession that saw no barriers between the different fields. For Hébert, they were all related to the same objective: improving peoples' lives and the built environment while allowing every social class access to quality products that were both functional and aesthetically pleasing.

Modern design education

Hébert was also committed to education, recognizing that teaching was the best way to influence future generations of artists and designers. In the mid-1950s, he tried with limited success to introduce design courses at the École des Beaux-Arts, but its director was rather uninterested.[16] Since he had experience in and a growing reputation for furniture design, Gauvreau met Hébert to discuss the possibility of a design studio at the École du meuble.[17] Hébert had to convince him that introducing design did not mean neglecting the importance of heritage and craftsmanship; on the contrary, design represented the continuity of the crafts. Scandinavian design was the ultimate inspiration for Hébert and the model to follow for the development of furniture in Québec. For him, designers like Alvar Aalto, founder of Artek, had successfully evolved a limited craft-based production toward industrial production, all the while maintaining the tradition of handmade quality in objects and furniture. Indeed, Hébert always promoted the idea of linking design with the various crafts instead of creating a barrier between the two worlds and regularly held up the success of the Danish designers in the production of local goods. Gauvreau was hard to convince, but in the late 1950s, it became clear that the École du meuble was not successfully meeting the primary objectives established in the 1930s of creating a dynamic craft-based industrial sector. In the context of the post-war baby boom, along with the influence of television and the expansion of suburban life, the furniture school's archaic model with its Art Deco influences was increasingly irrelevant in Québec society. Gauvreau, pressured by his students who became more and more interested in modern design, was also seeing the influence of Scandinavian design appearing in the work of students in the class of Guy Viau, a cabinetmaker interested in exploring new avenues such as modular furniture and simplified construction methods (see Figure 3.6). For all these reasons, in 1958,

Figure 3.6 Scandinavian-influenced chair assembly projects made by the students of Guy Viau at the École du meuble, 1951. Unknown photographer. Fonds de l'École du meuble, Archives du Cégep du Vieux Montréal.

58   Martin Racine

he eventually hired Hébert, but not wholeheartedly; perhaps he saw in him the shattering of his dream for a strong and distinct craft sector.

Hébert wished to share the great potential of industrial design with his students. He also wanted to explore new construction methods in wood and not simply rely on traditional cabinetmaking assemblies. In his practice, he had realized the potential of aluminum for furniture construction and wished to further explore innovative creations with this material. Increasingly, Hébert sought a broader community of designers beyond the borders of Québec and Canada. In 1953, he participated in a design workshop and colloquium at the Massachusetts Institute of Technology and attended a conference by Buckminster Fuller, whose creativity and vision left a deep impression on him. He also discovered the ingenious furniture designed by Charles and Ray Eames, Eero Saarinen, and the unique steel rod furniture of Harry Bertoia. He witnessed how companies such as Knoll and Herman Miller were integrating and promoting modern design and using new materials with great success.

Given his interest in such innovations in form and materials, Hébert was critical of the École du meuble's continuing focus on solid wood furniture. Although he valued the qualities of local wood products, for him, aluminum held just as much potential for expressing the province's identity. In the 1950s, the province became one of the world's largest aluminum producers, thanks to its hydroelectrical power sources. Hébert perceived aluminum as closely tied to the modernization of Québec, and for him, Québec designers ought to lead in exploiting its aesthetic as well as structural potentials.

The decline of the École du meuble and the rise of industrial design

By the late 1950s, Gauvreau's influence was in decline, and most progressive designers considered the École du meuble outdated. Although Hébert introduced modern design at the school, he felt there was a need for a more in-depth education in industrial design. The occasion to play a more influential role as an educator came in 1958, when the school was relocated to a building next to the École Polytechnique. Its name was also changed to Institut des arts appliqués, a move that more closely corresponded to the type of instruction the school was dispensing, which put less emphasis on traditional furniture design. It was at the Institut des arts appliqués that Hébert trained the first generation of young industrial designers. He mentored such successful designers as Michel Dallaire, Albert Leclerc, and Marcel Girard, who consider him the father of modern design in Québec.[18]

The Quiet Revolution that took place during the political leadership of Liberal Prime Minister Jean Lesage (1960–6) heralded a period of significant reform. Elected in 1960, his government recognized the need for a broader system of education. A major educational restructuring was introduced in 1966, and the Institut des arts appliqués came under the jurisdiction of a professional college, the Cegep du Vieux-Montréal. This was a disappointment for Gauvreau, who was hoping to see his school merge into the university system, as in the case of the École des Beaux-Arts, which was integrated within the Université du Québec à Montréal in 1969. The Institut des arts appliqués essentially became a technical program, with little remaining of the former École du meuble's prestige as an arts and crafts school. Hébert actively participated in the 1963–4 commission responsible for revisiting education in Québec – better known as Commission Parent – and lobbied for the implementation of a university degree in industrial design. In 1961, he received a grant from the provincial Ministry of Trade and Commerce to study different design promotion centers in Europe and traveled in West Germany, France, England, Sweden, and Switzerland to visit each of them and to meet their directors. Upon his return, he prepared an ambitious project for an Institute of Design in Montréal, which included a graduate program where world-renowned designers would be invited to teach. The impetus for such a school was bolstered by the aluminum industry. In his efforts to establish a design school and promotion center, Hébert had the support of Henri Strub, one of Alcan's directors, and collaborated with both local and international designers.[19] Hébert's initiatives finally led to the creation in 1969 of the École de design industriel at the Université de Montréal, where he taught until the late 1970s.

How to reconcile tradition with modernity?

Hébert's battle to integrate modern design education at the university level and the decline of Gauvreau's École du meuble perfectly capture the evolution of design and the dismissal of traditional crafts in favor of modernity. Although he had been critical of the École du meuble, Hébert was not in direct opposition with Gauvreau's perspective as he also recognized the importance of preserving traditional craft know-how, but he did not understand Gauvreau's dismissal of modern design and industrial production. Although severely judged by Hébert, Gauvreau's rejection of the industrial manufacturing has to be put in its historical context because, for him, handiwork was a cultural patrimony to reclaim. In the early twentieth century, craftsmanship was extremely coded in Québec for political and economic reasons.[20] It encompassed many significant roles and functions in society and seemed to be an instrument for economic growth that was fully autonomous from the Anglophone world. The actualization of this idea was of fundamental importance for a society looking for both cultural and economic emancipation. The solution proposed by some Francophone intellectuals such as Gauvreau was to break the continuity of a subordinate role in creating an indigenous economy closely tied to local resources. This is why Gauvreau integrated business courses into the school's program to strengthen the French-speaking representatives' presence in the economy of Québec, which, up until then, essentially had been dominated by the English-speaking business elite. What was required was the formation, from the ground up, of a middle class able to perform all of the necessary productive and commercial activities of an active and well-integrated society.

It is in this complex social as well as cultural and political context that Gauvreau defined his vision for the École du meuble, and attempted to make a personal contribution to the development of Québec. He had a clear view of his mandate, to find a way for Québec to repossess its productive capacities in a framework of economic and cultural independence. Throughout his career, his teaching was centered on cabinetmaking, wood construction, and the history of furniture since the French colony. He traveled across Québec to collect traditional furniture, seeking rare ancient models built by the first settlers, and created a museum at the school to expose the pieces with the objective of raising students' and visitors' awareness of the richness of Québec's heritage.[21] He advocated the use of wood right down to such details as handles or drawer pulls. As Lesser notes: "Committed to developing Canadian resources rather than metal – Gauvreau eschewed the industrial aesthetic in favor of the craftsman's natural affinity for material."[22] At the École du meuble, solid wood was definitely seen

60   Martin Racine

as the primary material to value as its use would symbolically create a clear historical link with the traditions and know-how found in the origins of French Canadian furniture.

Even though he was only fourteen years younger than Gauvreau, Hébert's influences were quite different and he did not feel the necessity of seeing both traditional crafts and French influences shape the identity of local furniture design. Hébert wanted design to evolve in Québec as it did in Finland, Sweden, and Denmark, and hoped that traditional crafts would transition into modern design and become one of the province's signatures. Hébert did not have the same admiration as Gauvreau for French Art Deco and wished to see Québec's furniture production innovate and adapt to modern living through new materials such as aluminum. In this regard he was disappointed by the provincial government's slowness in recognizing design, especially when compared to the federal government's efforts immediately after the Second World War. In 1953, Hébert was one of the founding members of the Canadian Association of Industrial Designers. Five years later, because of his leadership and professional reputation (by this time he held five or six patents), he was elected president. As a French Canadian, Hébert was definitely a pioneer, since commerce and industry, as we have seen earlier, were areas mostly dominated by the English-speaking community. The 1960s and the Quiet Revolution would open up a whole new era for the emancipation of Québec society and for the development of design. As such, Julien Hébert and several young Québec designers (many of whom were his former students) would play a key role in one of the most exciting events hosted in Montréal, Expo 67 – a World's Fair that would profoundly change the social, economic, and cultural identity of Québec.[23]

Notes

1 Gloria Lesser, *École du meuble, 1930–1950* (Montréal: Château Dufresne, Musée des arts décoratifs de Montréal, 1989), 14–22.

2 The school was named after André-Charles Boulle (1642–1732), a famous cabinetmaker to Louis XIV, and the creator of luxurious and very richly worked furniture and engravings.

3 Gauvreau mentions his trip to New York in his book *Nos intérieurs de demain* (Montréal: Librairie d'action Canadienne-Française, 1929).

4 Gauvreau, *Nos intérieurs*, 32–3: "L'exposition international des arts décoratifs de 1925 représente un moment historique dans l'histoire du mobilier, elle a acquis une influence mondiale et transforme profondément l'esthétique des arts décoratifs. Quant à nous, Canadiens, nous devons tirer le plus grand profit de nos relations avec les décorateurs français. . . . Mais, de grâce, n'allons pas chercher nos inspirations chez nos voisins. . . . Adoptons à notre vie un mobilier qui réponde vraiment à nos besoins quotidiens, et dont la tenue puisse symboliser notre caractère national"; unless otherwise noted, all translation are by the author.

5 Lesser, *École du meuble*, 19.

6 Gauvreau, *Nos intérieurs*, 33: "C'est vous, Mesdames et Mesdemoiselles, qui aurez un grand rôle à jouer dans la décoration de nos futurs intérieurs canadiens. Si vous jugez, un jour, qu'il est 'chic' d'avoir dans vos intérieurs des meubles de chez nous, fabriqués avec des bois de chez nous, par des artistes de chez nous, vous aurez fait là œuvre nationale."

7 Alain Findeli, *Le Bauhaus de Chicago, l'œuvre pédagogique de Lászlo Moholy-Nagy* (Québec: Septentrion, 1995).

8 "Jean-Marie Gauvreau est mort il y a quelques semaines. Il a eu beaucoup de vérités et je n'ai pas à les énumérer ici. Et c'était un bien brave homme que j'aimais bien. Il a eu un malheur: celui de partir sur de fausses prémisses. En fondant l'École du meuble il y a trente-cinq ans, il eut mieux valu mettre l'accent sur la production industrielle du meuble que sur les

traditions françaises et artisanales. Il eut mieux valu aussi développer l'artisanat comme départ de la petite industrie que de développer un artisanat 'fait main.' Gauvreau ne pouvait savoir. Il avait fait un stage en France à l'époque où la 'qualité' était 'française' dans l'esprit des Canadiens Français." Julien Hébert, personal memoirs, 1940–70, Fonds Julien Hébert, Musée national des beaux-arts du Québec.

9 "Que serait-il arrivé si Gauvreau, par un hasard quelconque, avait dû séjourner quelques mois en Scandinavie? Toute sa philosophie en eut été changée et son action aurait eu des répercussions extraordinaires sur l'industrie au Québec. Les artisans d'alors seraient aujourd'hui des industriels; leurs entreprises modestes seraient aujourd'hui considérables et bien des jeunes seraient prêts à prendre la relève. Il est toujours facile de refaire l'histoire à partir des soupirs mais voilà un cas qui montre en tous cas l'importance de l'inspiration du départ, d'une philosophie initiale valide. Gauvreau avait compris à la fin de sa vie et toutes les conversations que nous avons eues le prouvent." Hébert, personal memoirs.

10 On Julien Hébert, see Martin Racine, *Julien Hébert: Fondateur du design moderne au Québec* (Montréal: Les éditions du passage, 2016).

11 Julien Hébert, radio interview "Le travail de la création," *Radio-Canada*, July 7, 1982: "Si je suis devenu designer, c'est peut-être parce que j'ai fait en parallèle la sculpture et la philosophie à un certain moment. La sculpture, c'est la forme, le sensuel, le touché. La philosophie c'est la raison, alors de là à faire du design, il n'y avait qu'un pas."

12 Terry Smith, *Making the Modern: Industry, Art, and Design in America* (Chicago: University of Chicago Press, 1994).

13 John Bruce Collins, "Design for Use, Design for the Millions, Proposals and Options of the National Industrial Design Council, 1948–1960" (Master's thesis, Carleton University, 1986), 79.

14 Letter, Sigmund Werner to Julien Hébert, April 4, 1951, Fonds Julien Hébert, Musée national des beaux-arts du Québec.

15 *Domus*, no. 298 (November 1954): 58 (no author).

16 In 1954, Julien Hébert wrote to the director of the École des Beaux-Arts suggesting that he integrate design education into the school's curriculum. Fonds Julien Hébert.

17 Raymond Bernatchez, "Julien Hébert, l'un des pères du design québécois," *La Presse*, March 15, 1990.

18 Michel Dallaire, "Designer industriel, professeur, patron et ami," *Liberté* 223 (1996): 5–8.

19 According to a letter from Henri Strub to John Bland, director of McGill University's School of Architecture, November 14, 1960. University Archives, McGill University.

20 Cinzia Maurizia Giovine, "Jean-Marie Gauvreau: Arts, Handicrafts, and National Culture in Québec from the 1920s until the 1950s," *Design Issues* 10 no. 3 (Autumn 1994): 22–31.

21 This collection is now housed at the Musée des maîtres et artisans du Québec.

22 Lesser, *École du meuble*, 17.

23 See Martin Racine, "The Ambiguous Modernity of Julien Hébert," in *Expo 67, Not Just a Souvenir*, ed. Rhona R. Kenneally and Johanne Sloan (Toronto: University of Toronto Press, 2010), 93–108.

4 The interiors of the Belgian Royal Library

An expression of national identity with an international imprimatur

Fredie Floré and Hannes Pieters

The Belgian Royal Library, situated on Brussels Mont des Arts, is an impressive monumental building (see Figure 4.1).[1] The project was conceived as a new home for the collections of the Royal Library and as a memorial for King Albert I (1875–1934), who had been killed in a mountaineering accident in 1934. The beloved monarch had been a strong promoter of science and the arts, and a living memorial was considered a fitting monument to his legacy. Two competitions for the new library were organized in 1937–8, with Brussels- and Paris-trained architect Maurice Houyoux (1903–60) winning the final one. However, the outbreak of the Second World War, problems with the City Council, and several other disputes significantly delayed progress on the prestigious building project, and not until 1954 did construction work begin. More than thirty years after Houyoux won the competition, the library finally opened to the public in 1969. Interestingly there was an apparent discord between the building's architecture and its interior. While both of them have been closely analyzed in recent studies, this chapter further contextualizes and develops the discussion on the library's interior as a negotiator of political identity.[2] It opens with a discussion of the political background of the entire building project before focusing on the mediating role of the remarkable modern interior furnishings.

In his inauguration speech, young King Baudouin (1930–93), a grandson of Albert I, stated that the library showed itself as "a collective work of all Belgians" and as "an institution that unites the past, the present and the future."[3] This description, which speaks to the nationalist intentions behind the project, referred first and foremost to the library collections, which originally were conceived as a "memory of the nation"[4] and which, according to former head librarian Jan Frans Vanderheyden, were meant to provide future generations with stimuli for "the further development" of the nation's "spiritual patrimony."[5] However, in its own way the building also united past, present, and future. After all, it was part of a long and complex project of national representation.

Many features of the building and its location testify to that project. The urban layout of the Mont des Arts was inspired by the late nineteenth-century wish of King Leopold II to develop the strategic spot on the intersection of Upper and Lower Town into the cultural and intellectual heart of the nation. Parallel with contemporary nationalist-inspired building projects in other European cities, the king hoped to centralize, cluster, and represent the cultural and scientific riches of the young country on this location. Already in the 1880s plans for the Mont des Arts, the Royal Library was considered a significant part of this project. Although the second library competition stipulated the Botanique as the building site, in 1939, following a period

Figure 4.1 The Royal Library on the Mont des Arts, ca. 1969. Maurice Houyoux, architect (1954–69). Pol De Prins, photographer. Sint-Lukasarchief, collection Centre d'Information de Bruxelles.

of intense public debate on the choice of location, it was decided to return to the originally suggested site: the Mont des Arts.[6] The nineteenth century was also present in the choice of a classically inspired architectural language, which was considered appropriate for a royal project – a point of view that was in line with the 1930s architectural debate on monumentality. The library as built, especially the large formal staircase and impressive portico leading up to the entrance, reflect this language of monumental form.

Completing the project, however, proved difficult, as the task of representing the Belgian nation and its royal family had been severely complicated by events during and after the Second World War. For one thing, public support for the royal family and even the monarchy was severely threatened by the Royal Question, a political crisis triggered by debate on whether Leopold III (son of Albert I and father of Baudouin) could return to his position as king after he had surrendered to German forces during the war. Altered visions on national representation and cultural diplomacy also emerged during the Cold War. As this essay will show, these developments had a great impact on the library's interior design, conceived and executed in the 1950s and 1960s by the Kortrijk-based firm Kortrijkse Kunstwerkstede Gebroeders De Coene [Ateliers d'Art de Courtrai De Coene Frères or Kortrijk Art Workshops De Coene Brothers].[7] In striking contrast to the library's classicist inspired façade, the post-war interiors were given an unmistakably modern expression. This is exemplified in a representationally important space, the special collections reading room. A photograph taken shortly after the library's opening in 1969 shows a vast open space with a suspended ceiling and light-colored wall-to-wall carpet intended to optimize the acoustics (see Figure 4.2). The interior is defined by the position and elegant appearance of modern reading desks, accompanied by chairs designed by Finnish-American architect Eero

Figure 4.2 Precious works reading room of the Belgian Royal Library, ca. 1969. Pol De Prins, photographer. Sint-Lukasarchief, collection Centre d'Information de Bruxelles.

Saarinen from the American Knoll collection. As this chapter will examine, together the monumental building and its local version of "International Style" furnishings testify to an ongoing search for an up-to-date image for the Belgian kingdom during a critical episode in its history and a continuous revision of how to express that image within an increasingly globalizing world.

A long-term project of nation building

When in 1934 the idea first arose to build a new Royal Library in the heart of Brussels, a highly symbolic architectural and urban question was born. Founded in 1837, shortly after Belgium's independence and the establishment of the country as a constitutional monarchy, the Royal Library was conceived as a key element in the nineteenth-century strategy of nation building.[8] Being at once a royal and a national library, it was meant to safeguard the royal treasures and stimulate the young nation's literary and scientific production. The basis for the library collection was the Librije van Bourgondië, a unique collection of manuscripts that already in 1559 had received royal status when it became part of the established Royal Library of the Netherlands. The goal of the Belgian Royal Library, originally located in the Palais de l'Industrie, was to collect and preserve the literary heritage related to the nation's past and to register a copy of all publications made in Belgium. By fulfilling these tasks, the library contributed to

The interiors of the Belgian Royal Library   65

the creation, confirmation, and further development of a Belgian national consciousness, constructing a Belgian identity for the newly constituted kingdom along the way. Belgium had been conceived as a constitutional, popular, and hereditary monarchy whose incumbent is titled the King or Queen of the Belgians, indicating a direct link with the people of Belgium, whom he or she refers to as "fellow-countrymen."

In the mid-1930s, the library's special agenda was further intensified when King Albert I – much loved by the Belgian people for his unassuming lifestyle and harmonious family life – unexpectedly died and the idea surfaced to erect a new national library as what could be termed a "living memorial" to him – a useful project that is marked as a memorial.[9] By then the library collections had significantly grown and the institute was also in need of more space. Once the plan to construct a new building was approved by King Leopold III and his widowed Queen Mother Elisabeth, the Belgian government decided that the budget initially reserved for the erection of statues and other traditional forms of remembrance to the late monarch in different parts of the country should be entirely used to realize the Albert I or "Albertina" Library. Hence, the new Royal Library was directly connected to the Belgian royal family, which gave it an even stronger national meaning. This representative aspect was further enhanced by the choice to construct the library on the Mont des Arts, conceived by King Leopold II as the cultural and intellectual heart of the nation, where ideally also the national archives and the national museums would be clustered and staged. This project, however, implied the destruction and replacement of a considerable part of the existing dense urban fabric in the center of Brussels.

To move toward the realization of this complex project, the Belgian government in 1935 established an autonomous parastatal organ: the Fonds Bibliothèque Albert Ier [Albert I Library Fund]. This Fund, overseen by eminent figures from academia and politics, was assigned the responsibility to gather the necessary budgets,[10] to carry out preliminary studies on the requirements of the library, and, finally, to ensure its realization. One of the first tasks was to define the particular nature of the library. To address this question a council of librarians drawn from the country's main libraries was established.[11] On advice of the council and after much debate, the Library Fund decided that the new Royal Library should not be a public library, but rather a national book depository and study library devoted to higher education and scientific research. The new national and royal memorial thus was to become a showcase for Belgian science and literature.

The urban and architectural design of the project was the result of a long process that started with two design competitions. The first focused on the urban layout of the Mont des Arts and was won by Jules Ghobert. The second competition for the architectural design of the Royal Library was won by Houyoux. Even though neither of the winning entries was executed as initially designed, they did have a major influence on the way the building project was conceived both during and after the Second World War. The site was both symbolically and topographically demanding. To cope with the large differences in height of the building site, Ghobert designed a sequence of open squares, each symmetrically aligned along an axis that visually connects the Royal Square in the Upper Town with the City Hall spire in the Lower Town (see Figure 4.3). The vast middle square – the "esplanade" – was conceived as a large tray that subtly draws the attention to the central masterpiece: the Royal Library. Houyoux's architectural plans also expressed an outspoken sense of monumentality. Early drawings depict a library with an impressive portico with Doric columns, a large staircase, and sculpted

Figure 4.3 Winning competition entry for the urban layout of the new Mont des Arts area. Jules Ghobert, architect (1946). © Archives d'Architecture Moderne, Bruxelles.

decorations, which graciously complements the monumental urban setting. The manifold use of symmetrical and axial composition principles both in plan and elevation, the deliberate spatial *mise-en-scène*, the tendency to stress volume and vastness, and above all the use of a classical form vocabulary were all reminiscent of the competition projects designed in the 1930s.

The historical events of the Second World War and profound changes in the sociopolitical context after the war severely hindered the realization of the new library. After 1945, large-scale monumental projects increasingly triggered negative connotations due to associations with the architecture and urbanism of totalitarian regimes. By this time the project had also lost much of its social and political support. Not only did the Royal Question deeply trouble the ties between the Belgian people and its monarchy, it also highlighted the differences between the mainly Catholic Flemish part of the country where the majority of the citizens in a 1950 referendum voted in favor of Leopold III's return to his position as king, and the strongly socialist Francophone part where the majority opposed his return. Furthermore, the country experienced a series of very turbulent political shifts during the first post-war decade. No fewer than nine national governments were installed between 1946 and 1954. As a result the library project had moved from the center of a noncontroversial commemoration of a figurehead of the Belgian royal family and a celebration of the nation to that of an intense political and social conflict, which articulated the often opposing viewpoints of the country's different communities. On top of the problematic national circumstances, the project also had to cope with growing local protest against the large-scale transformation of the existing urban fabric of Brussels and the demolition of old heritage sites. Local protest actions against the destruction of the sixteenth-century Nassau Chapel, several other historical buildings, and Vacherot Park on the Mont des Arts culminated in the establishment of a "Comité d'Action pour la Défense du Mont des Arts" [Action Committee in Defense of the Mont des Arts].

Eventually, the 1958 World's Fair gave the project the boost it needed. During the 1950s, Houyoux and his collaborators (and later successors), architects Roland Delers and Jacques Bellemans, repeatedly adjusted the plans for the Royal Library. The final version of the designs shows that, even though some of the basic principles still reflected the original approach, remarkable changes had occurred in the way the "monumental" aspect of the library was conceived. The architects lessened their reliance on a classical form vocabulary and tried to create a more rational arrangement for the reading rooms. This second change was strongly influenced by the head librarian, who played a key role in the decision making. Nevertheless, because the commissioners kept associating the representative aspect of the library with a more traditional view of monumentality, this evolution could not be translated into the main façade, which, in the opinion of the authorities, had to have a truly "dignified" – code language for more classical – monumental appearance. Even though in the end both the interior spaces and the rear façades received a more contemporary post-war expression, the final design of the building's public face was clearly a post-war implementation of a pre-war monumental design approach. When the building was inaugurated, the architectural appearance of the library was severely criticized for this in the Belgian press. For example, in the national newspaper *De Standaard* journalist Guido Van Hoof stated: "The rigid lines of this building block do not esthetically move you, and what was supposed to be a piece of jewelry according to folklore fanatics – i.e. the so-called Nassau Chapel – rather resembles a sore wart on the architectural skin."[12]

Conceptualizing a modern library

A strong stimulus for the development of the library into a modern institution came in 1956, when Herman Liebaers (1919–2010) was appointed head librarian. Then just thirty-seven years old, Liebaers was a Germanist who had started working for the library in 1943 and in the early 1950s had acquired scholarly experience in the United States through a Fulbright scholarship.[13] Shortly after his appointment, Liebaers began to criticize the design, making a plea for a more functional and therefore less representative design where "service" toward the reader would be essential. According to him, Houyoux's 1946 designs did not sufficiently support this idea. In particular, Liebaers feared that the monumental character several of the architect's drawings suggested would stand in the way, as it would "hinder simple and direct relations between the library and its readers and also because it would impose standards that would drain resources towards accessory expenses" (see Figure 4.4).[14] The reading rooms with high ceilings described in Houyoux's early drawings resembled, in the eyes of the head librarian, "waiting rooms of railway stations" that would only widen the distance between library staff and users.[15] Liebaers argued that the budget necessary to finish the building according to Houyoux's designs – for example, the use of Belgian marble "gris d'Ardennes" for the floor of the grand vestibule – was better spent on the development, the equipment, and the access to the collections.[16] "Living collections are more important than flamboyant marbles," as the head librarian wittily put

Figure 4.4 Perspective for the periodicals reading room, Royal Library. Maurice Houyoux, architect (1946). Algemeen Rijksarchief, Brussels, Bibliotheekfonds Albert I.

it in 1958.[17] He supported the idea that the Royal Library needed to express a certain "architectural monumentality," but pointed out that the collections themselves should not be forgotten as they also strongly contributed "to the homage to the dedicated one."[18] Liebaers was here clearly referring to the identity of Albert I as an engaged supporter of science and the arts and saw this as an important stimulus to also conceptualize the library building as a modern house of an up-to-date library collection.

Liebaers's influence on the project would particularly show in the internal layout and furnishings of the building. In a 1958 letter to the president of the Albert I Library Fund, he pleaded for a "functional equipment and organization of the Albert I Library."[19] His interventions were based on thorough documentation of national and international reference projects. In 1957, he had sent two staff members on a study trip to Berlin and to several cities in Sweden, Copenhagen, and Aarhus to collect information on a diverse set of recently built or renovated royal libraries, university libraries, municipal libraries, etcetera.[20] He sent two other colleagues to France and Switzerland.[21]

Liebaers reserved the most distant research trip for himself, in 1959 going to the United States.[22] Based on this experience, he wrote a report on "the recent construction, organization, furnishings and technical equipment of American libraries."[23] Liebaers had studied a few prototypes of new library concepts, chief among them Lamont Library of Harvard University (1947–9); and several established libraries of an earlier period, including the New York Public Library (1902–11). He also consulted such ongoing projects as the Barnard Library (1958–60) and the United Nations Library in New York (1961), and had conversations with "qualified librarians" of whom he particularly mentioned renowned librarian Keyes Metcalf, former director of Harvard University Libraries.[24]

The interiors of the Belgian Royal Library 69

Figure 4.5 Periodicals reading room, Royal Library, ca. 1969. Roger Van Obberghen, photographer. Archive Stichting De Coene, collection Verzameling De Coene nv., Rijksarchief Kortrijk, no. 12.

Liebaers was clearly inspired by the American examples. Compared to the Brussels Royal Library, most of the new building projects in the United States seemed to be constructed without much delay. "When the first brick is laid, all plans are finished and there are no interruptions during the execution," Liebaers reported to the Albert I Library Fund.[25] He praised the standardized approach that had emerged in the United States since the construction of Harvard's Lamont Library, the Charles Hayden Memorial Library of the Massachusetts Institute of Technology (1950–1), and Princeton's Firestone Memorial Library (1946–9).[26] A limited number of floors, a subtle interface between the reading rooms and the stacks, and office spaces organized according to an open layout were some of the key features of this new approach.

According to Liebaers, "the same certainty characterizes the arrangement of the new libraries and their furnishings" in the United States.[27] He noticed that the floors of the new libraries were often covered with highly resistant and quiet materials, including rubber, vinyl, or asphalt tiles. More representative spaces were finished with terrazzo or marble stones. Conference rooms, executive offices, spaces for the consultation of special collections had wooden floors or were carpeted. Walls – mostly lightweight constructions – were plastered and painted in light colors, although Liebaers also took note of experiments with plastic wall coverings. Suspended ceilings were commonly applied and often a large part of their surface was used for lighting. In terms of furniture, Liebaers noticed that both wood and metal was used, but that the first seemed to become more popular than the latter, in particular in the public areas. Bookshelves were mostly free standing and appeared in several standardized varieties. Study areas were to be found in different sizes and forms in various parts of the library. The furniture in the public areas generally included wooden card catalogs, a low checkout desk, exhibition cabinets, reading tables with a horizontal or an inclined tabletop, more isolated reading carrels, and chairs of a "robust construction" type.

Liebaers acknowledged that the US examples could not simply be copied to the Belgian context as they were too closely related to a different educational system and its social, economic, and everyday life conditions. Nevertheless, he found their emphasis on functionality and concern for the comfort of the individual reader as well as the accompanying design solutions persuasive and succeeded in convincing the Library Fund directors and Houyoux to significantly adjust the library plans. As Liebaers later explained, it was decided to mainly "retrieve the modern library approaches from the Anglo-Saxon world" – "Anglo-Saxon" in this case mainly referring to the United States.[28] Several of the interior design characteristics mentioned in Liebaers's report on his US study trip would later appear in the Brussels library: the choice of wood as the dominant material, the suspended ceilings, the freestanding cabinets, and the availability of lecterns (inclined tabletops) in the reading rooms, etcetera. To address Liebaers's concerns and in accordance with developments within his own oeuvre toward a more modern architectural language, Houyoux simplified many of the interior designs and decorations and removed many of the classicizing architectural elements such as the barrel vault, pillars, and frieze in the grand vestibule (see Figure 4.5). He also added a mezzanine in the high-ceilinged reading rooms,[29] integrated more small-scale reading rooms into the overall library layout, and further expanded the space for directly accessible collections of reference works.[30]

De Coene's modern agenda

For the interior design and furnishings of the new library, the Albert I Library Fund chose to work with the Flemish furniture firm Kortrijkse Kunstwerkstede Gebroeders De Coene. This choice was at once remarkable and perfectly in line with the modern policy that Liebaers was advancing. By contracting De Coene, the Belgian government opted for a company that in the interwar period had built up a strong international reputation as a producer of high-quality Art Deco furniture. De Coene also had experience in representing the nation through the company's participation in international fairs such as the 1925 Paris *Exposition des Arts Décoratifs et Industriels Modernes* and the 1937 Paris *Exposition Internationale des Arts et des Techniques dans la Vie Moderne*.[31] However, as a result of its collusion with the enemy during the Second World War, De Coene's reputation had been severely damaged. The company had produced barracks, emergency housing, and furniture for the German military and civilian services, as well as a number of fake wooden airplanes meant to mislead the Allied air force.[32] After Liberation, De Coene's directors were convicted for economic collaboration and the company was sequestered by the government. Not until 1952 were the family members of De Coene and their close allies back in charge. Financial settlements between De Coene and the national government remained pending until 1957.

The interiors of the Belgian Royal Library   71

While these convictions would seem to make De Coene an unlikely choice for a project with such progressive ambitions and delicate politics, one of the key reasons De Coene succeeded in obtaining the large contract for the interior furnishings of the Royal Library had to do with the new direction the firm's management took in 1953. In the 1950s, the company risked having its profits confiscated. Stimulated by this situation, Pol Provost, the general director of the company who had already begun preparing a restructuring of the company during the war, decided to reinvest as much capital as possible into new technologies, in particular into new branches of the wood and furniture industries.[33] For example, the firm installed an up-to-date technical laboratory and bought an advanced press for the production of bakelized wood. Over the course of the 1950s, a whole range of new building products was launched: self-supporting panels, new types of plywood, doors, trailers, prefabricated houses, and a new type of glulams (glued laminated timber support beams), which allowed for the rapid construction of large halls or pavilions.[34]

Both the furniture and interior design departments were also reformed. This process was marked by the 1954 acquisition of the production and sale licenses of Knoll International furniture for the Benelux and the Belgian Congo. By this time, Knoll was well known for its modern domestic and office furniture with designs by such famous architects and designers as Eero Saarinen, Harry Bertoia, and Ludwig Mies van der Rohe. For De Coene, producing and selling this furniture signaled an important step in the modernization of its product range and distanced the company from its wartime activities. De Coene continued producing period furniture, but at the same time started its own post-war modern furniture lines. In a 1998 interview Adolf De Coene, member of the company's executive committee in the 1950s, underlined the enormous influence Knoll had on the Flemish company: "In that time, in '54, all companies in Flanders were old-fashioned. We stood nowhere in comparison with America. Before the arrival of Knoll De Coene already produced so-called modern furniture, but in the 1950s there was no comparison with the Knoll designs."[35]

In political terms, De Coene's deal with Knoll was also very meaningful, especially in the context of the Cold War. After all, collaborating with the American-based company helped De Coene in compensating for the company's commissions for the German occupation forces and in distancing itself from its much-discussed recent trial.[36] It also added to the growing visual representation of the American superpower in Western Europe.[37] From the early 1940s, Hans Knoll had cultivated connections within the Washington political elite, including the Office of Foreign Buildings Operations, a division of the State Department that oversaw the construction, planning, and maintenance of buildings and real estate in other countries.[38] Knoll was able to profit from the so-called counterpart funds of the United States in Europe created by the Marshall Plan and others by producing furnishings for use in the US diplomatic facilities expansion program.[39] The 1954 license contract between Knoll and De Coene confirms the strong ties between the American firm and the American authorities. It stipulated that Knoll Associates and Knoll International – respectively, the name of the New York-based parent company and that of Knoll's growing collection of foreign subsidiaries and franchises – reserved the right to sell directly "to the American government and to all public or semi-governmental American agencies or bodies on the territories assigned to the licensee and without having to grant compensation for this to the latter."[40]

The clean lines, modern materials, and sculptural forms of the Knoll furniture convincingly supported and visualized De Coene's efforts to neutralize its burdened recent history and reinvent itself as a fully fledged partner in the promulgation of the American example. Knoll products were presented to a Belgian audience in several ways, including explicit pro-American events. For example, the traveling exhibition *American Design for Home and Decorative Use*, organized by the Museum of Modern Art (New York) and sponsored by the newly formed United States Information Agency (USIA), came to Belgium in 1954.[41] Stimulated by several of these soft power strategies, over the course of the 1950s and 1960s in Belgium as in several other Western European countries, Knoll furniture became a key component of the interiors of many new office buildings and of the domestic interiors of the culturally progressive upper and upper-middle classes.[42]

Perhaps inspired by the Knoll Planning Unit – the interior design service set up by Florence Knoll in New York – De Coene started its own research and design office in 1956. It was led by Philippe Neerman (1930–2011), one of Belgium's most remarkable post-war industrial designers, who started working for the company only a year after graduating from the Brussels La Cambre architecture and visual arts school in 1953.[43] The name given to the research and design office, TVR-Contract Jobs, referred to its early focus on the design and production of encasements for televisions or radios. However, according to a former colleague, the office soon began receiving commissions for large-scale interior design projects and contracts for Knoll furniture and other furniture design series.[44] TVR-Contract Jobs was equipped with a separate drawing room and production space and quickly developed into a key department of De Coene. The Royal Library was one of its first and most important assignments. Neerman continued to work for the company until the mid-1960s, when the Kortrijkse Kunstwerkstede Gebroeders De Coene experienced financial problems and in 1966 was largely taken over by the Société Générale de Belgique, a powerful Belgian investment group. Neerman then established his own design office and continued to work for the Royal Library.[45]

The combination of De Coene's strong interwar reputation as a producer of high-quality furniture and interiors, its remarkable post-war modernization, the association with the powerful and internationally recognized Knoll brand, and the extensive network of contacts Provost had developed in the political world, business circles, and the emerging world of industrial design enabled the company to again attract large commissions with a high level of visibility. This included the interiors of the Royal Library where Knoll's "International Style" furniture was combined with other furnishings designed by Neerman and the De Coene company. According to a De Coene advertisement, the project called for: "6 km shelving, 500 desks and reading tables, 15000 card-catalogue cabinets, 300 cupboards and storage furniture, 2000 seats, 800 m² screens and partitions, 3000 m² wall coverings and panels, 60 display cases, 200 meter counters, 1000 m² carpet, 400 doors, 5 km plinths, 4000 m² ceiling."[46] De Coene furnished the cafeteria, no fewer than sixteen reading rooms, the executive offices and boardroom, the special collections section, the manuscripts cabinet, the main entrance hall, the museum space, and the incorporated Nassau chapel.

The Royal Library project was not the only "royal" assignment De Coene obtained. For example, the company was contracted to construct the interiors of the Institut Royale du Patrimoine Artistique [Royal Institute for Cultural Heritage] in a new modernist building (1955–8) in Brussels designed by architect Charles Rimanque. The interiors of the offices, studios, and laboratories were designed by Paris-trained interior architect Stéphane Jasinski (1907–2000), were produced by De Coene's design department, and included Knoll furniture.[47] Furthermore, De Coene contributed to several highly visible projects of national government representation, including the interior decoration of Belgian embassies or consulates in Bonn, Budapest, Canberra, The Hague, Copenhagen, Lisbon, Moscow, New York, and Washington, DC, in the period 1952–77.[48] Many of these projects were meant to project an image of a well-organized enterprise that valued high-quality construction – a mechanism that in turn would reflect positively on the government. De Coene's capacity to contribute to such image building was supported by its simultaneous involvement in prestigious international commissions such as the interior arrangements of the new UNESCO headquarters in Paris by architects Marcel Breuer, Pier Luigi Nervi, and Bernard Zehrfuss.[49] For this project De Coene produced a large series of conference desks, among other pieces.[50]

Straightforward modern interiors

Inspired by the combined post-war aspirations, activities, and technical expertise of Liebaers, Neerman, De Coene, Houyoux, and Delers, the interiors Houyoux had originally envisaged for the Royal Library were replaced with more straightforward modern versions featuring locally designed furniture and items from the Knoll catalog. Characterized by the elegant presence of Knoll's sculptural furniture elements – in particular the Saarinen executive chairs – some of the library interiors at first sight showed affinities with those of the UNESCO headquarters and many other modern buildings constructed at the time. Also in Brussels many new modern office buildings and skyscrapers appeared in the post-war decades. Inspired by foreign examples, the architecture and interiors of these buildings were often conceived as significant expressions of the commissioner's overall corporate identity. A telling example is the Banque Lambert in Brussels, a late 1950s office building designed by American architect Gordon Bunshaft of Skidmore, Owings and Merrill. The interiors of the bank were furnished by De Coene and Simonis, a Brussels-based furniture company. Simonis also chose to modernize its furniture collection in the mid-1950s and became one of the first distributors of Herman Miller products in Belgium. As in many contemporary office buildings, the lobby of the Banque Lambert featured Mies's Barcelona chairs, produced by Knoll since 1953.[51]

However, the Royal Library's interiors were also quite distinct from these projects. While Knoll products were obviously present in many of the rooms and offices, they did not dominate the interiors; rather, they were carefully integrated into the sophisticated overall interior design and furnishing concepts first developed by De Coene with Neerman and later by Neerman working independently. Inspired by Liebaers's ideas, this concept focused on providing a unique interpretation of modern service and comfort. This translated, for example, into the dominant use within the public areas of mobile wooden furniture elements with refined detailing. De Coene's design office developed reading tables with wooden tabletops and carefully integrated chromed metal rails along which several bookends could be positioned. For the special collections reading room, wooden lecterns with an adjustable inclination were produced. The book counters in the main reading room were specially conceived to endure frequent use and to absorb sound. Their tabletops were made of slats of beech fixed to an underlying structure with the use of a series of screws, which contrive to give the furniture elements a particularly playful appearance. The top floor cafeteria was equipped with chairs that Neerman had designed in 1960 for the Philips headquarters in Eindhoven (see Plate 4). The chairs consisted of an elegant, and in technical terms, complex framework of bent plywood (American walnut) with an unusually large and comfortable seat and armrests that widened to give more support as needed. The orange-red upholstery convincingly complemented and enlivened the room's contrasting color pallet dominated by dark wood paneling, light-colored natural stone cladding, black floor tiles, and white marble tabletops.

Modern library service also translated into the integration of state-of-the-art technical equipment in library interiors. To optimize the connections between visitors, books, and personnel, a technically sophisticated distribution center was installed in the heart of the main reading room. An electronic transport system allowed easy movement of books from the closed library stacks to the reading room and vice versa. Book requests were transported by means of a pneumatic device integrated in a modern wooden furniture element (see Figure 4.6). Communication between library visitors and the distribution counter was ensured by a discreet lighting system. When requested items were ready to be picked up, the library staff was (and still is) able to notify the reader through a switchboard connecting to smoothly integrated red lights indicating the numbered seats at the reading tables. When the library was inaugurated, the progressive technical equipment was considered a key feature of the new royal building. The newspaper *La Cité* reported that King Baudouin, accompanied by a series of personalities, visited the library, including its "technical installations."[52]

Figure 4.6 Distribution center in the main reading room, ca. 1969. Unknown photographer. Photo collection of the Royal Library.

Several published photographs highlighted the electronic equipment of the library, giving the whole enterprise an almost futurist touch.[53]

At the time of the opening, Baudouin had already built a solid reputation for himself and as such had significantly contributed to restoring the people's confidence in the Belgian monarchy. He was much appreciated as the new king of the Belgians and was guiding the monarchy with growing confidence through the post-war era, including the redefinition of its representation. The modern interiors of the royal library can be seen as an expression of this search for a renewed identity. The royal institute was a prestigious modern enterprise, up to date with foreign developments and confident enough to negotiate its own identity within an international frame of reference. There was no overly dominant use of royal symbols or a classicist vocabulary. While the boardroom later prominently displayed portraits of the reigning king and queen, the original focus was on the passions, rather than the images of the late Leopold II and Albert I (see Figure 4.7). The longest wall in the room was covered with a reproduction of a medieval engraving representing the city of Brussels. On the side, a display case for manuscripts was integrated into a wall covered in precious dark ebony veneer, making the books appear almost to float in space. The engraving and the manuscripts clearly referenced the library's core business of collecting, preserving, and facilitating consultation and highlighted its contribution to nation building through these activities. The boardroom also displayed a distinctive but at the same time internationally recognizable design language. The furniture in the room included a series of tables with a chromed foot and a lustrous ebony tabletop designed by Neerman and his

Figure 4.7 Main boardroom of the Royal Library, ca. 1969. Roger Van Obberghen, photographer. Photo collection of the Royal Library.

office, which acted like a mirror, reflecting the representations of the intellectual identity of the kingdom of the Belgians further into the room. The executive chairs upholstered in soft brown calfskin were designed by American designer Vincent Cafiero for Knoll and were produced by De Coene with dark wooden bases. One chair had a higher back and was meant to underline the prominent position of the president of the library board, a strategy De Coene also applied to its own chair designs and in other politically charged contexts, including board rooms of city halls.[54] In the case of the royal library, references to the key mission of the institute, high-quality local furniture production, and items from the renowned American collection of "International Style" furniture were skillfully combined into a well-balanced expression of a modern royal enterprise.

An ongoing search for an up-to-date image

The interior furnishings of the Belgian Royal Library were the result of a long-term project of national and royal representation within an increasingly manifest international and modern context. First of all, at the instigation of head librarian Liebaers, their design was informed by a study of many foreign, in particular American libraries. Furthermore they were produced by De Coene, a company that, motivated by a desire to erase the stigma of its own wartime activities, strongly invested in an up-to-date international and pro-American network of progressive business partners. Finally, the furnishings themselves carefully combined local production and designs by Neerman with icons of modern corporate identity from the collection of Knoll International, resulting in what can be described as a strong expression of national identity with an international imprimatur.

Today the interior of the Royal Library is in a problematic state due to the aging of the furniture, the absence of a conservation policy or renovation guidelines, and the new demands of library work. Combined with the fact that Belgium as a national project is increasingly questioned – a development stimulated by the continuous process of federalization, European unification, and the privatization of many national corporations – the original concept of the interiors and of the building as a whole appears to be highly vulnerable.[55] A 2007 intervention in the Royal Library serves as an example. To increase the accessibility of the institute – a key issue in the design of many contemporary libraries and government institutions – the main entry was relocated on the level of the "esplanade," leaving the original monumental entrance hall an empty residue. Populated by a series of the Italian design company Magis's 2004 Chair_One by German designer Konstantin Grcic, the new entrance lobby is an inviting place. However, despite this new international presence, the space doesn't seem to connect with the older interiors. It remains isolated from the existing discourses of national representation and from the embedded set of international references. A more conscious rereading of the Royal Library's original interior as a whole could reveal ample clues for a more engaging dialogue with Belgium's past, present, and future.

Acknowledgments

This essay is based on extensive research on the realization of the Mont des Arts and the Royal Library building, on the activities of the Kortrijkse Kunstwerkstede De Coene, and on the work of designer Philippe Neerman in a great variety of archives.

The interiors of the Belgian Royal Library   77

We wish to thank all archival institutions involved, in particular the Royal Library itself for supporting this research. In 2009, under the supervision of Fredie Floré, Johan Lagae, and Rika Devos at Ghent University, Hannes Pieters completed a master's thesis on the Royal Library building. Results of this research were published as a book titled *Bouwen voor de natie* and in an article in 2012. We want to thank the npo Stichting De Coene and in particular Philippe De Craene for their continuous advice, their willingness to share archival material, and their help in tracing the oral history of the company. Conversations with Philippe Neerman in 2001 and 2009 were of great value. With this chapter we hope to bring tribute to what the designer himself considered one of his major works. In 2015, we presented a first draft of this chapter at the "Changing Visions of Diplomacy by Design" conference at Brighton University. We wish to thank Harriet Atkinson and Verity Clarkson for hosting the event and for chairing a most inspiring discussion.

Notes

1 The Flemish name of Mont des Arts is Kunstberg.
2 Hannes Pieters, *Bouwen voor de natie: De Albertina op de Brusselse Kunstberg als monumentaal totaalproject* (Ghent: Academia Press, 2012).
3 King Baudouin stated the library was "une œuvre collective de tous les Belges," "une institution qui unit le passé, le présent et l'avenir." Cited in "Le Roi et la Reine ont inauguré officiellement L''Albertine'," *La Cité*, February 18, 1969, 7. All translations are by the author unless otherwise indicated.
4 Bert Populier, "Albertina op de Kunstberg: een kwarteeuw Koninklijke Bibliotheek Albert I," *Kunst en cultuur* 5 (1994): 4–7: "geheugen van het land."
5 Jan Frans Vanderheyden, "De Albertina Als Nationaal Monument," *De Bibliotheekgids* XIV 1 (1935): 1–5: "den verderen uitbouw" and "geestelijk patrimonium."
6 For a concise history of the competitions, see Pieters, *Bouwen voor de natie*, 226–47.
7 A first article on the interior of the library appeared in 2012: Hannes Pieters, "Het interieur van de Koninklijke Bibliotheek van België door de Kortrijkse Kunstwerkstede De Coene," *Bulletin KNOB* 4 (2012): 199–210.
8 Stefan Berger, "National Movements," in *A Companion to Nineteenth-Century Europe, 1789–1914*, ed. Stefan Berger (Oxford: Blackwell Publishing, 2006), 178. While Belgium was declared independent in 1830, the Belgian monarchy was established in 1831.
9 The term "living memorial" is a concept closely tied to wartime and post-war architecture and was not literally used in the context of the Brussels library. For a discussion of the concept, see, for example, Andrew M. Shanken, "Planning Memory: Living Memorials in the United States during World War II," *Art Bulletin* 84, no. 1 (2002): 130–47.
10 This included collecting the funds originally meant for the erection of statues in different parts of the country as well as managing additional funding from the different ministries involved.
11 For information on the members of the council of librarians, see "Verslag aan de regeering over zijn werkzaamheden sedert zijn stichting in 1935" (unpublished report, 1946), 87. Algemeen Rijksarchief Brussels, Bibliotheekfonds Albert I, III.0188, location: -6C 63.043–39. All subsequent references to Bibliotheekfonds Albert I refer to the fund with this title in the Algemeen Rijksarchief Brussels.
12 Guido Van Hoof, "Open boekenmijn," *De Standaard der Letteren*, February 14, 1969: "Door de strakke lijnen van deze blokkendoos word je niet estetisch bewogen en wat volgens folkloristische fanatici een sierraad moest zijn – de zogeheten kapel van Nassau – lijkt eerder op een zere wrat op de architektonische huid."
13 Van Hoof, "Open boekenmijn."
14 Herman Liebaers, "De la construction d'une nouvelle Bibliothèque nationale de Belgique," *Archives, Bibliothèques et Musées de Belgique* 2 (1958): 219–31: "entrave les rapports

78 *Fredie Floré and Hannes Pieters*

simples et directs entre la bibliothèque et ses lecteurs et aussi parce qu'elle impose un train de vie qui draine les ressources vers des dépenses accessoires."

15 Liebaers, "De la construction d'une nouvelle Bibliothèque nationale de Belgique," 226: "salles d'attente des gares de chemin de fer."

16 Maurice Houyoux, "Bibliothèque Albert Iᵉʳ. Project de l'Architecte M. Houyoux," *Architecture Urbanisme Habitation* 7 (1947): 97–112.

17 Herman Liebaers, "A propos de la Bibliothèque royale Albert Ier à Bruxelles," *Bulletin de l'UNESCO à l'intention des Bibliothèques* 1 (1956): 35: "Des collections vivantes sont plus importantes que des marbres flamboyantes."

18 Liebaers, "A propos de la Bibliothèque royale," 35: "monumentalité architecturale," "à l'hommage au dédicataire."

19 Letter from Herman Liebaers to E. J. Solvay, president of the Albert I Library Fund, June 11, 1958, Bibliotheekfonds Albert I: "équipement et aménagement fonctionnel de la Bibliothèque Albert Ier."

20 One staff member went to Berlin and visited the library of the recently established Freie Universität, the American Memorial Library (opened in 1954, an American open-access library), and the Public Scientific Library (Öffentliche Wissenschaftliche Bibliothek). The other visited the Royal Library of Stockholm, the libraries of Uppsala University and Lund University, the municipal and university libraries in Goteborg, the National Library and the Central Library of Frederiksberg in Copenhagen, and the Central Library in Aarhus. See Letter from Herman Liebaers to the president of the Albert I Library Fund, May 17, 1957, Bibliotheekfonds Albert I.

21 One staff member visited Paris (Bibliothèque Nationale, Bibliothèque des Facultés de médecine et de droit, Centre nationale de la recherche scientifique) and the university libraries in Caen, Aix-en-Provence, Clermont-Ferrand and Bourges. The other visited the National Library in Berne, the library of the Polytechnic School in Zurich and the UN Library, the library of the Bureau International du Travail and the library of the European Council for Nuclear Research in Geneva. See Letter from Herman Liebaers to E.J. Solvay, June 11, 1958, Bibliotheekfonds Albert I.

22 Letter from Herman Liebaers to E. J. Solvay, February 11, 1960, Bibliotheekfonds Albert I.

23 Herman Liebaers, "La construction, l'aménagement, le mobilier et l'équipement technique récents des bibliothèques américaines," unpublished report, February 1960, Bibliotheekfonds Albert I.

24 Keyes Metcalf (1889–1983) worked in various roles at the New York Public Library and in 1937 was appointed Director of University Libraries at Harvard, where he dealt with plans for three new buildings, including Lamont Library. After his retirement in 1955, he often served as a building consultant and published a manual on the planning of academic and research libraries: *Planning Academic and Research Library Buildings* (New York: McGraw-Hill, 1965).

25 Liebaers, "La construction, l'aménagement": "Lors de la pose de la première pierre, tous les plans sont terminés et aucune interruption n'intervient au cours de l'exécution."

26 The architects of Harvard's Lamont Library, Princeton's Firestone Memorial Library, and the Charles Hayden Memorial Library, are, respectively, Henry Shepley; Robert B. O'Connor; and Voorhees, Walker, Foley & Smith.

27 Liebaers, "La construction, l'aménagement": "la même certitude marque l'aménagement des nouvelles bibliothèques et leur équipement mobilier."

28 Van Hoof, "Open boekenmijn."

29 "P.V. van de zitting van de raad van beheer van het Bibliotheek Albert I Fonds van 22 mei 1959," May 22, 1959, 3, Bibliotheekfonds Albert I.

30 Pieters, *Bouwen voor de natie*, 146.

31 For a discussion of these contributions, see Werner Adriaenssens, "De Vlaamsche moderne woonkamer. De Kunstwerkstede op de tentoonstelling van 1925 in Parijs," and Norbert Poulain, "Het interbellum. Van art deco tot modern," both in *Kortrijkse Kunstwerkstede Gebroeders De Coene*, ed. Frank Herman and Ruben Mayeur (Kortrijk: Uitgeverij Groeninghe, 2006), 90–107; 108–31.

32 See Ruben Majeur, Lieven Douchy and Marc Goethals, "Ambachten en industrie onder één dak. Groei en ontwikkeling van de Kortrijkse Kunstwerkstede," in *Kortrijkse Kunstwerkstede*, 41–69.

The interiors of the Belgian Royal Library 79

33 Also Provost had been sentenced to several years in prison for economic collaboration. For more on Pol Provost, see Ruben Majeur and Lieven Douchy, "Pol Provost. Een nieuw elan," in *Kortrijkse Kunstwerkstede*, 170–81. For a discussion on De Coene's post-war investments in new branches of the wood and furniture industries, see Rika Devos and Fredie Floré, "Modern Wood: De Coene at Expo '58," *Construction History* (2009): 103–20.

34 In 1958, De Coene built more than twenty-three glulam pavilions at the Brussels World's Fair. See Devos and Floré, "Modern Wood," 103–20.

35 Hilde Bouchez, "Adolf De Coene, de trots van de oude blinde meubelmaker," *De Standaard Magazine*, October 16, 1998, 14.

36 As the De Coene trial was one of the first trials in Belgium on economic collaboration, it attracted a lot of public attention. See Majeur et al., "Ambachten en industrie onder één dak," 41–69. See also Fred Germonprez, *Jozef De Coene en de Kortrijkse Kunstwerkstede* (Tielt: Lannoo, 1983), 163–219. For an audio account of De Coene's position within the economic field in Belgium during the Second World War, see also "De Coene and the Second World War: A Historical Analysis. Prof. Dr. Dirk Luyten SOMA/CEGES, UGent – BE," in *Kortrijkse Kunstwerkstede De Coene gebr: Ateliers d'Art de Courtrai De Coene fr.*, ed. Terenja van Dijk and Frank Herman (Kortrijk: Erfgoedcel Kortrijk, 2009) (DVD).

37 This observation is developed in Fredie Floré, "Architect-Designed Interiors for a Culturally Progressive Upper-Middle Class: The Implicit Political Presence of Knoll International in Belgium," in *Atomic Dwelling: Anxiety, Domesticity, and Postwar Architecture*, ed. Robin Schuldenfrei (Abingdon: Routledge, 2012), 169–85.

38 Brian Lutz, *Knoll: A Modernist Universe* (New York: Rizzoli, 2010), 61. For a discussion of Knoll's early years, see also Paul Makovsky, "Knoll Before Knoll Textiles, 1940–46," in *Knoll Textiles, Nineteenhundredfortyfive–Twothousandandten*, ed. Earl Martin (New Haven, CT: Yale University Press, 2011), 74–101. On Knoll and the building projects of the FBO, see Jane Loeffler, *The Architecture of Diplomacy: Building America's Embassies* (New York: Princeton University Press, 1998), 57, 64, 67–8, 71, 75, 92–3, 190.

39 Eric Larrabee and Massimo Vignelli, *Knoll Design* (New York: Abrams, 1981), 176. On Knoll and the Marshall Plan, see also Greg Castillo, *Cold War on the Home Front: The Soft Power of Midcentury Design* (Minneapolis: University of Minnesota Press, 2010), 62–4.

40 "Convention" (unpublished document), Rijksarchief Kortrijk [Public Record Office Kortrijk], Archive of the Kantoor Controle Vennootschappen 2 in Kortrijk, pack 263, file tax assessment year 1965, 3. It looks like in these cases Hans Knoll wanted to ensure the right to directly sell furniture without De Coene as an intermediary. So it concerns compensation for the fact that De Coene doesn't have these American (government) agencies as a client, while they are located in the Benelux.

41 The exhibition visited cities in Finland, Sweden, Norway, Denmark, Belgium, and Italy from 1953 to 1955. See Castillo, *Cold War on the Home Front*, 111.

42 For further discussion of Knoll's promotional strategies in Belgium, see Floré, "Architect-Designed Interiors for a Culturally Progressive Upper-Middle Class," 169–85.

43 From 1954 until 1966, Neerman was head of the "Contract Jobs" department of De Coene. "Philippe Neerman," unidentified clipping, 1992. Knoll International France had a similar planning unit first led by Roger Legrand.

44 Carl Dehaen, *Historische evolutie van de dept: TVR-Knoll-Contract Jobs*, cited in Pieters, *Bouwen voor de natie*, 179.

45 Neerman's own office was named Industrial Design Planning Office Philippe Neerman & co. Johan Valcke, "Openbaar vervoer voor de mens. Philippe Neerman (1930), 47 jaar design vanuit Vlaanderen," in *Prijzen Henry Van de Velde 1999 van het VIZO voor loopbaan, jong talent, bedrijf en beste product* (Brussels: VIZO, 1999), 2–5. In 1966, the Kunstwerkstede De Coene was converted into the industrial group nv Houtindustrie De Coene & Company, over which the Société Générale held 60 percent control. See Mayeur, Douchy and Marc Goethals, "Houtindustrie De Coene: Opkomst en ondergang van een industriële groep," in *Kortrijkse Kunstwerkstede*, 140–69.

46 "In de Koninklijke Bibliotheek zijn er talrijke meesterwerken. Het eerste dat u zult zien . . . is het werk van De Coene," advertisement of the nv Houtindustrie De Coene and Company, unidentified newspaper clipping.

47 Gertjan Madalijns, "KIK. Het Koninklijk Instituut voor het Kunstpatrimonium" (master's thesis, Antwerp University, 2015).

80 Fredie Floré and Hannes Pieters

48 These projects are listed in Bernard Pauwels, "De Coene-projecten. Een eerste repertorium," in *Kortrijkse Kunstwerkstede*, 216–31.

49 For a thorough discussion of the architecture of and the art displayed in the UNESCO headquarters, see Christopher E. M. Pearson, *Designing UNESCO: Art, Architecture and International Politics at Mid-Century* (Burlington, VT: Ashgate, 2010).

50 These conference desks were still in use when in 2009 former project manager Jérome Dervichian was interviewed on site. "UNESCO-gebouw (1958–1960)," in *Kortrijkse Kunstwerkstede De Coene gebr: Ateliers d'Art de Courtrai De Coene fr.* (DVD).

51 See "Banque Lambert à Bruxelles," *L'Architecture d'Aujourd'hui* (September 1965): 100.

52 "Le Roi et la Reine ont inauguré officiellement L'"Albertine.'"

53 See, for example, "La famille royale inaugure la bibliothèque Albert Ier," *La Dernière Heure*, February 18, 1969.

54 For example, the boardroom of the Flemish municipality Merksem was equipped with the same "Philips" chairs as the cafeteria of the Royal Library. The chair for the mayor was executed with a higher back and imprinted with the emblem of the municipality.

55 Fredie Floré and Johan Lagae, "Een onbeminde Belgische 'lieu de mémoire,'" in Pieters, *Bouwen voor de natie*, V–VII.

Spaces of persuasion

5 Exhibitions for modern living

Lifestyle propaganda and the promotion of modern furniture and furnishings in the United States, 1930s–1950s

Margaret Maile Petty

Wherever we go and whatever we do, design is always with us – making itself felt in our lives. Physically, good design can go far to increase the efficiency of our actions. Spiritually, it can add much to our enjoyment of things around us. So it follows in a very real sense how much we know about design is a larger measure of how much we get out of life.[1]

Alexander Girard, 1949

The ideological continuum of 'good design' and quality of life was the beam upon which post-war rhetoric balanced modern design with the American consumer ethos and lifestyle. In the mid-twentieth century, modern design in the United States was sold not so much as a moral and social imperative as it had been in Europe and Britain, but rather as a conduit for and intensifier of 'better living' – used synonymously with the American 'way of life'. Within this ideological landscape, a variety of modes of persuasion were employed to re-cast modern design as lifestyle embodiment and expression. From the later 1930s leading up to the Second World War, awareness increased among a vocal minority of furniture manufacturers, retailers, designers, critics and curators of America's command of industry and marketplace despite the juvenile state of the nation's aesthetic development in comparison with that of European modernism. Working both collaboratively and independently, these agents for change employed sophisticated display strategies and focused rhetorical frameworks in the articulation of not only a distinctive approach to modern design and interiors, but also of a persuasive and scalable image of the American lifestyle. Curated for both retail and cultural contexts, such displays codified the American 'way of life' for domestic consumption and contributed to the imaging of US furniture, furnishing and ideology for international exportation. While the Cold War propagandizing of American consumer culture in Europe is beyond the scope of this chapter, what happened in the years leading up to the Second World War and in the years immediately following its conclusion was critical in the establishment of a cultural and commercial climate hospitable for and sustaining of 'good design' in the United States. From museum galleries to manufacturers' showrooms to more hybrid-collaborative exhibition models, the full sweep of modern design and furnishings was displayed and showcased with the didactic intent to educate industry, design professionals and the public as to the principles of good design as well as its role in popular notions of 'better living'.

84 *Margaret Maile Petty*

Taking these repeatedly paired objectives as a point of departure, this chapter will examine the ways in which the exhibition of modern design and furnishings served to convince industry of the importance of 'good design' as an ethical and financial imperative and similarly to demonstrate to the consuming public its inseparability from the American way of life. How and where these messages were delivered and the critical role of cultural and commercial networks in the promotion of modern design and furnishings forms a core theme of this chapter. Drawing upon popular and industry media, exhibition catalogues and archival material, this study explores some of the key design exhibitions from the 1930s through the early 1950s that aided in the reinvention of the American furniture industry and promoted a modern lifestyle predicated upon good design.

Window-shopping: modern design on display

From the outset modern design in the United States was defined within a commercial context and within close proximity to the marketplace. The merging of American commercial and cultural production was the focus of two exhibitions held in New York City in 1934 – the National Alliance of Art and Industry's *Industrial Arts Exposition* and the Museum of Modern Art's (MoMA) *Machine Art* exhibition. Edward Alden Jewell, art critic for the *New York Times*, reviewed both shows, underscoring their shared interest in defining a national style informed by the unique qualities of American industrial design and aesthetic sensibilities. Alon Bement, director of the National Alliance of Art and Industry and curator of the *Industrial Arts Exposition*, described the aim of his show as: "to demonstrate that beauty and sales value are complementary to our civilization; [and] to emphasize visually that there is a definite trend toward a national style."[2] On either side of this slender semi-colon, Bement put forth a tidy summary of the efforts throughout the second half of the 1930s to reconcile marketplace viability with the articulation of a modern American aesthetic within the context of a consumer lifestyle.

A month later Jewell revisited MoMA's *Machine Art* exhibition in a separate review, describing it as one of the "most engrossing ever held" at the Museum.[3] Certainly as a collection of thoughtfully curated industrial objects, *Machine Art* was highly successful in staging the products of industry as exemplary of a modern aesthetic. Philip Johnson, who curated and designed the exhibition for MoMA, used a host of novel display materials – including velvet, sheet copper, molded plastic and painted colored panels – along with clever groupings and dramatic lighting to glamorize the wide range of objects on display, from propellers to chemistry beakers to dental instruments (see Figure 5.1).[4] Rather than masking the commercial nature of the objects on display, the dazzling exhibition design enhanced these qualities, eliciting associations with department store showrooms from some reviewers.[5] Similarly, the exhibition catalog, not unlike a department store directory, included the name, manufacturer, designer and price for each object on display and reminded museum goers that "unless otherwise specified the object may be purchased from the manufacturer."[6]

Figure 5.1 Machine Art, Museum of Modern Art, New York, March 5–April 29, 1934. Philip Johnson, curator and designer. Unknown photographer. The Museum of Modern Art Archives. Acc. IN34.5 © Photo SCALA, Florence.

Useful Objects and the merchant of MoMA

Building on its initial endorsement of industrial design with the *Machine Art* exhibition, MoMA continued its commitment to educating the public about modern design with the first *Useful Objects* exhibition in 1938. Showcasing approximately 100 household items selected on the basis of their "good modern design," "availability at retail stores" and retail price of $5.00 or less, the exhibition aimed to demonstrate that "it is possible to purchase everyday articles of excellent design at reasonable prices."[7] Unlike Johnson's rarified exhibition that primarily emphasized the aesthetic qualities of industrially produced goods, *Useful Objects* sought to instruct consumers on how to identify affordable, well-designed household goods.[8]

After its inaugural showing, the annual *Useful Objects* exhibition opened every November and remained in MoMA's galleries throughout the Christmas shopping season. The focus of the displays remained largely on household items and the criteria held fast to the principles of good design as set forth by the museum – "a design suitable to the specific use; a material adequate to that use and respectfully handled; a concept congruous with the necessary method of production; and an imaginative rendering."[9] Ever aware of the importance of consumer accessibility, items selected for *Useful Objects* had to be readily available in retail outlets and at a price not exceeding the maximum allowed for an entry, which was $5.00 in 1938, $10.00 in 1940, and $25.00 in 1946.[10]

The didactic yet market-friendly focus of *Useful Objects* can be largely attributed to Edgar Kaufmann Jr., who proposed, curated and championed the exhibitions.[11] Son of prominent Pittsburgh merchant Edgar Kaufmann Sr., who strongly believed that the department store had a responsibility to contribute to "the cultural life of the community," Kaufmann Jr. was raised in an environment that prized the role of commerce in protecting and promoting culture.[12] During his tenure at MoMA, which stretched from 1937 to 1955 (with a pause during his wartime service), Kaufmann Jr. advanced a similar philosophy, innovating new ways in which the museum could engage with and harness the marketplace to achieve its aims.

Seeing potential to expand the reach of *Useful Objects*, Kaufmann Jr. sought MoMA's support in staging a design competition to identify "a group of designers capable of creating a useful and beautiful environment for today's living, in terms of furniture, fabrics, and lighting," and having done so, to "bring the best designs on the market."[13] To ensure the production and retail availability of winning designs, Kaufmann arranged partnerships with both manufacturers and a number of the nation's leading department stores. With such innovative arrangements, Kaufmann advanced his mission from educating consumers about good design to directly influencing the marketplace. Of additional importance, it is at this pivotal moment that Kaufmann also placed the rhetoric of 'today's living' at the center of his efforts.

Organic Design in Home Furnishings, as the 1940 competition became known, was overseen by Eliot Noyes, the director of MoMA's Department of Industrial Design, in consultation with Kaufmann, who was away for wartime service.[14] Noyes, like Kaufmann, believed that such partnerships were essential if the Museum was to have any real impact on the success of modern design in the United States. As Noyes described:

> [The] production of merchandise is a chain in which the designer depends on the manufacturer and the manufacturer depends on the retailer, who is the final control on what sort of design is presented to the public. . . . As we struggle with the problem of getting better design on the market, we can conjure up a pleasant picture of how it all might work. . . . In this idle dream we picture the retailer as someone with a great sense of his social responsibility and an understanding of the absolutely fundamental importance of good design in relation to his own good business. In this picture, it is the retailer who is the patron of design progress and forward thinking, in order that he may provide better ways of living through what he sells.[15]

Noyes, picking up the theme of design as a means to 'better ways of living', cleverly united the social responsibility of the retailer to the consuming American public through the manufacturer. This strategic framing of the ecosystem of modern design in the United States was echoed in the efforts of others in this period likewise seeking to bring change to the methods and practices of American industry.

Manufacturers in the marketplace: the independent furniture showroom

Parallel with Kaufmann's efforts, New York-based designer Gilbert Rohde distinguished himself within the nascent American design community of the 1930s as an outspoken critic of the nation's furniture industry. Like Kaufmann and Noyes, he recognized that modern design could not thrive in the United States without the support of the whole of the design industry. Writing for the trade newspaper *Retailing*, Rohde set out his critique of prevailing industry practices, suggesting that they were both economically and ethically untenable:

> All the conditions and practices existing in the furniture trade at present tend to inhibit the development of furniture that has a really superior economic value – from the physical set-up of factories to retail promotion. Factories are not equipped to permit a free use of modern materials and efficient production methods; retailers and magazines seek only to increase rapidity of obsolescence, and to cater to established prejudices.[16]

Before consumers could be persuaded to adopt modern design as a key factor in the American way of life, industry would need to be convinced to make dramatic changes to manufacturing methods and distribution practices. To this end, Rohde approached D. J. De Pree, president of Midwest furniture manufacturer Herman Miller, in 1932 with a provocation – move the company's focus away from traditional and historically derivative styles or live with the knowledge that these practices were unethical, aesthetically false and financially unsustainable. De Pree, well known for his strong Calvinist beliefs, took the warning to heart, appointing Rohde as director of design for Herman Miller and agreeing to restructure the company's manufacturing capabilities to produce modern furniture.[17]

Modernizing models, materials and manufacturing processes was just the start, however. The bigger challenge was the furniture industry's increasingly inhospitable distribution channels, which threatened to cancel out any gains achieved on the production side. A new distribution model that would allow greater control over the presentation of products as well as sustained contact with customers was also needed. The independent, manufacturer-operated furniture showroom appeared an ideal solution, allowing manufacturers to sidestep notoriously difficult retail buyers, to provide their own specially trained salespeople and, important, to control the display and merchandising of their products directly to the consumer.

Herman Miller opened its first independent showroom in Chicago's Merchandise Mart in 1939, followed in early 1941 by a second showroom located at One Park Avenue in New York City (see Figure 5.2). Both showrooms were designed by Rohde and adhered in their design and spatial arrangements to the model room approach common in department stores and museum displays of the later 1930s and 1940s.[18] Precise room settings were staged to look as convincing as possible with a host of decorative props – including live models posed with homey verisimilitude mid tea service for publicity photographs. The literal narrative elements and theatrical vignettes of Rohde's showrooms provided full-scale demonstrations of Herman Miller's new modern furniture lines, serving to familiarize their cliental with the role of these furnishings in the modern lifestyle and to entice them with their benefits.[19]

Figure 5.2 Herman Miller showroom, Merchandise Mart, Chicago, 1939. Gilbert Rohde, designer. Unknown photographer. Courtesy of the Herman Miller Archives.

In the mid-1940s, the progress of Herman Miller's modern design program was challenged by both wartime restrictions and the untimely death of Rohde in 1944. Committed to realizing Rohde's ideas for reinventing the company, D.J. De Pree brought in New York architect, designer and critic George Nelson in August 1945. Like Rohde before him, Nelson criticized the staid practices of the industry, arguing that they had a crippling effect on both manufacturing and aesthetic innovation.[20] Noting in particular the importance of controlling representation in the marketplace, Nelson identified the retailer as "the man who stands between the progressive manufacturer and the public . . . most buyers are not sympathetic to new ideas. The manufacturer knows it and generally conforms."[21]

Over the next five years, Nelson endeavored to overcome such problematic industrywide practices, illustrating how a manufacturer could successfully produce, market and sell modern design in the United States. Nelson's first steps included designing a seventy-seven-piece modular furniture collection, developing a new graphic program, bringing in a number of young talented designers – including Charles Eames, Isamu Noguchi and Paul Lazlo – and, important, redesigning the company's showrooms in Chicago (1949), Grand Rapids (1949) and New York City (1947). Expanding Herman Miller's representation on the West Coast, the company opened a showroom at 8806 Beverly Boulevard in Los Angeles in 1949, with architecture and interiors designed by the Eames Office (see Figure 5.3).[22]

Very much an expression of the Herman Miller philosophy, the new Los Angeles showroom was as much about demonstrating a modern lifestyle and individual choice as it was about showcasing the company's products. With custom-made demountable display partitions set on a modular grid for maximum adaptability and visual porosity, the showroom was intended, as Charles Eames described, not to "suggest rooms but rather space situations which occur whenever furniture is used. The objects and accessories, far from attempting to dictate any style, try to suggest an attitude which brings together good furniture honestly conceived and those objects of everyday life

Figure 5.3 Herman Miller showroom, 8806 Beverly Boulevard, Los Angeles, 1949. Eames Office, designer. Unknown photographer. Courtesy of the Herman Miller Archives.

of which all people grow fond."[23] Again, here the greatest emphasis was placed on the role of good design in the pleasurable experience of everyday living. The space and the objects on exhibit in Herman Miller's post-war showrooms weren't proscriptive as they had been in the early 1940s, but rather they were backdrops for fluid arrangements suggestive of different attitudes toward living.

At roughly the same time that Nelson began working with Herman Miller, Florence Knoll founded and began directing the Knoll Planning Unit (KPU) for Knoll Associates. Although the company began as a small furniture distributer specializing in modern European design, by the mid-1940s, the company was producing its own line of modern furnishing in the United States. As with Herman Miller, the showroom would become much more than a showcase for Knoll products. Working with the KPU, Knoll designed numerous showrooms for the company across the United States and internationally in the post-war period. Between 1949–51, Knoll opened showrooms in Chicago, Atlanta, Dallas and Boston, as well as designing a new flagship showroom at 575 Madison Avenue in New York City.

Again the Knoll showrooms were not organized as model rooms, but rather as abstract compositions harmonizing display architecture, graphic and sculptural elements and furniture groupings (see Figure 5.4). The effect was one of pleasurable arrangements, open to the imagination. Describing Knoll's 601 Madison Avenue

Figure 5.4 Knoll showroom, 601 Madison, New York City, 1948. Knoll Planning Unit, designer. Archives of American Art, Smithsonian Institution.

showroom in 1948, *Interiors* editors wrote: "As one turns, every direction offers appealing vistas of color and perspective. The patron's first impression is not that furniture is for sale, but how nice it would be to live there."[24] It would seem from the frequency of such comments in the media that the Knoll showrooms were very much designed with the intention of transporting clients to a realm of new possible engagements between architecture and design. Taking visitors out of the known, Knoll offered a host of three-dimensional 'ideas', spatial sketches that allowed for the imaging of new ways of living. As Florence Knoll recalled: "The [showrooms] were important because we had to do a lot of convincing. At the time there were very few clients who were interested in these ideas. They thought they had to have traditional furniture from Grand Rapids [Michigan]. These showrooms were what really convinced them."[25]

For Modern Living and *Good Design*: a collaboration of culture and commerce

Contemporary with the great expansion of manufacturers' furniture showrooms, in the immediate post-war period the Museum of Modern Art and other cultural institutions similarly focused on defining 'good design' for American audiences, with continued and increasing emphasis on its role in 'good living'. *For Modern Living*, an exhibition held at the Detroit Institute of the Arts in 1949, was one of the first comprehensive demonstrations of modern American furnishings and interior design following the war. Curated by designer Alexander Girard, the exhibition included traditional object displays as well as a variety of room settings, demonstrating "a new ideal of beauty" in the design of "homes and the other things we live with."[26] At the heart of *For Modern Living* was the aim of demonstrating the composition of the American lifestyle through the union of education, good design and the marketplace.

As had been the tradition with such design exhibitions since MoMA's *Machine Art*, the *For Modern Living* catalog included numerous product photographs and identifying information for designers and manufacturers, as well scholarly essays that situated these objects within a larger cultural framework. An essay of particular interest by John A. Kouwenhoven, a contributing editor at *Harper's Magazine*, charted the historical development of design in the United States, applying an exceptionalist framework in defense of (what he perceived to be) America's unrecognized position as the progenitor of modern design based on the intrinsic modernity of the national character and vernacular traditions. Kouwenhoven asserted: "In spite of the rather widespread feeling among some Americans that 'modern' furniture, like modern painting or modern architecture, is somehow foreign, many of its fundamental techniques and forms are thoroughly indigenous to the United States."[27] Encouraging consumers to proudly embrace modern design, Kouwenhoven reminded readers that on "historical grounds" Americans "might well feel more at home with a bent plywood cantilevered chair . . . than with the Grand Rapids Chippendale designs which most of us still think are more home-like."[28] Here Cold War rhetoric met that of good design and the American way of life.

Kaufmann Jr., who served on the exhibition's Committee of Advisors, also contributed an essay to the catalog. Moving from Kouwenhoven's nationalizing argument to the marketplace, Kaufmann called attention to the potential of the exhibition to do "great good as an exceptional and magnificent recommendation of the best of current design." As such, Kaufmann posited that it could "help build a stronger, happier, healthier community," if only "manufacturers, designers, retailers, shopmen, technicians, salesmen" would "look and think about what they see." The emphasis was once again on education, but in this instance Kaufmann pointed to producers and retailers rather than to consumers, as had Rohde and Nelson. Focusing on the ways in which modern design was "commissioned, produced, advertised, and sold" was the most likely pathway to the development and growth of good design in the United States, according to Kaufmann.[29]

While Kaufmann's criticisms were directed primarily at the American home furnishings industry, in this period a number of small manufacturers began to define themselves through the production and promotion of modern design, many with a focus on its suitability for the American lifestyle. Among the first generation of modern American furnishings manufacturers and retailers were Dunbar, Directional, Widdicomb, M. Singer and Sons, Herman Miller and Knoll Associates, among others. The latter two companies played a particularly important leadership role through their participation in a number of post-war lifestyle and design exhibitions, including *For Modern Living*. One might reasonably argue that Herman Miller and Knoll astutely recognized the broad benefit to their businesses of participating in and supporting such exhibitions, and therefore, actively cultivated relationships with museums and curators advocating for modern design. D. J. De Pree and Florence Knoll, for example, served on the *For Modern Living* Committee of Advisors, and designers associated with both companies participated in the exhibition. Knoll, Nelson and Eames were each given individual exhibition rooms in which to demonstrate an approach to the incorporation of good design within a modern lifestyle. In addition, Knoll, Nelson and Eames all served on the exhibition's Committee of Designers.

Particularly in the design and description of the 'model rooms' for the exhibition, Knoll, Nelson and Eames demonstrated the power of these arrangements to portray distinct approaches to modern design and the American lifestyle. Their individual personalities as designers and philosophies are evident as well in the descriptive statements composed by each for the exhibition catalogue. The designers were asked to describe the room settings they had created for the show. Eames, for example, proposed that his contribution, rather than presenting a "special room or section of a house," offered one example of an "attitude" toward both the space and objects of life, suggesting, "This kind of living expressed is an expansive one, enriched by the special selection and enjoyment of the objects used" (see Figure 5.5).[30] Similarly, Knoll described her installation as one in which, "Function and beauty are treated as an entity – not divorced from one another. And these gracious arrangements vividly suggest the many possibilities for a reconciliation of mass production and personal expression which is perhaps the greatest single contribution of modern design to today's living."[31] Both statements emphasize the opportunity for personal expression and enjoyment through the selection and arrangement of modern furniture and furnishings. Furthermore, in both instances the benefits of such efforts were situated within the promise of 'today's living'. The flexible, modern settings exhibited by both Eames and Knoll staged a personalizable lifestyle facilitated by modern design.[32]

The efforts, ideas and involvement of Eames, Nelson, Knoll and others at the fore of the modern design movement in the United States were also drawn upon for what would become one of the most ambitious, comprehensive and sustained design exhibitions of the post-war period – the Museum of Modern Art's *Good Design* program.

Figure 5.5 Eames room in *For Modern Living*, September 11–November 20, 1949. Illustrated in Alexander Girard and W.D. Laurie Jr., eds., *An Exhibition for Modern Living*, The Detroit Institute of the Arts, 1949. Unknown photographer. Courtesy of the Detroit Institute of Arts, USA/Bridgeman Images.

In many ways a continuation of the *Useful Objects* series, *Good Design* was the first large project taken up by Kaufmann after he returned to MoMA following his service in the war. Appointed head of the Department of Industrial Design, Kaufmann announced the collaboration between the Museum of Modern Art and Chicago's wholesale marketplace, the Merchandise Mart, to produce the *Good Design* program in November 1949. More than just an exhibition series, the program sought to identify everyday objects and furnishings meeting specific aesthetic and functional standards and brand them as 'good design' so that they would be easily distinguishable (even after the exhibition) within the marketplace. MoMA director René d'Harnoncourt and Wallace O. Ollman, general manager for the Mart, described the objectives for their collaboration around the *Good Design* exhibition series:

> It is the first time an art museum and wholesale merchandising center have co-operated to present the best examples of modern design in home furnishings. Now, at the mid-point of the century, these two national institutions, whose very different careers began just 20 years ago, believe and hope that in combining their resources they are stimulating the appreciation and creation of the best design among manufacturers, designers and retailers for good living in the American home.[33]

The *Good Design* program was comprised of three annual shows and the exhibition selections were disseminated through publications, symposia, advertising and branding, consumer opinion polls and a host of public programs. The first two annual shows were timed to coincide with the winter and summer home furnishings markets at the Merchandise Mart, while the third and final exhibition was held at MoMA in New York City and featured a smaller selection of objects exhibited earlier in the year. The inaugural *Good Design* exhibition opened on January 16, 1950, at the Merchandise Mart – the second Monday of the winter home furnishings market. It is significant that the first exhibition would be at the Mart, rather than MoMA, which historically opened traveling exhibitions in their New York City galleries before releasing them to be shown elsewhere. In launching the *Good Design* exhibition series at the Mart, the primacy of the commercial setting was acknowledged, as well as the essential role of the retail marketplace in defining and disseminating modern design in the United States. As Terence Riley and Edward Eigen have suggested in their study of the program, the primary aim of the *Good Design* exhibitions was to "inform customers and manufacturers about modern design products and to ensure that these products were made widely available through retail markets."[34] In partnering with the Mart, MoMA gained direct access to manufacturers, wholesale merchants and consumers, thereby moving closer to Kaufmann and Noyes' pre-war efforts to bring the influence of the museum to bear on the whole of the design, production and consumption cycle.

For *Good Design* Kaufmann called on the nation's leading designers to bring credibility, creativity and new products to the annual series, inviting Charles and Ray Eames to design the first *Good Design* exhibition held at Chicago's Merchandise Mart in January 1950. Subsequently, Kaufmann invited Danish designer Finn Juhl to design the annual Mart exhibition in 1951, and the following year American architect Paul Rudolph was selected to design the exhibition display. Joining the Herman Miller design team in 1952, Alexander Girard was given responsibility for the *Good Design* exhibitions in both 1953 and 1954. In addition to contributing the exhibition design, these individuals along with a number of other prominent figures from across industry and cultural sectors also participated on the annual *Good Design* selection committees, including Herman Miller's D. J. De Pree, Florence Knoll, Philip Johnson, Eero Saarinen, Serge Chermayeff and others, collectively defining 'good' modern design in the United States in the first half of the 1950s.[35]

Conclusion

Underscoring the sustained trajectory of these individual efforts – if often connected through people and purpose – from Philip Johnson's 1934 *Machine Art* exhibition to Kaufmann's more consumer-friendly *Useful Objects* series, to the post-war lifestyle-focused exhibitions *For Modern Living* and *Good Design*, to the rapid expansion of manufacturer-owned and -operated showrooms, one can easily identify shared recognition of the necessity of systemic change across the whole of the design industry if modernism was to have a chance of survival on American shores. While initiatives in the later 1930s and early 1940s focused more closely on raising consumer awareness, by the second half of the 1940s criticism was increasingly aimed at manufacturers, wholesale buyers and retailers. The popularization of modern design, and moreover the integration of these products and principles into the American lifestyle, required more than just consumer education; industry had to be persuaded to support and

Exhibitions for modern living 95

sustain modern design, a message that could then be taken to the marketplace. Thus, while the great post-war design exhibitions such as *For Modern Living* and *Good Design* were by all accounts well attended by the public and heavily featured in trade and popular media, they were perhaps most influential on American industry, helping to shape the presentation and representation of modern design in the marketplace as well as the rhetoric that placed it within the context of 'today's living'.[36]

It would seem such messages did not fall entirely on deaf ears in the post-war period, as a number of manufacturers adopted a modern design agenda and ethos, changing their manufacturing strategies, engaging designers and overhauling the ways in which modern design was promoted, marketed, displayed and distributed, not only through exhibitions such as *For Modern Living* and *Good Design*, but also with the increasing presence within the trade through manufacturer's showrooms and a wide breath of media coverage.

The persuasive mechanisms utilized in these displays were as various as the objects exhibited, from *For Modern Living*'s quaintly poetic sole Chippendale Chair reflected into infinity with a pair of flanking mirrors that greeted visitors and served as a symbolic reminder of the "futility of endless repetition of designs of the past" to the Knoll's invitingly abstract showroom landscapes of modern furniture to the unmistakable product branding of the *Good Design* selections that included hang tags and point of purchase signage.[37] Through such exhibitions, cooperative programs, showrooms and other commercial and cultural displays, the design industry and the public were reminded of what constituted 'good design' and its constitutive role in the American 'way of living'. Such displays also and importantly contributed to the material and ideological codification of the American lifestyle as expressed through such catch phrases as 'good living' and in the iconic imaging of furniture, furnishing and interiors produced by companies like Herman Miller and Knoll. These fundamentally American images and ideals were further deployed as a prime US tactic in the Cold War. The 'soft power' of the American lifestyle targeted the Achilles heel of communism, as Greg Castillo and others have argued.[38] However, as with all modern warfare, the outcome of such assaults was not so clear. The international exportation of modern American design did not always find eager or ready markets; often the messages were reinterpreted to suit other cultural traditions and beliefs and were stripped of their American consumerist connotations.[39] But if instead of looking for the success or failure of the exportation of US modern furniture, interiors and ideology, one explores its mutations and transgressions, the glare of propaganda is lessened and the core values of good modern design come into sharper focus, as do the efforts of the many individuals who believed in its role in making life better for everyone.

Notes

1 Alexander Girard, "Forward," in *An Exhibition for Modern Living, the Detroit Institute of the Arts* (Detroit, MI: Detroit Institute of the Arts; J. L. Hudson Company, 1949), 5.
2 Edward Alden Jewell, "Art Scans Its Niche in Industrial Plan," *New York Times*, February 26, 1934, 22.
3 Edward Alden Jewell, "The Realm of Art: The Machine and Abstract Beauty," *New York Times*, March 11, 1934, X12.
4 For period accounts, see, Walter Rendell Storey, "Machine Art Enters the Museum Stage," *New York Times*, March 4, 1934, SM12; and Edward Alden Jewell, "Machine Art Seen in Unique Exhibit," *New York Times*, March 6, 1934, 21. See also Mary Anne Staniszewski,

96   *Margaret Maile Petty*

The Power of Display: A History of Exhibition Installations at the Museum of Modern Art (Cambridge, MA: MIT Press, 1998), 152–60.

5   A critic from *The New Yorker* described with some irony, "The place itself looks, more than anything else, like a very elaborate hardware store." Quoted from "Machine Art," *The New Yorker*, March 17, 1934, 18.

6   "Machine Art," 18.

7   Press release no. 38831–23, The Museum of Modern Art, August 31, 1938, accessed www. moma.org/learn/resources/press_archives/1930s/1938/1; see also, "Beauty Begins in the Kitchen," *The Christian Science Monitor*, October 29, 1938, 6.

8   Press release no. 381013–27, The Museum of Modern Art, October 13, 1938, accessed www.moma.org/learn/resources/press_archives/1930s/1938/1.

9   Helen Johnson Keyes, "Good Design in Useful Objects," *The Christian Science Monitor*, December 17, 1940, 8.

10 Harvey A. Anderson and Alice M. Carson, "Useful Objects in Wartime: Fifth Annual Exhibition of Useful Objects under $10.00," *The Bulletin of the Museum of Modern Art* 2 (December 1942–January 1943): 3–21.

11 While Kaufmann claims credit for the concept and development of the *Useful Objects* annual exhibitions, the shows are affiliated in official MoMA publications with the respective director of industrial design, for example, John McAndrew in 1938, Eliot Noyes in 1940 and acting director Alice M. Carson in 1942. Press release no. 1488, "Biographical notes on Edgar Kaufmann, Jr., and Finn Juhl," The Museum of Modern Art and The Merchandise Mart, 1951, accessed www.moma.org/docs/press_archives/1488/releases/ MOMA_1951_0006.pdf?2010; Press release no. 649, "Democracy in Design Shown in Exhibition of Useful Objects at Museum of Modern Art," The Museum of Modern Art, accessed November 26, 1940, www.moma.org/momaorg/shared/pdfs/docs/press_ archives/649/releases/MOMA_1940_0080_1940–11–22_401122–71.pdf; and Harriet Schoenholz Bee and Michelle Elligott, *Art in Our Time: A Chronicle of the Museum of Modern Art* (New York: The Museum of Modern Art, 2004), 50.

12 Terence Riley and Edward Eigen, "Between the Museum and the Marketplace: Selling Good Design," in *The Museum of Modern Art at Mid-Century: At Home and Abroad, Studies in Modern Art, 4* (New York: The Museum of Modern Art; H. N. Abrams, 1994), 150–75.

13 Press release no. 40916–54, "The Museum of Modern Art Announces Terms of Two Design Competitions for Home Furnishings," The Museum of Modern Art, September 30, 1940, accessed http://www.moma.org/docs/press_archives/630/releases/ MOMA_1940_0061_1940–09–16_40916–54.pdf?2010.

14 While not formally a member of the department at this time, Kaufmann had been appointed chair of the Museum's Industrial Design Advisory Committee by Alfred Barr, and in this capacity was able to provide much support for Noyes and in particular with the Museum's trustee committees. See Gordon Bruce, *Eliot Noyes: A Pioneer of Design and Architecture in the Age of American Modernism* (New York: Phaidon Press, 2006), 58–9.

15 Eliot Noyes, "Report on the Department of Industrial Design," *MoMA, NY*, June 16, 1941; as quoted in Bruce, *Eliot Noyes*, 67, note 35.

16 Gilbert Rohde, "Does the Furniture Industry Continue to Live in a World of Long Ago?" *Furniture Retailing*, Home Furnishings Edition, May 14, 1934.

17 On the early history of the Herman Miller Furniture Company, see Marilyn Neuhart and John Neuhart, *The Story of Eames Furniture, Book 2* (Berlin: Gestalten, 2010), 451–89. On Rohde's furniture designs and wider contribution to the historical development of modern American design, see Phyllis Ross, *Gilbert Rohde: Modern Design for Modern Living* (New Haven: Yale University Press, 2009).

18 *The Story of Eames Furniture, Book 2*, 478–80. See Marilyn F. Friedman, *Selling Good Design* (New York: Rizzoli, 2003), for any number of examples of model room settings designed for display in American department stores and museums (particularly those at the Metropolitan Museum of Art in New York City) during the 1920s and 1930s.

19 *The Story of Eames Furniture, Book 2*, 487.

20 George Nelson, "The Furniture Industry: Its Geography, Anatomy, Physiognomy, Product," *Fortune*, January 1947, 106–11, 171–2, 174, 176, 178, 181–2. Secondary sources

addressing Nelson's *Fortune* article include Stanley Abercrombie, *George Nelson: The Design of Modern Design* (Cambridge, MA: MIT Press, 2000), 84–90; and *The Story of Eames Furniture, Book 2*, 501–4.

21 Nelson, "The Furniture Industry," 174.

22 John Neuhart, Marilyn Neuhart and Ray Eames, *Eames Design: The Work of the Office of Charles and Ray Eames* (New York: Harry N. Abrams, Inc., 1989), 102–5.

23 Steinhauser, Herman Miller press release, September 14, 1949.

24 "Knoll Associates Achieve Intimacy and Openness in a Colorful Plan," *Interiors + Industrial Design* 3 (October 1948): 108–11.

25 Paul Makovsky, "Florence Knoll Bassett: The Conversation," *Metropolis* 11 (July 2001): 11.

26 E. P. Richardson, "Introduction," in *An Exhibition for Modern Living*, 7–8.

27 John A. Kouwenhoven, "The Background of Modern Design," in *An Exhibition for Modern Living*, 10–26.

28 Kouwenhoven, "The Background of Modern Design."

29 Edgar Kaufmann Jr., "Modern Design in America Now," in *An Exhibition for Modern Living*, 27.

30 *An Exhibition for Modern Living*, 80–1.

31 *An Exhibition for Modern Living*, 76–7.

32 While Charles Eames is the only designer named in the exhibition publication, both Charles and Ray Eames worked closely on such projects in this period, thus it is more than likely that they collaborated on the installation *For Modern Living*.

33 Press release 491109–78, "Museum of Modern Art and the Merchandise Mart Announce Continuing Series of Exhibitions in a Joint Program: 'Good Design,'" The Museum of Modern Art and The Merchandise Mart, November 9, 1949, accessed www.moma.org/docs/press_archives/1371/releases/MOMA_1949_0085_1949–11–09_491109–78.pdf?2010.

34 Terence Riley and Edward Eigen, "Between the Museum and the Marketplace: Selling Good Design," in *The Museum of Modern Art at Mid-Century: At Home and Abroad, Studies in Modern Art, 4* (New York: The Museum of Modern Art; H.N. Abrams, 1994), 150–75, see p. 152.

35 The successful program ran from 1950 to 1955. MoMA has made a number of useful press releases related to various aspects of the *Good Design* program, from throughout the five-year run of the series, available online. See, for example: "Large New Group of Good Design," The Museum of Modern Art and the Merchandise Mart, June 22, 1950, accessed www.moma.org/momaorg/shared/pdfs/docs/press_archives/1441/releases/MOMA_1950_0050.pdf?2010; "Third Annual Good Design Exhibition Series announced," November 26, 1951, accessed www.moma.org/momaorg/shared/pdfs/docs/press_archives/1564/releases/MOMA_1951_0081_1951–11–26_511126–69.pdf?2010; and 521024–71; "Installation Designer and Selection Committee Chosen," October 31, 1953, accessed www.moma.org/momaorg/shared/pdfs/docs/press_archives/1656/releases/MOMA_1952_0078_71.pdf?2010.

36 See, for example, Mary Roche, "For Modern Living," *New York Times*, September 11, 1949, SM48; Margaret Warren, "'Modern Living' Exhibits, Light in Effect, Heavy in Symbolism," *The Christian Science Monitor*, October 20, 1949, 14; and Betty Pepis, "Art and Industry Linked on Homes: Exhibit by New York Museum and Chicago Merchandisers Marks New Collection," *New York Times*, January 17, 1950, 31.

37 Roche, "For Modern Living."

38 Greg Castillo, *Cold War on the Home Front: The Soft Power of Midcentury Design* (Minneapolis: University of Minnesota Press, 2010).

39 See, for example, Guy McDonald, "The Modern American Home as Soft Power: Finland, MoMA and the 'American Home 1953' Exhibition," *The Journal of Design History* 4 (2010): 387–408; Richard Pells, *Not Like Us: How Europeans Have Loved, Hated, and Transformed American Culture since World War II* (New York: Basic Books, 1998); and Paolo Scrivano, "Signs of Americanization in Italian Domestic Life: Italy's Postwar Conversion to Consumerism," *Journal of Contemporary History* 2 (2005): 218–340.

6 Knolling Paris

From the "new look" to *Knoll au Louvre*

Cammie McAtee and Fredie Floré

On Thursday, January 13, 1972, the exhibition *Knoll au Louvre* was inaugurated at the Musée des Arts Décoratifs in Paris. The event was very much a state affair, with an honor guard stationed along the stairway as Eugène Claudius-Petit, president of the museum, and Jacques Baumel, the French secretary of state, jointly opened the exhibition with Florence Knoll Bassett, Knoll's *éminence grise*, Robert Cadwallader, president of Knoll International, and Yves Vidal, president of Knoll International France, in attendance. The installation, designed by Lella and Massimo Vignelli, displayed the company's products in an impressive, playful and yet dramatic setting within the Pavillon de Marsan, one of the nineteenth-century terminating wings of the Louvre complex (see Figure 6.1).[1] The Vignellis took full advantage of the three-story space, removing a false ceiling to exploit its verticality and to draw luminosity from the skylights. A twelve-foot-high, three-dimensional "Knoll" drew visitors up the stairs and beneath the arch of the "n" to enter the grand central gallery (see Figure 6.2). The historicist backdrop framed a series of stacked Formica, aluminum, and Plexiglas cubes scattered through the center of the gallery. These jewel boxes contained Knoll's "modern classics": iconic chairs, tables, and other pieces by Ludwig Mies van der Rohe, Marcel Breuer, Florence Knoll, Eero Saarinen, Harry Bertoia, Hans Wegner, and Don Albinson.[2] They were followed by cubes holding furniture by Roberto Matta and Kazuhide Takahama – the two designers representing Knoll's 1968 purchase of the Italian firm Gavina SpA – and a final cube introducing the company's newest innovation, William Stephens's 1971 Landscape office system. More pieces by second-generation Knoll designers and other Gavina designers were placed in niches along the side aisle looking into the Tuileries Garden.[3] Color was used to unite the various elements – Knoll's signature shade of orange-red was used for most of the upholstered furniture – and a fifty-foot-high display of Knoll textiles ran along one side of the gallery. A visual presentation of the company's history projected onto linen screens accompanied by three sound environments further heightened the already dynamic installation.[4]

It was a moment of public celebration, the exhibition paying homage to Knoll's considerable contributions to modern design. But it had another significance for the most famous modern furniture manufacturer in the world, for it was through this retrospective that Knoll conquered a new and powerful representational space. Although its products had early on entered museum collections and had been featured in countless exhibitions, for the first time Knoll was the main focus of an entire exhibition in not only a major European institution, but, if the title *Knoll au Louvre* was to be taken at face value, in the world's most prestigious museum.[5] "Knoll scores another

Figure 6.1 "The brilliant exhibition designed by Massimo and Lella Vignelli," *Knoll au Louvre*, Musée des Arts Décoratifs, Paris, January 13–March 13, 1972. Jacques Primois, photographer. Florence Knoll Bassett Papers, 1932–2000, Archives of American Art, Smithsonian Institution.

first" was the jubilant headline of the company's press release. Olga Gueft, the editor of *Interiors*, reported that Knoll had at last been "formally accorded official recognition as one of the epoch-making forces in the history of design."[6]

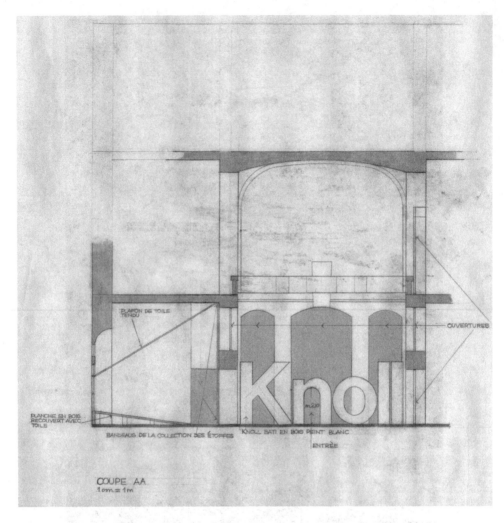

Figure 6.2 Section for *Knoll au Louvre* showing the height of "Knoll" within the central gallery, October 1971. Vignelli Associates, designers. Massimo and Lella Vignelli papers, Vignelli Center for Design Studies, Rochester Institute of Technology, Rochester, NY.

But as great an achievement as it was for the company, the exhibition was nothing less than a triumph for the director of Knoll's French subsidiary, Yves Vidal (1923–2001), and his partner, interior designer Charles Sévigny (b. 1918). For more than twenty years, Vidal and Sévigny had assiduously worked to create a distinct look for Knoll International (KI) France (1951–92), one that moved it away from the International Style toward new associations with luxury and pleasure. As this essay will examine, they forged a relationship of equals between modern and historical furniture and interiors, an especially significant association for the French market, and brought new meaning to Knoll's modern furniture by presenting it in contexts that were highly desirable to French and in turn American consumers. These were markedly different approaches to the one Hans and Florence Knoll carefully cultivated in the late 1940s and 1950s. Whereas the first "Knoll look" was conceived to relate to the coolness, austerity, and efficiency of modern architecture, the "new look" developed in France brought a sensuous and sophisticated cachet to the company's products.[7] If the Knolls gave modern furniture its post-war imprimatur, Yves Vidal and Charles Sévigny succeeded in making Knoll "chic."

Knoll International France

In 1951, on the strength of receiving a large contract for furniture for employee housing in Europe from the US State Department, the newly established international arm of Knoll opened its first two subsidiaries. According to at least one close associate, from the very start Hans Knoll favored Paris over the Stuttgart office, lavishing a disproportionate amount of money on it despite the West German operation's greater financial success.[8] Although family and other personal reasons have been cited to explain this preference, Hans Knoll clearly understood that success in Paris translated into symbolic capital, a priceless asset for a manufacturer of high-end modern furniture.

The company's expansion into France was greatly aided by an American expert in factory planning and control and planning methods, who had reorganized Knoll's US factories and redesigned its business system in the late 1940s. As one of the few American business consultants then working in France, Kenneth B. White was well placed to advise on the company's introduction into Paris.[9] A longtime admirer of Knoll furniture and the business and design minds behind it, White provided some of the initial capital and briefly acted as one of KI's directors.[10] His office in the well-heeled 8th arrondissement, the center of haute couture, and his home in the prestigious 16th also functioned as an unofficial Knoll showroom; both were exclusively furnished with the company's products.

It was thus with great expectations that Knoll's first European showroom opened in Paris in 1951. According to White, it was his wife who found the location at 13, rue de l'Abbaye, a small street near the sixth-century Benedictine Abbey of Saint-Germain-des-Prés.[11] The Left Bank address immediately distinguished Knoll from both the traditional center of Parisian furniture manufacturing – the Faubourg Saint-Antoine on the other side of the city – and the factories producing metal furniture in the suburbs. The 6th arrondissement was instead closely associated with Paris's intellectual and artistic communities, and known for its bookstores and art and antique galleries. Café de Flores was just around the corner. The location nevertheless had a distinguished modern architecture connection: Le Corbusier's rue de Sèvres office and Pierre Charreau's Maison de Verre were close by, and Eileen Gray lived on the rue Bonaparte. But as design historian Constance Rubini has noted, it was also the affluent and professional population of company directors, doctors, dentists, and lawyers, as well as decorators and couturiers that drew Knoll and other design galleries to the area.[12]

Knoll thus entered Paris quietly, choosing an understated way into the city's decorative arts-oriented design culture. Although the company's immediate future was secured by State Department contracts, Hans Knoll saw the European home furnishings market as the next one to conquer.[13] The Paris location suggests that from the very start Knoll sought to integrate the company into the historic fabric of Paris. Occupying the ground and first floors of a garden-fronted building, the showroom, designed by Florence Knoll with Charles Niedringhaus, who worked with her in New York in the Knoll Planning Unit (KPU, Knoll's in-house interior design firm), and Charles Sévigny, presented the company's products in the rooms of a real apartment rather than in the idealized space of a customized showroom (see Figures 6.3 and 6.4).[14] Glimpses through the net textile onto the street or into the seventeenth-century courtyard signaled that a complete break with the past was not possible, or, perhaps, even desirable. The setting also emphasized the furniture's flexibility and thus liveability inside the city's historic perimeter. If the entrance strategy for the company's introduction into the Paris furniture and design scene was in some ways unexpected, the connection to art it was cultivating – the showroom faced two art galleries – was in perfect continuity with Florence Knoll's efforts.[15] She had consistently designed spaces that played two ways, as Hans Knoll's Madison Avenue office well demonstrates. While on one hand, the furniture bespoke efficiency in industrial design and rational office

Figure 6.3 Knoll International France showroom, 13, rue de l'Abbaye, Paris, between 1951 and 1961. Unknown photographer. Courtesy of Knoll, Inc.

Figure 6.4 Knoll International France showroom with Knoll Series 72 chair (Eero Saarinen, 1950), desk (Franco Albini, 1950), Arteluce floorlamp (Gino Sarfetti, 1950), cylinder lamp (Isamu Noguchi, 1944), Womb chair with ottoman (Saarinen, 1946–8), and tripod table (Hans Bellman, 1946), between 1951 and 1955. Jean Collas, photographer. *Maison & Jardin* (August 1955).

planning, on the other, the inclusion of a Paul Klee painting hanging on the wall and a Bertoia model for a screen along the window ledge directly connected the company's products to the world of modern art. Regular exhibitions of contemporary art in Knoll's showrooms further reinforced these connections.

Designer Pierre Perrigault, a graduate of the prestigious École Boulle school of furniture design and craftsmanship, remembered Knoll's Paris opening as nothing less than a revelation: "To enter in the small showroom was to penetrate the petit monde Knoll, which was distinct from everything that existed."[16] Yves Vidal, initially hired by the Knolls in 1952 as a salesman, and designer Roger Legrand, who joined him in 1953, carefully cultivated the showroom as a place to see and be seen, using it as a venue for book launches, art exhibitions, and parties.[17] But at the same time, with the boundary between gallery and showroom so artfully blurred, it was not surprising that many early visitors did not understand exactly what the company was selling.[18]

The first Knoll showroom also left its mark on Paris by establishing the 6th as the center for modern design. The bookstores on nearby boulevard Saint-Germain were gradually edged out by design *échoppes*, a fundamental change in the neighborhood's identity.[19] KI France directly contributed to the street's redevelopment in 1961, when it closed the first showroom and opened a large two-story storefront at 268, boulevard Saint-Germain. But even if it was now more easily recognized as a commercial

104 *Cammie McAtee and Fredie Floré*

space, Vidal continued to engage the world of art; for example, commissioning a mural from popular OP artist Victor Vasarely in 1967.[20]

Knoll au Printemps

If the rue de l'Abbaye quickly became a magnet for the design intelligentsia – known as *Knollese* – the reach of the small showroom into the vast French home furnishings market had obvious limitations. Knoll's products, however, were not entirely unknown to French consumers. They had been included in several of the exhibitions that the US State Department had toured across Europe.[21] Yet while such presentations were designed to create desire for the objects and the lifestyle they represented, from a business point of view they were hardly the ideal means to reach the individual consumer, especially if their products were as expensive as Knoll's were. Reaching KI France's target market, the financially prosperous sector of society, was a doubly difficult task, for even if Knoll's products were "good design" in American parlance, the world of French interior design was notoriously conservative. What Knoll needed was a respected intermediary that would not only introduce its products to the conservative bourgeoisie, but one that would "distinguish" them, as sociologist Pierre Bourdieu termed this process of legitimization.[22]

The company's formal *entrée* came in late 1954, when Le Printemps, the Parisian *grand magasin* most closely associated with luxury goods, invited Knoll to present its products in the store's prestigious boulevard Haussmann building.[23] Billed as the first presentation of KI France's complete collection of furniture and textiles adapted to real apartments in France, the display was presented on the third floor for the entire month of February 1955 (see Plates 5 and 6).[24] Occupying 600 square meters, *Sens de l'espace et de la couleur* (*The Significance of Space and Color*), as the exhibition was dramatically titled, allowed the designers to fully explore the dual themes.[25] Designed by Legrand, now director of the Paris *bureau d'études* (Planning Unit), the scenography was closely based on the vocabulary Florence Knoll had established in the American showrooms.[26] To set the stage for the dramatic interpretation, all daylight was blocked, and ceilings were painted in blocks of black and grey to modulate the sense of height; the ingenious space frame device was used in combination with screens, curtains, and horizontal and vertical panels to create rooms; and flowers, plants, artwork, and other accessories were employed to warm up the domestic settings. The more sculptural, stand-alone chairs and tables by Bertoia, Mies, Saarinen, and Franco Albini were the stars of the show, with Florence Knoll's tables, sofas, and other pieces characterized by rigorous geometries and sleek silhouettes serving their familiar background role. Herbert Matter's brilliant technique of suspending the seating shells and then front lighting them to cast dramatic shadows also found its way into the exhibition.

Where the display irrevocably broke from its American predecessors was in the intensity of its color palette, which was remarkably vivid and more varied than the primary colors combined with black, white, and beige that had so far characterized Florence Knoll's showrooms. As the combination of a purple shag carpet with an orange Womb sofa and a fuchsia Womb chair alone shows, textures were similarly played up, almost to the point of distortion. The variegated color scheme culminated in a dramatic presentation of textile samples, which one reviewer described as "a large three-dimensional mural standing out from the black background."[27]

While the colors were chosen for their shock value, the text that accompanied the display placed the furniture in a suggestive historical continuum that began with Louis XIV at Versailles, passing to Josephine at Malmaison, and then to the Third Republic.[28] The writer, most likely Vidal, lamented that rather than surrounding themselves with furniture that spoke of their time – as did the Sun King – contemporary "gens de goût" adopted a facile solution by looking backward in time and furnishing their homes with antiques. These styles were ill-suited to modern life and the aesthetics of contemporary architecture, the United Nations in New York and Le Corbusier's Unité d'Habitation in Marseilles specifically cited.[29] By contrast, Knoll International's furniture was a full participant in the renewal of the art of architecture, designed by contemporary architects, painters, and sculptors, and fabricated by technicians using the latest industrial developments. But Vidal clearly wanted to play it both ways, for the idea that Knoll's furnishings were compatible rather than hostile to earlier styles was also repeatedly asserted.[30]

By all accounts the exhibition achieved the goals of both Printemps and KI France. The store's personnel journal reported on the strong reactions the show elicited, reasoning that if it "has baffled many people, it is because some of its [design] aspects have broken with acquired habits, and that it requires an effect to judge without relying on preconceived ideas."[31] Vidal later recalled the near scandal the color scheme and unexpected material choices caused:

> It was the first time they saw gravel on the floor, the first time they saw net on the windows, the first time they saw two colors close to each other like pink, orange, and red and blue and green. It was unheard of at that time – it wasn't done. You couldn't even put gray and beige together. It was the first time they saw tweeds on chairs . . . the first time they saw lighting the way we did it in spots.[32]

There were other refreshing differences. While the manufacturers located in the Faubourg Saint-Antoine sold furniture ensembles, the brochure on hand at the Knoll exhibition made clear that the buyer could purchase single pieces and was free to use them to compose original arrangements. The textile line also made it possible to customize some of the furniture elements, an important selling point in the interior furnishings market. It was thus that Knoll's products were presented to Printemps's discerning clientele. The imprimatur of the powerful tastemaker secured Knoll a prestigious place within the French home furnishings market. In the decades to come, sales of Saarinen's pedestal chairs and tables in France would surpass those in the United States, becoming, along with Bertoia's wire chairs, almost *objets standards* or basic equipment in the chic French interior.[33]

The opening in French attitudes toward modern design in general may also stem from significant changes in the position of the world of *haute couture* toward mass production. If *prêt-à-porter* had previously been anathema of French high fashion, in the late 1940s, Christian Dior reconceptualized it as a means of bringing good design to, if not the masses, a broader market, while at the same time providing a means of retaining greater control over the unlicensed copying of his work.[34] *Couture-création* (made-to-measure) now coexisted with well-made, factory-produced, ready-to-wear clothing. This broadening in the definition of what constituted designer fashion may have aided KI France's efforts to establish its "label." Just as the *griffe* attached to a product of *prêt-à-porter* designer fashion distinguished it as a work of quality and

106 *Cammie McAtee and Fredie Floré*

authenticity, Knoll's products not only physically bore the name of a reputable maker, but were further distinguished by their associations with individual designers, whose works were serially produced by highly skilled technicians following strict guidelines and using only the very best materials.[35]

Knolling Paris

While the combination of intense colors in the Printemps exhibition brings to mind the coming revolution in the French fashion world led by Yves Saint-Laurent, an early *Knollese* himself, Knoll's French identity would quickly transition from shock to chic sophistication. This turn can be felt in what was likely the first piece of furniture designed and produced under the direction of the French subsidiary: an elegant adjustable table with cross-braces (ca. 1954) by Paris-based interior designer Charles Sévigny.[36] Sévigny, however, is much more important to Knoll's history as a stylist and interior designer than as an occasional furniture designer. Despite his name, he was American and served in the US Army in France during the Second World War.[37] After the war, he studied interior design at the Parsons School of Design in New York. In his final year, Sévigny was awarded the school's prestigious Hollis S. Baker Prize. The selection of his project for the design of a "contemporary living room for a person of taste and adequate income . . . based on the best principles of contemporary architecture and stressing proportion, scale, and taste in the choice of furniture, objects and painting" by a jury that included not only highly successful interior designer Eleanor McMillen Brown, but the art director of *Town and Country*, the editor of *House and Garden*, and Edgar Kaufmann Jr., director of the Department of Industrial Design at the Museum of Modern Art, all but foretold Sévigny's later success.[38] He also won a scholarship for a four-month study trip in Europe, which allowed him to return to France in August 1948. As well as taking classes at the École des Beaux-Arts, Sévigny made important contacts in the fashion world, Christian Dior among them. Sometime between 1948 and 1951, he and Vidal met and began a life together that would last for half a century.[39]

In 1951, Sévigny was hired to work for the US State Department under the direction of architect Alan Jacobs, the head of the Paris-based regional office of the Federal Buildings Operation. Jacobs was responsible for the acquisition and subsequent renovation of ambassadorial residences in Europe. He was also a great admirer of Knoll furniture.[40] As regional decorator for the Federal Building Office (FBO), Sévigny worked on "practically every U.S. ambassador's residence in Europe, including Moscow, Warsaw, Sofia and Budapest," experience that enabled him to work confidently on a grand scale, as he later put it.[41] It seems likely that it was through his work for the State Department that Sévigny met the Knolls. The direct heir to such influential American expatriate designers working in Paris, including Elsie de Wolfe and Van Day Truex, Sévigny has been credited for helping to establish the direction of post-war "haute décoration française."[42]

If often characterized as the *incontournable* figure in the French world of post-war design, Yves Vidal had a less direct entry into modern design than did his partner. Born into a Marseillaise family of industrialists, Vidal studied medicine and law before finally graduating as a pharmacist from Aix-en-Provence Université.[43] After the war, he worked for the American chemical firm Celanese and as an assistant to British fashion photographer Richard Dormer.[44] Despite the fact that Vidal lacked expertise in either modern design or furniture manufacture, when she met him in late 1951 or early 1952, Florence Knoll immediately recognized that he possessed assets that went beyond professional experience.[45] Charmed by his good looks and ambition – qualities he shared with Hans Knoll – she saw that Vidal had the "right personality" for the project to promote Knoll furniture in a culture still focused on historical styles:

> He helped build [the idea of Knoll] in the world of chic. He made it elegant to have Knoll furniture. . . . Whether they liked it or not, certain people were [at the parties he threw in the showroom], they were seen there and gave the whole thing an elegance and acceptance, which was important to breaking into the market in France.[46]

In 1955, the year Hans Knoll died, Vidal was promoted to director of KI France.

Although Sévigny is only occasionally mentioned in connection with Knoll in the 1950s and 1960s, he played a major role in the company's development as Vidal's design and life partner. The couple's close connections within not only the decorating, but also the fashion world of Paris were critical to KI France's success. Indeed, compelling parallels can be drawn between the strategies they developed and those of *haute couture* in the late 1940s and 1950s, a period of time in which the French fashion industry struggled to reassert its supremacy in a very different competitive environment. The "New Look," as Christian Dior's 1947 collection was dubbed by Carmel Snow, editor in chief of *Harper's Bazaar*, turned fashion back to *luxe et plaisir*. Hubert de Givenchy, whose Faubourg Saint-Germain apartment Sévigny redesigned in 1968, memorably characterized the elegant space as "a perfect mixture of the sumptuous and the simple."[47] Knoll entered this world of luxury through Vidal and Sévigny's design. Through their second business of acquiring, renovating, and furnishing apartments with Knoll pieces and antiques, sold *clé en main*, they perfected the artful combination of historical styles and Knoll's clean lines, an approach that found favor with their conservative clientele.[48] In Sévigny's hands a piece of Knoll furniture brought a sophisticated modern touch to a highly personalized space – a Barcelona chair complementing rather than competing with a Louis XV bergère, its formal homologue.

Powerful stage sets

But what Vidal was also peddling was glamour, a quality Knoll's furniture had not yet acquired in the United States. Extremely elusive and difficult to pin down, glamour is both image and experience. It is defined by "those in the know" and it requires an audience prepared to recognize it. Cultural historian Stephen Gundle sees glamour as a phenomenon closely tied to consumption. As he writes, it is "an enticing and seductive vision that is designed to draw the eye."[49] As members of the *beau monde* themselves, Vidal and Sévigny were perfectly placed to craft a glamorous European image for Knoll. Every design decision they made put forward an image intended to conjure up associations with culture, art, fashion, and international travel.

This subtle, but highly seductive strategy drove KI France's publicity campaigns in the 1960s. Although early on KI France advertised in home decorating magazines like *Maison & Jardin* and *La maison française*, such publications placed the company in the uncomfortable, even distasteful position of appearing to compete with other modern furniture manufacturers. Conversely, the Knoll ads that appear in André Bloc's journal *Aujourd'hui: Art et Architecture* between 1955 and 1961 show the company struggling to assert a clear identity within a more avant-garde milieu. Whereas publicity for the design *échoppes* Galerie Mai and Galerie Steph Simon adopted the understated look and language of contemporary art, Knoll's ads were sales-oriented and missed the same mark (see Figure 6.5). These images serve to underscore the fact that the avant-garde was not Knoll's world.

Toward his goal of reaching the wealthy and cultivated bourgeoisie, Vidal instead turned to art and culture journals. This strategy was obviously modeled on Knoll's long-running campaign in the *New Yorker* in the 1950s.[50] *L'Œil*, a progressive monthly established in 1955 by Georges Bernier and his American wife, Rosamond Bernier,

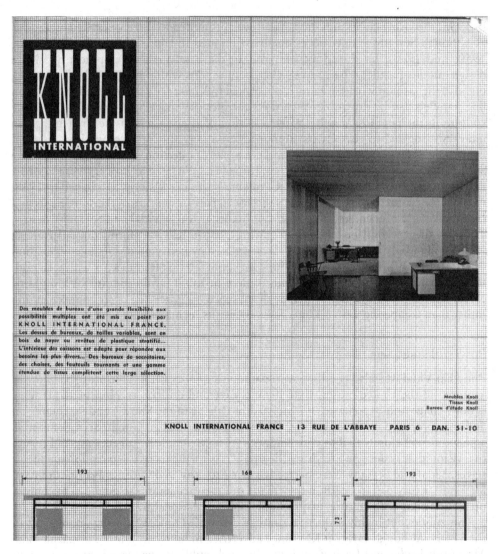

Figure 6.5 Knoll International France advertisement in *Aujourd'hui: Art et Architecture* (March/April 1955). Herbert Matter, graphic designer. Courtesy of Knoll, Inc.

was one of the magazines KI France advertised in. Dedicated to presenting "tous les arts, tous les pays, tous les temps" ("all the arts, all the countries, all the time"), the magazine included articles on architecture and design and in 1958 launched a special section on interior design titled "L'Œil du décorateur" ("The Eye of the Decorator"). The articles in this section show that Vidal, Sévigny, and the Berniers shared the same vision of the French interior – an eclectic world of diverse objects, styles, and periods that created a unique look. Like KI France, L'Œil was based in the 6th arrondissement; its offices were located only a short distance from the rue de l'Abbaye showroom.

A few times a year Knoll purchased the advertising space of L'Œil's back cover, and it is in these eye-catching color ads that the emergence of a French version of the "Knoll look" can be discerned.[51] At first the magazine ran Herbert Matter's visually playful and often humorous Knoll advertisements, but in the early 1960s L'Œil began publishing Knoll publicity images that broke away from the pattern of the American ads. An early example appears in the March 1962 issue (see Plate 7). The advertisement focuses on a Florence Knoll pedestal table desk and a black Saarinen chair from the 72 series. A flash of primary color from a bouquet of yellow daffodils (Florence Knoll's signature touch) and the red letter K at the bottom of the page enlivens the almost monochromatic image. However, an additional presence suggests other concerns were guiding the composition. In the bottom left corner a ceramic cat, a hand-painted ceramic from Tolalá, Mexico, is positioned. While it established the foreground and its quirkiness referenced Matter's famous images and the tone of L'Œil, the juxtaposition subtly raises the question of what constitutes a work of art. Like the folk art cat, the chair and table were the products of the artist's sensibility and the highly advanced craft expertise of a culture. The ad also reinforced the message that Knoll's products were capable of negotiating a harmonious relationship with eclectic elements. At every turn, the message conveyed in these sophisticated ads was that Knoll was in a class of its own.

However, the most powerful marketing tool Vidal and Sévigny employed were their two homes, which they regularly used for Knoll ads. In 1961, Vidal bought York Castle in Tangier, Morocco, and in less than a year with the help of Sévigny and Belgian expatriate architect Robert Gérofi, transformed the crumbling monument into a glamorous weekend residence.[52] Its interiors, which had served many purposes in the past, reputedly ranging from harem to prison, were reconceived, equipped with Knoll furniture, and decorated with artworks, exotic objects, antiques, and textiles gathered from all over the world (see Plate 8). L'Œil was among the many magazines that published lavish photographic spreads of York Castle.[53] Two years later, Vidal bought the Moulin des Corbeaux, a seventeenth-century mill located along the Marne River just outside Paris, and shortly thereafter renovated and redecorated it with Sévigny.[54] In addition to becoming a photography set for Knoll furniture, Vidal used the Moulin in tandem with the boulevard Saint-Germain showroom for Knoll events.

The merger of historical elements, contemporary design and art, and luxurious materials into a distinctly French take on what constituted post-war glamour is no better represented than in a joint advertisement for Knoll and the Revillon frères fur company shot at the Moulin around 1963 (see Plate 9). Undoubtedly intended for diffusion in fashion magazines, the ad is set in the house's elegantly paneled and papered dining room, its focus on two Saarinen Womb chairs upholstered in dark mink, a Bertoia Diamond chair covered in zorrino fur, and a low Saarinen pedestal table holding books and objets d'art from Vidal and Sévigny's collection. The bowls, vases and candlesticks arranged on the mantelpiece and table complement the chairs' structures, chrome becoming analogous to silver, modern fabrication methods implicitly equated with hand craftsmanship. The presence of Vidal's miniature whippet in a corner of a Womb chair not only identifies Vidal as the author of the image, the dog's comfortable position on the mink also restates the identification of Knoll with luxury, pleasure, even decadence.

It was through these images of chic sophistication that KI France's "new look" began to seep into the United States. Diffused through fashion, decoration, and lifestyle magazines as well as Knoll sales brochures, these scenes of afternoon lunches in the French countryside and exotic dinners in Morocco proved extremely effective marketing devices in the United States as well as in Europe. For example, in January 1964, the popular biweekly *LOOK* ran a lengthy "lifestyle" article – part travelogue, part fashion shoot, part cooking lesson – about a weekend party at York Castle. Vidal's position as president of KI France was mentioned, but it was his role as "host *extraordinaire*" that was celebrated in Robert Freson's photographs, which included Vidal dressed in "Arabian robes" seated in a Womb chair, and a formally attired Sévigny accompanied by fashion model Nathanaele Catherinet awaiting an intimate dinner at a Saarinen pedestal table and chairs on the terrace (see Figure 6.6). As architectural writer John Peter commented, "York Castle's

Figure 6.6 Yves Vidal seated in a Womb chair on the terrace of York Castle, September 1963. Robert Freson, photographer. *LOOK* (January 28, 1964). © Robert Freson.

counterpoint of contemporary and traditional, of richness and simplicity superbly illustrates the Moorish look. Increasingly popular here, its monochromatic walls, multicolored tiles bring an air of exotic elegance into U.S. homes."[55] By constructing a glamorous story, articles like this one brought Knoll's "new look" into the American home in another way.

The penetration of this eclectic or more personalized approach to using Knoll furniture into American interior design is no better expressed than in the Stamford, Connecticut home of Robert Cadwallader, who rose through the Knoll ranks to become vice president of marketing in 1965. When planning his move to the East Coast, Cadwallader had imagined living in a house "as modern as Philip Johnson's glass box," but instead, he and his wife, Laura, purchased an eighteenth-century converted barn. After telling *New York Times* journalist and longtime Knoll observer Rita Reif that the "attitude at home and the attitude in the office are somewhat different," Cadwallader, who would become Knoll's fourth president in 1971, expressed a surprisingly iconoclastic position for an executive of a modern furniture manufacturer, lashing out against "a hell of a lot of sacred things about modern design."[56] Following the example set by Vidal and Sévigny, the Cadwalladers did not hesitate to combine Victorian antiques with Barcelona chairs and tables, an early American sleigh bed with Bertoia chairs; they used a "clutter of objects" as a means to "relax" rooms, this last technique an American take on European eclecticism. Laura Cadwallader, a needlework artist, went so far as to decorate Saarinen pedestal stools with floral patterns.[57] Although Cadwallader distanced the company from the décor of his home, Reif recognized that something fundamental was changing: "There will probably never be a Knoll look that approximates the cozy interiors of Mr. Cadwallader's home, but some relaxation of the attitude is apparent." With the exception of perhaps the Womb chair, Knoll's attitude or style had never been relaxed. The "Knoll look" was evolving in directions neither of its founders could have anticipated.

Knoll au Louvre

Reif's article also hinted that a greater sea change was under way on the business side of Knoll. Although Florence Knoll's continuing leadership as director of design had ensured the company's transition after she sold it in 1960 to Art Metal, Inc., her definitive retirement five years later left Knoll without either a strong in-house designer or a clear vision of the future. Looking for new strategies to distinguish Knoll in an increasingly competitive world of design, Knoll president W. Cornell Dechert decided to emphasize the company as a global force. In 1969, the parent company headquartered in New York exchanged the slightly diminutive "Associates" for Knoll International, Inc., with the international side of the business in turn becoming Knoll Overseas, Inc.[58] Though these changes suggest that Hans Knoll's expansionist vision for Knoll had been realized, the company struggled to reassert a distinct brand. The acquisition of the Italian Gavina company in 1968 gave more weight to its international identity, but integrating its different design aesthetic into a cohesive "Knoll look" proved difficult.

The 1972 exhibition in Paris came at a crucial moment in Knoll's search for a new identity. In working with the Vignellis, the company clearly demonstrated on European soil the new direction it was taking in terms of image building. However, the applied visual language of the exhibition – especially the dialogue between the

112   *Cammie McAtee and Fredie Floré*

modern furniture and the historic context – made reference to the eclectic approach developed by Vidal and Sévigny. And perhaps unconsciously, the Vignellis' exhibition design also referenced connections with the world of *haute couture*. The installation can be read as a fashion show: the "stars" in the Knoll collection occupying the center of the gallery, with the newcomers positioned in the side galleries.

For his part, Vidal saw the exhibition as the perfect opportunity to expand KI France's presence in Paris and in 1972 opened a four-story showroom on the Right Bank in the center of high fashion design and other luxury goods. Just as the rue de l'Abbaye and boulevard Saint-Germain showrooms had drawn their distinction from the art and intellectual world of the Left Bank, the 9, rue du Faubourg Saint-Honoré showroom designed by Sévigny took its cues from the fabled fashion houses that were its neighbors. The placement of Breuer's Cesca and Wassily chairs and Mies van der Rohe's MR chairs against a backdrop of contemporary Knoll textiles in the showroom's large windows summarized exactly twenty years of work to establish Knoll as the furniture equivalent to haute couture fashion.

The street, however, is also the address of the symbolic site of French power, and two of France's greatest supporters of modern design as well as art, Georges and Claude Pompidou, were then its occupants. While much has been written about the Pompidous' commission to Pierre Paulin for the redesign of rooms in their private apartment on the first floor of the Élysée, Claude Pompidou made significant modern adjustments to the composition of these spaces prior to this ambitious project.[59] As photographs taken for *Paris Match* record, among other contemporary additions including works of modern art from the couple's collection, she brought a Saarinen table and chairs and a pair of Mies van der Rohe Barcelona ottomans into a private dining room and personal office (see Plate 1).

Knoll's arrival at the Élysée suggested that the prospects for KI France's move into the most prestigious neighborhood of Paris were extremely propitious. Vidal ensured that the new showroom opened to coincide with *Knoll au Louvre* and exploited the publicity it generated.[60] But despite his efforts, the Saint-Honoré showroom envisioned as the apogee of KI France's achievements was instead a flop and Vidal was out, dismissed as company director before year's end.[61] Evidently, the time for this kind of expansion had passed unnoticed. Though it is unlikely anyone took note of it at the time, there was also a troubling discrepancy in Knoll's presence in the Élysée. While its introduction into the period rooms was proof positive of the success of Vidal's long campaign to bring the company's products into the "best" society, the mix of the pedestal set and eighteenth-century furniture raised the idea that Knoll represented the past rather than the present, let alone the future of modern furniture. And Paulin's Pompidou apartments showed that modern design was going in other directions.

Although the response to *Knoll au Louvre* was generally adulatory, a few commentators saw cracks in Knoll's once impenetrable chromed armor. As critic Jacques Michel succinctly put it in his review in *Le Monde*, Knoll "no longer occupied the avant-garde position that was once its domain."[62] He interpreted the Italian turn in the company's collection as representing a fundamental break with the very past the exhibition had highlighted: "The demanding honesty of the Germano-American architects remains unanswered in the face of new design talents, which generally come from Italy bringing brilliant ideas and baroque humor. They quickly please and just as quickly tire. The new Knoll is, in reality, anti-Knoll, if not to say, anti-Mies-van-der-Rohe."[63]

Knoll was renewing its collection, but by embracing the Italian design scene – known to be critical of the establishment – it seemed to contradict its identity as a producer of modern classics.

Rather than a year of celebration, 1972 was quickly becoming one of introspection.[64] Not surprising, the company redoubled efforts to update its image. But here it was caught in a quandary. Vidal had introduced elements into the Knoll "look" that the company was loath to lose. The company's executives recognized that the images integrating modern as well as historical furniture, interiors and architecture, fashion, and the sensuality of *la belle vie française* had made Knoll's products extremely desirable on both sides of the Atlantic. While their publicity images never again engaged the "simple and sumptuous" world created by Sévigny and Vidal, Massimo Vignelli's art direction leveraged another rarified world, that of high architecture. He had Knoll furniture photographed not only in buildings by the architect-designers who had created Knoll's great classics – Mies van der Rohe's Seagram Building and Saarinen's TWA Terminal among them – but also in less expected sites like Palladio's Villa Caldogna, which hosted a photography shoot of Gae Aulenti's collection in 1976.

There is some truth to Florence Knoll Bassett's claim in the late 1970s that "even today in France, all modern furniture is called Knoll."[65] Post-war design in France, as the 1972 exhibition paid homage, was deeply indebted to the sleek lines, elegant forms, and luxurious textiles that Knoll designers brought to modern furniture. It is hard to imagine that Paulin's dining room set for Georges and Claude Pompidou could have been designed without Saarinen's famous pedestal series as its formal predecessor. While Yves Vidal alone deserves recognition for his role as the mastermind behind Knoll International's successful implantation in France, his greatest achievement, which Charles Sévigny shares in, was in making Knoll's furniture "classic," in the sense that it could hold its own beside any historical style. Through their careful orchestration, modern furniture, once an *arriviste* in the hermetic world of French decoration, now had an established place within the tasteful bourgeois interior. If once it would have seemed an oxymoron, this conceptualization was, if not born in France, significantly advanced there by Vidal and Sévigny in the 1960s and 1970s to the point where today, Knoll is synonymous with "classic" modern design.

Acknowledgements

This essay is the first product of our research project on Knoll International. For their help with our research, we are grateful to Katie Okamoto, Knoll, Inc.; Jennifer Whitlock, Vignelli Center for Design Studies; Dominique Forest, Laurence Bartoletti, and Rachel Brishoual, Musée des Arts décoratifs, Paris; Laura Coustans, Archives historiques du Printemps, Paris; John Davison of the Tangier American Legation; Sarah Lichtman, and her research assistant Catherine Powell at the Parsons School of Design; Arnaud Inglebert, Knoll International France showroom, Paris; Jayda Karsten, Canadian Architectural Archives; and the KU Leuven library. Our special thanks go to Charles Sévigny and Thomas Michael Gunther, who shared recollections and insights into the world of KI France with us. Finally, we would like to extend our appreciation to Javier Gimeno Martinez, Amelie Rennolds, Estelle Thibault, Alice Thomine-Berrada, Niké Vanderpoorten, Annie Vanhoutte, and Moniek Bucquoye, as well as to Penny Sparke and the community of the Modern Interiors Research Centre at Kingston

114 *Cammie McAtee and Fredie Floré*

University for their response to our work on KI France, and to Robin Schuldenfrei and Rika Devos for their insightful comments on the penultimate version of this essay.

Notes

1 Discussions about the exhibition began in October 1969, when François Barré, who was in charge of the museum's Centre de Création Industrielle, approached Robert Cadwallader, then Knoll's vice president of marketing. According to this letter, it was Italian designer Gae Aulenti who suggested that the museum organize a retrospective on Knoll. Barré to Cadwallader, October 7, 1969; exhibition file "392," Centre de documentation, Musée des Arts Décoratifs, Paris. According to the museum's records, the exhibition was held between January 13 and March 13, 1972. The earliest drawings for the installation are dated June 17, 1971. Massimo and Lella Vignelli Archives, Vignelli Center for Design Studies, Rochester Institute of Technology.
2 Although closely associated with Knoll, the company's right to produce Marcel Breuer's furniture only came in 1968 with the purchase of Gavina SpA. The following year Knoll purchased Wegner's distribution rights.
3 After considerable debate, the work of Gae Aulenti, Cini Boeri, Vincent Cafiero, Marc Held, Andrew Morrison & Bruce Hannah, Max Pearson, Warren Platner, Charles Pollock, Jorgen Rasmussen, Tobia Scarpa, Richard Schultz, and Bruce Tippett was exhibited. "Knoll Scores Another First," press release, January 13, 1972; Knoll, Inc. archives, New York.
4 Designed by Ann and Nicholas Chaparos (Chaparos Design), three phases of Knoll furniture history – the 1920s, 1940s, and 1960s – were projected onto the screens. The sound environments were among the earliest professional works of New York sound artist Charles Morrow.
5 The exhibition's French title was *Knoll au Musée*.
6 Olga Gueft, "Knoll au Louvre," *Interiors* 131, no. 9 (April 1972): 136.
7 As Bobbye Tigerman has shown, Florence Knoll developed the distinct "Knoll look" in the showrooms she began designing in 1948. The "Knoll look," Tigerman explains, focused on a restrained color palette, pronounced textures, and the strong geometric forms Knoll preferred. See Bobbye Tigerman, "'I Am Not a Decorator': Florence Knoll, the Knoll Planning Unit and the Making of the Modern Office," *Journal of Design History* 1 (2007): 61–74, esp. 67–72.
8 Peter Lotz, Hans Knoll's Stuttgart attorney, n.d. [ca. 1977], 2; Knoll, Inc. archives. Lotz's dates, however, are not always reliable. This interview was part of historical research by Richard Saul Wurman, Christine Rae, and Massimo Vignelli that formed the basis for the first official company biography, Eric Larrabee and Massimo Vignelli's *Knoll Design* (New York: Harry N. Abrams, 1981).
9 Before and after the war, White maintained a second office in France, where one of his biggest clients was the aluminum company Pechiney. On White, see Matthias Kipping, "The U.S. Influence on the Evolution of Management Consultancies in Britain, France, and Germany since 1945," *Business and Economic History* 25, no. 1 (Fall 1996): 114 n.3, 116.
10 K. B. White, interview, likely with Wurman, conducted in the showroom of KI France, Paris, n.d., Knoll, Inc. archives.
11 White, interview, 4. The name and nationality of Mrs. White are so far unknown.
12 Constance Rubini, "Éditer, diffuser," in *Mobi Boom: L'Explosion du design en France. 1945–1975*, ed. Dominique Forest (Paris: Les Arts Décoratifs, 2010), 229.
13 Yves Vidal stated these intentions in an interview, presumably in the late 1970s, which is quoted in Brian Lutz, *Knoll: A Modernist Universe* (New York: Rizzoli, 2010), 62.
14 In an interview in the late 1970s, Florence Knoll Bassett spoke of working with Niedringhaus on the design of the first showroom. Florence Knoll Bassett, interview likely by Wurman and Rae, n.d., 14; Knoll, Inc. archives. However, Sévigny recalls being involved in the design of the showroom, and his name is often mentioned in connection with it. Charles Sévigny and Thomas Michael Gunther, "Notes on Knoll International France for Fredie Floré and Cammie McAtee" (unpublished document), July 2016.
15 The Galerie Manteau occupied no. 14 and the Galerie Zak occupied no. 16, rue de l'Abbaye. *Annuaires de Paris*, 1954. Microfilm, Bibliothèque nationale de France.

16 Pierre Perrigault quoted in Patrick Favardin, *Les Décorateurs des années 50* (Paris: Éditions Norma, 2002), 316: "Entrer dans le petit showroom de la rue de l'Abbaye, c'était pénétrer dans le petit monde Knoll, distinct de tout ce qui existait"; unless otherwise noted, all translations are by the authors. In 1954, Perrigault established KI France's second showroom in Lyon in collaboration with Vidal, engineer Paul Beucher, and Michel and Théo Schulmann, directors of Mobilier International. The influence of Knoll on post-war French design has been considered by design scholars, including Anne Bony, Patrick Favardin, and researchers for the 2010 exhibition *Mobi Boom: L'explosion du design en France 1945–1975* organized by the Musée des Arts Décoratifs, Paris.

17 Rubini, "Éditer, diffuser," 229. Vidal recalled meeting the Knolls in 1952. Lutz, *Knoll: A Modernist Universe*, 62. Roger Legrand (b. 1925) first met Florence Knoll while he was traveling on a study course in the United States (1949–51). He then worked with Jorge Ferrari-Hardoy, designer of the Butterfly chair (and Legrand's future brother-in-law), on studies for furniture in Buenos Aires. When he returned to Paris in 1953, he was hired as the technical director for the Paris Knoll Planning Unit and assistant to Vidal, a position he held until 1964. The French title of Legrand was "directeur du bureau d'études, section France." On Legrand, see Thibaut Varaillon, "Roger Legrand et Pan-U" (Master's thesis, École du Louvre, 2015); Centre de documentation, Musée des Arts Décoratifs.

18 As characterized by Vidal in an interview quoted in Larrabee and Vignelli, *Knoll Design*, 195; and Lutz, *Knoll: A Modernist Universe*, 62.

19 On the diffusion of modern design in France, including the role showrooms played, see Rubini, "Éditer, diffuser" 206–35.

20 This work is reproduced in Knoll's internal newsletter, "Notes from Abroad," *Knoll World* 3 (April 1967): n.p.

21 On Paris as a venue for these exhibitions, see especially Gay McDonald's research on the Museum of Modern Art's *50 Years of American Art*, conceived specifically for a French audience and presented at the Musée national d'Art Moderne in the spring of 1955 as part of the USIS-produced "Salute to France" festival. It included Knoll and Herman Miller furniture. Gay McDonald, "Selling the American Dream: MoMA, Industrial Design and Post-war France," *Journal of Design History* 17, no. 4 (2004): 397–412.

22 Pierre Bourdieu developed these ideas in his study of French culture in the 1960s. The English translation of the book is *Distinction: A Social Critique of the Judgment of Taste*, trans. Richard Nice (London: Routledge & Kegan Paul, [1979] 1986).

23 Though surviving archival records do not contain any correspondence, it must have been initiated by Colette Gueden, director of the store's in-house decorating department, who was responsible for a series of exhibitions intended to open up the public to a larger view of contemporary design and shake it out of its post-war torpor.

24 Advertisement announcing the exhibition, 1955; Archives historiques du Printemps, Paris.

25 For descriptions of the exhibition, see especially "Actualités: Sens de l'espace et de la couleur," *Aujourd'hui: Arts et Architecture* 1, no. 2 (March–April 1955): 92–5; and "Knoll ou le triomphe de l'architecture," *Sud-Ouest Bordeaux*, May 11, 1955; press clippings, Archives du Printemps.

26 On the KPU, see Tigerman, "'I Am Not a Decorator.'"

27 "Actualités: Sens de l'espace," 92: "une grande fresque à trois dimensions se détachant sur le fond noir du mur." The same issue also featured a two-page article on Harry Bertoia's wire chairs (78–9).

28 The text is recorded only in press clippings, including two newspaper reviews: "En voulez-vous du 'fonctionnel'?" *Vie des Métiers* (Lyon), March 1954; O.M., "L'Ameublement Moderne ou le 'sens de l'espace et de la couleur,'" *L'Alsace* (Mulhouse), February 13, 1955. Clippings in "Dossier de rendement presse for 'Knoll' 1955–1956," Archives du Printemps. Vidal's authorship is confirmed by an article with a similar narrative published in a Belgian architectural journal: Vidal, "Permanence du 'meuble moderne' par Yves Vidal," *Architecture* 54, no. 9 (1954): 350.

29 The positive relationship between Knoll's furniture and modern architecture was also cited in reviews of *Art 1955*, an exhibition at the Musée des Beaux-Arts de Rouen that included Knoll furniture in a survey of contemporary art, design, and architecture. See Jérôme

116   *Cammie McAtee and Fredie Floré*

Mellquist, review of *Art 1955, Aujourd'hui: Arts et Architecture* 1, no. 2 (March–April 1955): 20–1.

30   *Printania* cited Roger Legrand on this question: "Y a-t-il incompatibilité entre l'ancien et le moderne? M. Legrand . . . ne le croit pas" ("Is there incompatibility between the traditional and the modern? M. Legrand . . . doesn't think so"). "Sens de l'espace et de la couleur," *Printania* 24 (1955): 18; Archives du Printemps.

31   If the exhibition "a déconcerté maintes personnes, c'est que certains de ses aspects, rompant avec les habitudes acquises, exigeaient un effort d'adaptation pour les juger sans s'appuyer sur des idées préconçues." "Sens de l'espace et de la couleur," 15.

32   Vidal quoted in Larrabee and Vignelli, *Knoll Design*, 195.

33   On sales of Saarinen pedestal chairs, see Rubini, "Éditer, diffuser," 229. Knoll also extended a concession to Printemps to sell its furniture. By 1958, Knoll's products were distributed in France through some thirty franchised dealers in the provinces and North Africa. "Knoll International Limited," internal report, October 1957; Knoll, Inc. archives.

34   *Prêt-à-porter* designer fashion was entirely controlled by the maison; it was, as fashion historian Alexandra Palmer writes, a "couture-based product" that allowed the designer to mass-produce his/her ideas instead of having them copied. Alexandra Palmer, *Couture & Commerce: The Transatlantic Fashion Trade in the 1950s* (Vancouver: University of British Columbia Press, 2007), 183–94.

35   As the brochure available at the exhibition stated, scientific methods "ont donné aux meubles Knoll et à leur éléments en bois, en plastique ou en métal, une haute qualité d'exécution et de finition" ("have given to Knoll furniture and to their elements in wood, plastic and metal, a high quality of execution and finishing"). Brochure, "Knoll au Printemps," n.d. [1955]; Archives du Printemps.

36   Designed around 1954, the table was made by Knoll until the early 1960s, but only rarely appears in the company's records.

37   Relatively little has been written about Sévigny; the best published source for his biography is Patrick Favardin and Guy Bloch-Champfort, *Les Décorateurs des années 60–70* (Paris: Editions Norma, 2007), 294–301.

38   "[Parsons School of Design] Alumni News" (August 1948), 4; The New School Archives and Special Collections, The New School, New York.

39   The auction catalog of Sévigny and Vidal's collection offers a sketch of their life together. See Thomas Michael Gunther, "Préface," *Collection Charles Sévigny – Yves Vidal* (Paris: Christie's, October 22, 2009), auction catalog, 6–7.

40   On Alan Jacobs, see Jane C. Loeffler, *The Architecture of Diplomacy: Building America's Embassies*, 2nd ed. (New York: Princeton Architectural Press, 2011), 53.

41   Sévigny quoted in "Sévigny in Spain," *Architectural Digest* 30, no. 1 (July/August 1973): 64. An article on American embassies states that Sévigny "has been with the FBO since 1951 during which time he has planned the interiors of our properties throughout Europe, Africa and the Middle East." "Interior Design Staff of FBO," *Interior Design* 8 (1958): 64. The decorator Eleanor McMillen Brown, a director of the Parsons School who had close contacts with several American ambassadors, or the school's director, Van Day Truex, may have recommended Sévigny. Sévigny recalls it was Van Day Truex who advised him to take the job. Sévigny and Gunther, "Notes on Knoll International France for Floré and McAtee."

42   Favardin and Bloch-Champfort, *Les Décorateurs des années 60–70*, 27.

43   Biographical information from "Vidal (Yves, Antoine, Adrien), *Who's Who in France / Qui est Qui en France*, 10th ed. (Paris: Éditions Jacques Lafitte, 1971–2), 1546.

44   According to Lutz, Vidal worked at Celanese before he met Hans and Florence Knoll. Lutz, *Knoll: A Modernist Universe*, 62. On Vidal's work with Dormer, presumably based on information from Sévigny, see Gunther, "Préface," *Collection Sévigny – Vidal*, 6.

45   Florence Knoll Bassett later recalled that they met through Charles Niedringhaus, who was with her in Paris in 1951 to set up the showroom. Knoll Bassett, interview, n.d., 14; Knoll, Inc. archives.

46   Knoll Bassett, interview, 15.

47   Jean-Louis Gaillemin, "*Architectural Digest* Visits: Hubert de Givenchy. Interior Design by Charles Sévigny," *Architectural Digest* 35, no. 5 (June 1978): 82–9, 148.

48 According to Favardin, a few decorators, including Sévigny, had been exploring the potential of combining the old and the new in the 1950s. However, he states: "il revient à Yves Vidal, le directeur de France de Knoll International, secondé par le décorateur américain Charles Sévigny, d'avoir magistralement démontré la pertinence de cette juxtaposition" ("It was the merit of Yves Vidal, president of France of Knoll International, assisted by American decorator Charles Sévigny, to have masterly demonstrated the pertinence of that juxtaposition"). Favardin, "Se meubler, ou la difficulté d'être de son temps," in *Mobi Boom*, 58.

49 Stephen Gundle, *Glamour: A History* (Oxford: Oxford University Press, 2008), 5. For a more focused study of glamour and modern architecture and design, see Alice T. Friedman, *American Glamour and the Evolution of Modern Architecture* (New Haven, CT: Yale University Press, 2010).

50 On Knoll's US marketing strategy, see Christine Rae, "Knoll: Portrait of a Corporation," *Graphis* 26, no. 148 (1970/71): 154–62, 188, 193–4.

51 Our reading of *L'Œil*'s role in the development and diffusion of Knoll's "new look" is indebted to research Niké Vanderpoorten conducted for her thesis "First Class Seat to Modernity. De import van het modern Amerikaanse interieur in België en Europa (1945–1965)" (Master's thesis, Ghent University, 2009).

52 Vidal describes the project in Landt Dennis, "York Castle in Tangier," *Architectural Digest* 45, no. 1 (January 1988): 14, 18, 104–11. Though romantically known as York Castle – supposedly named after the Duke of York and future James II of England – the building was built in the late seventeenth century as a Palais de Pacha. On the myths and true origins of "York Castle," see Martin Malcolm Elbl, *Portuguese Tangier (1471–1662): Colonial Urban Fabric as Cross-cultural Skeleton* (Toronto/Peterborough: Baywolf Press, 2013), 766 ff.

53 Pierre Berdoy, "York Castle [A Photographic Report]," *L'Œil* (December 1962): 92–103. Berdoy also did photographic work for KI France.

54 The building most likely dates to the seventeenth century with significant renovations in the nineteenth. On Vidal's renovations, see "Moulin des Corbeaux," *Architectural Digest* 29, no. 3 (March/April 1973): 12–19.

55 John Peter, "Castle in the Casbah," *LOOK*, January 28, 1964, 53. Food and fashion editors Susanne Kirtland and Marilyn Kantor also contributed to the article.

56 Rita Reif, "A 1760 Barn for 1968 Living," *New York Times*, March 22, 1968.

57 Interestingly, Laura Cadwallader's "personalization" of the stools predates the interior designer Alexander Girard's application of needlepoint to modern furniture. It was in 1974 that he designed a series of needlepoint patterns for the seats of Eero Saarinen's pedestal chairs in the dining room of the Miller House in Columbus, Indiana (Eero Saarinen; 1953–7).

58 "Knoll Associates Goes International," press release, August 25, 1969; Knoll, Inc. archives.

59 On Georges and Claude Pompidou's integration of modern furniture into the Élysée Palace, see Jean Coural, *Le Palais de l'Élysée: histoire et décor* (Paris: Délégation à l'action artistique de la Ville de Paris, 1994), 133–5. At the Pompidous' request, a Saarinen table and chairs were also installed in the presidential vacation home in the Mediterranean, Fort de Brégançon. On Pierre Paulin's project, see the recent exhibition catalog Cloé Pitiot, *Pierre Paulin* (Paris: Centre Pompidou, 2016).

60 The timing, if not the decision to open a second showroom in Paris, followed talks about the exhibition that began in 1969. On the design of the Faubourg Saint-Honoré showroom, see "25 ans de design de l'avant-garde," *L'Œil* 34, no. 2 (February/March 1972): 65–9.

61 Through these years of change, Vidal had continued to ascend through the company's ranks, named a vice president of Knoll International in 1966, a position he maintained alongside his direction of KI France. K. B. White attributed the failure of the new showroom to bad planning by Vidal (interview, 4). But, according to Jean-Paul Larçon and Roland Reitter, Vidal's firing was also tied to pressure from Knoll's parent company, Walter E. Heller, which was pushing for cheaper mass-production methods. Vidal was replaced by a new management team charged with changing production methods. Larçon and Reitter, "Corporate Imagery and Corporate Identity," in *Psychoanalysis and Management*, ed. Michael Hoffman and Monika List (Heidelberg: Physica-Verlag, 1994), 258.

62 Jacques Michel, "Le système Knoll. Le 'design' au carrefour de l'architecture," *Le Monde*, January 19, 1972, 13: "n'occupe plus la situation 'avant-gardiste' qui fut naguère la sienne."

118 *Cammie McAtee and Fredie Floré*

63 Michel, "Le système Knoll," 13: "La probité exigeante des architectes germano-américains est restée sans suite face aux nouveaux talents du *design*, généralement venus d'Italie avec des idées brillantes et de l'humour baroque. Ils plaisent et lassent rapidement. Le nouveau Knoll est, en réalité, de l'anti-Knoll,' il faudrait dire de l'anti-Mies-van-der-Rohe'."

64 These challenges are addressed in internal reports, including "The future – Knoll au Louvre, beginning or end?," n.d. [1972]; and "Knoll Sales Meeting – 1972," n.d. [1972], both in the Knoll, Inc. archives.

65 Knoll Bassett, interview, 15.

7 Corrections fairs and Japanese furniture made in prison

Yasuko Suga

In 2007, aprons branded with a prison logo were worn by prison officers at the Corrections Fair in Tokyo. The apron's strong and "cool" logo has made it very popular and the mass media's enthusiastic promotion has made it a huge sales hit (see Figure 7.1).[1] The apron is, however, just one of many ordinary products made behind bars every day in Japan. The origin of these products is never explicitly stated; it is never printed or otherwise indicated that it is "prison made." A variety of prison-made goods have entered the Japanese home through the invention in 1959 of the correctional fair: an annual exhibition for prisons and the prison industry organised by the Ministry of Law. From the start, visitors appreciated the products made in prison and carefully read the panels explaining the reality of prison life and prison industry on display. It was a good opportunity for each prison to publicise its productivity and diligence.

One of the industry's most important products was furniture designed after Western mainstream models, as well as traditional handicraft furniture. The variety of furniture styles produced in prison since World War II was a direct consequence of post-war reconstruction processes. Japanese furniture production underwent a huge change after World War II. It was revived through a process of forced internationalisation or what the contemporary interior designer Shigeru Uchida described as "the reception of a new lifestyle."[2] This was originally achieved through dealing with mass commissions from the US Occupation Army. Japanese industry learnt new processing technology and modern mass-production systems, and adapted them for Japanese society. At the same time, the Western way of life became more dominant, and this required new types of products for Japanese homes. Beds, drawing room sets (a low table and a few sofas), sideboards, and Western-style clothing closets in a mix of Japanese and Western styles were in huge demand.

The prison industry, very quietly, contributed to changing the Japanese home during this significant period of transition and recovery that lasted for a few decades after the war. Although they did not directly deal with the US commissions, some prisons received mass commissions to create desks and chairs for modern school use from local governments, and others strived hard to meet the need for a variety of goods such as soaps, handbags, and home furniture. In addition, the production of traditional handicraft furniture also began behind bars after the war.

While Michel Foucault and others have analysed notions of obedience and control in prison, the place itself has been forgotten from the perspectives of design history and material culture studies. The central historical narrative of furniture design in post-war Japan has been constructed around heroic designers like Isamu Kenmochi, companies like Tendo Mokko (renowned as the manufacturer of the Butterfly stool

120 *Yasuko Suga*

Figure 7.1 Prison-made aprons with a logo described in a famous television show as "enviously nice!!" "a novel speciality," and "priced 1029 yen." *Keisei* (October 2007).

Figure 7.2 Butterfly stool. Sori Yanagi, designer (1954). Tendo Mokko, manufacturer. Mushashino Art University, Tokyo.

designed by Sori Yanagi, one of the most iconic designs representing post-war Japanese furniture), and Karimoku that specialise in fine wood furniture, and products selected by the Good Design Award project starting in 1957 (see Figure 7.2).[3] The study of the prison industry would provide us with an alternative design history, which is sometimes closer to the reality of post-war consumer culture. This chapter discusses how furniture production in the Japanese prison industry, likely the remotest sphere of the furniture industry, developed and changed after the war, and how publicity strategies affected the ways in which prisons and society were connected.

What is prison industry?

Today in Japan, there are seventy-seven correctional institutions with 61,000 prisoners (both male and female) working in some type of industry within the prison system.[4] This is the second largest group of workers in the country, falling between the Toyota company, the largest workforce in Japan, which employs just under 70,000 workers, and Japan Railways' 52,000 workers. What constitutes prison industry is largely categorised into three fields: productive work (some of the materials are provided by the state, or a company commissions the work and the nation provides the prison workforce); vocational training (acquiring knowledge, techniques, and qualifications for post-prison life); and self-supporting work (washing, cleaning, cooking, and mending). There are three categories within vocational training: mass production for state use and commissions from private and public companies, such as printing and papermaking, metalwork, or sewing; furniture and everyday goods, such as clothes and shoes; and traditional handicraft works using local materials (woodwork, weaving and dying, metalwork, etc.). Thus furniture is produced both through mass production and craft within the prison.

The historical background of furniture production in prisons was, arguably, partly driven by the ancient tax system of *So-yo-cho* (labour or alternative goods collected as tax), implemented from the seventh century until the ninth century. Historically, crafts and carpentry work have been officially included within the pool of national labour. Specific localities were ordered to pay taxes with their craft products under the system of taking advantage of local craftworks and using their skills nationally to provide exterior and interior decorative design work.[5] Although it is unclear when prisoners began to practise woodcarving and carpentry, it must have occasionally happened whenever a craftsperson was imprisoned and generally whenever there was a need for furniture – self-sufficiency has always been a strict tenet for prisons.[6] However, for a long time, craft-making in prisons was arguably just a one-off occasion, because prison labour was considered a penalty well into the nineteenth century. Inmates were forced to labour for the sake of the public good, doing such tasks as mending roads or reclaiming land. In this way, prisoners were used as cheap labour.

After Japan opened to the West in 1854, this standard became problematic from an international perspective and, in 1888, the Japanese Correctional Association was established to demonstrate to the world that, under unequal treaties, Japan was modernising internally. The notion of punishment changed for the better with the introduction of the Penal Code of 1908, which required that the prison industry be hygienic and economical instead of inflicting physical and mental hardship. But the main focus of the industry was still work service. Another large shift occurred in 1933, when the prison law was altered to define the role of a prison as one of rehabilitation. This led to the understanding of prison as a type of re-education. Inmates were also compensated for their labour; a shift that signalled how much the concept of punishment had changed. These reforms were internationally recognised in the 1930s. However, during World War II, the prison again became a convenient source of

122 Yasuko Suga

forced labour, prisoners were exploited for shipbuilding and airport construction, and all humane reforms abruptly stopped. After the war, prisoners' fundamental human rights were reconsidered, and vocational training was implemented in 1956.

The emphasis of the prison industry has thus shifted, moving from a punishing philosophy of physical pain and forced labour to an ethic of correctional work for rehabilitation in society. The content of the work has also varied, including woodwork, printing, sewing, metalwork, chemical-related manufacturing, paper production, knitting and bag making, pottery, and leatherwork. Especially after the war, furniture production has played a significant role in the prison economy: on average, it has accounted for a quarter of the total revenue of the prison industry (more than 4 billion yen in 1963 and 10 billion in 1974).[7] This was due to the increasing awareness of furniture making behind bars as a means of re-education and job training, and the social demand for new types of furniture.

Western-style drawing room unit furniture

The formal introduction of furniture making in prisons began in the 1960s, and many prisons chose to specialise in some specific line of production or style that would differentiate them from other prisons. There are many notable examples of furniture that showcased the specific character of a prison. For example, Okayama Prison made steel office furniture. Chiba Prison produced wooden chests of drawers admired for their durable construction. Hiroshima Prison became famous for creating chests of drawers designed as wedding gifts, while Nagoya Prison has successfully specialised in folding tables and chairs. One of the strongest trends, however, was Western-style drawing room unit furniture. The post-war establishment of US army, navy, and air force bases across the country – there were more than 650 institutions in 1955, which was reduced to around 270 by 1959 – stimulated this trend.[8] Japan quickly had to prepare housing for the occupation army. Furniture companies across the country were commissioned to supply furniture for what was called the American Dependent Houses (off-base housing for American soldiers staying in Japan with their families, with an American-style arrangement of the rooms) (see Figure 7.3). This was, in fact, opportune for the reincarnation of the Japanese furniture industry. Designers Isamu Kenmochi and Kappei Toyoguchi from the governmental body and Kogei Shidosho of the Industrial Art Institute in Sendai organised the production for this large order of Western-style furniture. The magazine *Kogei Nyusu* (*Industrial Art News*) issued by the Industrial Art Institute frequently carried articles explaining mass-production methods for furniture and discussing reconstruction housing and the trends and practicality of American furniture. The magazine thus tried to integrate new knowledge of Western-style furniture and furniture production to address the urgent demands for domestic recovery. The aforementioned Tendo Mokko furniture company (est. 1940), well known for its technique of moulding plywood furniture, was one of the companies that began to introduce Western-style furniture series when it received a mass commission for modular furniture for the Dependent Houses.[9]

An appetite for Western-style furniture had existed since Japan opened to the West in the mid nineteenth century. Limited production and consumption of Western-style furniture began around cities like Yokohama and Kobe, where foreigners were

Figure 7.3 Living room in a B-2 type Dependent House. Unknown photographer. GHQ Design Branch Japanese Staff and Shoko-Sho Kogei Shidosho, eds., *Dependents Housing* (Tokyo: Gijutsu Shiryo Kanko-kai, 1948).

allowed to settle. Such furniture was displayed in and distributed through department stores in big cities, notably by Mitsukoshi, which in 1904 declared itself the first department store in Japan and began dealing in fashionable Western furniture.[10] European artistic movements such as Art Nouveau, Art Deco, and Bauhaus were also introduced to the public by professional artists and designers. However, the lifestyle of ordinary people was very distanced from such fashions and slow to change, so much so that in 1919 the Movement for the Improvement of Living was inaugurated. Led by Seikatsu Kaizen Doumei-kai (Union of Life Improvement), the organisation was affiliated with the government, which advocated the pursuit of efficiency in fashion, eating, manners, and any other aspect of life considered important for the goal of improving the nation's industrial productivity.

After World War II, the modernisation of lifestyle was much more strongly voiced, which in practical terms meant the introduction of "chairs" and "tables" into the Japanese home. Many companies began to produce modern (code word for Western-style) furniture, as represented in the exhibition of Western-style furniture at the first Exhibition of National Excellent Furniture held in Tokyo at the Metropolitan Industrial Hall in 1955. In the same year, *Kogei Nyusu* carried long articles on the "analytical study of the chair" discussing the appropriate size and function of "chairs" in a Japanese home setting.[11] Major furniture makers like Karimoku and Kosuge also followed a similar strategy of producing "European" (again, practically meaning Western) models, backed up by the strong social aspiration for the "American way of life" promoted through television shows like

124   *Yasuko Suga*

Bewitched (first shown in Japan from 1966 to 1970), and by the consumer demand the housing boom had created.[12]

Right after the war when so many people had lost their homes and were poverty-struck, the expensive Western-style furniture high-end makers produced was simply inaccessible for the average consumer. However, starting in the 1950s there was a sharp increase in demand for new types of furniture for ordinary homes. Small, low-cost homes became common, and the *danchi* (housing complex) style home, with its combined dining room and kitchen, was prevalent.[13] More homes were designed with Western-style plans and with Western-style furnishings in mind, with a dining room and a living room using tables and chairs (often used on the typical *tatami* straw mat floors as well as on wooden flooring). But it was also recognised that what the average citizen practically needed in order to realise the modern way of living was economy: the cheaper, the better.

The challenge of making Western-style furniture at Kofu Prison

Prison officers had studied the market trend, as the raison d'être of the prison industry as self-sufficient, efficient, and economical as well as educational was repeatedly discussed. In 1963, they estimated that the annual demand for furniture was 250 billion yen, and that by 1965, the demand would double.[14] Many prisons chose to produce furniture that was in steady demand. The prisons in the cities of Kofu and Fuchu were quick to introduce these furniture types in the Western styles.

In Kofu Prison's case, it started the production of furniture after the war with no experience. To set their products apart from those of other prisons, the prison officers decided to focus production on drawing room sets. They went through much trial and error. The prison technical officers started with research on how and where to collect the necessary materials. The technical side also proved challenging, for, although sewing machines for factory use had been widely utilised in prisons, they could not handle thick leather parts for sofas. The complex curved forms of wooden parts were also very difficult to design precisely, and officials had to repeat experiments many times.

Another of the difficulties Kofu Prison faced was adjusting the Western-style furniture designs to address physical differences and prevailing patterns of use and home environments in Japan. A technical officer later recalled:

> To adapt the drawing room furniture set that was made for the average Westerner to the average Japanese body size, and yet to keep the real feeling even in a smaller compact size, we drew plan after plan for adjustment. You cannot just downsize the products, because then the products will lose the comfort in sitting.[15]

Furthermore, size and weight had to be taken into consideration in the design, for the furniture could not be too imposing in smallish rooms, and had to be light enough to be moved by a homemaker when she cleaned the room. Although modelled on large and heavy mainstream Western prototypes, the sofa and armchairs were thus scaled down for the Japanese context (see Figure 7.4). The merger of two very different furniture cultures demanded a new design decision-making process.

Figure 7.4 Drawing room unit furniture based on Western models produced by Kofu Prison in the early 1990s. *Keisei* (October 1992).

Publicity for prisons

The post-war years were also the time when prisons were under increased pressure to gain more commissions in the face of intense competition with mechanised private companies. Prisons could fill national orders at a very low cost – the inexpensiveness of prison-made goods had been the only selling point up to that time – which drew commissions. But the prices the prisons offered began to be challenged by private companies in a time of economic growth characterised by rapid industrialisation. Eventually, even the low labour costs in prisons for handmade furniture, such as that produced in Kofu Prison, were threatened by the inexpensiveness of mechanical production.[16] Suffering from multi-layered organisational stagnation, prison directors, for the first time, felt that publicity would be needed to make their industry – processes and later products – known to society. The first step was the organisation of large-scale trade exhibitions. In 1957, power press machines and metal products made with them in Osaka and Kobe Prisons, and some arts and crafts works from other prisons were exhibited at the United Nations Asian Conference held in Tokyo. The following year, when the International Trade Fair was held in Osaka, the same two prisons again exhibited the machines to more than 3,500 buyers from thirty countries, who were surprised by the high standard of the products.[17]

Following such encouraging experiments, the Ministry of Law decided to inaugurate an annual exhibition event for prisons and the prison industry. In 1959, the first National Prison Industry Exhibition, or corrections fair, was held at the Tokyo Municipal Industrial Hall, a major venue for industrial trade fairs. The exhibition comprised five sections: woodwork, printing, sewing, leatherwork, and other crafts. Nationwide prison-made products, including clothes, shoes, and furniture, were displayed under one roof for the first time and sold on the spot. Prizes for excellence were awarded, such as the Minister of Law Prize and other honourable mentions. This also served to provide both the prison officers and the prisoners with a concrete motivational target. In addition, the exhibition proved an efficient direct medium to inform society about the prisons' contributions, which were generally totally unknown; their authorship of these products, unmarked, was invisible.

In the first years, the two-day exhibition attracted more than 5,000 visitors (this increased to 25,000 visitors by 1976).[18] The publicity posters were hung at national railway stations, and it was opportune that, in addition to radio, television broadcasting publicly began in 1953 in Japan, with colour broadcasting following in 1959 (stimulated by the event of Crown Prince Akihito's wedding).[19] TV and radio stations made a good popular appeal to consumers by reporting that prisons produced many cheap but high-quality goods.

Contemporary reports and early pictures show how furniture dominated the woodwork section from the beginning. At the second exhibition (1960), the displays were of very simple forms with no fancy decorations, and most furniture pieces – shelves, closets, and low tea tables – were supposed to be presented on traditional *tatami* mats (see Figure 7.5). But there was absolutely no doubt that furniture was the main attraction. As the first baby boom generation in Japan reached marriageable age, a big demand for furniture, in particular to furnish new Western-style homes, was created. Many of the visitors were female homemakers and would-be homemakers, and they found the prison-made products much cheaper than comparable commercially made goods (around half the market price), and very durable, if not fashionable.

Figure 7.5 Furniture sets displayed at a corrections fair, Tokyo, 1960. *Keisei* (September 1960).

It is notable that compared with the first few years of exhibitions when furniture items were mainly designed for use on *tatami* mats, the types of furniture exhibited became more Western and by the 1970s included the standard living room unit furniture used in Western-style rooms. In parallel, records show that the drawing room set furniture made in Kofu Prison increased in presence throughout the decade. It received the honorary prize as early as 1960 at the corrections fair, and in 1968, finally won the highly coveted Minister of Law Prize, the highest award given at the annual exhibition and therefore all the prisons' aim. Kofu Prison has won this prize many times since.

Sales at the corrections fair provided a good competitive event in addition to the prizes. A draw at the end of the fair for an especially popular product that many wished to purchase was instituted early on. The Western-style furniture set was always the centre of attraction, with many applications for the purchase draw. The popularity at the corrections fair directly reflected social demand, from which the prison staffs learned much, later weaving their experience of the visitors' reactions into their future production. More than just giving the prison staff consumer feedback, the corrections fair in general functioned as an important interface between society and the prison; visitors were very impressed to discover that so many productive activities took place behind bars. Moreover, some parts of the fair also provided a voyeuristic gaze into the daily living environment of prisoners. For example, beginning in 1976, a model room of an average shared cell attracted great interest.[20] A compact cell of the humblest kind on display, in contrast with the wide-ranging products, convinced taxpayers that their money was justly used on prisons.

Handwork as an added value: *karaki* products

As prison-made products became better known in society, their drawbacks also became clear, chief among them their aesthetic limitations. The lack of attractive product designs was criticised from the earliest years of the corrections fair.[21] This was a big challenge in the 1970s when the effect of Japan's rapid economic growth was widely felt in the design arena. The International Council of Societies of Industrial Design held its first international conference in Japan in 1973. By this time, Shiro Kuramata, Masanori Umeda, Sori Yanagi, and other notable Japanese furniture designers occupied important places on the world stage. The choices of domestic consumers, who could now afford to select products by their design, were taken more seriously than ever, even after the two oil shocks of 1973 and 1979. In fact, the year of the first oil shock was defined by the Ministry of International Trade and Industry as the "design year," with many related local and international events organised to highlight design. In addition, for the first time, women's opinions became decisive in designing manufactured goods.[22] In this context, the design of goods took on increasing importance.

However, without full-time art directors or designers for guidance, prison-made goods, mainly planned by technical officers and produced by inmates, frequently lacked a cohesive sense of design and aesthetic attraction. As the examples exhibited at corrections fairs demonstrate, clothes were not fashionable, and bags and shoes used too much alligator skin (popularly associated with the mafia) almost to the point of being grotesque. Furniture was regularly criticised for not being crafted in the best proportions. If prison-made furniture had once been praised for its unaffected and simple qualities, this was no longer enough for the increasingly design-literate consumer.

128   *Yasuko Suga*

Prison officials turned to traditional local "craft" handwork as an answer to the design problem. This played into pre-existing notions about the local and handmade qualities of prison-made furniture. Corrections fairs became even more popular and impressive when displays of independent "handicrafts" sections began appearing in the late 1970s. Various demonstrations of special local crafts were also conducted by instructors, actual prison staff members who had trained with the prisoners. It quickly became clear that being handmade was now a distinctive feature of prison-made products.

As mass production and corresponding mass consumption became common domestically, consumers sought to differentiate themselves from their peers by what they bought. Many homemakers expressed a preference for handcrafted goods over machine-made goods. From the economic point of view, prison craftwork was again also attractive because it was much cheaper: professional craftspeoples' prices were two or three times higher than the prisoners' prices. But from the design point of view, there were also limitations in traditional crafts, which can have a rigidly set style and a set material – and a limited scope with regard to improvising new designs.

The movement towards craft production in prison matched the national strategy of promoting Japanese special crafts beginning in the 1970s. The combination of traditional Japanese style and modern utility in furniture and living design – suitable for the post-war living conditions in Japan – was in high demand. In 1974, the Minister of Economy and Trade enacted a law to encourage traditional craft industries to promote the revival and survival of local crafts and communities. One good example of such special craft-based furniture was and is made at Osaka Prison: the traditional craft industry of *karaki* products. *Karaki*, which originated in China and passed into Japan in the eighth century, became the special technique in Osaka prefecture by the eighteenth century. It is a technique of woodcraft using ebony, red sandalwoods, Chinese rosewood, and other woods. No nails or screws are used in assembly, and *karaki* pieces are beautifully lacquered. Decorative shelves, flower stands, and paperweights are the main products of this highly prized art, and over the centuries excellent pieces were offered to the imperial family.

In 1973, the officers at Osaka Prison were ambitious enough to tackle *karaki*. This decision was again motivated by the desire to distinguish the prison's production from that of other prisons. Because its mastery took several years of practice, *karaki* was considered suitable for prisoners serving sentences of eight or more years. The prison officially set up a two-year course for elementary training, and asked the well-known instructor Tomitaro Fujii, the director of the Cooperative Society of Osaka Karaki, for guidance. Fujii taught around thirty prisoners. He enthusiastically taught the inmates the whole process: how to choose materials, and how to design, assemble, and lacquer the pieces. There is no record of the prisoners' voices, but it was later reported that under Fujii's "whole-hearted" instruction, the prisoners eagerly developed their skills.[23] This example also shows that the success of craft production at prisons is dependent on the presence of an enthusiastic supporter in the local community.

At the 1977 corrections fair, a *karaki* decorative shelf of the prison won the Minister's Prize, an award it has repeatedly held ever since (see Figure 7.6). The *karaki* products always received commissions despite their high price.[24] In 1986, among the 59,000 products for sale on the spot, a piece of *karaki* furniture was the most expensive on display (2,500,000 yen; then roughly 14,500 British pounds); yet seven people applied for the purchase draw.[25] More significant, however, was the fact that this was the year that Osaka Prison's *karaki* products were officially recognised as "traditional crafts of Japan," based on the Act on the Promotion of Traditional Craft Industries

Japanese furniture made in prison 129

Figure 7.6 Visitors looking at the award-winning works at a corrections fair, Tokyo, 1977 (upper left); prize-winning *karaki* work of Osaka Prison (upper right); visitors queuing for the opening (lower). *Keisei* (August 1977).

specified by the Minister of Economy, Trade and Industry. This validation came after winning the Minster of Law Prize thirteen years in a row, which was considered good evidence of durable production. It was the first such achievement for any prison industry product, and the event was widely covered by the mass media.

130 *Yasuko Suga*

One of the unexpected outcomes of the move towards prison-based craft production was recognised by Kunio Sato, editor of the *Asahi* national newspaper, in 1987:

> In the contemporary time of automatisation and mass production in modernization, for many localities it is extremely hard to find successors of their traditional crafts. Prisons are starting to become the home protecting such traditions. . . .
> Now is an amazing period, to think that the excluded people diligently strive to handmade.[26]

Prison-made craft furniture had come to contribute to maintaining local crafts in danger of dying out.

Corrections fairs as spaces of persuasion

In 1976, the 10,000 people visiting the two-day fair were happy to find that "everything is cheaper than the market price," and it was reported that "the popularity of handmade products rises every year."[27] Every exhibit sold out. The exhibition was described as "just as crowded as a bargain basement of a department store," and the phenomenon of the purchase draw was reported as follows: "woodworks such as furniture are especially highly popular, and those who want to buy them rush to order. So, the winner is decided by drawing lottery on the final day."[28] Following the success of the corrections fairs, more opportunities to display and publicise the prison manufacturing industry were sought. Permanent displays were installed in many local prison sites. At Maebashi Prison, it was reported that it sold an average of 40,000 to 50,000 yen worth of products per day in 1996, bought by families visiting the inmates and other visitors.[29]

The invention of the corrections fair was, however, *the* critical element in the success of prison-made products, especially furniture. They promoted the positive image of prisons and their inmates, and thus enlightened the people of the value of the Japanese prison system. They were a key space of persuasion for the Japanese audience and for the prisoners, to visualise that the prisoners were an integrated part of society. At the same time, from the prisoners' point of view, the corrections fairs reassured them that they had worth in society. In the words of Sachiyo Yoshida, a former technical officer who established the design company Prisona: "It is certain that the prisoners feel a sense of accomplishment in making things in their everyday monotonous lives. I think they feel that they are connected with the society through what they have made, and this feeling keeps holding them up mentally."[30] The moral role of the corrections fairs was and is considered very significant.

The corrections fairs offered a view into how prisons supported Japanese consumer culture from different angles. On one hand, prisons supported the average consumer's ability to purchase the popular Western-style furniture by providing it at the cheapest possible price. The prisons' production was promoting an interesting aspect of Japan as a modernising nation, and the distance between the prisons and the larger society was practically reduced thanks to the accessibility in price the former openly provided to the latter. On the other hand, it satisfied the national need for continuing the tradition of local special crafts. When traditional furniture fell out of fashion, the corrections fairs and related events provided a good number of handwork furniture products constantly on show in society. It can be argued that modernity and tradition

Japanese furniture made in prison   131

thus coexisted in the prison industry, with the corrections fairs as the main venue of communicating the positive message.

The making of Japanese furniture has been discreetly supported by the prison industry for decades. There are, however, important differences to recognise between products made inside and outside of the prison system. The art and design critic Kyoichi Tsuzuki discusses how an inmate making goods differs from what a designer does in his/her creation to pursue originality. At prisons, inmates pursue sheer "ordinary-ness."[31] This may be true in the modern age; however, it may also be said that the support of "ordinary-ness" through creation, not just high design models, has always been the social task of a designer. The quiet and anonymous contribution of the prison industry, full of goodwill projected by the multi-level publicity, can be regarded as such a design activity.

Notes

1 For four years starting in 2008, prisons sold 52,000 items with the logo, amounting to 60 million yen – an unheard-of best seller. Ukai Hidetoku, "'Horino naka' no roudouryoku wo ikase," *Nikkei Business*, 10 December 2012, 14–15.

2 Shigeru Uchida, *Sengo Nippon Dezain-shi* (Tokyo: Misuzu Shobo, 2011), 16.

3 For Japanese post-war furniture, see, for example, Hitoshi Mori, Katarina Posch, Bonnie Rychlak, and Tetsu Matsumoto, *Design: Isamu Noguchi and Isamu Kenmochi* (New York: Five Ties Publishing, 2008); Ryuji Arai, *Post-war Japanese Wooden Furniture* (Tokyo: Kagu Shinbunsha, 2014).

4 For more information, see the official homepage of the Japanese Correctional Association, www.e-capic.jp/capic.htm.

5 Officials in Hida Province, a mountainous area famous for its woodwork, sent their excellent carpenters and woodworkers to the central government (around 100 craftspeople every year) instead of paying the tax with money. These craftspeople were called *Hida-no-takumi* (master craftspeople of Hida) and were very highly esteemed. These master craftspeople would build houses, palaces, and temples, as well as make furniture such as low tables, drawers, and cupboards. Because of the national importance of woodcarving, carpentry, and pottery, Japan has had a series of legendary craftspeople like a Buddha sculptor, Kuratsukuri no Tori, a sword craftsperson, Amakuni, and a potter for tea ceremony vessels, Mosan, to name a few. The legendary craftspeople were considered almost saints. Their stoic nature and strong mentality of devotion to a craft were highly admired in society.

6 For example, there are pictures of furniture such as a brazier and a flower stand made by prisoners in the nineteenth century.

7 Editor, "Kyosei Sagyou toshiteno Ichiendama zukuri," *Keisei* (*Bulletin of the Society of Penitentiary*) (November 1963): 10; Takehiko Fujii, "Keimu Sagyo no Genjo to Hitotsu no Koan," *Keisei* (September 1974): 10.

8 The data was prepared by Okinawa prefecture, which the United States occupied until 1972. "Okinawa no Beigun Kichi oyobi Jieitai Kichi," www.pref.okinawa.jp/toukeika/yearbook/50/beigun.html.

9 Mitsumasa Sugasawa, *Tenndo Mokko* (Tokyo: Bijutsu Shuppansha, 2008).

10 For the history of Japanese department stores, see Taketoshi Yamamoto and Tamotsu Nishizawa, ed., *Hyakkaten no Bunkashi: Nihon no Shohi Kakumei* (Tokyo: Sekai Shisosha, 1999).

11 "Analytical Study of Chair (1)," *Kogei Nyusu*, 23, no. 6 (1955): 19–48; "Analytical Study of Chair (2)," *Kogei Nyusu*, 23, no. 12 (1955): 8–13.

12 The number of houses rose from 5,000 in 1962 to 45,000 in 1967. Akiko Takehara and Akiko Moriyama, ed., *Nippon Dezain-shi* [*The Concise History of Japanese Modern Design*] (Tokyo: Bijutsu Shuppansha, 2003), 100.

13 The dining-room-and-kitchen style was introduced in 1951 by the Japan Housing Corporation for all the apartment houses it built. See Housing Research and Advancement

132 *Yasuko Suga*

Foundation of Japan, *Nippon ni okeru Shugo Jutaku no Hukyu Katei – Sangyo Kakumei ki kara Kodo Keizai seichoki made –* (Tokyo: Housing Research and Advancement Foundation of Japan, 1997), 147–51.

14 Editors, "Zadankai: Gikan no Mita Keimu Sagyo," *Keisei* (July 1963): 34–5.

15 Shiro Kitayama, "Kofu Keimusho ni okeru Ousetsu setto no Seisaku," *Keisei* (October 1992): 60. Shiro Kitayama was a prison officer at Kofu Prison.

16 Ritsuyuki Hanayama, "Keimu Sagyo to Ippan Roumu oyobi Sangyo tono kyogo," *Keisei* (November 1955): 43–7. The wage struggle was not limited to Japan; for example, Denmark, Austria, and Belgium had the same problem. The United States and the United Kingdom did not suffer much from it.

17 Editors, "Kokusai Mihon-ichi to Keimu sagyo," *Keisei* (July 1958): 84–5.

18 Editors, "Sagyo Seihin Tenjikai nitsuite," *Keisei* (September 1960): 58–9; Editors, "Keimusho Sagyo Seihin Tenji Sokubaikai," *Keisei* (August 1976): n.p.

19 The year 1953 was called the "First Year of Domestic Electric Appliances." A washing machine, a refrigerator, and a vacuum cleaner were called the "Three Sacred Treasures" of modern homes. However, after a decade, consumers' tastes changed and a car, a cooler (air conditioner), and a colour television (together called the "3 Cs") became the sought-after, symbolic home products.

20 Editors, "Kyokai Dayori," *Keisei* (August 1976): 110.

21 Toranobu Kudo, "Zenkoku Keimusho sagyo seihin tenjikai wo mite," *Keisei* (October 1964): 98.

22 For instance, in the 1970s, colourful floral patterns were widely applied to electric appliances mainly used in kitchens.

23 Akiro Hatakeyama, "Karaki Seihin ni 'Dento Kogeihin' no Shitei," *Keisei* (September 1986): 57.

24 For example, in 1985, although it was priced at such a high value of 1,800,000 yen, the product received a commission. Editors, "Keimu sagyou kyouryoku jigyoubu dayori," *Keisei* (July 1985): 106.

25 Editors, "Keimu sagyou kyouryoku jigyoubu dayori," *Keisei* (July 1986): 116.

26 Kunio Sato, "Keimusho ga mamoru dento kogei," *Asahi Shinbun* (Tokyo district), 9 July 1987, 3. Recently, other prison-made craft furniture has been recognised as a "traditional craft of Japan," such as the woodwork made at Shimane Prison, following the Osaka example.

27 "Ninki ari Jukeisha Sakuhin," *Asahi Shinbun* (Tokyo district), morning ed., 18 June 1976, 22.

28 "Tokubaijo nami," *Asahi Shinbun* (Tokyo district), evening ed., 18 June 1976, 10.

29 "Shokuhin kara Mikoshimade Tasai: Keimusho no Sagyo seihin wo miru," *Asahi Shinbun* (Gunma district), 31 October 1996.

30 The aim of the company is to give new ideas to the prison industry's sales and advertising campaigns to make prison-made goods more attractive to the public. At first, it ran an online retail shop that opened in 2007; however, in 2010, a brick-and-mortar shop was set up in the city of Kobe. The company has annual sales of around 40 million yen. Junko Ishida, "Nikkei Design," *Nikkei Business* (June 2010): 12.

31 Kyoichi Tsuzuki, *Keimusho Ryo-hin: Made in Prison* (Tokyo: ASPECT Corp., 2008), 8.

Plate 1 Claude Pompidou seated at a Knoll pedestal dining table set (Eero Saarinen, 1957) in the private presidential dining room, Élysée Palace, Paris, December 1971. Patrice Habans, photographer. *Paris Match* (January 1, 1972). © Getty Image HABANS Patrice/Contributor.

Plate 2 Brochure for the Caribe Hilton featuring the incorporation of tropical nature indoors along with Womb chairs (Eero Saarinen, 1946–8) and ARKLU furniture (1944–8) early 1950s. Toro, Ferrer and Torregrosa, architects (1947–9). Unknown graphic designer. Courtesy of the Hospitality Industry Archives, Conrad Hilton College, University of Houston.

Plate 3 Promotional brochure showing Rolando López Dirube's *La Religión del Palo* (1957) encircled by spiral staircase in the Havana Riviera ca. 1957–8. Polevitsky, Johnson & Associates, architects (1956–7). Unknown photographer. Courtesy of HistoryMiami.

Plate 4 Philips chairs (Philippe Neerman, 1960) in the cafeteria of the Royal Library, Brussels, 2009. Maurice Houyoux, architect (1954–69). Hannes Pieters, photographer.

Plate 5 *Sens de l'espace et couleur*, exhibition of Knoll International furniture and textiles at the Grands Magasins du Printemps, Paris, February 1955 (left-right): seating shells, Womb chair, and ottoman (Eero Saarinen, 1946–8), Diamond chair and side chairs (Harry Bertoia, 1952). Roger Legrand, designer. Jean Collas, photographer. Fonds Jean Collas, Les Arts Décoratifs, Paris.

Plate 6 Sens de l'espace et couleur: (background) Knoll textiles; (middleground left-right) desk and chair (Franco Albini, 1950), Womb chair (Eero Saarinen; 1946–8), Arteluce floorlamp (Gino Sarfetti, 1950), tripod table (Hans Bellman, 1946), and Womb sofa; (foreground) bench (Florence Knoll, early 1950s). Roger Legrand, designer. Jean Collas, photographer. Fonds Jean Collas, Centre de documentation, Les Arts Décoratifs, Paris.

Plate 7 Knoll International France advertisement featuring Series 72 chair (Eero Saarinen, 1950) and table desk (Florence Knoll, 1961), *L'Oeil* (March 1962). Claude Michaélidès, photographer. Chassin, advertising agency. Courtesy of Knoll, Inc.

Plate 8 Pedestal stools and low table (Eero Saarinen, 1957) on the roof terrace of York Castle featured in a Knoll International brochure from the 1970s. Charles Sévigny, set designer. Jacques Primois, photographer. Unimark International London, graphic designers. Massimo and Lella Vignelli papers, Vignelli Center for Design Studies, Rochester Institute of Technology, Rochester, NY. Courtesy of Knoll, Inc.

En associant des fourrures et des meubles de classe, Knoll et Revillon ont réalisé un subtil accord de qualité, de confort et de raffinement : la douceur de la fourrure répond à la souplesse des formes et enveloppe la sobriété des lignes. Ici, le fauteuil de Bertoïa est en zorrino (sorte de mouffette proche du skunks), tandis que les deux canapés de Saarinen sont recouverts de vison brun foncé.

Revillon

Plate 9 Advertisement for Knoll International France and Revillon frères featuring Womb chair (Eero Saarinen, 1946–8), Diamond chair (Harry Bertoia, 1952), and pedestal table (Saarinen, 1957), in the dining room of the Moulin des Corbeaux, Saint-Maurice, ca. 1963. Charles Sévigny, set designer. Unknown photographer. Centre de documentations, Les Arts Décoratifs, Paris. Courtesy of Knoll, Inc.

Plate 10 Top floor banquet hall of Itamaraty Palace, Brasília showing the *Vegetation of the Central Plateau* tapestry (Roberto Burle Marx, designer, 1965), wooden table (attributed to Bernardo Figueiredo), and nineteenth-century Brazilian chairs, 2015. Oscar Niemeyer, architect (1960–7). José Airton Costa Jr., photographer. Collection of the Ministry of Foreign Affairs, Brazil.

Plate 11 Portinari Room of Itamaraty Palace, Brasília showing two baroque angels hung against a mirrored wall, 2015. Oscar Niemeyer, architect (1960–7). José Airton Costa Jr., photographer. Collection of the Ministry of Foreign Affairs, Brazil.

Plate 12 Seating in the visa and passport services section, US Embassy, London, ca. 1960. Eero Saarinen, architect and furniture designer (1955–60). Balthazar Korab, photographer. Balthazar Korab Collection, Prints and Photographs Division, Library of Congress.

Plate 13 Visa and passport services section, US Embassy, London, ca. 1960. Eero Saarinen, architect and furniture designer (1955–60). Balthazar Korab, photographer. Balthazar Korab Collection, Prints and Photographs Division, Library of Congress.

Plate 14 Hostesses seated in the Grant Featherston-designed Talking chairs at the Australian Pavilion, Expo 67, Montréal, 1967. Robin Boyd, exhibit designer; James Mccormick (Commonwealth Department of Works), architect (1964–7). Unknown photographer. Image No. AA1982/206, 28 (Barcode 7649625), National Archives of Australia.

Plate 15 Salon of the ambassador's apartment, Australian Embassy, Paris, France, 1978. S35 tubular steel armchairs by Marcel Breuer. Artworks: (left) Syd Ball, *Heriot Wall* (1973); (on rear wall, part obscured) David Aspden, *Free form Red* (1976). Harry Seidler & Associates, architects (1973–7). Max Dupain, photographer. © Copyright Penelope Seidler. Eric Sierins Photography.

Plate 16 David Moore photography exhibition, ground-floor gallery, Australian Embassy, Paris, 1978. Harry Seidler & Associates, architects (1973–7). Max Dupain, photographer. David Moore Photography Exhibition, photographs © Lisa Moore; interior photograph, Max Dupain, 1978. © Copyright Penelope Seidler. Eric Sierins Photography.

The diplomacy of furniture

8 National identity and modern furniture in Brasília's Itamaraty Palace

Luciana Saboia, Elane Ribeiro Peixoto and José Airton Costa Junior

This essay analyzes the relationship established between modern Brazilian architecture and furniture design from two perspectives: the consolidation of Brasília as the federal capital, and the ambiguous idea of modern Brazil. For its supporters, the new capital, built between 1956 and 1960 more than 1,000 kilometers away from the coast, represented an opportunity for the development and cultural emancipation of Brazil, a goal clearly targeted by President Juscelino Kubitschek's policy and slogan: "50 years of development in five years." Its defenders glorified the project enthusiastically, considering it a key factor for national integration, including a more balanced distribution of the population across the territory and a market expansion linking the industrialized zone to the hinterland, thus promoting the latter's development. Its detractors considered it an unnecessary endeavor of colossal proportions. Many did not believe Brasília would actually be built, as the political rants of parliamentarians opposed to Kubitschek illustrate. All the difficulties, the improvisations and the urgency that accompanied the construction of an entirely new city led to an epic adventure that translated into a series of new institutional buildings and interior spaces.

The focus of this essay is the relationship between modernity and identity, which comes to the fore in modern furniture in Brasília. While the capital's architecture and planning have been closely studied, the individual governmental palaces that occupy the center of the monumental plan have received far less attention, especially the design of the interiors and their furnishings.[1] What role did Brasília's individual palaces play in disseminating a vision of a country destined to modernity? What message did their interiors communicate before and after the coup? To answer these questions, we will focus on the Ministry of Foreign Affairs, the famous Itamaraty Palace (Oscar Niemeyer, architect, 1960–7) that was designed to house administrative offices and to host international ceremonies and commendations (see Figure 8.1). Built between 1962 and 1967, but officially inaugurated only three years later, the palace embodies many contradictions and ambivalences. It can be considered a summary of the main issues related to Brazil's economic and industrial development in the 1950s and 1960s and as the affirmation of a national identity based on references to both the colonial tradition and 1920s European modernism.

The façades of Itamaraty Palace mark the landscape around the National Congress and are composed of exposed concrete arches, of which the image is reflected in the surrounding pool. The main access ramp – covered in white marble – ceremoniously leads to the palace interior, passing beneath the archway and connecting to the glass box that encloses the building. The sole work of art in the garden designed by Roberto Burle Marx, Bruno Giorgi's sculpture *Meteor* (1968), seemingly floats on the water.[2]

Figure 8.1 View of Itamaraty Palace showing access ramp, water gardens (Roberto Burle Marx, landscape architect, 1965) and the sculpture *Meteor* (Bruno Giorgi, 1968), 2015. Oscar Niemeyer, architect (1960–7). José Airton Costa Jr., photographer. Collection of the Ministry of Foreign Affairs, Brazil.

Accessible only to registered visitors and the diplomatic staff, the palace's immense internal spaces prioritize emptiness and a view outside into the rear garden, also designed by Burle Marx. Inspired by the planning of the former Itamaraty Palace in Rio de Janeiro, the new building has a central reception area flanked by two wings, one containing offices for the general secretary, and the other housing the office of the minister of foreign affairs.[3] The palace's internal spaces are connected on different levels, forming a spatial continuum. The ground floor, reserved for large receptions, is almost empty. The only objects that animate the open space are Mary Vieira's sculpture *Ponto de encontro / Meeting Point* (1970), and the surrounding curved benches that explain its title (see Figure 8.2).[4]

Configured as a mezzanine, the second floor is reserved for commendation ceremonies and includes an open garden. Its focal point is the Treaties Room, a space animated by a light wooden lattice screen designed by artist Athos Bulcão (see Figure 8.3). International acts and agreements are signed on the only piece of furniture on the entire floor: a nineteenth-century jacarandá table on which the 1888 Golden Law that abolished slavery was signed. The table, a French marquetry piece in Napoleon II style, was transferred to Brasília from the former Ministry of Foreign Affairs in Rio de Janeiro.

The top floor comprises rooms of different sizes for receptions and dinners, which are all connected to an open roof garden (see Figure 8.4). From here visitors have an unobstructed view of the Esplanade and the National Congress. The interiors received a great deal of attention to detail, comparable in Brazil only to that given to the Ministry of Education and Health in Rio de Janeiro, a masterpiece of the Brazilian

Figure 8.2 Main floor of Itamaraty Palace showing sculptural staircase, and in the background, internal gardens (Roberto Burle Marx) and the *Ponto de encontro / Meeting Point* sculpture (Mary Vieira, 1970), 2015. José Airton Costa Jr., photographer. Collection of the Ministry of Foreign Affairs, Brazil.

Figure 8.3 Second floor Treaties Room of Itamaraty Palace showing nineteenth-century table on which the 1888 Golden Law was signed and lattice screen (Athos Bulcão, designer, 1967), 2015. José Airton Costa Jr., photographer. Collection of the Ministry of Foreign Affairs, Brazil.

Figure 8.4 View of the top floor of Itamaraty Palace overlooking the Esplanade of Ministries and showing Eleh Side Table/Bench (Sergio Rodrigues, designer, 1965) and the *Duas amigas/Two Girlfriends* sculpture (Alfredo Ceschiatti, 1968), 2015. José Airton Costa Jr., photographer. Collection of the Ministry of Foreign Affairs, Brazil.

modern movement. The furniture and objects were designed by Athos Bulcão, Rubem Valentim and Alfredo Volpi, among other modern artists.

Itamaraty Palace signifies a turning point in the appreciation of the Brazilian modernist tenets configured in Brasília. Planned during a democratic period, the city was criticized especially in view of the newly formed political context of the Cold War. Four years after the capital was inaugurated, the ideals that both inspired and justified it were replaced by the uncertainties associated with the military dictatorship, instated by means of a coup in 1964. Alvorada Palace (1956–8) and Planalto Palace (1958–60), both designed by Oscar Niemeyer as an affirmation of Brazil's modern identity, were increasingly viewed as isolated objects, denying the utopian ideals that inspired their conceptions. Because of the new political scenario during the Cold War and its completion after the coup, Itamaraty Palace, like the others palaces built during this period, incorporated a double image. Its wide internal spaces were still perceived as an expression of the concept behind the modern program, in which the idea of freedom and collectivity prevails, while isolated objects or construction details were increasingly interpreted as symbols of national history, monumentality and power. In order to clarify contemporary connotations of Brazilian modernism and the role of modern design, this essay presents the construction of Brasília from the point of view of its critics and highlights Itamaraty Palace and its interiors as a configuration of ambivalences. In doing so it develops a reflection on architecture, furniture, Brazilian identity and cultural recognition.

The Brazilian modern movement:
in search of a modern national identity

Until the eighteenth century, the economy of the American Portuguese colony was based on the production of large sugarcane plantations located on the Atlantic Coast and sustained mainly by slave labor.[5] During this period, there were only a few urban settlements along the coast, like Rio de Janeiro and Salvador, and there was no developed urban network into the hinterland. The establishment of gold mines in the southwest region of Brazil during the eighteenth century led to the development of several villages with numerous baroque churches and buildings that were the locus of trade and control of gold production. For this reason, one of the most important Brazilian movements for independence from Portugal originated in this region. The 1789 revolt of the mining region formed the basis for Brazil's foundational myth, a narrative that includes heroes and martyrs inspired by the French Revolution.

Brazilian independence was achieved in the nineteenth century as a result of the economic weakness of Portugal as the kingdom was ravaged by the Napoleonic Wars.[6] Then, in 1822, the imperial era began in Brazil and the country was ruled from Rio by the descendants of the Braganza dynasty. During this period and even with the proclamation of the Republic (1889), Brazil was dependent on industrialized nations, mainly England. The situation began to change during the First World War. The interruption of international trade between 1914 and 1918 boosted industrial development, especially coffee production that was still controlled by rural oligarchies.

Brazil's first republic ended with the coup d'état of Getúlio Vargas, who became president in 1930.[7] The 1929 crisis also helped transfer political power from rural powers to the newly formed industrial urban bourgeoisie. Under Varga's dictatorship labor laws were introduced and the industrialization of the country was fostered. The pioneers of Brazil's modern movement converged around the nationalist and patriotic discourse that came out of Varga's administration. Brazilian modernity needed to be expressed and seen, and who could play such a heroic role better than the country's own artists? Undertaking this noble mission, the architects gathered by Lucio Costa turned to Le Corbusier, who came to Brazil as a project consultant for the new Ministry of Education and Health Building in Rio de Janeiro (1936–45).[8]

The sixteen-story slab building served as a field of experimentation for artists as well as architects. Several leading modern artists participated in its construction: Burle Marx designed its gardens, Cândido Portinari was in charge of the tile panels covering the building's walls and Niemeyer specially designed tapestries for the building.[9] The furniture was also notable; some of the pieces were designed for the Ministry of Education and Health Building by Niemeyer himself. The movable partitions were similarly custom-designed, and reinforced the typical flexibility of modern spaces.[10]

The building made waves internationally even before it was officially inaugurated in 1945. This was achieved by Philip Goodwin and G. E. Kidder Smith's 1943 publication *Brazil Builds: Architecture New and Old 1652–1942*, the catalog of a circulating exhibition organized by the Museum of Modern Art in New York.[11] According to architectural historian Lauro Cavalcanti, the catalog, distributed in more than forty-seven countries over a three-year period, gave modern Brazilian

140 Saboia, Peixoto and Costa

architecture great visibility.[12] The Ministry of Education and Health Building was an especially notable project, for it revealed the talent of young Rio de Janeiro architects. It acquired a special importance, even the value of a manifesto, and served to inspire the construction of the government buildings in Brasília a decade later.[13] The young architects' and artists' efforts resulted in a building that responded to the European modernist attempt to integrate the arts within a social agenda.

The desire to define and establish a Brazilian identity is what distinguishes the country's modern movement from its European counterpart. The watchword associated with the intellectuals involved was cultural autonomy. Having read Marx, Freud, André Breton and Rousseau, writer Oswald de Andrade proposed an attitude in his "Cannibal Manifesto" (1928) that he believed would redeem Brazilian culture: cultural cannibalism.[14] The analogy could not be clearer, since cannibalism means assimilating the enemy's strength and courage. Rousseau's myth of the noble savage was completely inverted, turning the enemy or foreigner into one's own flesh. The proposition was based on the "permanent transformation of Taboo into Totem," as Andrade phrased it.[15] By digesting and thus assimilating external forces the native becomes a civilizing agent; the warrior is strengthened while reinforcing his traditions and beliefs. The enemy, in this case European civilization, is sacrificed and later deified. Cannibalism, in itself a taboo, thus becomes sacred and turns into a totem.

Whereas the European modern movement at first demanded a complete break with cultural tradition, the Brazilian movement legitimatized the country's modernity by evoking tradition. This is also the reason the baroque art of the gold mining region and the folk art were considered manifestations of the Brazilian spirit and genuine expressions of national identity. According to art historian Roberto Conduru, theoreticians and ideologists of the modern movement intended to establish modernity through the country's reencounter with itself.[16] From the modernist point of view, artists and intellectuals needed to break with nineteenth-century conservative academicism and restore Brazil's "genuine" identity. For Eric Hobsbawm, the identity dynamics claim the legitimacy of the tradition, even if it is invented.[17]

This generation of artists and intellectuals, in line with the nationalism of the Vargas era, was committed to creating representations of the country expressive of its future potential, its social and economic development, and to overcoming its tragic history of slavery. For that reason, many intellectuals, artists and architects such as Rodrigo Mello Franco de Andrade (1898–1969), Mário de Andrade (1893–1945), Carlos Drummond de Andrade (1902–87) and Lucio Costa were also involved in the creation of the National Artistic Heritage Service in 1937.[18] They believed it was important to consider the tradition of eighteenth-century art and towns as part of Brazilian identity, as well as to combine traditional elements of folk art into a modern language in order to develop autonomous modern creations. This approach was not restricted to architecture, but also translated into furniture design through the use of local materials and craftsmanship. Interior spaces and furniture designs provide countless examples to illustrate this peculiar operation between the search for emancipation and the valorization of Brazilian memory and culture. The exposed wooden trusses in houses designed by Costa and the use of vegetal fiber in Portuguese artist Joaquim Tenreiro's chairs are good examples of this. Tenreiro's production methods were easily associated with a possible Brazilianess: the furniture's simple lines were achieved not by industrial methods, but through the use of traditional handicrafts and local woods, such as jacarandá (see Figure 8.5).[19]

Figure 8.5 Three interconnected jacarandá and straw conversation chairs (Bahia, Brazil, second half of the nineteenth century), 2015. José Airton Costa Jr., photographer. Collection of the Ministry of Foreign Affairs, Brazil.

Important furniture designers were similarly inspired and presented their versions of Brazilian identity. Such is the case of Italian architect and designer Lina Bo Bardi, who, after resettling in Brazil in 1946, discovered Brazilian popular culture and interpreted it through simple and ingenious solutions in her furniture designs. One of her most famous designs, the Bowl chair (1951), is inspired by the bowls of the indigenous Caiçaras people (see Figure 8.6). The chair illustrates how vernacular objects served as a starting point for Bo Bardi.

In the halls of the Alvorada and Planalto Palaces in Brasília – the president's residence and official workplace, respectively – the desired synthesis between modern architecture and furniture was achieved. The few carefully chosen pieces were selected by Niemeyer himself, and then either purchased from the world's most renowned modern design companies or ordered from Brazilian architects and furniture producers. The open spaces of the palaces held classic pieces of international modern design, including Le Corbusier's Grand confort sofa and Basculant sling chair (1928), designed in partnership with Pierre Jeanneret and Charlotte Perriand; Mies van der Rohe's Barcelona chair and couch (1929), manufactured by Knoll International; and Eero Saarinen's Womb chair (1946–8), also produced by Knoll. Many foreign iconic pieces were retailed by the Rio de Janeiro store Loja Oca, where Knoll International furniture was first represented in Brazil.[20]

Both palaces, Alvorada and Planalto, were also furnished with designs by Brazilian architects that were made by local furniture producers. In addition to Tenreiro's jacarandá

Figure 8.6 Lina Bo Bardi seated in Bowl chair (Lina Bo Bardi, designer, 1951), 1953. Francisco Albuquerque, photographer. Instituto Moreira Salles. Reproduced courtesy of the Instituto Lina Bo and P. M. Bardi.

chairs, Jorge Zalszupin, Bernardo Figueiredo and, later on, Sérgio Rodrigues all contributed pieces. Most of these chairs were produced with local materials, including various woods, vegetable fiber and leather, and required less demanding fabrication techniques in industrial terms. It is important to note that Loja Oca's owner was architect and designer Sérgio Rodrigues, known as one of the renovators of Brazilian design. His famous 1957 Mole armchair, which brought the designer international recognition once the new capital was built, has a simple design and utilizes local materials, which do not require sophisticated industrial resources. Described by Rodrigues as a "big sofa bed," it consists of a robust structure in jacarandá with strap-supported upholstery that drapes over the arms.[21] It is a very comfortable and trim armchair.

The modern Brazilian furniture chosen to furnish the interior spaces of the government buildings recognized local culture as well as the aesthetic standards of the European avant-garde. In doing so, a discourse based on miscegenation and symbolic cannibalism emerged, which in turn produced a very remarkable and enduring self-portrait of a nation.

Brasília: synthesis or antithesis?

It is against this complex identity that the planning of Brasília must first be considered. The government buildings in Brasília succeeded in bringing together urbanism, architecture and interior architecture. Planned by Lucio Costa in 1957, the design of the new capital is based on the crossing of two perpendicular axes: the north-south residential axis and the east-west monumental axis. Along the residential axis, the landscape of the superblocks conforms to the city's daily life through the alignment of rows of trees and in-between blocks, where local commerce takes place. At the crossing between the monumental and the residential axes the Central Bus Station is situated, from where the capital's landscape is revealed along the Ministries Esplanade and the Plaza of the Three Powers. The monumental axis, as its name suggests, is home to the main buildings Niemeyer planned, such as the National Congress, Planalto Palace and the Supreme Court of Justice building. The monumental axis also links the plaza to Alvorada Palace.

But even before its inauguration on April 21, 1960, the Brazilian capital-to-be was the subject of hot discussion. Foreign visits were particularly important to foster the debate concerning the construction of the city on the international stage. When the French minister of culture, André Malraux, visited Brasília in August 1959, he praised the Brazilian government's audacity, energy and confidence to build the capital, which he considered a symbol of hope, development and emancipation. In his own words, "To achieve development, great nations have often found their symbol and Brasília, it is probably a symbol of this sort."[22] A very different position was articulated by critic Sibyl Moholy-Nagy, who wrote in an article published in the American journal *Progressive Architecture*: "The rigid skeletons of the ministries rise left and right of the triumphal axis like late shadows of the 1922s City of Three Million People. One wonders about communication between government agencies across a public square of such dimensions."[23]

Criticism of the interior spaces in the federal capital buildings was equally harsh. French critic Françoise Choay saw a lack of coherence, arguing that they did not represent the premise of total design as conceived by Le Corbusier, Mies van der Rohe or Alvar Aalto. For her, Niemeyer's lack of interest in interior design was a sign of two contradictions: "On one hand, it translates the spirit of Brazilian architecture – theatrical, spectacular and outward oriented; on the other hand, the lack of industrial design in Brazil and the poorness of the proposed solutions in the country of interior decoration, an area ruled by syncretism."[24]

Moholy-Nagy and Choay both went to Brazil in September 1959, when the Extraordinary Congress of Art Critics was held in São Paulo, Rio de Janeiro and Brasília. The meeting, organized by art critic Mário Pedrosa, was aimed at analyzing the Brasília experience under the theme "New City – Synthesis of the Arts." Topics included the relationship between the city and art, thus fomenting the debate on the awareness of artistic activities in the social and cultural spheres. Pedrosa explained that the "synthesis of the arts" theme did not refer to a mere collaboration among architects, sculptors and painters, but rather to a spiritual affinity and a shared awareness of the dignity associated with their social and ethical mission as it could manifest in Brasília.

The congress attracted national and international critics, architects and authorities, such as Lucio Costa, André Bloc, Giulio Carlo Argan, Bruno Zevi and Richard Neutra, in addition to Choay and Moholy-Nagy. Most foreign critics took a stand against the city's empty monumental spaces, as well as the plasticity of its buildings. The plan for the capital was faulted for being a state imposition. The modern urban structure was criticized for its lack of human scale, and the architecture for being distant from the country's social agenda, which faced severe socioeconomic and political challenges.[25]

Yet even if the initial enthusiasm that greeted Brasília had diminished as opposition to the military coup and international criticism increased, Niemeyer was at the peak

144 *Saboia, Peixoto and Costa*

of his career when he designed the Ministry of Foreign Affairs building. As diplomat and architecture critic André Aranha Corrêa do Lago writes:

> When Brasília's heroic stage ended . . . , Niemeyer was able to focus on new experiences. . . . Apart from its great sobriety, Itamaraty Palace breaks in many ways with previous palaces: there are no differences among the four façades, its body does not rest on an elevated base, but rather directly on water, and there is a clear division between the building itself – the glass box – and the arches. Niemeyer minimized structural virtuosity, one of the most modern characteristics of his palaces, but eliminated the "classic" marble revetment in order to consolidate his first representative building in reinforced concrete.[26]

This attitude of revealing materials was also embodied in furniture design. The use of local materials and crafts techniques was part of appropriating modernity as well as creating a proper identity. What most critics could not understand about the construction of Brasília, its palaces and the pieces furnishing them, was the weight of their symbolic value, properly and abundantly expressed by their interior spaces through a mixture of baroque and contemporary furniture, a dichotomy that legitimated its very modernity by acknowledging its relationship to tradition. For that reason, Choay was surprised by the unusual mixture of what she perceived as randomly gathered pieces of furniture and paintings. According to Fernanda Fernandes, the wide and flexible interior spaces established a dialogue between painting, sculpture and landscape design within the material framework of architecture.[27] This synthesis, however, revealed conflicts and dialectics between architecture and art, between the universal and the national and between modernity and tradition.

Itamaraty Palace: design and diplomacy

Costa's 1957 Report of the Pilot Plan described the Ministry of Foreign Affairs and the Ministry of Justice as different from the other ministries planned for the Esplanade.[28] Unlike the ten-story (eight above the mezzanine) bar-shaped buildings, the Ministry of Foreign Affairs and the Ministry of Justice buildings were designed as relatively low pavilions symmetrically positioned on both sides of the National Congress. The Ministry of Foreign Affairs, better known as Itamaraty Palace, was the last ministry situated along the axis before the slope leading to the Plaza of the Three Powers. According to diplomat Wladimir Murtinho, the building was "oddly positioned, right at the entrance of the Plaza, almost as if it was a gateway."[29] The first version of the project did not include the arches around its perimeter or the large reflecting pool. These two important elements only appeared in the final version of the project, an addition that decisively marked the capital's monumental axis between the Esplanade and the Plaza of the Three Powers. The arches, represented in a stylized drawing, became a symbol of the ministry, and the building was often referred to as the "Palace of the Arches."

Wladimir Murtinho (1929–2002) was the diplomat in charge of executing the building plans for the new Ministry of Foreign Affairs. In 1963, he was appointed head of the commission to transfer the Ministry of Foreign Affairs.[30] Murtinho not only expedited the building's construction, but he also played an important role in formulating the building program by sharing his experience of working at the old

Brasília's Itamaraty Palace   145

ministry in Rio de Janeiro. He was responsible for contracting the construction work and decorating the palace, and it was Murtinho who hired Burle Marx to design the landscape and several decorative pieces, including the *Vegetation of the Central Plateau* tapestry (1965) and various paintings by other artists (see Plate 10).

However, his participation in the construction of Brasília went beyond Itamaraty Palace. Murtinho also took part in the public announcement of Brasília's construction abroad. In a 1990 interview, he recalled:

> The Ministry of Foreign Affairs had a huge impact upon the launch of Brasília, literally a launch. . . . The Ministry deemed it very important to use this [palace] as a theme for the country's cultural dissemination. And so we did; the first thing that was done was in East Berlin, at a large exposition entitled *Brazil builds Brasília* [1958], during which Brasília was introduced for the first time. . . . That was the title [the Ministry] came up with, meaning to say we were capable of doing it. Very well, I reused that very same theme later that year, at the universal exposition in Brussels. We made a gigantic photographic reproduction of the model, along with the caption "Brasília to be inaugurated on April 21." That was in 1958. Laughter ensued . . . no one believed, not even the Brazilian participants, especially the Brazilian participants, no one ever believed.[31]

Despite the drawn-out construction phase, it was always the explicit intention of the government to furnish and decorate the palace using only Brazilian pieces. Murtinho, who took an active role in this project, managing all the contracts and services, recalled the reasoning behind this: "because we wanted to give the palace a very important character, that of only including Brazilian items or items closely related to our history. And for many years, there was virtually nothing that was not either Brazilian or historical." While "Brazilian items" referred to art and furniture designed by modern Brazilian architects and designers, "items closely related to our history" constituted pieces brought from the old palace in Rio de Janeiro and gifts from foreign embassies and illustrious visitors.

In 1968, a year after construction was completed, the palace welcomed England's Queen Elizabeth II, who attended several festivities and inaugurations, including that of Bo Bardi's Museum of Modern Art in São Paulo (1956–68). Her visit was part of a British–Latin American economic integration program. It coincided with a period of huge popular protests against the military dictatorship. The repression of opposition movements culminated in the Institutional Act AI-05, promulgated on December 13, 1968, which limited civil rights and cracked down on opponents of the regime. The queen's visit, a major event closely covered by both national and international media, and the glamorous palace that served as its backdrop overshadowed the political debate (see Figure 8.7).[32] The palace was the focal point of all discussions. Its exuberant design, detailing and functionality had positive repercussions in diplomatic relations, as explained by diplomat Jorge Carvalho, who was the general secretary between 1969 and 1974. According to Carvalho, they strengthened an image of "a diplomacy that anticipates new challenges in the world surrounding us, and which is also a response to the country's new development requirements."[33]

Murtinho recalled that the queen's visit to Brasília revealed how successful the design of the palace was: "At that time, we held receptions for, it seems, some 5 to 6 thousand guests. . . . When the Queen of England came to Brasília, it was a party like

Figure 8.7 Dinner reception in the banquet hall of Itamaraty Palace for Queen Elizabeth II of England, 1968. Seated from left to right: Vice President Pedro Aleixo, Queen Elizabeth II, President Artur da Costa e Silva, and his wife, Iolanda Barbosa Costa e Silva. Marcel Gautherot, photographer. Instituto Moreira Salles.

never before seen around here. Everybody wanted to attend this reception, and it was then that we realized that the palace worked very well."[34] Although there had initially been resistance within the international community to moving their embassies from Rio to the new capital, the success of the royal visit encouraged foreign ambassadors and diplomatic authorities to consider taking up the Brazilian government's offer of land for the construction of new embassies. Furthermore, after the September 1969 kidnapping of the American ambassador in Rio by members of far-left organizations, Brasília seemed an ideal refuge for the foreign diplomatic body. At the official opening of the palace on April 20, 1970, the full transfer of the Ministry of Foreign Affairs to

Brasília was initiated. A year earlier it had been determined that all embassies should be installed and operating normally in Brasília by September 7, 1972. When this goal was achieved under the watchful eyes of the new military administration, Brasília was consolidated as the new capital.

But in many respects the meaning of the government palaces changed under the military rule. For many people, the modern buildings and their interior spaces containing furniture with bold and simple lines became associated with excessive austerity, thus creating a dissociative image of external plastic architecture and internal rigidity, monotony and bureaucracy. The modern pieces chosen to furnish ministry offices and the interiors of apartments destined for government representatives were considered sober and lacking artistic value by their users. This judgment was due to the habit of seeing sumptuously decorated halls in French neoclassic style, such as the ones in Rio de Janeiro's previous Itamaraty Palace. It was only a matter of time before the original furniture began to be replaced. In a few cases, some pieces were gradually removed from the noble halls and relocated to warehouses or sold to buyers of second-hand items. Sérgio Rodrigues commented: "The military regime didn't understand anything about design. They didn't realize what they had. They undervalued everything."[35]

The contradiction was the fact that under the military dictatorship, Brasília, its buildings and interior spaces, acquired a new meaning: they became bastions. The Brazilian identity modern artists imagined, seen as a force capable of overcoming the challenges put to the historical democratic nation, was overcome by a regressive nationalist vision well expressed by the popular slogan of the military dictatorship: "Brazil, love it or leave it." Brazilian governmental palaces became examples that could illustrate Manfredo Tafuri's critique of the monumentality of projects financed by governments, considering them expressions of bureaucratic architecture.[36]

Between object ostentation and cultural recognition

The function of a ministry of foreign affairs is to put into practice the country's policies in relation to those of other countries, while at the same time representing the country of origin. For the latter function, it is crucial to develop an easily accessible synthetic image of the country's culture. Itamaraty Palace, its furniture, both modern and antique, and its art collection contributed to the construction of such an image. They also assisted in the mediation, development and affirmation of a national identity and of what could be called Brasília's "founding myth." Gilbert Durand defined a myth as "a narrative permeated by a belief that spotlights characters, a usually unreal scenario, and this category includes the divine, the utopian and the surreal."[37] In his memoir on the city's design, Lucio Costa highlights some of the key ingredients of the myth on which Brasília is based. He starts by evoking a sacred symbol: the structuring axes of cities are designed as a crucifix, a mark placed on the land, a sign for whoever takes over the site.[38] This initial gesture is combined with a "desert" place, affirmed as emptiness. The modern city built on a plateau, a point of cosmic connection, vows to make a new social order viable, one that implies coexisting without any tensions among different individuals, overcoming obstacles that prevent the country from reaching its destiny: modernity.

Following this mythic narrative, every monument, every object reflects its own meaning. From this perspective, Itamaraty Palace acts as a mytheme. Inside the palace, furniture made by modern Brazilian designers confronts historical Brazilian furniture and objects from the eighteenth and nineteenth centuries. Two third-floor reception rooms, the Bahia Room and the Portinari Room, are examples of contrasts between different periods. The first, a small meeting room, is decorated with an eighteenth-century ceiling in polychrome wood and furnished with modern furniture (see Figure 8.8).[39] Named for the artist of the two great modern paintings that it contains, the second, a large hall and meeting room, contains a jacarandá and cedar table from the eighteenth century, Cândido Portinari's paintings *Os Gaúchos* and *Os Jangadeiros* (1939) and two Baroque angels salvaged from St. Peter of the Clerics in Rio, which hang on a mirrored wall that reflects back a view of the terrace (see Plate 11).

Figure 8.8 View of the Bahia Room of Itamaraty Palace showing modern furniture (unknown designer) in contrast to the eighteenth-century ceiling in polychrome wood, 2015. José Airton Costa Jr., photographer. Collection of the Ministry of Foreign Affairs, Brazil.

Brasília's Itamaraty Palace   149

In other palaces, there was a mixture of national and foreign furniture located in the same interior spaces. In Itamaraty Palace, modern furniture incorporated modern tenets but also used natural materials, noble woods, leather, natural fibers, fitting solutions derived from ancient objects and traditional crafts associated with the drawing of smooth and sensual lines. The latter represent the "other" in relation to steel structures, produced by a sophisticated industry inaccessible to Brazilian artists. The limits of production, however, were no obstacle to the expression of a culture capable of linking its traditions with whatever modernity is possible. This will to achieve modernity resulted in objects that express the promise of constant overcoming.

Itamaraty Palace began to represent what Tafuri described as an elliptical circularity found between different positions: between the negation and the acceptance of value. There is an ambivalence of meanings related to modern architecture in a dialectics between different stands: between the negation of the object in its wide internal spaces and the acceptance of its value as a means of cultural affirmation. Negating and affirming objects in the modern space are not isolated extremities; on the contrary, they are part of a narrative thread, a positive action of reading those ceremonial spaces, sometimes silent, other times magnificent, as "acts of conscious freedom," placing it at the core of a virtually endless thread of relations, both established and yet to be established. Fictitious stories and historical fictions make up a thread involving what has been planned and what has been built. If, on one hand, the construction of some sort of modernity has contributed to the fostering of a hegemonic and iconic discourse regarding the Brazilian identity, on the other hand, architecture, art and design have started to represent new reading potentials of a culture in formation, regardless of the dominant external relations or political orientation.

Acknowledgements

The authors gratefully acknowledge the support of the Ministry of Foreign Affairs especially Heitor Sette Ferreira Pires Granafei and the assistance of Eduardo Rossetti, professor at the Faculty of Architecture and Urbanism – UnB.

Notes

1 On Brasília's architecture and urban planning, see especially Elcio Gomes da Silva, *Os palácios originais de Brasília* (Brasília: Câmara dos Deputados do Brasil, 2014); Sylvia Ficher e Pedro Paulo Palazzo, "Os paradigmas urbanísticos de Brasília," *Cadernos PPG-AU/UFBA* 4, n. Special issue (2005): 49–71; Matheus Gorovitz, *Brasília, uma questão de escala* (São Paulo: Projeto, 1985); and Aldo Paviani, *Brasília, ideologia e realidade: espaço urbano em questão* (São Paulo: Projeto, 1985).

2 Bruno Giorgi (1905–93), along with Athos Bulcão (1918–2008) and Roberto Burle Marx (1909–94), were artists of the Brazilian vanguard who actively participated in partnership with architects like Lucio Costa and Niemeyer in Rio de Janeiro and later in Brasília. Their colleagues Rubem Valentim (1922–91) and Alfredo Volpi (1896–1988) also went on to collaborate on the Itamaraty Palace.

3 The name Itamaraty Palace refers to the old Itamaraty Palace, a nineteenth-century building located in Rio de Janeiro.

4 Mary Vieira (1927–2001) was part of the neo-concrete movement. Her "Manifesto Neoconcreto" (1959) was signed by artists who claimed the expression of subjectivity in abstract art in opposition to the dogmatism of the Brazilian concrete movement of the early 1950s.

5 While sugarcane was produced for export, the estates also produced textiles for consumer goods for the masters and slaves. See Gilberto Freyre, *The Masters and the Slaves* (New

York: Knopf, 1946) [first edition published in Rio de Janeiro by Maia & Schmidt in 1933]; and Sérgio Buarque de Holanda, *Roots of Brazil*, trans. G. Harvey Summ (Notre Dame, IN: University of Notre Dame Press, 2012). *Roots of Brazil* was first published in 1936 by José Olympio and is considered one of the most important classics of Brazilian historiography and sociology. See also Mario de Andrade, *O turista aprendiz* [*The Apprentice Tourist*] (São Paulo: Livraria Duas Cidades: Secretaria da Cultura, Ciencia e Tecnologia, 1976). *The Apprentice Tourist* is the result of Mario de Andrade's daily notes during his ethnographic trips, conducted between 1927 and 1929, in the north and northeast of Brazil. Some of the articles published in this book were first published in newspapers of the 1920s.

6 For example, the Portuguese policy on the gold fields was rigid. No productive activity was permitted unless it was for the extraction of gold. The exorbitant collection of tax and the rigorous laws fueled the Brazilian independence movement during the eighteenth century.

7 Vargas stayed in power for fifteen uninterrupted years, although he was officially elected only once, in 1950.

8 Lucio Costa (1902–98), who in 1956 won the competition for the pilot plan of Brasília, was one of Brazil's most influential modern architects. In 1930, he became director of the National School of Fine Arts. In 1936, he founded the National Artistic Heritage Service, and he was one of the first to come in contact with the modernist avant-garde.

9 Cândido Portinari (1903–62) was best known for his paintings dealing with Brazilian social issues.

10 See Elizabeth Davis Harris, *Le Corbusier: Riscos Brasileiros* (São Paulo: Nobel, 1987), 165.

11 This exhibition was part of the US State Department's "Good Neighbor" policy, initiated at the Pan-American Conference held in Montevideo in 1933. This policy consisted of a US economic and cultural move toward Latin American countries, a compensation resulting from Roosevelt's interventionist policy. An example of this policy was the interest in singer Carmen Miranda and the creation of Zé Carioca by Walt Disney Studios, both presented as symbols of Brazilian culture.

12 Lauro Cavalcanti, *When Brazil Was Modern: Guide to Architecture, 1928–1960*, trans. Jon Tolman (New York: Princeton Architectural Press, [2001] 2003), 9.

13 There are numerous studies on the relationship between the Ministry of Health and Education Building and its role in the construction of Brasília, including: Yves Bruand, *Arquitetura contemporânea no Brasil* [*Modern Architecture in Brazil*] (São Paulo: Perspectiva, 1981); Carlos Eduardo Comas, "Protótipo e monumento, um ministério, o ministério [Prototype, monument, a ministry, the Ministry]," *Projeto* (August 1987): 137, 149; and Hugo Segawa, *Arquiteturas no Brasil 1900–1990* [*Architectures in Brazil 1900–1990*] (São Paulo: EDUSP, 1999).

14 Oswald de Andrade (1890–1954) was one of the intellectuals from São Paulo most committed to modern art. He was a journalist, a lawyer and a writer. He lived in Paris in 1912 in an environment convulsed by the avant-garde. He founded several magazines in Brazil that have become references for writers and modern poets.

15 Oswald de Andrade, "Manifesto Antropófago [Cannibal Manifesto]," *Revista de Antropofagia* 1 (May 1928): 3, 7.

16 Roberto Conduru, *Vital Brasil* (São Paulo: CosacNaify, 2000).

17 Eric Hobsbawm and Terence Ranger, ed., *A invenção das tradições* [*The Invention of Tradition*] (Rio de Janeiro: Paz e Terra, [1983] 1984).

18 The National Artistic Heritage Service was the first federal agency focused on the preservation of historical and artistic heritage. It was created a few days after the coup that established the dictatorship of Getúlio Vargas. The first president was Rodrigo Mello Franco de Andrade, who headed the agency until 1967.

19 Luís Henrique Haas Luccas, "Da integração das artes ao desenho integral: interfaces da arquitetura no Brasil moderno [From Arts Integration to Total Design: Architecture Interfaces in Modern Brazil], *Arquitextos*, 160.02 (September 2013): 7.

20 A decisive moment in the history of modern Brazilian furniture occurred in 1952, when the Artesanal Móveis firm – owned by the Hauner brothers, pioneers in Brazil's furniture industry – changed its name to Forma and was incorporated into Knoll International. Granted exclusive rights to Knoll's products, Forma started to produce Knoll International's collection, comprising items made by renowned modern architects and designers from

Brasília's Itamaraty Palace 151

all over the world. On this subject, see Maria Cecilia Loschiavo dos Santos, *Móvel moderno no Brasil* [*Modern Furniture in Brazil*] (São Paulo: Studio Nobel, FAPESP and Editora da Universidade de São Paulo publishers, 1995).

21 Sérgio Rodrigues, interviewed by Juliana Contaifer, "A poltrona molenga que ganhou o mundo [The Softie Chair that Won the World]," *Correio Braziliense*, January 13, 2014, accessed September 2, 2016, www.correiobraziliense.com.br/app/noticia/revista/2014/01/19/interna_revista_correio,406060/a-poltrona-molenga-que-ganhou-o-mundo.shtml.

22 Original quotation: "Au cours de leur développement, les grandes nations ont souvent trouvé leur symbole, et sans doute Brasilia est-elle un symbole de cette sorte." André Malraux, "Brasília napalavra de André Malraux [Brasília in the Words of André Malraux]," (Presidency of the Republic, Documentation Service, 1959).

23 Sibyl Moholy-Nagy, "Brasília: Majestic Concept or Autocratic Monument?" *Progressive Architecture* 40, no. 10 (October 1959): 88–9.

24 Françoise Choay, "Une capitale préfabriqueé [A Prefabricated Capital]," *L'Oeil* 59 (November 1959): 82. "Il traduit d'une part l'esprit de l'architecture brésilienne, théâtrale, spectaculaire et orientée vers l'extériorité, et, d'autre part, la carence de l'*industriel design* au Brésil, la pauvreté des solutions apportées dans ce pays aux problèmes de l'aménagement intérieur, domaine dans lequel règne le syncrétisme." Authors' translation.

25 This has been analyzed by Fernanda Fernandes. See her article "Architecture in Brazil in the Second Postwar Period: The Synthesis of the Arts," in *Architecture + Art: New Visions, New Strategies*, ed. Eeva-Liisa Pelkonen and Esa Laaksonen (Helsinki: Alvar Aalto Academy, 2007), 84–93.

26 André Aranha Corrêa do Lago, "A arquitetura do Palácio do Itamaraty de Brasília [The Architecture of Itamaraty Palace in Brasília]," in *Palácio Itamaraty Brasília: Brasília, Rio de Janeiro* (São Paulo: Banco Safra, 2002), 26. Lago is a diplomat, economist and architecture critic. In 2013, he was appointed Brazil's ambassador to Japan. He was the curator of the exhibition of Brazil at the XIV Venice Biennale (2014).

27 Fernandes, "Architecture in Brazil in the Second Postwar Period," 15.

28 Lucio Costa, "Memória Descritiva do Plano Piloto" [Pilot Plan Report], in *Lucio Costa, Registro de uma vivência* [*Lucio Costa: Record of a Lifetime*] (São Paulo: Editora das Artes, 1995), 283–97.

29 Wladimir Murtinho, interviewed by Luis Carlos Lopes and Marli Guedes da Costa, Oral History, Federal District Public Archive, 1990, transcript, 24. Authors' translation.

30 Manuel Mendes, *O cerrado de casaca* [*The Cerrado in Tailored Jacked*] (Brasília: Thesaurus, 1995), 42.

31 Murtinho, interviewed by Lopes and da Costa, 24. Authors' translation.

32 Mendes, *O cerrado de casaca*, 85. A film made of the Queen's tour of Brazil demonstrates the ceremonial function of the Itamaraty Palace. "Visita da Rainha Elizabeth II," *Cinejornal Informativo* 118 (1968): 10:02; Arquivo Nacional Brasília, accessed May 23, 2016 http://video.rnp.br/portal/video/video.action;jsessionid=7F04A3159EFBF 38D3D5DC5D7 6BBED17C?idItem=3989.

33 Jorge Carvalho e Silva, "The Transference," in *Palácio Itamaraty Brasília*, 18.

34 Murtinho, interviewed by Lopes and da Costa, 8. Authors' translation.

35 Sergio Rodrigues quoted by Rainbow Blue Nelson, "Dreaming of Brasilia," *Wall Street Journal*, June 23, 2011.

36 Manfredo Tafuri, *Theories and History of Architecture*, trans. Giorgio Verrecchia (London: Granada, 1980).

37 Gilbert Durand, "Sobre a exploração do imaginário, seu vocabulário, métodos e aplicações transdisciplinares: mito, mitanálise e mito crítica [An Imaginary Exploration about Vocabulary, Methods and Disciplinary Applications: Myth, Myth Analysis and Myth Criticism]," *Revista da Faculdade de Educação* 1–2 (1985): 244–56. The essay was first published in 1977 and translated from French into Brazilian Portuguese by José Carlos de Paula Carvalho.

38 Costa, "Memória Descritiva do Plano Piloto," 283–97.

39 Although the furniture in this room has been credited to Bernardo Figueiredo, no documentation in the Ministry of Foreign Affairs archives has been found to support this attribution.

9 All-over inside-out
Eero Saarinen's United States Embassy in London

Cammie McAtee

In 2017, the American delegation to the Court of St. James will leave the embassy on Grosvenor Square for a new building in South London.[1] The twenty-first-century building and the park it is set within designed by the Philadelphia-based architectural firm KieranTimberlake have been conceived in response to the security and safety concerns that plagued the Grosvenor Square building virtually since it opened its doors in 1960. Designed by Eero Saarinen in two phases between 1955 and 1956, the soon-to-be former embassy was sold to a Qatari investment fund in 2009 and is slated for redevelopment as a boutique hotel (see Figures 9.1 and 9.2).[2] Only its façade and ground floor public spaces, which were given landmark status by English Heritage soon after plans for the embassy's decommissioning were announced, are likely to remain intact.[3] Theodore Roszak's sculpted eagle, which has watched over innumerable protests, lines of 9/11 mourners, and the daily grind of seemingly endless queues from its perch on the cornice, will now preside over comings and goings of a very different nature.

In architectural terms, it seems an anticlimactic, if not a prosaic fate for a building that generated so much debate as it neared completion, and again when it was considered for heritage designation in 2007. Best known for the hostility it provoked in 1960, the embassy was criticized for its Cold War politics and pretensions, for its retrograde eclecticism, historicism, symbolism, and formalism, before finally being dismissed as an unfortunate error in judgment by an otherwise good architect.[4] Although these assessments were made almost sixty years ago, they continue to weigh heavily on the building, making it difficult to see it or the intentions behind its design. And if the heritage designation given to the façade may be somewhat unexpected for a building so reviled, its extension to the main floor interiors may very well come as a total surprise. For if the exterior expression has been debated at length, the interiors have never been the subject of any sustained discussion or interpretation. They are thus in need of critical assessment. But to begin this reevaluation of the interiors, it is necessary to look at the connection between interior and exterior, between the contained and the container. This demands a rereading of the whole architectural project as well as a reconsideration of the architect's overall intentions.

Most scholars have focused on the building as an architectural expression of the "special relationship" between the United States and the United Kingdom. In the 1990s, Jane Loeffler and Ron Robin published important interpretations of the building that considered it through the lens of the US State Department's ambitious post-war foreign building program and both historians pay close attention to the important London project. While Loeffler's excellent research formed the basis of an interpretation of the

All-over inside-out: US Embassy in London 153

Figure 9.1 US Embassy, Grosvenor Square, London, ca. 1960. Eero Saarinen, architect (1955–60). Balthazar Korab, photographer. Balthazar Korab Collection, Prints and Photographs Division, Library of Congress.

embassy from the perspective of the US State Department's Office of Foreign Buildings Operations (FBO) and the goals of its Architectural Advisory Committee (AAC), Robin's analysis placed it more fully within the political goals of American foreign policy.[5] More recently, British architectural historian Murray Fraser has considered the embassy within a study of the influence of American models and buildings on British post-war architecture, a perspective that helps situate the British response to Saarinen's project. The decision, however, to focus on the issue of monumentality – a term Fraser connects to a powerful and very conservative member of the AAC, Ralph Walker, who wrote of the need to address the site through "a new monumentality, quiet and restrained, without any sense of the stunt" – again limits Saarinen's design to the symbolic confines of Grosvenor Square.[6] Drawing on more recently discovered sketches

Figure 9.2 View into Grosvenor Square from the main entrance, ca. 1960. Balthazar Korab, photographer. Balthazar Korab Collection, Prints and Photographs Division, Library of Congress.

and archival documents, Timo Tuomi has brought another dimension to the building's interpretation, reading the London embassy, along with Saarinen's two other State Department projects – an unrealized addition to the Helsinki Embassy (1952–3), and the Oslo Embassy (1955–9) – as carefully thought-through responses to their urban contexts.[7] As the architect's first substantial urban projects, they represent a breakthrough in his thinking about the place of modern architecture within the historical city.

While the focus on the architecture as a response to the Anglo-American "special relationship" has revealed much about the project, it has obscured the possibility that other motives lay behind the embassy's tight wrapping of concrete and Portland stone panels or the confident composure of its public spaces. This essay examines

All-over inside-out: US Embassy in London   155

Saarinen's design strategies toward the goal of revealing the embassy to be a complex work of diplomatic stagecraft, one that looked beyond its host nation to the larger field of the Cold War. Soft power, the ability to persuade through influence rather than through brute force, is the primary tool of diplomacy. Inspired by an argument first put forward in the 1970s about the use of Abstract Expressionism as a Cold War weapon, I argue that Saarinen deliberately engaged modern art as well as architecture and design as a means of constructing an image of the United States as a beacon of democracy and freedom.[8] Seen by many but spatially experienced by a relative few, the building was intended to convey a multilayered statement of American values that would resonate beyond London, perhaps as far as Moscow. The public interiors and their furnishings, critical actors in this work of statecraft, have been largely left out of scholarly considerations. They can be understood only in relation to the entire project and Saarinen's efforts to make every part of the embassy "sing with the same message" as he often referred to the challenge of total design. The photographs of the embassy reproduced in this essay are by architect and photographer Balthazar Korab, who worked in both capacities for Saarinen.[9]

London

As Loeffler has well chronicled, the extreme care with which the FBO approached the project speaks to the important political and historical alliance between the United States and the United Kingdom. The fact that the architect was selected through an invited design competition – the only one organized during the period – alone attests to its significance. The site itself demanded great respect. Not only is Grosvenor Square one of Mayfair and Central London's great spaces, it has also been closely associated with the United States from the young nation's beginnings in the eighteenth century. A succession of ambassadors leased private apartments on the square and offices in various buildings on or near it. The first attempt to architecturally formalize this connection was made in 1934. Commissioned to redesign the façade of a building on the southeast corner and to design new offices and ceremonial rooms, New York architect John Russell Pope proposed a Portland stone façade with elements recalling the work of Robert Adam.[10] The Grosvenor Estate rejected the project, forcing the architect to adopt the dominant architectural materials and forms of the square, namely red brick with Portland stone details. It was this stylistic and material character, what Nikolaus Pevsner later referred to as "genteel neo-Georgian," in which the estate planned to rebuild the square after the Second World War.[11] The American association intensified in 1942, when Major General Eisenhower established his wartime headquarters on the square, which became popularly known as Eisenhowerplatz and "Little America." The erection in the park of a statue of President Franklin Delano Roosevelt, a gift of the British people in honor of the Grand Alliance, in 1947 formally recognized this connection. Having significance for both the host country and the diplomatic mission, the post-war project obviously required a deft architectural and urban touch as previous accounts have emphasized.

How Saarinen responded to the project's contextual exigencies has been rigorously considered. However, there were, as there always are in such complex commissions, unstated demands or unconscious desires behind the publicly stated ones. Whether an architect wins or loses a competition usually comes down to whether these desires, which sometimes oppose or even trump the official ones, are answered. Saarinen, who

156   *Cammie McAtee*

had recently learned through psychoanalysis that the unsaid is often more significant than the said, understood that success lay in giving the jury a statement that went beyond the competition brief.[12] To win it would be necessary to address the underlying representational demands. Whereas the FBO had been following an architectural policy that privileged diplomatic responses – materials and forms that reflected specific contexts and climates – the London project was complicated by representational issues, not the least of which was the desire to make an architectural statement that would express the autonomy, maturity, and geopolitical position of the United States. When it came to judging the competition entries for London, the capital of the country that the United States had broken from in 1775 and fought against until achieving its freedom in 1783, there was no doubt that the jurors anticipated a sufficiently strong statement of political independence. The fact that plans for a new British chancery in Washington had been announced in 1955 upped the project's competitive dimension.[13]

London was, of course, important to the State Department for reasons that went beyond the "special relationship." The city was a key center of the Cold War. During the war London hosted a large Office of Strategic Services (OSS), the United States' first intelligence-gathering agency, the wartime headquarters of which were located on Brook Street near the site of the future embassy. This mission was taken over by the Central Intelligence Agency (CIA) after the war. Plans for the new embassy included space for both the CIA and the Federal Bureau of Investigation (FBI). Another competitive element stood on the other side of the buffer zone of the great green expanse of Hyde Park. The Soviet Embassy was located to the west in a mid-nineteenth-century townhouse on Kensington Palace Gardens. Mayfair was later discovered to be a veritable hub of Soviet spy activity. The fact that FBO advisor Henry R. Shepley took note of the new Soviet Embassy in New Delhi during his visit to the Indian capital in the spring of 1955 – "an undistinguished modernistic building" – suggests that architecturally outdoing the enemy also quietly entered into the jury's deliberations.[14]

Surviving sketches for the competition project, many in Saarinen's hand, show that from the very start he recognized that the main challenge lay in reconciling the (stated) programmatic realities of an office building with the (largely unsaid) representational demands of the public face of the United States in this most historically sensitive of capitals.[15] The drawings he made before, during, and after his visit to London in early December 1955, and those of the draftsmen he assigned to the project, show Saarinen simultaneously thinking through the building's dual nature as a palace and as an office building. Entirely in keeping with his design practice, Saarinen closely considered historical precedents. Sketch after sketch imagined neoclassical façades and grand gates, among them John Nash's Regent's Park (a model put forward by Ambassador Winthrop W. Aldrich), and monumental porticos reminiscent of Edwin Lutyens's British Embassy in Washington, considered the *nec plus ultra* of embassies. Others consider Roman rostral columns, symbols that allude to war (and/or) revolution. One of the most imaginative schemes turns to inverted arches, the same defining shape that would dominate Oscar Niemeyer's presidential palace in Brasília (1956–9) (see Figure 9.3). The presence of these historical explorations tells us that Saarinen dealt with the context of the square in a nuanced manner that layered responses to character, building typologies, urban form, and even symbolism.[16] Another group of drawings considered the embassy's other guise: the government office building. Its two main public functions – consular and passport services, USIS library and exhibition areas – are considered in studies for their entrances on Upper Brook and Upper

All-over inside-out: US Embassy in London 157

Figure 9.3 Eero Saarinen, sketches for US Embassy, London, late 1955/early 1956. Balthazar Korab, photographer. Balthazar Korab Collection, Prints and Photographs Division, Library of Congress.

Grosvenor Streets, respectively, as well as the main entrance to the office floors facing the square. The ideas for the architectural expression of the façade emerge through studies of the effect of reflective surfaces, stone panels, the combination of red brick with white stone or concrete (for a truly Neo-Georgian response) and with a black stone or composite, and various heavily patterned combinations.

The final competition project harnessed these diverse forces in a symmetrical façade facing the square, the Great Seal of the United States marking the location of the official entrance (see Figure 9.4). The upper floors project over an inset ground floor screened by a grille of natural bronze. The overall impression, however, is dominated by the façade, a load-bearing wall made up of Portland stone grilles interspersed with precast concrete box frames that wrap around the upper volume. The shift from the two registers is made through a bronze frieze intending to bear the (then) forty-eight state seals. A rather decorative cornice of thin grilles, described as sand-molded and black oxidized bronze, completes the composition.

Reviewing the eight submissions, the jury brought its deliberations down to those by Saarinen and Edward Durell Stone, both of whom were already working on FBO commissions. Saarinen, a native of Finland, had already been tapped for two Northern European projects: an addition to the embassy in Helsinki, and the embassy in Oslo, Norway, the commission of which he received just a few months before the invitation to compete for London came. Stone, however, was the indisputable frontrunner. By 1955, his project for the US Embassy in New Delhi (1953–9) had the AAC's

Figure 9.4 Model for the US Embassy, London, 1955–6. Balthazar Korab, photographer. Balthazar Korab Collection, Prints and Photographs Division, Library of Congress.

full support.[17] Saarinen was well aware that Stone had the edge; his "grille" scheme was clearly indebted to Stone's "Indian" screen-based approach as well as to the heavy window surrounds of Georgian architecture. His sketches also include many studies for a colonnade similar to the one realized in New Delhi. Jury members later recalled debating the two projects at length before deciding against Stone's project for a tall office tower behind walls. Though Saarinen's project reputedly elicited little initial enthusiasm from the jurors, by addressing the underlying duality of the project, he succeeded in expressing the building as both a palace *and* an office building. Or, as Henry-Russell Hitchcock phrased it in 1947, by balancing his project between the exigencies of the "architecture of genius" and the "architecture of bureaucracy."[18] It is this "and" strategy that needs to be kept in mind when considering the rest of the building, inside as well as outside.

Architectural Cold Warrior

Before developing an alternative interpretation of Saarinen's design intentions, it is necessary to bring the architect's wartime service into consideration. Though critics of the time – American Lewis Mumford as well as Briton Reyner Banham – liked to portray Saarinen as a bit of a naïf who gave the State Department what it wanted, few architects were as savvy as he when it came to understanding issues of representation and the symbolic value of architectural expression. As Barry Katz revealed two decades ago, Saarinen spent the war in the Office of Strategic Services.[19] In 1942, Saarinen, whose talent for designing exhibitions had been proven through his work on Norman Bel Geddes's *Futurama* exhibition at the 1939 New York World's Fair, was invited to join the OSS's Presentation Branch. As chief of the Special Exhibits Division, Saarinen, directing a team of artists, graphic designers, architects, and landscape architects, designed a series of OSS-sponsored exhibitions. Although the impact of his wartime projects on his later work has yet to be the subject of close study, Mina Marefat has introduced the compelling suggestion that Saarinen's chair designs – especially the swiveling pedestal series for Knoll in the late 1950s – were rooted in his projects for situation rooms for the president and upper military brass.[20]

While these intriguing ideas connect Saarinen's furniture designs to wartime innovations, it is important for the present context to consider how the OSS's mission to conceive, produce, and diffuse propaganda informed his later work for the State Department. Under the leadership of Hubert Barton, the Presentation Branch's work was devoted, as Katz has assessed, to the communication of highly complex intellectual ideas. Barton later summarized what the division's work came to embody: "Presentation is the selection, production and use of whatever medium or combination of media will transmit most effectively a particular body of facts to a particular audience."[21] These concepts were tested in the model situation room, which was presented alongside a graphic presentation of key ideas regarding the military situation that were intended to wake up the public to the realities of the war. Although no child of Eliel Saarinen, the celebrated author of many Finnish nationalist symbols and the creator of the visual identity of Henry Booth's educational community at Cranbrook, could have been indifferent to the symbolic dimension of architecture, through his OSS work the younger Saarinen gained a very different experience. He was part of the team that went to San Francisco to set the stage for the June 1945 United Nations Conference. It was there that the first version of the UN symbol, designed by Donal McLaughlin and Oliver Lundquist, was presented to the world.

The point of bringing up Saarinen's wartime experience is to suggest that the design for the embassy was filtered through what he had learned in the OSS about communicating political messages and creating meaningful symbols. As Katz concluded, "Like the new sciences of atomic physics and cryptanalysis, design evolved under the exigencies of war; owing nothing to conventional academic categories and everything to the job that needed to be done. In this case, that job was to put intelligence data into forms that could be quickly assimilated and, just as quickly, translated into action."[22] It also suggests that Saarinen was trained to see the embassy as the vehicle for communicating information or ideology. The fact that the nature of war had changed in the intervening decade – a chilling cold replacing raging hot – complicated the task. If not exactly a cultural Cold Warrior, Saarinen well understood the exigencies involved in crafting a complex message through an architectural image and the manipulation of haptic and optic effects in an interior space.

Duality and duplicity

It is here that we need to return to the complex façade of the embassy. Soon after winning the competition, Saarinen was directed to develop the internal plan, rework parts of the overall design, and increase the office building's size to accommodate workspaces for 700 State Department employees in approximately 600 rooms. As the model for the revised project shows, the diagrid structural system, designed in collaboration with the brilliant young British structural engineer Frank Newby, worked with the heavy load-bearing walls (see Figure 9.5). Left exposed over the main floor, the diagrid would also play a major aesthetic as well as structural role by establishing the formal language in the ground floor public areas. To further distinguish this main floor from the upper-floor offices, the height was raised and the office block further cantilevered over the ground floors. The façade was further refined, conceived as an unrelieved, even relentless surface of alternating registers of box frames projecting from the structure. Critics were quick to point out that this general scheme had been developed for the Oslo Embassy, the start of which predated the London by only a few months. Oslo's intricate façade expression, however, was apparently not part of the first project presented in early November 1955, which featured a reflective surface.[23] Given that Saarinen traveled to London just three weeks later leaves it an open question as to which project inspired the other.

Presented to the AAC as a contextual reference to the heavy window surrounds associated with Georgian architecture, the Portland stone frames were released from their classical strictures. In his initial description of the design, Saarinen emphasized their changeability; the façade, he argued, would alter over time as the Portland stone weathered. He later told an audience in London: "We knew when we designed the façade, that if we gave the wall sufficient texture of in and out surfaces that time and the London soot and rain and wind would make this a dramatically dark building."[24]

Figure 9.5 Model for the US Embassy, London, 1956–7. Balthazar Korab, photographer. Balthazar Korab Collection, Prints and Photographs Division, Library of Congress.

The exterior, therefore, was envisioned as having a built-in mutability that would evolve as the years went by. This key aspect of the design was not respected; the building's conscientious stewards regularly cleaned the façade.

Although I want to leave aside the critical reception of the building as much as possible toward seeing Saarinen's design intentions anew, two reactions bear reconsideration. Something more than hostility can be drawn out of assessments by Banham and those of his American counterpart Mumford. Both argued that the embassy suffered from an acute identity problem. It seemed to be a building that didn't know what it was supposed to be. In a review published after Saarinen's death, Mumford harangued the project, which at every turn he described as "just an office building," for its reliance on (cheap) monumentality that came off as a "literal misconstruction" of "our [diplomatic] purposes."[25] What should have been a representation of "friendly diplomacy" had had the "effect of a calculated insult": "our London embassy presents a cold, unsmiling face, a face unfortunately suggesting national arrogance and irresponsive power."[26] For Mumford, "this blank bureaucratic-military mask" concealed "the true face of America."[27]

Banham pointed to an unsettling sense of doubleness, even dark duplicity in Saarinen's design. The embassy looked like a modern building "when seen in raking views along the front, but contradicts itself when seen from further away."[28] By engaging in the State Department's questionable foreign policies, the architect, Banham opined, had missed the mark by trying to make the embassy something it wasn't: it should have simply been a "high quality office block, and hang the [State Department's] brand image." If here presented as a negative quality, this sense of doubleness suggests another level to Saarinen's design. It is toward discovering this hidden layer that I propose to now turn to Saarinen's intentions for the façade.

The soft power of Abstract Expressionism

In March 1960, as the building neared completion and heated reactions to its design began to be heard and published, Saarinen wrote to the *New York Times*. While his primary motivation was to defend the decision to place an eagle on the cornice, he also restated his intentions with an emphasis on the contextual references the Portland stone frames made to London's textures and colors. He made an important statement about the effect of the overall façade:

> [I]t seemed appropriate to use a traditional American symbol in an important way on a building which, although it functions as an office building, has a significance and character beyond that of an office building . . . we [also] considered it part of the total composition, where it would be a central motif, like a pediment, emphasizing the main entrance and making a climax to the deliberately *all-over* structural pattern.[29]

By this time Saarinen had been married to New York art critic Aline B. Louchheim for more than six years. Soon after joining Saarinen in Bloomfield Hills, Aline Saarinen had taken over Eero Saarinen & Associates' press relations and nothing about the firm released in print escaped her "scalpel-like pen" as her husband fondly referred to her criticism. Without doubt, this letter to the editor was a joint effort.

But Aline Saarinen's role in the architect's career was not limited to shaping his public persona. A snapshot taken during the design of the IBM Manufacturing and Training Facility in Rochester, Minnesota (1956–8) – a project that similarly relied on an unbroken patterned surface, albeit one of enameled aluminum panels – records the couple and Saarinen's head designer, Kevin Roche, engaged in an intense review of schemes for various patterns and color combinations (see Figure 9.6). Possessing an expert eye as well as a critical ability to read such design gestures through the lens of contemporary art, there is every reason to believe that she encouraged the architect to see his work, especially such formal values, within the broader world of art. The use of the phrase "all-over" in the *Times* article is, of course, an unmistakable, and, as I will argue, a very intentional reference to Abstract Expressionist painting.

The term was introduced to modern art in 1948 when Clement Greenberg deployed it to describe Jackson Pollock's work as possessing an "even, all-over design," a description that fits Saarinen's façade well.[30] As modern architects have long been wont to do, Saarinen was establishing a connection between architecture and art as a means of justifying his aesthetic choices. But there is more to this connection than rhetoric. It would be wrong to suggest that a creative artist as intuitive as Saarinen was simply transposing a new aesthetic from another field of art on his work. In retrospect, it is remarkable that although Saarinen has been taken at his word by virtually every critic and historian who has considered the embassy since 1960, the words he

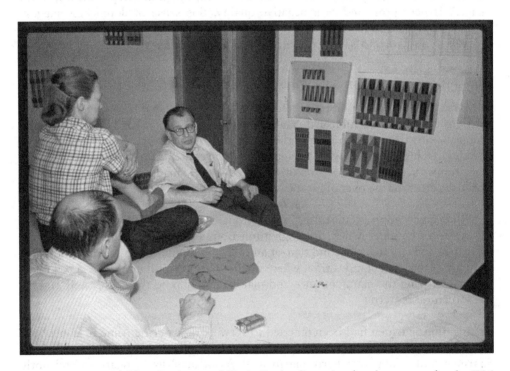

Figure 9.6 Eero and Aline Saarinen and Kevin Roche discussing façade patterns for the IBM Manufacturing and Training Facility in Rochester, Minnesota (1956–8), ca. 1956. Balthazar Korab, photographer. Balthazar Korab Collection, Prints and Photographs Division, Library of Congress.

chose to describe the overall effect of the façade have escaped notice. It is this description of the façade as an "all-over" that needs to be fully considered toward a more balanced reading of the architectural expression of the building and the design and diplomatic intentions lying behind it.

Any reference to Abstract Expressionism in the late 1950s must also be considered through the lens of Cold War cultural propaganda. In 1974, Eva Cockcroft revealed in a very potent article that US political rhetoric consciously appropriated Abstract Expressionist art in the 1950s and 1960s, piggybacking on the international success of artists associated with the movement, especially Jackson Pollock, and the goodwill their work engendered toward their home nation. She exposed a series of connections between key individuals associated with the Museum of Modern Art and government agencies involved in the creation of Cold War cultural propaganda, laying bare for the first time a profound political agenda in the Museum's traveling exhibition program. As she pinpointed, Abstract Expressionism "was the ideal style for these propaganda activities. It was the perfect contrast to 'the [Soviet Union's] regimented, traditional, and narrow' nature of 'socialist realism.' It was new, fresh, and creative."[31] The "freedom of expression" these artists enjoyed in an "open and free society" implied liberty from political intervention, though, as Cockcroft shows, nothing could be further from the truth when it came to the use of Abstract Expressionism in American foreign policy.

If we are cynical about these metaphors today, they resonated with the educated majority in the 1950s. And as the Cold War heated up, those Americans who questioned the direction or value of their government's cultural propaganda efforts recognized that Abstract Expressionism had succeeded where powerful individuals and institutions had failed as an international ambassador. Poet and critic Kenneth Rexroth captured what many saw as truth in his review of the 1958–9 European tour of the Museum of Modern Art's *The New American Painting* exhibition: "Everybody knows that from Barcelona to Warsaw, probably even Moscow, in spite of all the billions spent by the American government to lose friends and influence people, the most powerful American influences are modern jazz and these very painters. 'Everybody knows' that these paintings were the beginnings of a new way of seeing things."[32]

Although this discussion of the co-option of Abstract Expressionism by the State Department and its agencies may seem to lay the ground for a cynical interpretation of Saarinen's "all-over" gesture, it is intended to reframe its role in the design of the embassy. The appeal is obvious; Saarinen had every reason to think that such a reference was completely in keeping with the State Department's desire to project a positive image of contemporary America. What could be better than a façade loosened from the strictures of classical architecture, a regular pattern of rectangular frames released across the surface of the building, to suggest what was generally seen as the United States' greatest attribute, artistic freedom? As others have described, the painting was young, unfettered to the past, untraditional. And, interestingly for the present study, the public response to the Abstract Expressionists had been more positive in London than in many other European centers. As one art historian summarized, Pollock captured the "spirit of the age in London as in New York."[33] While knowledge and appreciation of the artist's work began to filter into the United Kingdom in the late 1940s, his work was first shown in 1953 in a group exhibition at the ICA. The world of architecture took note. Reviewing the show for *The Architectural Review*, art critic Robert Melville encouraged architects to look closely: "They are

164   Cammie McAtee

not pictures in any accepted sense of the term, but they are superb wall treatments, quite beyond the range of the 'interior decorator.' Those architects who acknowledge the humanizing functions of inner and outer, smooth and rough, and so on, should find his large ICA canvas particularly interesting."[34] As Jeremy Lewison has closely chronicled, as the years went by and Pollock's work was presented in different contexts, the positive reviews increased. During the years in which Saarinen refined his design for the embassy, Pollock's work dominated the London art scene. Peter Smithson, who offered one of the harshest criticisms of the embassy, later wrote of the intense effect of seeing his first Pollock painting, calling it "the Pollock of my liberation."[35]

In turning to Abstract Expressionism, Saarinen was deliberately engaging an art of expressing intense feeling. The painters and sculptors associated with it created strong, emotionally pitched forms through the exploitation of the tactile materials of their chosen media, whether paint or melted metals, and sometimes of scale (as in very large paintings), the use of intense color and/or charged line. If their forms were abstract, many artists engaged themes drawn from religion, myth, and the unconscious world to create works that engaged their viewers empathetically as well as visually. If his letter to the *New York Times'* editor represents Saarinen's only unambiguous reference to Abstract Expressionism, the London embassy was not the only project where he turned to its expressive power.

Saarinen first encountered the work of Theodore Roszak during a visit to New York in early 1953.[36] By this time the sculptor's heavy molten welded forms tortured in handling and violent in feeling had become closely associated with Abstract Expressionism. The impact of the artist's shapes and their rough, pock-marked surfaces evidently stayed with Saarinen, for he approached the artist to design the bell tower for his MIT Chapel later that year (1950–5) (see Figure 9.7).[37] The sculptor's work evidently struck him as an appropriate foil for the form, texture, and play of shadows in the chapel's brick cylinder. What Saarinen was seeking was a work that would simultaneously challenge and complement the architecture and, most important, create a tension within the overall project.

As the sheer number of drawings and cardboard study models for the façade for the London embassy alone demonstrates, Saarinen again put significant effort into bringing more values out of the texture and play of light and shadow in the façade. The imagistic painterly quality of the façade was strengthened by the decision to leave open half frames on the corners of every second floor, which leaves the impression of a tableau arrested by the limits of the support rather than by any preconceived plan. But even as the rhythm of the box frames was resolved, Saarinen still had some doubts. He turned to the building's details – the "fence" on the ground floor and the "frieze" space where the volume of the upper four floors of the building projected over the inset ground floor, and the cornice terminating the building – and again to Roszak. Abstract Expressionism was surely on the architect's mind for reasons beyond either fashion or politics.

The model for the revised project shows a highly textured fence topping the raised base of the building, and two types of lamp standards, the ones at the far corners close in form to the design that was eventually adopted (see Figures 9.1 and 9.5). Roszak played some role in the design evolution of these elements; scale models for lamps were recently rediscovered in the artist's studio (see Figure 9.8). Their jagged

All-over inside-out: US Embassy in London 165

Figure 9.7 Bell tower of the MIT Chapel, Cambridge, Massachusetts, ca. 1955. Theodore Roszak, sculptor (1953–5); Eero Saarinen, architect (1950–5). Balthazar Korab, photographer. Balthazar Korab Collection, Prints and Photographs Division, Library of Congress.

edges and contorted forms are entirely consistent with Roszak's work at the time; if the project had been carried out they would have significantly amplified the façade's tactility, complicated the values of light and shadow, and provided a formal counterpart to the rhythmic tableau of stone frames. Given that the creation of new art for a government building was a contentious issue at the best of times and the FBO was feeling considerable heat from Congress about the embassy-building program, it seems unlikely that these details were even proposed. They may, however, help explain the genesis of the building's highly criticized details. As the grille and bronze elements on the model for the first project illustrate, Saarinen was intent on bringing texture and deep tone values to the façade. It seems likely that when any hope to bring sculptural elements directly into the building details was gone, Saarinen, still trying to heighten the façade's texture, assimilated what he had learned through studies with the artist. The exposed ends of the concrete diagrid supporting the office block and the entire span of the cornice were capped

Figure 9.8 Maquettes for lamps for the US Embassy, London, ca. 1957. Theodore Roszak, sculptor. Amanda Millet-Sorsa, photographer. © Estate of Theodore Roszak/Licensed by VAGA, New York, NY.

with pieces of folded anodized aluminum, a jagged edge was introduced into the negative spaces between the projecting box frames, and their windows were divided in two by another piece of anodized aluminum. Taken together, these gestures all point toward a desire to amplify the emotional intensity through means derived from Abstract Expressionist painting and sculpture.

The design trajectory of the eagle reflects the difficulties in bringing modern art into the project. Previously unpublished study models for the sculpture show that Roszak also explored other forms that were, if still not consistent with his abstract work, more expressionistic than the monumental eagle raised onto the embassy's cornice on July 29, 1960 (see Figure 9.9).[38] The fact that the artist and the architect eventually decided to take a work of folk art as a model reads like a symbolic retreat.[39] In his letter to the editor, Saarinen praised the sculptor for creating a work as powerful as those by "anonymous American craftsmen." From this perspective, it now seems more than a little ironic that an architectural design rooted in what was arguably the best of contemporary American art was pilloried for a work of art that was consistently read as a pompous symbol of power.[40] In the end, the eagle fully obscured Saarinen's design intentions, becoming a lightning rod for all that was wrong about American architecture as well as foreign policy.

All-over inside-out: US Embassy in London 167

Figure 9.9 Early maquette for the eagle sculpture, US Embassy, London, ca. 1957. Theodore Roszak, sculptor (1957–60). Amanda Millet-Sorsa, photographer. © Estate of Theodore Roszak/Licensed by VAGA, New York, NY.

Outside in

Having made a case for reframing Saarinen's architectural motivations through the complicated lens of Cold War propaganda and global posturing, it is time to turn to the public spaces and their furnishings, the importance of which was underscored by English Heritage.[41] Even Banham recognized that these interiors and the entrance halls through which they were reached possessed "a lightness and spaciousness about them that no British architect has approached in recent years."[42] The public areas these entrances opened into – the Consular Section and the various facilities of the United States Information Service (USIS) – as well as the embassy's main lobby, are located on the slightly raised ground floor and a partially below-ground floor. This lower level is illuminated by a light well encircling the building (the infamous "moat") that was specifically intended to reduce any "gloomy basement" feeling.

Accessed through a dedicated entrance on the south side, the consular area comprises a large reception room, open workspaces for clerks processing visa and passport applications, and glass-walled offices for managers and consular officials (see Plates 12 and 13). Any British citizen who wanted to travel to the United States needed to go to the embassy. The reception area where visa applicants would wait, possibly for considerable periods of time, had great potential to shape perceptions about the United States, as Saarinen well understood.

The second large public area on this floor and part of the lower floor was given over to the activities and functions of the USIS (see Figures 9.10 and 9.11). Established

Figure 9.10 US Information Services library, ca. 1960. Balthazar Korab, photographer. Balthazar Korab Collection, Prints and Photographs Division, Library of Congress.

Figure 9.11 US Information Services auditorium, ca. 1960. Balthazar Korab, photographer. Balthazar Korab Collection, Prints and Photographs Division, Library of Congress.

All-over inside-out: US Embassy in London   169

in 1953, the mandate of the USIS was to be an educational and cultural outreach service to promote the United States and check the growth of anti-American sentiment.[43] Typical facilities in embassies and other foreign bureaus included broadcasting operations for radio and television, exhibition areas, auditoria for cultural events, and press and publication offices. The generous spatial allotment in the London embassy was directly proportional to how important the agency's mission was considered to be; there were ongoing concerns about anti-American sentiment in the United Kingdom.[44] Visitors entered on the north side through a lobby/exhibition space from where they could either ascend to enter the library or main gallery space, or descend to the lower level auditorium and cafeteria. These facilities saw substantial traffic flow; by the mid-1960s, the library alone welcomed more than 100,000 visitors annually.[45] The design of these very public interiors was therefore of top importance.

Between these two divisions Saarinen inserted the official entrance to the building and its central lobby (see Figure 9.2). After mounting the exterior staircase and passing the glass doors and a tall metal grille bearing the Great Seal of the United States and backing the elevator boxes, visitors were directed up one of two narrow stairwells to enter the largely ceremonial lobby area. Although Saarinen specified travertine for the walls as well as floors, Ambassador Aldrich (1953–7) criticized this space for not being magnificent enough and strongly recommended that the screened corner stairwell leading to the ambassador's floor be replaced with a "grand stairway."[46] Saarinen rejected this suggestion, recognizing it for what it was, a tired symbol of class power and entitlement. He kept the modest stairway, its message both discreet and discrete, choosing instead to focus the lobby on a long fountain that bisected the space. This element brought a sense of dynamic movement into the lobby during the years in which it operated. The sound of falling water also created a feeling of repose.

There were thus three distinct faces of America that needed to be expressed on the ground and lower floors. But at the same time, as Saarinen wrote to his two designers who were working with the associate architects in London, "nothing pays as well as keeping everything sort of within the same philosophy so that you don't have changes of material, changes of design without any change of mood."[47] This "sing with the same message" philosophy carried through the design of the two floors. The diagrid, which played a supporting role on the façade, was fully expressed on the ground floor, its cross-pattern carried down onto cruciform columns.

The consular services area occupies a corner of the ground floor overlooking the square. In a detailed letter describing the revised project to his London associates in October 1956, Saarinen discussed how he wanted both visitors and staff to feel in this space: "The general atmosphere . . . [is] one of openness, efficiency, and cleanliness – the European's picture of U.S.A."[48] At every turn, an analogy between the principles of modern architecture and American democratic value seems to be drawn by the open plan and the transparent walls. Not only is the consular office dominated by an open-concept office of desks, the few walled offices along the inner periphery are demarcated by clear glass partitions. The message is that nothing in America is hidden from view. The office is a masterful testimony of light manipulation: knowing how dark London can be, Saarinen, after consulting lighting designer Stanley McCandless, employed virtually every architectural trick in the book to bring in light from outside and then manipulate it to maximize its effect in support of the political message it symbolized.[49] As Korab's photographs

170 *Cammie McAtee*

show, natural light from outside pierced the chain metal curtains, and then, joined by fluorescent light from cruciform fixtures inserted within the coffers created by the diagrid, bounced off the highly polished terrazzo floors, the glass wall surfaces and the long glass counter that extends along almost the entire length of the room (see Plates 12 and 13). The gold-toned anodized aluminum surfaces covering the interior columns also picked up this light, suffusing the space with a warm glow. One wonders if Saarinen was familiar with Sir John Soane's Museum – a magisterial essay on the handling of the effects of natural light – perhaps touring it when he visited London in December 1955.

USIS libraries and information centers, ubiquitous elements in the post-war embassy, and the cultural events programmed in their exhibition spaces and auditoria were the State Department's most direct means of wielding soft power. Some USIS libraries were lending libraries, and contained not only book and magazines, but also American mail order catalogs, which were extremely popular in post-war Europe and a veritable force of state propaganda.[50] Though the experience of turning the pages of a Sears-Roebuck catalog was limited to one or two people at a time, it probably had as much if not more effect on creating desire for the American 'way of life' as attending one of the USIS's major traveling exhibitions. The librarians at the USIS Berlin branch are said to have had to resort to chaining the catalogs to the reference desk to keep them from being stolen.[51] For these reasons, as well as the special resonance of libraries in London, the embassy library was given pride of place.

Openness was expressed in a myriad of ways: through the floor to ceiling glazing, by the mezzanine floor, and the self-service book stacks. But at the same time, to balance this sense of transparency, the corner reading room and the visa area were if not completely veiled, subtly obscured from view from outside by means of loose weave metal drapes. Net curtains were hardly unusual in the 1950s; the textile department of Knoll made net fabric and Philip Johnson, an architect whose work Saarinen closely watched, had recently installed a more elaborate version to great effect in the Four Seasons Restaurant in the Seagram Building (1959). There the curtains soften the harsh outside light and keep the elite diners veiled from the prying eyes of passersby. The embassy's gently swaying curtains may similarly function to reconcile the ideological need to emphasize transparency and the Cold War need for obscurity. They may also have brought a musical quality to these spaces like the Four Season drapes. Taking a break from his diatribe, Lewis Mumford found much to admire in the library, applauding its organization, natural lighting, and easy access to its impressive collection of 25,000 volumes of Americana.

Saarinen's concern that art should have a prominent role continued inside the building. A memo in March 1957 reveals that he had not only begun discussing the eagle sculpture with Roszak, but that he also envisioned a fountain by Seymour Lipton for the court lobby, and two relief sculptures of the Great Seal of the United States by Marshall Fredericks.[52] That Saarinen believed these artworks were integral to the messages communicated by the different services in the embassy is shown in his description of the entrance to the USIS, which he saw as requiring something "less pompous and governmental looking."[53] If he was not yet sure of the right artist for the work, he was clear that it "should be some kind of modern sculpture such as Noguchi or possibly Calder hanging in front or out of the wall." At the very least, the eagle on the wall of this entrance "should have a friendly smile."[54]

The softest power?

It is important to consider the furniture in the embassy's public spaces as more than an extension of the architectural forms. Although Knoll furniture had virtually been standard issue in State Department projects in the early 1950s, as the decade progressed, complaints from the diplomatic core and from members of Congress had had an impact on how embassies were furnished.[55] Although he was a Knoll designer, Saarinen did not use any of the company's furniture in the embassy. For the upper floor and behind-the-scenes offices, he instead chose workaday teak desks and chairs designed by Edward J. Wormley for the Indiana-based furniture company Dunbar (see Figure 9.12). Here he was following a trend within the FBO: Dunbar furniture was also specified for Marcel Breuer's embassy in The Hague and for Stone's embassy in New Delhi, both completed in 1959. Whereas the furniture for The Hague was obtained through Belgian designer Jules Wabbes, who in 1958 signed a license agreement with Dunbar to manufacturer its furniture in his Brussels workshop and distribute it within Europe, the furniture in the New Delhi embassy was a mix of imported Dunbar furniture and Dunbar furniture produced in India through a special agreement with the company as a means of reducing costs.[56] But by the time the London embassy was furnished, State Department policy had fully shifted to "buying American."[57]

When it came to furnishing the embassy's representational spaces, Saarinen took on the task himself, his firm designing brown leather-upholstered lounge and side chairs, sofas, benches, and low glass-topped tables for the consular waiting room and

Figure 9.12 Typical office furnished with Dunbar furniture, ca. 1960. Balthazar Korab, photographer. Balthazar Korab Collection, Prints and Photographs Division, Library of Congress.

172   *Cammie McAtee*

the USIS library (see Figure 9.10, Plates 12 and 13).[58] The fact that the FBO agreed to very expensive custom designs indicates that the furniture and furnishing were recognized as having a significant role in conveying the subtle political message of the interior. While the heavily padded chairs might be read as modern interpretation of their Victorian precursor, a source Saarinen had previously looked to when designing his Womb chair (1946–8), their cruciform bases were intended to harmonize with the architectural forms and heighten what Saarinen termed the overall "stateliness" and "formality" of the spaces. The fact that they are apparently extremely uncomfortable – after trying out the side chairs in the library, Mumford grumbled that "they achieve a maximum of cushioned discomfort" – only underlines their representational role.[59] Sometimes soft power isn't very comfortable.

Although Ambassador Aldrich had requested a private dining room (in fact two) on the ambassador's floor, the architect kept the dining facilities together on the lower floor, undoubtedly recognizing that a separation between employees, the diplomatic corps, and members of the public who occasionally used the cafeteria would create a very un-American class distinction.[60] Saarinen filled the cafeteria with gleaming white molded fiberglass-reinforced plastic chairs, some with arms, some armless, and matching tables, all designed by his close friends and competitors, Charles and Ray Eames. The simple seating shells brought into mass production by Herman Miller in 1950 were upholstered with a straw-colored fabric – as Saarinen termed the distinctive golden tone of the anodized aluminium used for the building's details – and fitted with pedestal supports that immediately bring to mind his own earlier dining series for Knoll (1954–7). But whereas the leg of Saarinen's chairs and tables grows organically into the seat and tabletop, the one chosen for the cafeteria furniture was fitted with a cruciform base that echoed the ever-present diagrid.[61] Seeking a different mood in the adjacent dining room destined for the use of the ambassador and visiting guests, Saarinen brought in his overstuffed chairs upholstered in emerald-green leather.[62] The reasons Saarinen did not specify his own chairs and tables are unclear, but the danger of a conflict of interest may have played a role given that he received royalties based on Knoll sales.[63] Geopolitics, however, may very well have been behind this design decision. The Eameses' stacking plastic chairs had had a prominent place in the United States Information Agency's 1959 American National Exhibition, an event intended "to project a realistic and credible image of America" to Muscovites.[64] The presence of ubiquitous consumer goods was central to this strategy and famously fueled the Nixon–Khrushchev Kitchen Debate. The desire to make a similar statement in the embassy's public cafeteria may thus have guided the choice of a chair that was popularly associated with American democratic values.

On some level the cultural officials in the London embassy seem to have understood the complex relationship between the building's architecture and Abstract Expressionism. The USIS galleries were – appropriately enough – inaugurated by an exhibition of modern painting featuring Jackson Pollock's powerful *Black and White No. 15, 1951* (1951).[65] By contrast, none of the ambassadors assigned to the new building in the 1950s or 1960s found much in it to like. Despite being the brother of one of the founders of the Museum of Modern Art, Aldrich tried to intervene before and after the competition results were announced, arguing that the right architectural approach was a traditional not a modern one. Nor did the new embassy's third ambassador, David Bruce (1961–9), find favor in the building constructed to Saarinen's revised designs. His first recorded impression referred to it as

All-over inside-out: US Embassy in London 173

an "architectural monstrosity."[66] For David and Evangeline Bruce, it was Winfield House, the ambassador's official residence, that was the place of prestige, and like the Aldrichs before them and the Annenbergs after them, they lavished their attention and personal funds on its refurbishment and decoration.

Time has not been kind to either the exterior or interior of the embassy. While the impression of the former has been obscured by layers upon layers of security perimeters, changes to the interiors reflect very different concerns. It is unclear when the modern desk, chairs, sofas, and tables in the ambassador's office were removed, but photographs from the late 1970s show that they had been replaced by unimportant historical pieces that reflected the earlier ambassadors' fixation on equating diplomacy with traditional styles. The long expanses of white walls that made Lewis Mumford so uneasy when he visited were soon punctuated by large framed oil portraits of former ambassadors, a project Bruce initiated in 1961.[67] The addition of the portraits seems a deliberate attempt to trump modernity with tradition, to impose historical convention on the tabula rasa of modernity. But if the ambassador succeeded in injecting some sense of tradition into the uncompromisingly modern interior, the desires motivating these changes and additions can also be read as expressing a sense of inferiority. Although the pendulum has swung backward with midcentury modern architecture now prized where it was once censured (a factor that no doubt helped efforts to preserve the façade and public areas of the building), it has come too late to save the Grosvenor Square embassy.

For anyone sympathetic to Saarinen, there is poetic justice in knowing that his chief critic, Reyner Banham, was forced to cool his heels in the embassy's visa waiting room when he became one of the more than 67,000 Britons who visited the United States in 1961.[68] Perhaps he rethought some of his criticism of the building that day. We will never know, but it is worth recalling that Banham was traveling to the United States for the first time to face Philip Johnson in a much-hyped debate at the Metropolitan Museum at the end of March. To the great disappointment of the East Coast architectural intelligentsia, the sharp-tongued critic failed to take the bait and the whole affair fell flat, nothing but a tempest in a teapot. Had the leather sofas and the music of the swaying metal curtain worked their soft power magic on him?

Acknowledgements

For their help in my research, I thank Dennis Wolf, then deputy press attaché for the London embassy, for welcoming me into the building in September 2004, and in connection with that visit, the late Massachusetts Senator Edward M. Kennedy; Sara Jane Roszak and Amanda Millet-Sorsa, archivist of the Roszak archive; and Mary Daniels, now retired archivist at the Frances Loeb Library, Harvard University. I am grateful to Neil Levine and Sarah Williams Goldhagen for their comments on a preliminary version presented in a graduate seminar at Harvard. I would also like to acknowledge Harriet Atkinson and Verity Clarkson's University of Brighton conference in November 2015. Although I was unable to present due to twenty-first-century spatial politics, their "soft power" theme inspired new directions in my reading. I have benefited from challenging discussions about this building, its architect, and ideas about it with Réjean Legault over many years. I thank him for his intellectual generosity and constant support.

174 *Cammie McAtee*

Notes

1 This chapter will refer to the building as an embassy, which encompasses "all the offices of a diplomatic mission represented by an ambassador," rather than as a chancellery (US) or chancery (UK), which refers to the "office of the ambassador." Jonathan Colman, "Portrait of an Institution: The US Embassy in London, 1945–53," *The Hague Journal of Diplomacy* 4 (2009): 340, n.1. As early as 2000, the US Department of State had begun looking for the site for a new embassy.

2 The competition was announced in the fall of 1955. Each architect was required to visit the site. Saarinen was in London from December 1–8, 1955. The jury selected Saarinen's project on February 14, 1956. Saarinen presented a revised design on May 15, 1956. The design was further developed through 1957, with structural engineering designed in collaboration with Felix J. Samuely and Partners. The working drawings were produced in London by the associate firm Yorke, Rosenberg and Mardall, and construction began in 1957. The embassy was officially inaugurated in 1960.

3 The Grade II designation was supported by the following assessment: "Special architectural interest for the strongly articulated design and dynamic façades, well-detailed stonework and consistency of detail. Of particular note is the innovative application of the exposed concrete diagrid – an intelligent combination of structural expression and decorative motifs which provides cohesion to the whole and which illustrates Saarinen's principles of marrying form to structure, interior to exterior – and his close involvement in detail and execution. Eero Saarinen is an outstanding figure in C20 architecture and design and this is an early example of a modernist yet contextual approach to design in a sensitive urban location. Internal interest is largely confined to the ground-floor public spaces." English Heritage, "United States of America Embassy: List Entry Summary," 2009, accessed May 20, 2016, https://historicengland.org.uk/listing/the-list/list-entry/1393496.

4 Although the number of reviews and later commentaries on the embassy is too long to list here, of the British reviews, see especially those by [J. M. Richards], "Critical Appraisal of New American Embassy: Structure Versus Façade," *The Times* (London), October 28, 1960, 19; Robert Furneaux Jordan, "Office Block or Embassy?" *Architect and Building News* 218, no. 23 (December 7, 1960): 724–5; Reyner Banham, "Monument with Frills," *New Statesman* 60, no. 1552 (December 10, 1960): 918, 919; Peter Smithson, R. Furneaux Jordan, Reyner Banham, and Eero Saarinen, "Criticism: "Controversial Building in London," *Architectural Forum* 114, no. 3 (March 1961): 80–5; Fello Atkinson, "Criticism: U.S. Embassy Building, Grosvenor Square, London," *Architectural Review* 129, no. 770 (April 1961): 252–8. For critical appraisals in the United States, see Ada Louise Huxtable, "Sharp Debate: What Should an Embassy Be?" *New York Times*, September 18, 1960, SM36; Walter McQuade, "Architecture," *The Nation* 192, no. 12 (March 25, 1961): 270–1; and Lewis Mumford's late review, "The Sky Line: False Front or Cold-War Concept," *The New Yorker*, October 20, 1962, 174, 176, 178, 180–8.

5 Jane C. Loeffler, *The Architecture of Diplomacy: Building America's Embassies*, rev. 2nd ed. (New York: Princeton Architectural Press, [1998] 2011); Ron Robin, *Enclaves of America: The Rhetoric of American Political Architecture Abroad, 1900–1965* (Princeton, NJ: Princeton University Press, 1992). The present study is much indebted to Loeffler's in-depth research.

6 Murray Fraser with Joe Kerr, *Architecture and the "Special Relationship": The American Influence on Post-war British Architecture* (London: Routledge, 2007), 348.

7 Timo Tuomi, "Embassies and Chanceries: The Necessity of Unity," in *Eero Saarinen: Shaping the Future*, ed. Eeva-Liisa Pelkonen and Donald Albrecht (New Haven, CT: Yale University Press, 2006), 286–99.

8 Eva Cockcroft, "Abstract Expressionism, Weapon of the Cold War," *Artforum* 15, no. 10 (June 1974): 39–41.

9 Saarinen maintained an informal policy of hiring architects trained in other countries. Hungarian émigré and Beaux-Arts–trained architect and photographer Balthazar Korab worked for Saarinen from 1955 until 1958. He remained one of Saarinen's favorite photographers.

10 On Pope's project, see Steven McLeod Bedford, *John Russell Pope: Architect of Empire* (New York: Rizzoli, 1998), 152, 156–7.

11 Nikolaus Pevsner, *The Buildings of England: London: I The Cities of London and Westminster* (Harmondsworth, Middlesex: Penguin Books Ltd., 1957), 513–14.

12 On Saarinen's psychoanalysis in 1952–3, see Cammie McAtee, "Taking Comfort in the Age of Anxiety: Eero Saarinen's Womb Chair," in *Atomic Dwelling: Anxiety, Domesticity, and Postwar Architecture*, ed. Robin Schuldenfrei (London: Routledge, 2012), 3–25.

13 The new office building (1955–61), designed by Eric Bedford, chief architect of the Ministry of Public Building and Works, ultimately proved underwhelming.

14 Shepley quoted by Loeffler, *Architecture of Diplomacy*, 188. Murray Fraser raises the specter of Soviet activity in his discussion of the embassy's use, but he does not consider it as part of its design. Fraser, *Architecture and the "Special Relationship,"* 351.

15 A large group of Saarinen's drawings was donated to the Canadian Centre for Architecture in 2000 by David Powrie, who joined Saarinen's firm in 1955.

16 As Saarinen's former associate Cesar Pelli recalled about the embassy: "He had covered a wall with alternative designs. Some of those that he would always like to do were versions of Renaissance palaces, including lions by the entrances because they helped him to organize his mind about what was the symbolic nature of this kind of building. There were really about 30 kinds of designs but he just pondered over those. None of them ended up in his final design. But those were very critical in his exploration. He was really exploring, and the reason he had all of those alternative choices of forms was just to see which one would fit best with the problem as he understood it with his interpretation of what modern design requires, of what the nature of the project was." Eero Saarinen: Form-Giver of the "American Century" Symposium, Yale University, April 2, 2005.

17 Loeffler, *Architecture of Diplomacy*, 183–91.

18 Henry-Russell Hitchcock, "The Architecture of Bureaucracy and the Architecture of Genius," *Architectural Review* 101, no. 601 (January 1947): 3–6.

19 Barry Katz, "The Arts of War: 'Visual Presentation' and National Intelligence," *Design Issues* 12, no. 2 (Summer 1996): 3–21. More recently, Mina Marefat considered the import of Saarinen's wartime work for the OSS in her exhibition *Eero Saarinen: A Reputation for Innovation*, organized by the Finnish Embassy, Washington, DC, in 2010. Jean-Louis Cohen also briefly explored Saarinen's work for the OSS in his exhibition and book, *Architecture in Uniform: Designing and Building for the Second World War* (Montréal: Canadian Centre for Architecture, 2011), 322–3, 344, 386–8, 421.

20 Mina Marefat, "Documents Reveal Eero Saarinen's Second World War Secrets," *Architectural Review* 228, no. 1365 (November 2010): 22–4.

21 Hubert Barton, "Proposed State Department Presentation Division," February 1, 1945; cited in Katz, "The Arts of War," 12, n.25.

22 Katz, "The Arts of War," 12.

23 According to Loeffler, Saarinen received the Oslo commission in June 1955 and made his first presentation to the AAC on November 10, 1955. She notes that the project was accepted rather quickly, taking just two meetings (Saarinen made his second presentation in March 1956) to be approved. *Architecture of Diplomacy*, 191–2.

24 Saarinen, quoted in "Recent Work by Eero Saarinen," *RIBA Journal* 68, no. 1 (November 1960): 16.

25 Mumford, "False Front," 174.

26 Mumford, "False Front," 178, 184.

27 Mumford, "False Front," 185.

28 Banham, "Monument with Frills," 920.

29 Eero Saarinen, "Letter to the Editor," *New York Times*, March 6, 1960. Author's emphasis.

30 Which artist Greenberg first recognized this quality in is a matter of some dispute – he may have used it in the earlier 1940s – but he first applied it to Pollock in his review of the artist's first solo exhibition at the Betty Parsons Gallery. Greenberg, "Review of Exhibitions of Worden Day, Carl Holty, and Jackson Pollock," *The Nation*, January 24, 1948; reproduced in John O'Brian ed., Clement Greenberg: The Collected Essays and Criticism. Volume 2. Arrogant Purpose, 1945–1949 (Chicago: University of Chicago Press, 1986), 202.

31 Cockcroft, "Abstract Expressionism, Weapon of the Cold War"; reproduced in *Pollock and After: The Critical Debate*, ed. Francis Frascina (New York: Harper & Row, 1985), 128–9.

32 Kenneth Rexroth, "2 Americans Seen Abroad," *Art News* 58, no. 4 (Summer 1959): 54.

33 Jeremy Lewison, "Jackson Pollock and the Americanization of Europe," in *Jackson Pollock: New Approaches*, ed. Kirk Varnedoe and Pepe Karmel (New York: Harry N. Abrams, 1998), 228. Lewison does not consider the reaction to Pollock in the architectural world. He does, however, draw Aline Louchheim into his discussion of the reception of Pollock's work in Europe.

34 Robert Melville, "Review of the Exhibition *Opposing Forces*, ICA, January 28–February 28, 1953," *Architectural Review* 113, no. 676 (April 1953): 272.

35 Peter Smithson writing under the pseudonym Waldo Camini, "Entr'acte," *Architectural Design* 35, no. 5 (May 1965): 213.

36 In addition to an exhibition of Roszak's drawings at the Pierre Matisse Gallery, Saarinen may also have seen his entry into the international competition for a monument to "The Unknown Political Prisoner," which was on view at the Museum of Modern Art.

37 Recounted by Aline Louchheim in a letter to Ray and Charles Eames, October 4, 1953; folder 40, box 2, Aline and Eero Saarinen Papers, Archives of American Art, Smithsonian Institution.

38 I thank Amanda Millet-Sorsa for sharing her thoughts with me on the consistent theme of birds and flight in Roszak's work, among them welded steel sculptures *Flight* (1959), *Golden Hawk* (1961), and *Night Flight* (1962).

39 Aline Saarinen may have found the model for the eagle. While doing research for her book *The Proud Possessors* (1958), she spent considerable time at Shelburne Museum in Vermont, where the early American sculpture it was based on is located.

40 For a sense of the controversy sparked by the eagle, see Richard B. Morris, "Is the Eagle Un-American?" *New York Times*, February 14, 1960; "Gilded US Eagle Rides to Perch Above London Critics," *New York Times*, July 31, 1960; Toni Howard, "The Case of the Impudent Bird," *Saturday Evening Post*, September 24, 1960, 43, 46–7, 49.

41 English Heritage's justification for the preservation of these public areas made a clear contrast between them and the offices that "are (and always were) of little distinction." Citation Report, 2009.

42 Banham, "Monument with Frills," 920.

43 For a sense of the mission USIS officers felt, see Wilson P. Dizard's account, *The Strategy of Truth: The Story of the U.S. Information Service* (Washington, DC: Public Affairs Press, 1961).

44 Funding for USIS propaganda programs greatly expanded at just the moment when the new embassy was first being planned. In 1953, the London branch expanded to ninety-three staff members and controlled a huge budget ($850,000). Colman, "Portrait of an Institution," 348.

45 Wilson P. Dizard, *Inventing Public Diplomacy: The Story of the U.S. Information Agency* (Boulder, CO: Lynne Rienner Publishers, 2004), 186.

46 Memo from Earnest J. Warlow, FBO Regional Director, to William P. Hughes, FBO Director, March 28, 1956. Box 1, Jack M. Goldman Collection, Cranbrook Archives.

47 Saarinen memo to Glen Paulsen and Bob Burley, n.d., Goldman Collection.

48 Letter from Saarinen to E. J. Warlow, Cyril Mardall, and Henry Lawrence, September 21, 1956, p. 2; Goldman Collection.

49 Saarinen summarized his discussions with McCandless about the lighting of the public spaces on the lower floors, which were carefully conceived to avoid the "gloomy basement" effect, and those on the main floor, specifically the consular areas and USIS exhibition area, in detail in a letter to Glen Paulsen and Jack Goldman, who were working on site in London. Though the letter is undated, it was written as working drawings were in production in 1957. Saarinen to Paulsen and Goldman, n.d.; Goldman Collection.

50 On the libraries, see Dizard, *Inventing Public Diplomacy*, 179 ff.

51 Laura A. Belmonte, *Selling the American Way: U.S. Propaganda and the Cold War* (Philadelphia: University of Pennsylvania Press, 2008), 129.

52 Saarinen internal ESA memo, March 26, 1957; Goldman Collection. Lipton would later design a pair of sculptures for Saarinen's IBM Research Center (1957–61). Fredericks was a former student of Saarinen's mentor Carl Milles.

53 Saarinen memo, March 26, 1957.

54 Saarinen to Warlow, Mardall, and Lawrence, September 21, 1956, p. 3.

All-over inside-out: US Embassy in London 177

55 As Loeffler documented, the FBO first specified Knoll furniture for the US Chancery in Brussels, designed by Alan Jacobs (1948–50). *Architecture of Diplomacy*, 66.

56 Anita Möller (later Laird), chief interior decorator for the FBO from 1948 until the early 1970s, was in charge of furnishing all US embassies and foreign buildings. Responsible for buying and contracting as well as interior design, she had an increasingly strong role in the selection of furniture for the embassies as the 1950s progressed and Congress took a firmer line on the FBO building program. On Möller, see Joan McHale, "The Embassy Look," *Women's Wear Daily*, June 14, 1961; and on Möller and the New Delhi embassy, see "American Embassies Around the World," *Interior Design*, 29, no. 8 (August 1958): 62–4, 75. On Jules Wabbes's contributions to the diffusion of Dunbar furniture in Europe, see Fredie Floré, "Diplomatic Encounters: Jules Wabbes and the Production of American Dunbar Furniture in Brussels," in *Tradition, Transition, Trajectories: Major or Minor Influences?* ed. Helena Barbosa and Anna Calvera (Aveiro: UA Editora, University of Aveiro, 2014), 335–40.

57 This policy change was noted by McHale in "Embassy Look." The source for the Dunbar furniture in the London embassy is unclear.

58 Slides of the furniture prototypes and furniture as manufactured are held in the Eero Saarinen Collection, Manuscripts and Archives, Sterling Library, Yale University. It is unknown if the custom furniture was produced in the United States or the United Kingdom. If the latter, it could have been manufactured by International Interiors, a subsidiary of the Letchworth furniture maker D. Meredew Ltd, which held the British license to produce Knoll designs. The close relationship between the embassy's glass-topped tables and Mies van der Rohe's Barcelona table, which Meredew produced, might support this identification. According to Rosamond Allwood, Meredew received the British license to produce Knoll furniture in the late 1950s. Unable to use the Knoll name due to a successful name infringement suit brought by British furniture manufacturer Parker Knoll, Meredew established its Knoll subsidiary as Interiors International. A Knoll showroom opened in Bedford Square in 1959, later moving to a street near Tottenham Court Road, where a Knoll Planning Unit was also established. Knoll furniture was produced in one of Meredew's factories in Letchworth until the mid-1960s, when the British company lost its Knoll license. Allwood attributes this loss to changes in Knoll's direction when the company was sold in 1967. Rosamond Allwood, "Meredew of Letchworth: A Brief History," *Furniture History* 33 (1997): 308–9.

59 Mumford, "False Front," 180.

60 Communicated in the memo from Warlow to Hughes, March 28, 1956.

61 These cruciform supports were introduced to the Herman Miller plastic chair series in 1956, when the Eameses brought out their lounge chair and ottoman. On the chairs, see John Neuhart, Marilyn Neuhart, and Ray Eames, *Eames Design: The Work of the Office of Charles and Ray Eames* (New York: H. N. Abrams, Inc., 1989), 139–43, 206–7, 209. For a view of a molded chair similar to the embassy model, see 253.

62 The chairs are described in drawings dated August 1959. Saarinen Collection.

63 While cost may have been a factor (Herman Miller's molded plastic chairs were much less expensive than Knoll's pedestal series), the Eames chairs were then only manufactured in the United States. By the mid-1960s, however, D. Meredew Ltd was marketing Herman Miller furniture in the United Kingdom. "News: An International Event," *Design* 224 (August 1967): 61.

64 *Facts about the American National Exhibition in Moscow* (January 1959), 2–3, cited by Hélène Lipstadt, "'Natural Overlap': Charles and Ray Eames and the Federal Government," in *The Work of Charles and Ray Eames: A Legacy of Invention*, ed. Donald Albrecht (New York: H. N. Abrams, Inc., 1997), 160, 175 n.31.

65 The London weekly *The Tatler & Bystander* reported on the inaugural exhibition. See Alan Vines' photographic essay, "Grosvenor Square West," *Tatler & Bystander*, December 14, 1960, 647–50. See especially Vines's photograph of Stephen Munsing, the USIS cultural affairs officer, and an assistant hanging the Pollock painting (649). This exhibition was followed by several others on Abstract Expressionism, including *Vanguard American* Painting, 1962, which included the work of Pollock, Mark Rothko, Jasper Johns, and Robert Rauschenberg and traversed the public spaces of the embassy; *Rauschenberg: Illustrations*

178   *Cammie McAtee*

for Dante's Inferno, 1964; *Jasper Johns: Lithographs*, 1964–5. On these three exhibitions, see Frank G. Spicer III, "'Just What Was It That Made U.S. Art So Different, So Appealing?' Case Studies of the Critical Receptions of American Avant-Garde Painting in London, 1950–1964" (PhD diss., Case Western Reserve University, 2009).

66 David Bruce, diary entry, March 9, 1961, in *Ambassador to Sixties London: The Diaries of David Bruce, 1961–1969*, ed. Raj Roy and John W. Young (Dordrecht: Republic of Letters Publishing, 2009), 2.

67 John Young, *David Bruce and Diplomatic Practice: An American Ambassador in London, 1961–9* (London: Bloomsbury, 2014), 18.

68 This figure was cited by Ray Vickers, "Uncle Sam Abroad: US Embassy in Britain Illustrates Complexity of Modern Design," *Wall Street Journal*, November 30, 1964. I am grateful to Brook Bender, reference librarian at the State Department, and an anonymous specialist on visas for information on UK visa applications in the 1950s and 1960s.

10 Designed diplomacy

Furniture, furnishing and art in Australian embassies for Washington, DC, and Paris

Philip Goad

In 1969, the Commonwealth Government of Australia completed construction of its first high-profile, purpose-built embassy since the opening of Australia House in London in 1918.[1] Designed by Melbourne-based firm Bates, Smart & McCutcheon, the Australian Chancery (1964–9) in Washington, DC, represented a defining moment in Australian diplomacy. It was the physical confirmation of a relationship that had been building since 1942 when the United States of America entered World War II and Australia's ties with Great Britain began to inexorably wane. The defeat of the Japanese, Australia's ready engagement in the Korean conflict from 1950, the emergence of the Cold War and the threat of communism posed from Asia meant that Australia's position in the world politically and to a significant degree economically, was, by the mid-1960s, defined by its relationship to America.

In the midst of the nation's most intense involvement in Cold War politics, questions of nationalism and internationalism were intrinsic to projections of cultural identity and its malleable connection to international politics. Under the leadership of conservative Liberal Prime Minister Robert Menzies, Australia had escalated its involvement in the Vietnam War from 1962 and famously from mid-1966 went "all the way with LBJ."[2] However, by the early 1970s, Australia's desire to champion trade through agriculture and mining, and to engage in an internationalist, nonaligned position within Europe was clear. In 1972, when Sydney architect Harry Seidler was commissioned by William McMahon's Liberal government to design the Australian Embassy in Paris, it was the sole European embassy amongst six diplomatic projects Parliament formally announced in 1973. All others were planned for construction in Asia.[3] Design – through architecture, furniture and art – in Washington and Paris was implicated in this shifting diplomatic strategy.

Australian diplomacy and design

Australia constructed its very first embassy between 1913 and 1918. On a landmark site on the Strand, Australia House, designed by Scottish architects Alexander Marshall Mackenzie & Son, was the oldest purpose-built chancery of any foreign mission in London. It was a suitably pompous example of Edwardian Baroque: Australia symbolized as a faithful and prosperous servant of empire. The building displayed its nationality through materials: externally, with a base of Australian trachyte and internally, with marbles from the states of Victoria, New South Wales and South Australia, and joinery, panelling and flooring featuring timbers from all Australian states, especially black bean. It also had an exhibition hall, a space that would appear in all subsequent purpose-built Australian missions, based on the assumption that

180 *Philip Goad*

there was a need to explain the nation through collections of art and furniture and occasional display rather than through permanent symbols.

Despite such a grand entrée into the world of diplomatic architecture, for the next fifty years, Australian missions occupied existing buildings. There appeared to be no need, apart from the hoisting of the Australian flag, to assert identity through any specially commissioned architecture.[4] Furniture, interior design and art, as executed through buildings for diplomacy, were thus necessarily limited in their potential as part of an overall ensemble bespeaking the nation abroad. The only other avenue where they might perform some form of diplomatic role for Australia was through trade and the exposition pavilion.

At the Paris International Exposition (1937) and the New York World's Fair (1939) in each Australian pavilion's travel section, a table and set of cantilevered tubular steel chairs were faced in different Australian timber veneers.[5] The chairs, based on Marcel Breuer and Mart Stam's tubular steel chair designs (1925), had been produced in Australia since 1931 by Healings, the retail arm of A.G. Healing, a Melbourne bicycle manufacturer and radio dealer.[6] By 1938, three other companies in Melbourne had begun producing tubular steel furniture.[7] In addition to this evidence of being up to date with overseas trends in modern furniture, the pavilions' exhibits relied, for the most part, on large-scale photographic images of Australian landscape, flora and fauna, agriculture and industry, all set within modernist interiors that reflected the exhibits artists' expertise in commercial art and the architects' expertise in hospital design rather than any specific national style.[8]

An exception was the Australian Pavilion at Expo 67 in Montréal, where exhibits architect Robin Boyd (1919–71) designed the interior as a giant living room (see Plate 14). Against a backdrop of white shag-pile carpet and James Mccormick's air-conditioned, serviced and structural Nervi-inspired 'trees' faced in Tasmanian blackwood, visitors could sit on stereophonic 'talking chairs' designed by Melbourne-based Grant Featherston and browse through books placed on coffee tables. Close at hand were 'hostesses' dressed in hot orange and olive green outfits. In Montréal, national character was portrayed explicitly as relaxed and informal, read through not just the exhibits, but also through interior design: 'national' colours that combined 'Eucalyptus' (charcoal green), 'Desert' (a golden orange), wool (a thick off-white carpet that crossed the entire pavilion floor and swept up the angled side walls) and aluminium (natural anodized). Boyd's use of natural materials, his free arrangement of Featherston's iconic chairs and even a rear Australian native garden with live kangaroos provided a modernist vernacular that was both casual and urbane.[9] The interior's politics-free and trade-focussed message was simple: everything on show was Australian-made.

Australian-made

The question of locally designed and manufactured furniture was a preoccupation of the immediate post-war years in Australia. Modernist furniture designers from the late 1920s and 1930s like Fred Ward (1900–90) were joined by émigré designers and cabinetmakers such as Schulim Krimper (1893–1971), Paul Kafka (1907–72) and Fred Lowen (1919–2005), and a new generation of locally born and trained designers like Grant Featherston (1922–95) and Clement Meadmore (1929–2005), and English-born, New Zealand-raised and self-taught designer Douglas Snelling

Designed diplomacy: Australian embassies   181

(1916–85). Different from the French and American influences on the ground-breaking modernist furniture designs seen at Sydney's Burdekin House Exhibition in 1929,[10] Australian furniture of the 1940s had a new focus: the soft textures and naturalistic lines of Scandinavian designs by Bruno Mathsson and Hans Wegner, and the designs emanating from the wartime experiences of Americans like Danish-born Jens Risom, Ralph Rapson (both designing for Knoll from 1945) and Charles Eames (designing for Herman Miller from 1946). The American designs were heavily advertised in John Entenza's Los Angeles-based journal, *Arts and Architecture*, and local interest was so strong that in 1952, young architect Peter Burns established an Australian version of the journal, *Architecture and Arts*, which promoted similar themes of contemporary architecture, furniture design and sometimes art.[11]

A key figure who promoted the latest American modern furniture in Australia was Viennese-born émigré architect Harry Seidler (1923–2006). After graduating from Harvard and studying under Josef Albers at Black Mountain College (June–August 1946), Seidler worked in New York for Marcel Breuer and painted the walls of his Riverside Drive apartment as if a De Stijl composition using black and yellow lines.[12] Inspired by Piet Mondrian and Theo Van Doesburg's 'space constructions', he wanted to create three-dimensional sculptural tableaus within his interiors. It would become a lifelong commitment.

Seidler arrived in Australia in 1948 to oversee the completion of a house he had designed for his parents at Wahroonga, north of Sydney. He brought with him various pieces of modernist furniture that he used to furnish his one-room Point Piper studio: two plywood and steel chairs by Charles Eames (1945), a Womb chair (1946–8) by Eero Saarinen, a tubular aluminium BARWA lounge chair (1947)[13] and desk and wall lamps (ca. 1946) by the General Lighting Company (GLC). He complemented these international pieces with a Hardoy Butterfly chair (1938; produced by Knoll since 1947),[14] also purchased from Knoll's first New York showroom at 601 Madison Avenue, as well as built-in pieces of his own design (a white Mondrian-style bookcase and black suspended cabinet) and fabricated by Viennese émigré furniture maker Paul Kafka.

In October 1949, Seidler published the article "Painting Toward Architecture."[15] It was a concise statement of his aesthetic philosophy of architecture as three-dimensional non-representational sculpture, where compositional tactics of transparency and opposition, dematerialization of space and mass, simultaneity, polarity and counterpoint were rigorously followed, just as an artist might. Significantly, *Painting Toward Architecture* had been the title of Henry-Russell Hitchcock's 1947–8 exhibition at the Wadsworth Atheneum (which travelled to twenty-four venues) and also its 1948 catalogue.[16] An image accompanying Seidler's article was Van Doesburg's *Space-time construction #3* (1923), which he had seen at the exhibition's showing at New York's Museum of Modern Art and was then owned by Miller Company President G. Burton Tremaine and his wife, Emily Hall Tremaine.[17] It would become influential to Seidler's design practice and also his favourite artwork.[18] It would also find special echo three decades later, reinterpreted in the ground floor public exhibition space of the Australian Embassy in Paris.

Even at this early stage of his career, Seidler's preference was to use chair designs by others. Unlike his mentor Breuer, Seidler did not consider himself a chair designer. As his wife, Penelope Seidler, has observed: "He did not ever design a chair, he thought other designers were so much better than he could ever do."[19] Seidler preferred instead

182   *Philip Goad*

to design fixed pieces like floating cabinets or free-standing tables and then specify iconic designer furniture pieces as timeless sculptural counterpoints to his own, more architectural "space-time constructions."

On its completion in 1950, the Seidler House was a revelation for Australian architecture culture, not just for its assured American East Coast modern vocabulary, but also for its furniture and fittings. These included a mixture of fixed and moveable pieces of his own design (again fabricated by Kafka) and significantly, pieces specially bought and imported from Knoll in New York, including Saarinen's Womb chair, two Saarinen Grasshopper chairs (1946), twenty Eames dining and lounge plywood and steel chairs, four steel-frame Hardoy Butterfly chairs, four types of spun aluminium spotlights and a twelve-person dinner, tea and coffee and cutlery set (1946–8) by Russel Wright.[20]

The Seidler House, along with Seidler's Waks House, Northbridge, New South Wales (1949–50), was beautifully photographed and published in the US journal *Interiors*, where both houses were described in condescending fashion by Jane Fiske as "undisguised progeny of an idiom personalized by Marcel Breuer."[21] Fiske concluded:

> But is that style really International enough to survive – without a certain amount of mediation and mutation – another transplantation to the crust of a large sandy pie in the Pacific? In Mr. Seidler's interiors (which look as newly-Knolled as any we've seen) everything but the persistent invasion of native vegetation insinuates that this could be New Canaan, which is in Connecticut, USA.[22]

Fiske misunderstood Seidler's intention as others would do subsequently and over the ensuing decades.[23] Seidler firmly believed in the internationalism of his aesthetic and its geographic universality. Furniture along with architecture and art was part of that universality. It was to be timeless, modern and, like a global citizen, able to cross continental borders. Conservation architect Peter Emmett summarized this position succinctly when he observed that Seidler "saw 'the modern' not as American or German but as synonymous with 'civilization' and urban reconstruction in the post-war world."[24]

In all of Seidler's subsequent houses and into the 1960s and 1970s with his commercial office buildings, he would, where possible and where clients could afford it, specify furniture from Knoll and Herman Miller, or at the very least try to source good copies. This was not always easy. As Kirsty Grant notes, the duties on importing goods to Australia in the late 1940s and 1950s were extremely high.[25] Thus Seidler's importation of furniture directly from Knoll Associates in New York in 1948 was unusual and made even more so by the frequent appearance of these iconic pieces of furniture in all publications of his work, especially *Houses, Interiors, Projects*, the 1954 monograph he published on his work after just six years of Australian practice.[26] There was a reason for this: Seidler had special access to locally produced versions of the international designs. Before 1951, he sourced them from former employee architect Peter Makeig, who, Grant points out, "reproduced by hand versions of the internationally designed chairs" that Seidler had shipped out from New York for his parents' house.[27] After 1951, Makeig began mass-producing Eames chairs (described as Plyform chairs), Hardoy chairs (described as Hammock chairs) and Saarinen's Grasshopper chair (described as the Contour or the Descon Easy chair) at Descon Laminates, the company factory that he had established in the northern Sydney suburb of Brookvale. Each piece was given a new name because as mass-produced items, each was not covered by copyright law – so long as Makeig

Designed diplomacy: Australian embassies 183

didn't use the original designer's name as a point of sale. In 1952, *Australian Home Beautiful* cited Seidler as "Consulting Architect"[28] for Descon Laminates, which operated successfully until 1962, by which time the first locally made pieces from Knoll International (Saarinen, Risom and Bertoia) and Herman Miller (Eames) were being made under licence by the Melbourne furniture manufacturer William Latchford & Sons.[29] Earlier, however, in Brisbane, Queensland, furniture maker Laurie West had held the exclusive Australian license with Knoll since 1956, only to be given up when the strict import licences introduced by government were lifted in 1960.[30] West lost his exclusive licence, and by 1963 his store and business in Wickham Street, The Valley in Brisbane, had closed.

In the late 1950s, Harry Seidler had been a customer at West's[31] mainly for domestic clients but, in the early 1960s, with the ability now to import directly from Knoll, he turned his attention to the office interior. With his largest commission about to be completed – the fifty-storey Australia Square (1960–7) in Sydney, then Australia's tallest office building – Seidler ensured that any interior photographs included pieces from the Knoll range, including Charles Pollock office chairs, Max Pearson executive chairs and Florence Knoll marble coffee tables. Included too were exemplary international artworks by Le Corbusier, Victor Vasarely, Norman Carlberg and Alexander Calder, which adorned public foyers, the top office floor and the George Street plaza.

Seidler's furniture choices at Australia Square had made the fundamental step from domestic interior to office workspace. In this he followed the design choices of Charles Eames and Florence Knoll after him, who, as Penny Sparke has observed:

> understood the level of interchangeability that was possible between the domestic interior and the workspace. Working with "classic" furniture items developed by Mies van der Rohe and others, she developed a new aesthetic for corporate America in the 1950s and 1960s which was based on a simple interior language made up of classic chairs, a coffee table and plants and other appropriate decorative items.[32]

It was a design palette that would find suitability across the world in corporate office foyers. But it was also eminently suited to the spaces of diplomacy where the subtle suggestion of domesticity imparted understatement and invitation, a form of humane and not overbearing efficiency. It was a palette that spoke across international borders. At the same time, underlining it all was the undisputed market presence of Knoll, whose assured aesthetic guaranteed a new form of classic interior design that was modern and driven largely from America.

While Seidler made the shift from the domestic to commercial interior with relative ease in 1967, other Australian firms had been active in corporate office interior design since the mid-1950s. At the forefront was Melbourne architectural firm Bates, Smart & McCutcheon (BSM), a national leader in glazed curtain walled skyscraper design and in effect Australia's version of Skidmore, Owings & Merrill (SOM). From 1965, BSM became architects in association with SOM's San Francisco office in the documentation of the Chuck Bassett-designed AMP Square/St James Building, Melbourne (1963–9). BSM staff members worked in San Francisco on structural and services engineering aspects of the project, and Harold Strachan (head of BSM's interiors section since 1950) visited to collaborate with SOM

184 *Philip Goad*

interiors expert Margot Grant. American expertise in corporate interior design was openly embraced and emulated. In architecture as in politics, it was "all the way with LBJ."

Australian Chancery, Washington

In 1964, BSM was appointed to design the Australian Embassy's new chancery in Washington, DC, by Australia's Department of External Affairs.[33] This was an unusually high honour: the first purpose-built Australian embassy building in more than fifty years. Despite BSM's small number of government commissions in Canberra, there is little doubt that existing connections with SOM played in its favour. Located on an excellent site on Scott Circle and Massachusetts Avenue, the chancery's design was led by Osborn McCutcheon (1899–1983) and Hugh Banahan (1920–93), and governed by a strict brief that required fall-out shelters and high security, height restrictions that protected views of the Capitol and contextual respect for the city's dominant architectural style, Beaux-Arts Classicism. Clad in off-white Tennessee marble with bronze-tinted glass in bronze anodized frames, the chancery was an abstract palazzo, an elegant seven-level classical cage with a ground-floor, giant-order colonnade indicating public areas on the two lower floors, and a mid-level loggia indicating ambassadorial and diplomatic suites on the fourth floor. It echoed not just the marble-faced monumentality of pre-war Italian Rationalism, but also the subdued Classical Modernism of the late 1950s US embassy building program described by Jane Loeffler[34] that admitted precious material facing and the judicious inclusion of national regalia, in this case, a bronze coat of arms by Sydney artist Tom Bass (1916–2010).

The Australian Chancery could also be seen as an example of US "Good Neighbour Policy" but in reverse. Instead of the United States being the 'good neighbour' as it had been in 1930s Latin America, it was Australia in the 1960s which chose diplomatically (and through necessity) to follow Washington's aesthetic 'rules,' leaving the ground- and first-floor interiors to be expressions of national identity. They were conceived as public floors, as if the nation was on show. Identity and sophistication were imparted through furniture and finishes, art and temporary exhibitions. If externally, the building was suitably diplomatic, almost neutral in language, internally the nation was promoted through using specifically Australian materials, both natural and manufactured. This had been a long-tried strategy of Australian architecture and design abroad, especially at expositions since the mid-1930s, when Australia's presence architecturally in the form of temporary pavilions was deliberately modernist as a statement of independence from the cloying ties of empire. Internally, the contents of these pavilions were, by contrast, conscientiously 'Australian,' presenting 'unique' aspects of the country's attributes and characteristics.

In Washington, the chancery's ground level was floored in Australian walnut from Queensland. Carpets and curtains were made in Australia with substantial wool input and advice from the Australian Wool Board.[35] The focus of the double-height reception hall was an almost square panel of white Australian marble and an encircling upper wall of Western Australian wandoo timber lining. Above, a completely illuminated ceiling matched a vast white woollen rug below: the impression was of a light-filled atrium of a modern palazzo. A dramatic feature of the double-height foyer with its spiral stair and coffered ceiling were two large fourteen-foot square blue kangaroo skin rugs, which, according to the official brochure printed for the building's opening,

Figure 10.1 Entry foyer showing Steelcase swivel chairs on blue kangaroo skin rug and aluminium screen (left) by Vincas Jomantas, Australian Chancery, Washington, DC, 1969. Bates, Smart & McCutcheon, architects (1964–9). Australian News and Information Bureau, photographer. Image No. A1200, L82324 (Barcode 11664468), National Archives of Australia.

gave "a strong Australian flavour to this area" (see Figure 10.1).[36] The chairs placed on these rugs were US-made Steelcase leather swivel chairs, copies of the famous Pollock office chair. A further counterpoint was the sculptural screen of densely packed aluminium tubes separating the lobby from the main reception hall: a large-scale version of the maquette designed by émigré Lithuanian sculptor Vincent (Vincas) Jomantas (1922–2001), which in 1968 had won the inaugural Comalco Invitation Award for Sculpture in Aluminium in Australia. The fact that aluminium was being celebrated was not without some point. By the early 1960s, bauxite was being mined in Western Australia by Alcoa and in far north Queensland by Comalco, and its export to the United States accounted for huge export dollars for Australia as well as massive investment in mining and smelting infrastructure in Western Australia, Queensland and Victoria by the mid-1960s. Visible directly on entry to the chancery foyer, it was a financial handshake, a symbol of shared interests in vast capital investment of serious material interest to both countries rather than any marker of national symbolism.

An extensive collection of contemporary Australian art was selected for the chancery by a committee led by painter William Dargie (1912–2003), chair of the

Commonwealth Art Advisory Board (1969–73), and four architects from BSM (Sir Osborn McCutcheon, Hugh Banahan, John Hitch and Robert Bruce). Dargie, famous for his traditional portraiture, was the favoured artist of former Prime Minister Robert Menzies, whose antagonism toward modern art was well known. However the committee's subsequent choices reflected broad acceptance of contemporary Australian art, though all works were figurative in nature.[37] Significantly there was no presence of works by indigenous Australian artists. All paintings and prints were reserved for the ambassadorial suites, significant corridors and waiting areas of various diplomatic sections. With the exception of the Jomantas screen, this left the public floor at the ground level entirely free of fixed artworks.

When the Australian Chancery officially opened on June 20, 1969, there was an accompanying exhibition installed to the design of Robin Boyd and located in the ground floor gallery space. A year after Expo 67, Boyd had designed for the Industrial Design Council of Australia *The First Two Hundred Years* exhibition at Seidler's Australia Square in Sydney, where visitors moved between twenty cylinders suspended from Pier Luigi Nervi's isostatic coffered ceiling.[38] In Washington, he conceived an exhibition about contemporary Australia, also a series of cylinders but now six clear acrylic vertical posts enclosing vertical photographic poles contained within a passage of multiple curving screens (see Figure 10.2). Perhaps unconsciously so, it was like

Figure 10.2 Opening exhibition, Australian Chancery, Washington, DC, 1969. Robin Boyd (Romberg & Boyd), exhibit designer. Australian News and Information Bureau, photographer. Image No. A1200, L82239 (Barcode 11664394), National Archives of Australia.

a series of indigenous Australian burial poles.[39] Separating the exhibition from the chancery's reception hall was a line of eleven Featherston-designed Expo 67 Talking chairs specially shipped across for the opening.[40]

The new Australian Chancery represented the typical split of an external architecture of international diplomacy matched with national content internally that, by and large, was intended to be inclusive and serve many goals. Yet, as a complete work, it was without aesthetic assurance. While the architecture, furniture, furnishings and art were by Australian standards high, the underlying and none too subtle message was trade rather than a propagation of Australian cultural identity. While each component was in of itself worthy of inclusion in an ambassadorial role for Australia, as a curatorial project, the longevity of the 1969 ensemble depended heavily on the ongoing currency of the works of art, furniture and finishes, and the strength of each occasional exhibition that followed.

Australian Embassy, Paris

In 1973 when the Australian Parliament announced that six new embassies were being constructed in Asia, it was symbolic of newly found political confidence in being a player in the Asia-Pacific region. But Australia's growing diplomatic presence in Southeast Asia had not sprung up overnight. Prime Minister Harold Holt had been instrumental in shifting attention to Asia during his brief tenure as prime minister (1966–7), not just to assuage Cold War fears and complement American presence in the region, but also for the purposes of trade and to shift focus away from economic reliance on the British Commonwealth. By 1967, for example, Japan had replaced the United Kingdom as the largest market for Australian exports. Thus the decision to build an embassy in Paris just four years later was significant and not uncontroversial.

In 1971, during the tenure of the Liberal federal government under Prime Minister William McMahon, it was decided that two new buildings were required in Paris, one for the Australian Chancery, Australian missions to the OECD (the United Nations Organization for Economic Co-operation and Development) and UNESCO, and an ambassador's residence, the other to contain thirty-four apartments for diplomats and their families with a second ambassador occupying the top-floor apartment. Rights to purchase a site on Quai Branly, close to the River Seine and the Eiffel Tower, were secured by Alan Renouf, then Australia's ambassador to France. By September 1972, Seidler had been commissioned by the Liberal government to design the new Paris embassy, an appointment that raised eyebrows given that Seidler's wife, Penelope, was a member of the Evatt family, scions of the intellectual left and prominent in politics and the law. Seidler believed and claimed that recommendation for the commission came via John Overall, recent chairman of the National Capital Development Commission (NCDC) in Canberra.[41] It was not a political appointment. Then on December 2, 1972, the Australian Labour Party swept to power in Australia and three days later Gough Whitlam was sworn in as prime minister.

For the new Whitlam Labour government, intent on national reform across health and education, there was also a desire to reform its tactics of diplomacy. While in opposition, the charismatic Whitlam had stunned Australians and the incumbent Liberal government by travelling to the People's Republic of China and meeting with Premier Zhou Enlai in Beijing in July 1971. This was just days before US National Security Adviser Henry Kissinger had made his famous reconnaissance trip to China,

188   *Philip Goad*

paving the way for US President Richard Nixon to meet Chairman Mao Zedong in Beijing in 1972. The Chinese were impressed by Whitlam, and almost overnight he became an international statesman. Just three days after coming to power, Whitlam instructed Ambassador Renouf to open negotiations with his Chinese counterpart Huang Chen. It was Whitlam's top foreign affairs priority, along with the withdrawal of troops from Vietnam. On December 21, 1972, Renouf and Chen signed a joint communiqué on behalf of both countries, agreeing to establish formal diplomatic relations. Australia's Cold War policy was now potentially obsolete. It was an historic moment and it took place in Paris at what was then the official Australian residence on rue Lacaze.[42]

In many respects, therefore, the new Australian Embassy in Paris promised to be a special form of neutral meeting ground between Australia and China, to build new political and trade links that were to reap huge rewards for Australia in the short and long term. For the Whitlam government, therefore the design of the Paris embassy was important: it marked a new position for Australia, at arm's length from the United States and confidently international in outlook and behaviour. In early 1973, Seidler showed Minister for Overseas Trade Dr Jim Cairns and Minister for Urban and Regional Development Tom Uren his Trade Group Offices in Barton, Canberra (1970–4), which were nearing completion. They were suitably impressed, strengthening Seidler's endorsement as architect for the Paris embassy.[43]

Wanting to associate with a local practice in France, Seidler chose to work with US émigré architect, ex-Bauhaus master and his former employer Marcel Breuer, who had designed the UNESCO Building in Paris (1953–8) and had an office there.[44] Seidler also chose to collaborate with brilliant Italian engineer Pier Luigi Nervi, with whom he had worked on Australia Square and was again working with on the MLC Tower, Sydney (1972–5). Nervi had worked with Breuer on the UNESCO commission. Hence in Paris, it was a strong design team with a distinguished history of collaboration.

Seidler's desire to work with Breuer was important. There was prestige in the association. He knew well the curved arms of Breuer's Y-shaped UNESCO headquarters – he visited the site with Breuer in 1955 and again in 1960.[45] Also, given the comparable scale and function, there is little doubt that Seidler would also have been familiar with the sweeping curve of Breuer's headquarters building for the US Department of Housing and Urban Development in Washington, DC (1963–8).[46] For Seidler, Washington and Paris therefore had excellent precedents for uncompromising modern architecture within carefully controlled urban settings. There also was the added advantage that Breuer had a Paris office.

Australia was to be perceived as a model modern *citoyen du monde* – citizen of the world. Described by architecture critic Deyan Sudjic as an "elegant iceberg design",[47] Seidler's double crescent forms were brought into dialogue with the curving forms of the Champ de Mars. The chancery bulged towards the Eiffel Tower with the ambassador's apartment on the top having panoramic views from a rooftop terrace. A centrally located salon and dining room opened onto this terrace as well as an internal roof garden. At ground level, Nervi's structural concrete legs formed a porte-cochere and, by chance, appeared to denote a giant 'A' for Australia, though this was never the intention (see Figure 10.3). Inside, the main public areas were located at the entrance level: reception, an exhibition area leading to a multi-purpose space for functions, a 150-seat theatrette, and the Australian Information Service. The second nine-storey crescent housed the staff apartments, all the living spaces curving away from the street with views to the Eiffel Tower.

Designed diplomacy: Australian embassies 189

Figure 10.3 Australian Embassy, Paris, France, 1978. Harry Seidler & Associates, architects (1973–7). Max Dupain, photographer. © Penelope Seidler. Eric Sierins Photography.

For the interiors, Seidler was not overly interested in displaying Australian materials or the work of Australian furniture designers. In fact, there was no official requirement to do so. Indeed, for reasons of cost, it was more expedient and more economical to commission and purchase from within Europe. Unlike the Washington chancery where there had been a focus on displaying Australia through the physical fabric of the interior, art and the building's furnishings, in Paris, Seidler was keen to internally show Australia as a *citoyen du monde* whose tastes were impeccable and modern. He intended to specify the best international furniture available set within spaces that continued his long-held interests in visual polarity, counterpoint and capturing distant

190   *Philip Goad*

views as part of an overall visual field. The only overtly Australian content admitted would be in the selection of art (which would ultimately prove controversial) and in his aesthetic conception of the typical Australian habit of the exhibition hall, and in the content of its opening exhibition. Seidler did, however, use noted Australian landscape architect Bruce McKenzie to design the building's landscaping, and at one point, he suggested to McKenzie that 'snow gums' be considered for the upper-level courtyards.[48] McKenzie, however, chose not to specify Australian plants and trees, instead selecting other European and Asian varieties of plants according to the rigours of a northern climate.[49]

Seidler travelled widely in Europe to research furniture, finishes and light fittings, their costs and manufacturers' ability to supply. In January–February 1976, with office employee Peter Hirst, he made trips to the German factory of ERCO light fittings in Ludenscheid and the International Furniture Fair in Cologne.[50] Seidler used Washington-based lighting consultant Claude R. Engle to give advice on lighting the embassy's artworks and the building's exterior. Seidler wanted it to be a Parisian showpiece for Australian modernity and political maturity. He even included pictures he had taken of I.M. Pei's Everson Museum in Syracuse, New York (1965–8) as a suggestion for lighting the embassy's car ramp.[51] In Paris, furniture suppliers such as Knoll International France, IMMOB, INT, Flos, Artifort, amongst others were visited and a budget submission incorporating all findings was compiled. Then in June, Seidler proposed to the Australian government, on Breuer's suggestion,[52] that he appoint a consultant for the embassy interiors, the interior designer Charles Sévigny, who would later be described in Australia in 1980 as "the world's most exotic and flamboyant decorator."[53] Sévigny's role was to assist with suggestions for colour schemes, fabrics and furnishings. For Seidler, dealing with bureaucratic clients, this was a shrewd move. Sévigny, who had previously worked for the Foreign Buildings Operations of the US State Department, and had a close connection to Knoll International through his partner Yves Vidal, who was the former director of the French subsidiary of the company, was well placed to assist Seidler.

It was little surprise then that the final furniture choices presented to the Department of Foreign Affairs would be sourced mainly from Knoll. Indeed Seidler's spiral-bound report of April 1976 contained several pages of the Knoll International brochure from the Paris showrooms at 268, boulevard Saint Germain and 9, rue du Faubourg St-Honoré pasted directly in.[54] Knoll's Stephens system (for desks, cabinets and workstations) and chairs designed by Marcel Breuer, Charles Pollock, Morrison & Hannah and Max Pearson were recommended for the general office floors. For the ambassador's offices and apartment, the range was expanded to include Otto Zapf office chairs (1975), black aluminium wastepaper bins, black marble ashtrays and flowerpots, all sourced from Knoll. Important, in the ambassador's dining room, Mies van der Rohe leather cantilevered Brno dining chairs (1929) were specified. For the ambassador's salon, there were leather couches and black granite coffee tables, as well as S35 tubular steel armchairs (1930) by Marcel Breuer and a series of Breuer-designed Laccio coffee tables (see Figure 10.4 and Plate 15). For the apartments, Seidler added Breuer's Cesca tubular steel dining chairs with rattan seats and the occasional Eames plywood and leather armchair. Included in the April 1976 report, there were also photographs of furniture used in a real-life setting, most notably, Harry and Penelope Seidler's own home at Killara (1967) in suburban Sydney. Photographs of the Seidlers' Le Corbusier chaise, Breuer Wassily chairs, Saarinen tulip desk chair, round black granite coffee

Figure 10.4 Salon of the Ambassador's apartment, Australian Embassy, Paris, 1978. S35 tubular steel armchairs by Marcel Breuer. Artworks: (left, part obscured) David Aspden, *Free form Red* (1976); (right, near fireplace) Gunter Christmann, *Brightscape* (1972). Max Dupain, photographer. Harry Seidler & Associates, architects (1973–7). © Penelope Seidler. Eric Sierins Photography.

table, wall-hung telephone table, silk curtains and fake fur throw rugs were used as examples. It was clear that Seidler believed that his own domestic setting was equal to and ideal for the domestic setting of an Australian embassy. Seidler had also taken advantage of Knoll's acquisition of Gavina SpA in 1968, specifically to include all the Breuer-designed pieces which until that time had not been part of the Knoll range, namely the Laccio table (1924), Wassily chair (1925) and Cesca chair (1928) – all pieces with a Bauhaus heritage.[55] Just four years before in January–March 1972, there had been the sensational Lella and Massimo Vignelli–designed exhibition *Knoll au Louvre*, a retrospective of Knoll held at the Museum of Decorative Arts. Seidler's choice to use Knoll in Paris thus made the Australian embassy appear utterly contemporary and aligned the nation with indisputable artistic pedigree in terms of interior design. As finally realized, in the ambassador's offices, Seidler's overall vision was largely carried through. Walls were covered in tufted wool and adorned with a single modern painting, select pieces of furniture (each with a modernist pedigree) and one entered from a brilliant red anteroom, which journalist Anne Matheson described as "like coming into a lovely snowstorm."[56]

192 *Philip Goad*

If Seidler had orchestrated a seamless internationalism in the chancery, ambassador's apartments and diplomatic apartments, he reserved special interest for the ground-floor lobby and exhibition area. Once inside, visitors were greeted by a sweeping, open space. In Seidler's words:

> The furnishing of the main entrance to the Chancellery, aside from the black granite reception desk and deep pile fawn coloured wool carpet on the wall containing the lift doors, opposite the entrance, consists of a dramatic exhibition of photographs depicting Australian scenery and other subjects. This is seen as the focal point of the Embassy's entrance environment.
>
> It is proposed to impart an instantly recognizable image of 'Australia' to any visitor. The exhibition is felt to be the most convincing way of portraying the essence of the country in preference to any display of art collections, artefacts etc.[57]

The exhibition, conceived by Seidler, was a series of eight very large panels suspended from the Nervi-designed T-beam structure above and floating above the floor and covered on both faces by huge colour photographs by celebrated Sydney photographer David Moore (1927–2003) (see Figure 10.5 and Plate 16). As Seidler stipulated:

> The twenty-five pictures were selected on the criteria that each had to have not only a uniquely Australian story to tell, but each had to be far more than an illustration – it had to have the quality of a work of art.[58]

Figure 10.5 David Moore photography exhibition, ground-floor gallery, Australian Embassy, Paris, 1978. Max Dupain, photographer. David Moore Photography Exhibition, photographs © Lisa Moore; interior photograph, Max Dupain, 1978. © Penelope Seidler. Eric Sierins Photography.

Designed diplomacy: Australian embassies 193

Images of Uluru (Ayers Rock), the Sydney Harbour Bridge, Pitjantjatjara Children at Ernabella in South Australia, a sheep muster at Merna Merna Station in South Australia were just some amongst a graphic and evocative impression of the world's oldest continent. Seidler had created his own space-time construction in the tradition of Van Doesburg and avoided the potentially crass connotations of diplomacy as trade. In front of the hanging exhibition were a shag pile carpet and four Wassily chairs centred on a black granite coffee table where visitors could read Australian newspapers and other publications. Seidler envisaged the exhibition to be easily removable, but for the most part, he wanted it to be on display at all other times[59] – as if a permanent art piece commissioned for the space. Art and a single curatorial voice was Seidler's message for the diplomatic interior.

But Seidler's splendid vision was to be challenged as the opening date for the embassy loomed. Labour Prime Minister Gough Whitlam was controversially dismissed in November 1975, and a new Liberal federal government in Canberra led by Malcolm Fraser immediately began to slash public spending. For the Paris embassy, this meant a cut to the project's $100,000 art budget. In 1976, instead of purchasing new Australian artworks for the embassy interior, Seidler was only permitted to borrow twenty-five works from the Australian National Gallery in Canberra. However by August 1977, only six paintings were permitted to be sent. Further, the Liberal government refused to pay to freight the paintings to Paris for the building's opening. Seidler was appalled and was reported in the Australian press as saying: "It is unthinkable for the building to be opened to the public with empty walls."[60] In the end, he paid $8,000 of his own money to send the paintings to Paris,[61] where he was also forced to personally supervise the reassembly of their frames, re-stretching and hanging.[62] As a personal gesture, Seidler donated artworks to the embassy, namely an aboriginal bark painting, *Kinga, The Legendary Crocodile* by Curley Barrdjungka, member of the Yiritja group, Gunwinggu Tribe, from the Liverpool area at Oenpelli in the Arnhem Land of the Northern Territory (none had been available from the National Collection) and four lithographs of work by Sydney artist John Coburn.[63]

The Australian Embassy in Paris was officially opened to much fanfare on Australia Day, January 26, 1978. A thousand guests looked on as Australia's ambassador to France, David Anderson, and French Foreign Minister Louis de Guiringaud jointly opened the granite-clad structure. While Anderson continued to live in the old ambassador's residence on the rue Lacaze, thirty-two of the staff (many with families) had already moved into the embassy's apartments, and the Australian ambassador to the OECD, Patrick Donovan, and his wife moved into the specially designed ambassador's apartment on the ninth floor. On the building's opening, public reception was overwhelmingly positive though there was acknowledgement that government cuts had compromised Seidler's interior vision for the embassy offices. Journalist Anne Matheson observed that alongside Seidler's carefully chosen modernist furniture from the Knoll catalogue was "much of the shabby, indeed shoddy furniture from the old embassy."[64] Adding insult to injury was the fact that the Donovans had removed much of the modern furniture and replaced it with period furniture and some pieces of their own. Seidler was distressed and made formal complaints to the Department of Foreign Affairs, but to no avail. Despite this, the building and its public interior spaces were considered, publicly and professionally, a triumph.[65] Remarkably, the architect was not at the building's opening – he had not been invited. In retrospect, this must be

194 Philip Goad

seen as one of Australia's lowest points in post-war cultural diplomacy and an insult to one of its most successful and internationally respected architects.

Seidler was to ultimately be vindicated when he organized eminent Australian photographer Max Dupain (1911–92) to document the completed embassy in late May 1978. Dupain's photographs capture Seidler's vision for the embassy unsullied and pure.[66] The furniture, the artworks and the ground-floor exhibition of David Moore photographs are all in place. Further vindication came when former Prime Minister Whitlam was appointed OECD ambassador to Paris in 1980, and he and his wife, Margaret, diligently reset the ambassadorial furniture to Seidler's original layout. Two internationalists, one in politics, the other in architecture – Whitlam and Seidler – at last had their showpiece in place.

A diplomatic coup

Alongside the Paris embassy, Australia constructed new diplomatic mission buildings in Kuala Lumpur (1973–8), Bangkok (1973–8) and then, in the 1980s, in Beijing (1982–92), Riyadh (1985–7) and Tokyo (1986–90), and more recently in Jakarta (2010–14)[67] – all part of a major shift to focus heavily on Asia in regional politics, inward migration and export trade. None of the subsequent buildings, their interiors, furniture and art – while all designed by distinguished Australian architects and respectful of their respective urban contexts – have carried the same aesthetic and political import as the Australian representations in Washington, DC, and Paris. The interior, furniture, furnishings and artworks of the Australian Chancery in Washington, DC, marked the nation's complicity in Cold War politics, signalling diplomacy as a matter of trade, tourism and friendly collaboration between corporate and militarily aligned cousins. By contrast, the Paris embassy was a new phenomenon for Australian diplomacy overseas. It was a statement of independence. Its assured modern aesthetic crossed international boundaries and made alliances with other accomplished works of modern architecture in Paris, namely Breuer's UNESCO Headquarters. It bespoke cultural identity and aesthetic sophistication rather than trade. Seidler's extensive use of furniture from Knoll International in Paris was not obeisance to US-style corporate office interiors but instead, like his conception of the ground-floor photographic exhibition, part of a lifelong and single-minded commitment to achieving fully integrated visual ensembles of architecture, furniture and art. Additionally, in the aid of diplomacy, iconic modernist pieces of furniture designed by acknowledged masters of design were the markers of international taste – they could travel anywhere. If by 1978 this was a dated idea in terms of contemporary aesthetics, it was not in the area of diplomacy. Australia had finally transcended the bonds of empire, placed itself at arm's length from the United States, and aesthetically put itself on equal footing with the rest of Europe – its Paris embassy was an aesthetic diplomatic coup.

Acknowledgements

The advice and assistance provided by Penelope Seidler, Polly Seidler, Peter Hirst, Eric Sierins, Robert Dunster, Robert Riddell, Deborah van der Plaat, Cammie McAtee, Fredie Floré, the National Archives of Australia and the Mitchell Library, State Library of New South Wales in the preparation of this chapter is gratefully acknowledged.

Notes

1 Australia's chancery at Djlman Tharmin 15, Jakarta, Indonesia, completed in 1967, had been under construction since 1962. An Australian Chancery opened in New Delhi, India in 1966.

2 The phrase "all the way with LBJ," famous in Australia, comes from a speech Australian Prime Minister Harold Holt (1908–67) gave in front of US President Lyndon B. Johnson in Washington, DC, in late June 1966.

3 "Australian Architects Chosen for New Embassy Buildings," M/134, September 19, 1973, Parliamentary Transcripts, Commonwealth of Australia. Projects were announced for Saigon, Suva, Singapore, Kuala Lumpur, Bangkok and Paris. While most of Australia's foreign diplomatic facilities are referred to as chanceries, the Paris building project was defined as an embassy because in addition to its function as a chancery (office building), it also housed offices for missions to the OECD and UNESCO, as well as housing for the diplomatic corps.

4 An exception was the Australian High Commissioner's Residence, Chanakyapuri, New Delhi (1955), designed by American architects Joseph Allen Stein and Benjamin Polk.

5 "The Australian Pavilion at the Paris Exhibition," *Art in Australia*, May 15, 1937, 33; G.H. Beiers, "The Australian Exhibit at the New York World's Fair," *Art in Australia*, August 15, 1939, 78.

6 *Australian Home Beautiful* 9, no. 12 (December 1931): 13. See Nanette Carter, ed., *Savage Luxury: Modernist Design in Melbourne 1930–1939* (Bulleen, VIC: Heide Museum of Modern Art, 2007), 62–3.

7 K.R. Devling of William Street, William Bedford Company and D.F. Cowan. See Carter, *Savage Luxury*, 63.

8 See Philip Goad, "Collusions of Modernity: Australian Pavilions in New York and Wellington, 1939," *Fabrications* 10 (August 1999): 22–45.

9 Ann Stephen and Philip Goad, "Good Evening America: Australia's Pavilion Diplomacy," in *Modern Times: The Untold Story of Modernism in Australia*, ed. Ann Stephen, Philip Goad and Andrew McNamara (Carlton, VIC: Miegunyah Press, 2008), 184.

10 Heather Johnson, "Modern Rooms," in *Modern Times*, 22–9.

11 Paul Hogben, "*Architecture and Arts* and the Mediation of American Architecture in Post-war Australia," *Fabrications* 22, no. 1 (2012): 30–57.

12 Philip Goad, "The Architect's Studio, 1948–89: An Interview with Penelope Seidler," in *Modern Times*, 117.

13 The BARWA lounge chair (1945) was designed by Edgar Bartolucci and Jack Waldheim. Initially made of steel, the BARWA lounge was produced in aluminium in mass quantities from 1947.

14 The BKF, Hardoy or Butterfly chair was designed in Argentina in 1938 by Jorge Ferrari-Hardoy, Antonio Bonet and Juan Kurchan.

15 Harry Seidler, "Painting toward Architecture," *Architecture* (October 1949): 119–24. This article, based on Seidler's essay "Aesthetics in Modern Architecture," written when he was at Black Mountain College (1946), also appeared in *Royal Architectural Institute of Canada Journal* (October 1946): 245–9.

16 Henry-Russell Hitchcock, *Painting Toward Architecture: The Miller Company Collection of Abstract Art* (New York: Duell, Sloan and Pearce, 1948).

17 Seidler, "Painting Toward Architecture," 121. See also Peter Blake, *Architecture for the New World: The Work of Harry Seidler* (Cammeray, NSW: Horwitz Australia, 1973), 32 and Harry Seidler, *The Work of Harry Seidler: Work in the Mainstream of Modern Architecture* (Canberra, ACT: Royal Australian Institute of Architects, 1980).

18 In 1992, the Seidlers bought *Space-time construction #3*, which Penelope Seidler subsequently donated in 2010 to the National Gallery of Australia, Canberra. See Accession No.: NGA 2010.14, where the artwork is noted as Seidler's favourite.

19 Penelope Seidler, personal correspondence with the author, September 17, 2014.

20 For a complete account of the Seidler House furniture, see Peter Emmett, *Rose Seidler House, Wahroonga 1945–50: Conservation Plan* (Sydney: Historic Houses Trust of New South Wales, 1989), 56–85.

21 Jane Fiske, "Two Houses from Down Under," *Interiors + Industrial Design* 111, no. 5 (December 1951): 87.

196 Philip Goad

22 Fiske, "Two Houses from Down Under," 87.

23 For example, see Paul Rudolph, "Regionalism in Architecture," *Perspecta* 4 (1957): 12–19.

24 Emmett, *Rose Seidler House, Wahroonga 1945–50*, 95.

25 Kirsty Grant, ed., *Mid-century Modern: Australian Furniture Design* (Melbourne: Council of Trustees of the National Gallery of Victoria, 2014), 14.

26 Harry Seidler, *Houses, Interiors, Projects* (Sydney: Horwitz Publications, 1954).

27 Grant, *Mid-century Modern*, 14. Makeig worked for Seidler from 1949 to 1950. See Blake, *Architecture for the New World*, 262.

28 Mary Jane Seymour, "New Style Chairs Being Made Here," *Australian Home Beautiful* (July 1952): 34.

29 "Controversy of the Chairs," *Australian Home Beautiful* (October 1962): 59.

30 Exhibition panel text, *Hot Modernism: Building Modern Queensland 1945–1975*, State Library of Queensland, July 9–October 12, 2014.

31 Letter, Harry Seidler to Laurie West, dated March 31, 1959. Private collection of Margaret West, Brisbane (exhibited at *Hot Modernism: Building Modern Queensland 1945–1975*).

32 Penny Sparke, "The Mid Twentieth Century Interior (1940–1970)," in *Designing the Modern Interior: From the Victorian to Today*, ed. P. Sparke, A. Massey, T. Keeble and B. Martin (Oxford: Berg, 2009), 154–5.

33 "Architects to Design New Chancery for Washington," *The Canberra Times*, October 3, 1964, 7. Construction was overseen on site by BSM project architect Robert Dunster. The building was completed in 1969.

34 Jane Loeffler, *The Architecture of Diplomacy: Building America's Embassies* (New York: Princeton Architectural Press, 1998), 167–86.

35 *Chancery: Australian Embassy, Washington* (Canberra: Government Printer, 1969), unpaginated.

36 *Chancery: Australian Embassy, Washington*, unpaginated. The blue kangaroo is the female Red Kangaroo and is distinguished by sections of blue-coloured fur.

37 The artists selected included painters Sidney Nolan, Albert Tucker, Charles Blackman, John Perceval and Leonard French and sculptors Inge King, Clifford Last and Arthur Boyd.

38 "Squares in the Round," *Architect* 2, no. 4 (July–August 1968): 2; Robin Boyd and Mark Strizic, *Living in Australia* (Sydney: Pergamon, 1970), 76–7.

39 Design Drawings, Opening Exhibition, Australian Chancery, Washington, DC, n.d., Romberg & Boyd. Grounds Romberg & Boyd Collection, Manuscripts Collection, State Library of Victoria. Courtesy Tony Lee, Robin Boyd Foundation.

40 Personal communication with Robert Dunster and the author, November 26, 2014.

41 Alice Spigelman, *Almost Full Circle: Harry Seidler* (Rose Bay, NSW: Brandl & Schlesinger, 2001), 294.

42 Billy Griffiths, *The China Breakthrough: Whitlam in the Middle Kingdom, 1971* (Clayton, VIC: Monash University Publishing, 2012), 69, 108; Stuart Doran and David Lee, ed., *Australia and Recognition of the People's Republic of China, 1949–1972* (Canberra: Department of Foreign Affairs and Trade, 2002), 827–31.

43 Spigelman, *Almost Full Circle*, 294.

44 Colin Griffiths, principal associate in the Seidler office, recalled that when the government was interviewing architects shortlisted for the Paris embassy, Seidler said he would partner with Breuer's office in Paris and that a member of the selection committee had said, "That sounds like a very good idea." Email communication with Polly Seidler, October 5, 2015.

45 Spigelman, *Almost Full Circle*, 256, 271.

46 The HUD Building (now the Robert C. Weaver Federal Building) most clearly realized John F. Kennedy's 1962 directive 'Guiding Principles for Federal Architecture'. See Judith Helm Robinson, Stephanie S. Foell, Robinson & Associates, Inc., *Growth, Efficiency and Modernism: GSA Buildings of the 1950s, 60s and 70s* (Washington, DC: US General Services Administration, 2003), 42–5, 86–7.

47 Deyan Sudjic, *Australian Embassy Tokyo: Architects Denton Corker Marshall, Blueprint Extra 02* (London: Worldsearch Ltd., 1991): 7.

48 Letter, Harry Seidler to Bruce McKenzie, October 3, 1975. Folder: "Australian Embassy, Paris and Paris Art," MLMSS7078/14, Harry Seidler Collection, Manuscripts Collection, Mitchell Library, Sydney.

Designed diplomacy: Australian embassies   197

49 This is despite mention of Australian eucalypts and other flora being planted in indoor gardens and on patios. See Anne Matheson, "The New Australian Embassy: A Gilt-Edged Investment in Paris," *The Australian Women's Weekly*, May 11, 1977, 4. See also "Descriptive Notes for the Landscape Development, Australian Embassy, Rue Jean Rey, Paris," prepared by Bruce McKenzie & Associates for the Australian Government Overseas Property Bureau, October 1976. Folder: "Australian Embassy, Paris and Paris Art", MLMSS7078/14, Seidler Collection.

50 Report: Australian Embassy, Paris – site visit by Harry Seidler and Peter Hirst, January–February 1976, MLMSS7078/29, Seidler Collection.

51 Letter, Harry Seidler to Claude Engle, dated November 24, 1975. Folder: "Australian Embassy, Paris and Paris Art," MLMSS7078/14, Seidler Collection.

52 Spigelman, *Almost Full Circle*, 302.

53 Elizabeth Murphy, "French Style for an Australian Restaurant," *The Australian Women's Weekly*, January 23, 1980, 6–7.

54 Report, "Interior Design for the Australian Embassy, Paris."

55 Eric Larrabee and Massimo Vignelli, *Knoll Design* (New York: H. N. Abrams, 1981), 168.

56 Anne Matheson, "Brilliant Opening for Our Paris Embassy," *The Australian Women's Weekly*, March 1, 1978, 17.

57 Report, "Interior Design for the Australian Embassy, Paris."

58 Report, "Interior Design for the Australian Embassy, Paris."

59 Report, "Interior Design for the Australian Embassy, Paris."

60 "Paying the Freight for a Paris Opening," *Sydney Morning Herald*, July 30, 1977.

61 "Decoration," *The Canberra Times*, August 2, 1977, 3.

62 The six paintings finally sent were *Heriot Wall* (Syd Ball, 1973) – seventh-floor salon; *Bright Scape* (Gunter Christmann, 1972) – ambassador's dining room; *June 1969* (Gunter Christmann, 1969) – west wall of salon, seventh floor; *Black and White* (David Aspden, 1976) – ambassador's fifth-floor office; *Free form Red* (David Aspden, 1976) – reception hall, seventh floor opposite pivot door; *Veronese* (Michael Johnson, 1974) – inside reception, fifth-floor lobby.

63 The four Coburn lithographs were *Biennale of Sydney '73'*; *Temple '75'*; *Flame Tree '76'*; and *Wasteland '76'*.

64 Matheson, "Brilliant Opening," 17.

65 The embassy was published widely and response was uniformly positive. See, for example, William Marlin, "A Paris Accord," *Architectural Record* (November 1978): 103–12.

66 See Peter Blake, *Harry Seidler, Australian Embassy = Ambassade d'Australie, Paris* (Sydney: Horwitz, 1979).

67 An exception was the Australian Embassy, Berlin (2002), a major refurbishment of an existing building undertaken by Bates Smart (formerly Bates, Smart & McCutcheon).

Index

Note: Page numbers in *italic* indicate figures.

AA *see* Airborne
AAC *see* US State Department Office of
   Foreign Buildings Operations
Aalto, Alvar 57, 143
Abstract Expressionism 161–3, 172, 177n65;
   Cold War tool 155, 163; materiality of 164–6
Académie de la Grande Chaumière (Paris) 53
Adam, Robert 155
Airborne 19, 27, 31n45
Air France 31n47, 31n49; Hôtel N'Gor
   (Dakar, Senegal) 31n46; Hôtel Relais
   (Brazzaville) 24–5, 26, 27, 28, 31n53
Air France residence (Brazzaville) 27, 28,
   31n46
Akihito, Crown Prince (Japan) 126
Albert I (Belgian king): memorial to 62, 65,
   68, 75
Albert I Library *see* Royal Library (Brussels)
Albert I Library Fund 69, 70, 77n11
Albertina Library *see* Royal Library
   (Brussels)
Albini, Franco: chair 104, *plate 6*; desk *103*,
   plate 6
Albinson, Don 98
Alcan (Aluminum Company of Canada) 59
Aldrich, Winthrop W. 156, 169, 172, 173
Aleixo, Pedro *141*
all-over 161, 162–3
Allwood, Rosamond 2
Aluminium française 20
Alvorada (presidential) palace (Brasília) *see*
   Oscar Niemeyer
Amakuni 131n5
American Dependent Houses (Japan)
   122, *123*; impact on Japanese furniture
   industry 122
*American Design for Home and Decorative
   Use see* Museum of Modern Art (New York)
American National Exhibition (Moscow)
   172; *see also* Kitchen Debate

American 'way of life' 7, 20, 83–4, 87, 91,
   95, 170; influence on Japanese furniture
   119, 123–4; *see also* better living
Anderson, David 193
Andrade, Carlos Drummond de 140
Andrade, Mário de 140, 150n5
Andrade, Oswald de 150n14; *Cannibal
   Manifesto* 140
Andrade, Rodrigo Mello Franco de 140
Annenberg, Walter H. and Leonore 173
Arango Design Store (Miami) 41
Architectural Forum 38–9
Architectural Review 163
Architecture and Arts 181
Argan, Giulio Carlo 143
ARKLU 38; furniture: Caribe Hilton
   furniture 38, *plate 2*
Arneson, Stephen 38
Arquitectura 41
Art Deco (style) 48, 49, 60, 70; in Belgium
   70; interpretation in Québec 48–52, *51*, *52*
   54, 57, 60; in Japan 123
Artek 57
Arteluce *see* Sarfetti, Gino
Artesanal Móveis *see* Forma
Artifort 20, *25*, 28, 190; Congo chair
   (Theo Ruth) 30n22
Art Nouveau (style) in Japan 123
Arts and Architecture 181
Asahi 130
Aspden, David: *Black and White* (1976)
   197n62; *Free form Red* (1976) *191*,
   197n62, *plate 15*
Atelier de recherche et de création *see*
   Mobilier national
Ateliers d'Art de Courtrai De Coene Frères
   see Kortrijkse Kunstwerkstede Gebroeders
   De Coene
Aujourd'hui: Art et Architecture: 19, 20, KI
   France advertisements in 107–8, *108*

200 *Index*

Aulenti, Gae 114n1, 114n3; Knoll advertisement in Villa Caldogna 113
Australia House (London): architecture 179; exhibition hall 179–80; materials 179; significance of style 179
Australian ambassador's residence (Paris) 187, 193
Australian Chancery (Washington, DC) (US) 8, 179, 184–7, *185*, *186*; architecture 184, 10n33; artworks in 185–6; as expression of Cold War politics 8, 194; furnishings 184–5; inaugural exhibition 186–7, *186*; materials 184–5, 189, 196n36
Australian Embassy (Bangkok, Thailand) 194, 195n3
Australian Embassy (Beijing, China) 194
Australian Embassy (Berlin, Germany) 197n67
Australian Embassy (Jakarta, Indonesia) 194, 195n1
Australian Embassy (Kuala Lumpur, Malaysia) 194, 195n3
Australian Embassy (New Delhi, India) 195n1
Australian Embassy (Paris, France) 179, 181, 187–94, *189*, *191*, *192*, 195n3, *plate 15*, *plate 16*; ambassador's apartment 187, *191*, *plate 15*; architecture 188; artworks in 193, 194; Australian Information Service offices 188; diplomatic staff apartments 187; furnishings 190–2, 193, 194; inaugural exhibition 192–3, *192*, 194, *plate 16*; interior design 189–90; landscape architecture 190, 10n49; political significance of project 188, 193; program for embassy: missions to the United Nations Organization for Economic Co-operation and Development and UNESCO 187; reception of 193, 197n65; site 188; theatre: exhibition hall 188, *192*, *plate 16*; *see also* Charles Sévigny; Harry Seidler; and individual furniture designers
Australian Embassy (Riyadh, Saudi Arabia) 194
Australian Embassy (Saigon, Vietnam) 195n3
Australian Embassy (Singapore) 195n3
Australian Embassy (Suva, Fiji) 195n3
Australian Embassy (Tokyo, Japan) 194
Australian foreign policy: "Australian made" policy in official foreign buildings 180; and Cold War politics 179, 187, 194; embassy building program 195n3; establishment of Australian-Chinese formal relations 187–8; rise of importance of Asia-Pacific 187, 194; shift away from Great Britain 179, 187; shifts in Australian-US relations 179, 188

Australian High Commissioner's residence (New Delhi, India) 195n4
Australian Home Beautiful 183
Australian Information Service 188
Avery, Tracey 5

Ball, Syd: *Heriot Wall* (1973) 197n62, *plate 15*
Banahan, Hugh (Hubert P.) 184, 186
Banham, Reyner: criticism of US Embassy (London) 158, 161, 167; debate with Philip Johnson 173; first trip to US 173
Banque du Congo belge 24
Banque Lambert (Brussels) 73
Barcelona chair *see* Mies van der Rohe, Ludwig
Barnard Library, Barnard College (New York) 68
Barr, Alfred 96n14
Barrdjungka, Curley: *Kinga, The Legendary Crocodile* 193
Barré, François 114n1
Bartolucci, Edgar and Jack Waldheim: BARWA lounge 181, 195n13
Barton, Hubert 159
BARWA lounge chair *see* Bartolucci, Edgar and Jack Waldheim
Bass, Tom 184
Bassett, Charles (Chuck) 183
Bassett, Florence Knoll *see* Knoll, Florence Schust
Bates, Smart & McCutcheon: 179; AMP Square/St James Building (Melbourne) 183–4; comparison with Skidmore, Owings & Merrill 183; *see also* Australian Chancery (Washington, DC): architecture
Bates Smart: renovation of Australian Embassy (Berlin) 197n67
Batista, Fulgencio 42, 43; corruption under 39, 42, 45n20; reliance on tourism for economic development 39, 42
Baudouin (Belgian king) 62, 63, 74–5
Bauhaus 50, 53, 55, 191; in Japan 123
Baumel, Jacques 98
Bawa, Geoffrey 2
Bedford, Eric 175n13
Bel Geddes, Norman 159
Bellemans, Jacques 67
Bellman, Hans: tripod table distributed by Knoll *103*, *plate 6*
Bement, Alon 84
Berdoy, Pierre 117n53
Bernier, Georges *see* L'Œil
Bernier, Rosamond *see* L'Œil
Bertoia, Harry 5, 20, 71, 98, 183; furniture (Diamond chair series 109, *plate 5*, *plate 9*; model for screen 103; popularity in France 105; wire chairs 5, 20, 58, 104, 105, 111,

115n27, 183, *plate 5*, *plate 9*); inclusion of chairs in *50 Years of American Art* exhibition 5
better living (concept) 83; in Belgium and Belgian Congo 17; in Japan 123
Beucher, Paul 115n16
Bewitched (American television program) 123–4
BKF chair *see* Hardoy, Jorge Ferrari, Antonio Bonet and Juan Kurchan: Butterfly (BKF) chair
Blackman, Charles 196n37
Bloc, André 19, 27, 31n45, 143; *Aujourd'hui: Art et Architecture* 107; *L'Architecture d'Aujourd'hui* 19
Bo Bardi, Lina: Bowl chair 141, *142*; Museum of Modern Art (São Paulo) 145
Boeri, Cini 114n3
Borduas, Paul-Émile: teaching at École du Meuble (Montréal) 50
Bouchet, Léon-Émile 48–9; Art Deco furniture 51
Bourdieu, Pierre 104
Boyd, Arthur 196n37
Boyd, Robin: exhibition design (Australian Chancery [Washington DC] 186–7, *186*; Australian Pavilion, Expo 67 [Montreal] 180, 186, *plate 14*; *The First Two Hundred Years*, Industrial Design Council of Australia exhibition, Australia Square 186)
Brasília (Federal Capital of Brazil): construction of modern capital 135, 138, 140; ideals for 138; impact of coup d'état on architecture and design 135, 143, 147; inauguration of 143, 145; international acceptance as capital 146–7; planning 142–3; presentation of project at Expo 58 145; reception of 143–4; Report of the Pilot Plan 144, 150n8; *see also* individual architects, designers and buildings
Brazil Builds: Architecture New and Old 1652–1942 see Museum of Modern Art (New York)
Brazilian modernism *see* Brazilian Modern Movement
Brazilian modernity 147, 149–50n5, 150n8, 150n14; *see also* individual architects, artists and writers
Brazilian Modern Movement 136, 138, 139–42
Breton, André 140
Breuer, Marcel 181, 182, 188, 190: architecture (UNESCO headquarters [Paris] 73, 188, 194; US Department of Housing and Urban Development [Washington, DC] 188, 10n46; US Embassy [The Hague]

171); associate architect for Australian Embassy (Paris) 188; furniture 55, 98, 180, 190 (Australian copies 180; Cesca chair 99, 112, 190, 191; Laccio coffee table 190, 191; S35 tubular steel armchair 99, 190, *191*, *plate 15*; Wassily chair 99, 112, 190, 191, *192*, *plate 16*); Paris office 188, 10n44; production of furniture by Knoll 114n2, 191
Brown, Eleanor McMillen 106, 116n41
Bruce, David 172–3
Bruce, Evangeline 173
Bruce, Robert 186
Brussels World's Fair (1958) *see* Expo 58, Brussels (1958)
Buchanan, Donald 54
Bulcão, Athos 149n2; contributions to Ministry of Education and Health (Rio de Janeiro) 138; lattice screen, Itamaraty Palace (Brasília) 136, *137*
Bulletin de l'Union des Femmes Coloniales 15, 23
Bunshaft, Gordon 73
Burdekin House Exhibition (Sydney) 181
Burle Marx, Roberto 22, 139, 149n2; Itamaraty Palace (Brasília) gardens 135, 136, 145, *136*, *137*; Ministry of Education and Health (Rio de Janeiro) gardens 139; *Vegetation of the Central Plateau* (tapestry) 145, *146*, *plate 10*
Burns, Peter 181
Butterfly (BKF) chair *see* Hardoy, Jorge Ferrari, Antonio Bonet and Juan Kurchan: Butterfly (BKF) chair
Butterfly stool *see* Yanagi, Sori

Cadwallader, Laura 111; needlepoint work on Saarinen pedestal stools 117n57
Cadwallader, Robert 98, 111, 114n1; Stamford, Connecticut home 111; work for Knoll Associates and Knoll International 111
Café de Flores (Paris) 101
Cafiero, Vincent 76, 114n3; Knoll executive armchair *75*, 76
Caiçaras indigenous craftwork 141
Cairns, Jim 188
Calder, Alexander 170; artwork in Australia Square 183
Calsat, Henri-Jean: Hôtel Relais (Brazzville) 24, 26, 31n53
Camini, Waldo *see* Smithson, Peter
Canadian Association of Industrial Designers 60
Cannibal Manifesto see Andrade, Oswald de
Caribe Hilton (San Juan, Puerto Rico) 33, 34–9, 44; architecture 35–9; furniture

202 Index

(ARKLU 38, *plate 2*; furniture 36, 37–8: Jens Risom guest room furniture 37, 38; Womb chair 36, *plate 2*); importation of furniture from US 33; public-private co-production between Puerto Rican government and Conrad Hilton 34–5; *see also* Toro, Ferrer and Torregrosa

Carlberg, Norman: artwork in Australia Square 183

Carson, Alice M. 96n11

Carvalho, Jorge 145

Castillo, Greg 4, 5, 33, 95

Castro, Fidel 33, 42, *43*

Catherinet, Nathanaele 110

Cavalcanti, Lauro 139

Central Intelligence Agency: US Embassy (London) 156

Ceschiatti, Alfredo: *Duas amigas/Two Girlfriends* (1968) 138

Chair_One *see* Konstantin Grcic

Chaparos Design 114n4

Charles Hayden Memorial Library, Massachusetts Institute of Technology (Cambridge, Massachusetts) 69

Charreau, Pierre: Maison de Verre 101

Chassin *plate 7*

Chen, Huang 188

Chermayeff, Serge: member of *Good Design* selection committee 94; member of jury for *Design for Normal Living Requirements* competition 55

Chiba Prison 122

Choay, Françoise 143, 144

Christmann, Gunter: *Brightscape* (1972), *June 1969* (1969) *191*, 197n62

CIA *see* Central Intelligence Agency

Clarté 30n34

Claudius-Petit, Eugène 98

Coburn, John: *Biennale of Sydney '73'*; *Flame Tree '76'*; *Temple '75'*; and *Wasteland '76'* 193

Cockcroft, Eva 163

Cold War 2, 4–5, 8, 15, 20, 63, 71–2, 83, 91, 95, 138, 152, 155, 156, 158–9, 163–4, 167–8, 170, 179, 187–8, 194

Committee on the Design of Public Works (Puerto Rico) 38

Commonwealth Art Advisory Board (Australia) 185–6

Conduru, Roberto 140

Contour chair *see* Saarinen, Eero: Grasshopper chair

Contour chaise lounge *see* Hébert, Julien

Cooperative Society of Osaka Karaki 128

corrections fairs *see* Japan Ministry of Law and specific fairs

Corrections Fairs (Tokyo) 7, 119, 120, 125–7, *126*, 128–31, *129*

Costa, Lucio 139, 143, 147, 149n2, 150n8; and creation of National Artistic Heritage Service 140; houses by 140; Ministry of Education and Health (Rio de Janeiro) 139; participation in Extraordinary Congress of Art Critics 143; planning of Brasília 142–3, 147, 150n8; Report of the Pilot Plan (Brasília) 144

Cranbrook Academy of Art (Bloomfield Hills, Michigan) 159

cubanidad 41–2

Cuban Revolution 33, 42–3; destruction of casinos and hotels 42, *43*; occupation of Havana Hilton 42; press conference in Copa Room, Havana Riviera 42

Cubex kitchen *see* De Koninck, Louis-Herman

Dallaire, Michel 58

danchi 124

Dargie, William 185–6

Dechert, W. Cornell 111

De Coene *see* Kortrijkse Kunstwerkstede Gebroeders De Coene

De Coene, Adolf 71; *see also* Kortrijkse Kunstwerkstede Gebroeders De Coene

De Koninck, Louis-Herman: Cubex kitchen 19, 24

Delers, Roland 67, 73

Delétang, Maurice 19–20

De Pree, D. J. 87–8; advisor to *An Exhibition For Modern Living* 92; direction of Herman Miller 87; member of *Good Design* selection committee 94; roots and beliefs 87; *see also* Herman Miller Furniture Co.

Descon Laminates: manufacture of unlicensed copies of Eames, Saarinen, and Hardoy chairs 182–3; *see also* Makeig, Peter

Design for Normal Living Requirements competition, National Gallery of Canada (Ottawa) 54

Detroit Institute of Fine Arts: *An Exhibition For Modern Living* 9n4, 91–2, 93, 94–5; advisory committee 91–2; catalog 83, 91; Eames room 92, *93*, 97n32; Herman Miller room 92; Knoll Associates room 9n4, 92

D. F. Cowan (Melbourne) 195n7

d'Harnoncourt, René 93

Diawara, Mantha 32n61

Dior, Christian 5, 105, 106, 107: introduction of *prêt-à-porter* 105; "New Look" 107

Directional Furniture 92

Dirube, Rolando López: *La Religión del Palo* (1957) 41, *plate 3*; large relief, Havana Riviera 46n27

Index 203

D. Meredew Ltd. (Letchworth): manufacture of Knoll furniture 9n9, 177n58; UK distribution of Herman Miller furniture 177n63

Doesburg, Theo van 181, 193; *Space-time construction #3* (1923) 181, 195n18

Domus 56

Donckers, René: Belgian Congo pavilion, Paris World's Fair (1937) 22, 23

Donovan, Patrick 193

Dormer, Richard 106

Drew, Jane *see* Fry, Maxwell and Jane Drew: *Tropical Architecture in the Humid Zone*

Dunbar Furniture Co. 92, 171, *171*, 173; *see also* US Embassy (London); US Embassy (New Delhi); US Embassy (The Hague)

Dupain, Max *189*, *191*, *192*, 194, *plate 15*, *plate 16*

Duplessis, Maurice 47, 53

Durand, Gilbert 147

Dux furniture 20, 28, 31n41; armchairs in Air terminus building (Kinshasa) 24, *25*, 30n22; Kinshasa factory 20, 28, 31n41

Eames, Charles 89–90, 92, 94, 172, 181, 183; advisor to *An Exhibition For Modern Living* 92; furniture (for Herman Miller 89, 172, 181; lounge and ottoman 177n61, 190; moulded plastic chair 172; *Organic Design in Home Furnishings* competition furniture 54; plywood and steel chairs 181, 182; UK production of molded plastic chair 177n63; unlicensed copies of plywood and steel chairs in Australia 183)

Eames, Charles and Ray (Kaiser) 5, 58, 94, 172; exhibition design (Eames room, *An Exhibition For Modern Living* 92, *93*; *Good Design*, Merchandise Mart [Chicago] 94); exhibitions of work (American National Exhibition [Moscow] 172; *An Exhibition For Modern Living* 92, *93*; *50 Years of American Art* 5; furniture 58, 89, 172)

Eames Office: design of Herman Miller showroom, Los Angeles 89–90, *89*

École Boulle (Paris) 48–9, 103; model for École du Meuble (Montréal) 49, *50*; origins 60n2

École de design industriel, Université de Montréal (Montréal) 59

École des Beaux-Arts (Montréal) 48, 53, 57, 58

École des Beaux-Arts (Paris) 106, 174n9

École des Beaux-Arts (Québec City) 48

École des Hautes Études (Montréal) 48

École du Meuble (Montréal) 48–52, 54, 57–8, 59–60; creation and curriculum 48–52, 57–8; decline of 52, 58–9; furniture

produced at 50–1, *51*, *57*; location in Académie Marchand 51–2; museum of traditional French-Canadian furniture 59; relocation, name change and incorporation within a professional college 58; Scandinavian influence on 52, 57, *57*

École Polytechnique (Montréal) 58

École Technique (Montréal) 49

Eero Saarinen & Associates *see* Saarinen, Eero

Eisenhower, Dwight D. 155

Elisabeth (Belgian Queen) 65

Elizabeth II (Queen of UK, Australia, Canada, New Zealand and Head of Commonwealth): visit to Brazil 145–6, *146*

Élysée Palace (Paris): private apartments of Claude and Georges Pompidou 1, 112, *plate 1*; reception rooms and furniture by Pierre Paulin 1, 112, 113

Engle, Claude R. 190

Entenza, John 181

ERCO lighting 190

Espacio 41

Esplanade of Ministries (Brasília) 136, *138*, 143, 144

European Modern Movement 17, 123, 140

European reconstruction program *see* Marshall Plan

Exhibition of National Excellent Furniture (Tokyo) 123

Expo 58, Brussels (1958) 21, 67; *Brazil builds Brasília* 145; glulam pavilions by De Coene 79n34; model house for Belgian Congo "white colonizers," Expo 58 21, *21*

Expo 67, Montréal (1967) 48, 60; Australian Pavilion 180, 186, 187, *plate 14*; and Québec identity 60

Exposition international des arts décoratifs et industriels modernes, Paris (1925) 48, 49, 70; *see also* Art Deco

Exposition Internationale des Arts et des Techniques dans la Vie Moderne 70, 180; *see also* Paris World's Fair (1937)

Extraordinary Congress of Art Critics (São Paulo) 143–4

Fallan, Kjetil 6

FBI *see* Federal Bureau of Investigation

FBO *see* US State Department Office of Foreign Buildings Operations

Featherston, Grant 180; Talking chairs 180, 187, *plate 14*

Federal Bureau of Investigation: in US Embassy (London) 156

Fernandes, Fernanda 144

Ferreira, Angela 28

Ferrer, Miguel 45n10

Figueiredo, Bernardo 142, 151n39

204 *Index*

Firestone Memorial Library, Princeton
  University (Princeton University, New
  Jersey) 69
First World War 139
"First Year of Domestic Electric Appliances"
  (Japan) 132n19
Fiske, Jane 182
Flos 190
Fonds Bibliothèque Albert Ier *see* Albert
  I Library Fund
For Modern Living exhibition; *see* Detroit
  Institute of Art: *An Exhibition For
  Modern Living*
Forma 150–1n20
Foucault, Michel 119
Four Seasons Restaurant (New York) *see*
  Philip Johnson
Fraser, Malcolm 193
Fraser, Murray 153, 175n14
Frechet, André 48, 49
Fredericks, Marshall 170
French, Leonard 196n37
French Revolution: influence on Brazilian
  identity 139
Freson, Robert 110, *110, cover*
Freud, Sigmund 140
Freyre, Gilberto 149–50n5
Fry, Maxwell and Jane Drew: *Tropical
  Architecture in the Humid Zone* (1956)
  15, 17–18, 27, 31n50–1
Fry, Tony 4
Fuchu Prison 124
Fujii, Tomitaro 128; *see also karaki*; Osaka
  Prison
Fuller, R. Buckminster 58

Galérie 54 (Paris) *see* Eric Touchaleaume
Galerie Mai (Paris) 108
Galerie Manteau (Paris) 114n15
Galeries Lafayette (Paris) 49
Galerie Steph Simon (Paris) 30n27, 108
Galerie Zak (Paris) 114n15
Gaulle, Charles and Yvonne de 1
Gauvreau, Jean-Marie 7, 48–53, 56,
  57–8, 59–60; creation of museum of
  traditional French-Canadian furniture
  59; direction of École du Meuble 48–53,
  57–8; early education 48; education at
  École Boulle 48–9; furniture 51, *51*;
  study of French system of furniture
  manufacture and distribution 49;
  teaching at École Technique 49; vision
  for modern design 49–50, 56, 58,
  59–60; writing (*Nos intérieurs de
  demain* 49–50, 60n3)
Gavina SpA 98, 111, 114n2, 191
General Lighting Company: desk and wall
  lamps 181

Ghobert, Jules: winning entry for urban
  layout of Royal Library on the Mont des
  Arts, Brussels 65, 66
Giorgi, Bruno 149n2; *Meteor* (sculpture)
  135, *136*
Girard, Alexander: curator of *An Exhibition
  For Modern Living* 91, *93*; design of *Good
  Design* exhibitions 94; design philosophy
  83; Saarinen pedestal chairs for Miller
  House 117n57; work for Herman Miller
  94
Girard, Marcel 58
Givenchy, Hubert de 107
glamour 107, 109–10
Golden Law of 1888 (Brazil) 136; table on
  which law was signed 136, *137*
Goldman, Jack 176n49
good design (concept) 7, *16*, 83–4, 85–6,
  90–5, 104, *105*; in Canada 54; in Japan
  123–4
Good Design Award (Japan) 120
Good Design exhibition program (1950–5)
  7, 91–5; exhibition designers (Alexander
  Girard 94; Charles and Ray Eames 94; Finn
  Juhl 94; Paul Rudolph 94); philosophy
  behind 83–4, 85–6, 93; selection committee
  94; venues (Merchandise Mart [Chicago]
  94; Museum of Modern Art (New York)
  94); *see also* Edgar Kaufmann, Jr.
Goodwin, Philip 139
Grant, Margot 183–4
Grasshopper chair *see* Saarinen, Eero
Gray, Eileen: apartment on rue Bonaparte,
  Paris 101
Grcic, Konstantin: Chair_One 76
Greenberg, Clement 162
Griffiths, Colin 196n44
Grosvenor Square (Mayfair, London):
  association with US 155; post-war
  reconstruction 155; statue of Franklin
  Delano Roosevelt 155
Gueden, Collette 115n23
Gueft, Olga 99
Guiringaud, Louis de 193
Guys, Raoul 25, 27; furniture and interiors
  (Air France residence [Brazzaville] [with
  Charlotte Perriand and Jean Prouvé] 27,
  28; Cité Universitaire [Antony] [with
  Charlotte Perriand and Jean Prouvé]
  27: Fauteuil confort rotin 25, *26*; Guest
  house in the tropics 25, *26*; Hôtel Relais
  [Brazzaville] 25) *26*

Habans, Patrice 9n1, *plate 1*
Habiter en Belgique et au Congo 16, 30n37
Hannah, Bruce *see* Morrison & Hannah
Hansen, Per H. 4
Hardoy, Jorge Ferrari 115n17

Index 205

Hardoy, Jorge Ferrari, Antonio Bonet and Juan Kurchan 15, 195n14; Butterfly (BKF) chair 15, 19, 20, *21*, 22, *22*, 25, *26*, *90*, 115n17, 181, 182, 195n14; produced by Knoll *90*, 181; unauthorized copying in Australia 182

Harper's Bazaar 107

Harper's Magazine 91

Hauner brothers 150–1n20

Havana (Cuba): postwar economy 34, 39, 40, 42–3; US perceptions of 34, 42; *see also* Knoll International GmbH: subsidiaries

Havana Hilton (Havana): revolutionary headquarters 42

Havana Riviera (Havana) 33, 39–44, *40*, *plate 3*; Copa Room taken over by Fidel Castro 42; locally-produced furniture 40; sculpture by Rolando López Dirube 41, *plate 3*

Healings, A. G. 180

Healings (Melbourne): manufacture of Marcel Breuer and Mart Stam furniture 180

Hébert, Julien 7, 48, 52–60; creation of École de design industriel, Université de Montréal 59; design philosophy 53, 55–6; furniture (Contour chaise longue 55–6, *56*; hammock chair 54–5, *54*; Sun-Lite outdoor furniture 55, *55*); influence of Scandinavian design on 53, 57; perceptions of modern materials 54, 58, 60; president of Canadian Association of Industrial Designers 60; project for Institute of Design 58–9; promotion of industrial design 58–9; studies 53; teaching 57–8; winner of *Design for Normal Living Requirements* competition 54, 54–5

Hébrard, J. and J. Lefebvre: Air France residence (Brazzaville) 27

Held, Marc 114n3

Herbst, René 52

Herman Miller Furniture Co. 2, 5, 7, 9–10n10, 40, 58, 73, 87–90, 92, 94, 95, 115n21, 172, 177n63, 181, 182; exhibitions of products (American National Exhibition [Moscow] 172; *An Exhibition For Modern Living* 92, *93*, 95; *50 Years of American Art* 5, 115n21); design direction 87–90; influence on Australian furniture design 181; international distribution (Belgium 73; Cuba 40; UK 177n63); international licenses to manufacture (Australia 183); showrooms 7: (Grand Rapids 89; Los Angeles 89–90, *89*; Merchandise Mart [Chicago] 87, *88*, 89; New York 87, 89); unlicensed copying in Australia 182;

see also Alexander Girard; D. J. De Pree; Charles and Ray Eames; Finn Juhl; George Nelson

Hida-no-takumi 131n5

Hilton, Conrad: adoption of Caribe Hilton as model 39; Hilton International Hotel chain 24; preference for historical styles 35; and Puerto Rican government 34–5; *see also* Caribe Hilton; Havana Hilton

Hiroshima Prison 122

Hirst, Peter 190, 194

Hitch, John 186

Hitchcock, Henry-Russell 158, 181

Hobsbawm, Eric 140

Hollis, Edward 8–9

Holt, Harold 187, 195n2

Hôtel Aviamar (Kinshasa) 24; *see also* Claude Laurens; Sabena

Hotel Capri (Havana) 43

Hôtel Relais (Brazzaville) 24–5, 31n53, *26*; *see also* Air France; Henri-Jean Calsat; Raoul Guys

Houyoux, Maurice 62, 65–6, 67, 70, 73; architecture: Royal Library (Brussels) 62, *63*, *64*, *65*–6, 67, *68*, *69*, 70, 73, *74*, *75*, *plate 4*

IBM Manufacturing and Training Facility (Rochester, Minnesota) 162, *162*

IBM Thomas J. Watson Research Center (Yorktown Heights, New York) 176n52

IMMOB 190

Industrial Art Institute (Sendai) *see* Kogei Shidosho

Industrial Arts Exhibition (New York) 84

Industrial Design Council of Australia exhibition (Sydney): *The First Two Hundred Years* 186

Industrial Design Division, National Gallery of Canada 54; *see also* Buchanan, Donald

Industrial Design Planning Office Philippe Neerman & co. 79n45

Institut des arts appliqués (Montréal) 58; *see also* École du Meuble

Institut Royale du Patrimoine Artistique (Brussels) 72–3

INT 190

Interiors see Interiors + Industrial Design

Interiors + Industrial Design (New York City journal) 36, 91, 99, 182

International Council of Societies of Industrial Design (Kyoto) 127

International Furniture Fair (Cologne) 190

International Interiors 177n58; *see also* D. Meredew Ltd.; Knoll International GmbH

International Style 35, 64, 72, 76, 100

International Trade Fair (Osaka) 125

Itamaraty Palace (Brasília) 135–8, *136*, 137, *137*, *138*, *141*, 143–9, *146*, *148*,

206 *Index*

plate 10, plate 11; Bahia Room 148, *148*;
installation of historical works in 136,
137, 141, 147–8, *148*, 149, *plate 11*;
Portinari Room 148, *plate 11*; Treaties
Room 136, *137*; visit of Queen Elizabeth II
145–6, *146*; *see also* Oscar Niemeyer;
individual artists and designers
Itamaraty Palace (Rio de Janeiro) 136,
144–5, 147, 149n3; objects transferred to
Brasília 136, *137, plate 11*

jacarandá 136, 140, 141–2, 148; chairs from
Bahia, Itamaraty Palace (Brasília) *141*
Jacobs, Alan 106, 177n55
Jacobsen, Arne 20
Japanese Correctional Association 121
Japanese corrections fairs *see* Japanese
Ministry of Law
Japanese furniture production in prison:
importance to prison economy 121, 122,
125; input of women consumers 124,
126; introduction of handcraft into 125,
127–30, *129*; popularity of products 119,
120, 126, 127, 128; *see also* individual
prisons
Japanese Housing Corporation 131–2n13
Japanese Minister of Economy and Trade:
law to encourage and protect traditional
craft 128
Japanese Ministry of International Trade
and Industry: Act on the Promotion
of Traditional Craft Industries 128–9;
designation of 1973 as the "design year" 127
Japanese Ministry of Law: corrections fairs
119, 125–7, *126, 129*; prizes and purchase
draws 128, 130
Japanese prison industry: competition from
marketplace 125; crafts sustained by
127–30; history 121–4; impact of World
War II 121–4; mass production within
121; prison population 121
Jasinski, Stéphane 73
Jeanneret, Pierre: art trade of furniture 28,
32n61; furniture (Basculant sling chair 141;
Chandigarh 28; Grand confort sofa 141);
see also Le Corbusier; Charlotte Perriand
Jens Risom Design 45n16
Jewell, Edward Alden 84
Johnson, Lyndon Baines 179, 184
Johnson, Michael: *Veronese* (1974) 197n62
Johnson, Philip: architect of Glass House
Estate (New Canaan, Connecticut) 111;
curator and designer of *Machine Art*
exhibition 84, 85, *85*, 94; debate with Reyner
Banham 173; furnishing of Four Seasons
Restaurant (New York) 8, 170; member of
Good Design selection committee 94

Jomantas, Vincent (Vincas) 185, *185*, 186
Jones, Robin 2
Juhl, Finn 94

Kafka, Paul 180: manufacture of Harry
Seidler furniture 181, 182
Kandinsky, Wassily 53
karaki 127–9, *129*; high value of products
128; introduction into prison manufacture
128; origins and development in Osaka
128–9
Karimoku 120, 123
Kaufmann Jr., Edgar 19, 86, 87, 91–4,
106; contributions to *An Exhibition For
Modern Living* catalog 91–2; direction
of the Department of Industrial Design,
Museum of Modern Art (New York) 19;
juror at Parsons School of Design 106;
mission for design and the marketplace
92; Museum of Modern Art exhibitions,
competition, and programs (*Good
Design* 93–5; *Organic Design in Home
Furnishings* 86; *Useful Objects* 85–6)
Kaufmann Sr., Edgar 86
Kenmochi, Isamu 119, 122; American
Dependent Houses commission 122
Khrushchev, Nikita S. *see* Kitchen Debate
Kidder Smith, G. E. 139
KieranTimberlake 152
KI France *see* Knoll International France
King, Inge 196n37
Kissinger, Henry 187–8
KI Stuttgart *see* Knoll International Stuttgart
Kitayama, Shiro 132n15
Kitchen Debate (Moscow) 4, 172
Klee, Paul 53, 103
Klumb, Henry 38
Knoll 1, *3*, 21, 22, 26, 58, 64, 69, 73, 74, 75,
76, 90, 92, 99, *100*, 102, *103*, 108, 110,
181, 190, *191, 192, 193, plates 1, 2, 5–9,
15–16*; exhibitions of products (*American
Design for Home and Decorative Use* 72;
50 Years of American Art 5); globe 2, *3*;
graphics 109; high cost of international
importation 182; and Nordiska Kompaniet
2; recognition of importance of exhibitions
92; training facilities for sale and
marketing of Knoll products 2; unlicensed
copying of products (Australia 182–3; Sri
Lanka 2); US State Department projects
106, 171; *see also* individual designers
Knoll, Florence Schust 2, 98, 183; advisor
to exhibitions (*An Exhibition For
Modern Living* 92; *Good Design* 94);
creation of "Knoll look" 7, 101; design
of Hans Knoll Associates office (New
York) 102–3; design philosophy of 91,

Index 207

92, 183; exhibition designs (Knoll room, *An Exhibition For Modern Living* 9n4, 92); founding of Knoll Planning Unit 90; furniture 98 (bench *plate 6*, table desk 109, *plate 7*); marriage to Hans Knoll 2; retirement from Knoll 111; showroom designs (New York 2, 9n4, 90–1, *90*, 95; Paris 102, *102*, 103); *see also* Knoll Planning Unit

Knoll, Hans: death 2; early work with Jens Risom 45n16; marriage to Florence Schust 2; work with US State Department 71

Knoll Associates, Inc. 71, 92, 182; establishment in New York City 1; factories in East Greenville (Pennsylvania) 1–2; marketing strategies 109; name change to Knoll International 111; offices at 575 Madison Avenue, New York 102; purchase of distribution rights to Hans Wegner furniture 114n2; purchase of Gavina SpA 98, 111, 191; rights to produce (Breuer designs 114n2, 191; Hardoy Butterfly (BKF) chair 19); role of the showroom in market education 7; sale to (Art Metal. Inc. 111; Walter E. Heller 113, 117n61); showrooms 95 (Atlanta 2, 90; Boston 2, 90; Chicago 2, 90; Dallas 2, 90; Detroit 2; Los Angeles 2; Miami 2; New York 2, 90–1, *90*, 181; San Francisco 2; Washington DC 2); use of art and exhibitions in showrooms 103

Knoll au Louvre/Knoll au musée see Musée des Arts Décoratifs (Paris)

Knoll *bureau des études see* Knoll Planning Unit (Paris)

Knoll Design book project 114n8

Knoll International Brussels (Brussels): foreign license held by De Coene 20, 71–2

Knoll International France (Lyon): direction 115n16; showroom 115n16

Knoll International France (Paris) 1, 7, 100–13, 190, 191, 194; concession at Le Printemps 116n33; direction 100, 106–7, 112, 117n61; distribution through France 116n33; exhibitions (*Art 1955* [Rouen] 115–16n29; *Knoll au Louvre/Knoll au Musée* 7, 98–100, *99*, *100*, 111–13, 191; *Sens de l'espace et du couleur* 7, 104–6; *plates 5–6*); marketing strategies and parallels with fashion industry 104, 105–6, 107–11, 112; presence in France and North Africa 116n33; product development (rocking chair by Marc Held 114n3; table by Charles Sévigny 106); showrooms (9, rue du Faubourg Sainte-Honoré 112, 190; 268, boulevard

Saint-Germain 103–4, 190; 13, rue de l'Abbaye 101–3, *102*, *103*, 104; Victor Vasarely mural 104); use of showrooms for exhibitions and book launches 103; *see also* Roger Legrand; Yves Vidal

Knoll International GmbH: beneficiary of European reconstruction 2, 71; creation of European subsidiaries 2, 9n5; name change to Knoll Overseas, Inc. 111; sale of licenses 71; subsidiaries and licensees (Australia 2, 183; Belgian Congo 71; Benelux 2, 71–2; Brazil 2, 141; Canada 2; Cuba 2, 40; Cyprus 2; Finland 2; Germany 2, 101; Guatemala 2; India 2; Iran 2; Italy 2; Mexico 2; Morocco 2; Netherlands 2; Norway 2; Spain 2; Sweden 2; Switzerland 2; UK 2, 9n9, 177n58; Venezuela 2); UK name infringement suit 177n58

Knoll International Limited: incorporation in 1951 9n5

Knoll International Stuttgart 2, 101

"Knoll look" 7, 101, 109, 111

Knoll Planning Unit: display techniques and color palette 90–1, 104; as model for De Coene 72; international offices (London 177n58; New York 72, 90, 95, 102; Paris 79n43, 104, 115n17); showroom design (Atlanta 90; Boston 90; Chicago 90; Dallas 90; New York 90, *90*; Paris 102, *102*, 103); *see also* Charles Niedringhaus; Florence Schust Knoll; Roger Legrand

Knoll textiles 9n5, 98, 104, 112, 113, 170

Knoll World 115n20

Kobe Prison 125

Kofu Prison 124, 125, *125*; manufacture of Western-style dining and living room sets 124, *125*, 127

Kogei Nyusu (Industrial Art News) 122, 123

Kogei Shidosho 122; American Dependent Houses commission *123*

Korab, Balthazar *153*, *154*, *155*, *157*, *158*, *160*, *162*, *165*, *168*, *169–70*, *171*, *plates 12–13*

Kortrijkse Kunstwerkstede Gebroeders De Coene 63, 70; company history 70–2; furniture and interior design (Banque Lambert [Brussels] 73; Belgian embassies and consulates [Bonn, Budapest, Canberra, Copenhagen, The Hague, Lisbon, Moscow, New York, Washington DC] 73; conference desks for UNESCO 73; Institut Royale du Patrimoine Artistique [Brussels] 72–3; Philips chair for Philips headquarters [Eindhoven] 74, *plate 4*; Royal Library [Brussels] 63–4, 70–1, 72, 73–6); purchase of license for manufacture and distribution of Knoll furniture in the Benelux and

208   *Index*

Belgian Congo 71–2; research and design office 72; sequestering of company, wartime activities 70, 76; *see also* Philippe Neerman; Pol Provost; TVR-Contract Jobs
Kosuge 123
Kouwenhoven, John A. 91
KPU *see* Knoll Planning Unit
K. R. Devling (Melbourne) 195n7
Krimper, Schulim 180
Kubitschek, Juscelino 135
Kuramata, Shiro 127
Kuratsukuri no Tori 131n5

La Cambre (Brussels) 72
La Cité 74
La Concha Hotel (San Juan, Puerto Rico) 44
La femme au Congo. Conseils aux partantes 23
Lago, André Aranha Corrêa do 144
Laird, Anita Möller *see* Möller, Anita
La Maison 22
La maison française 107
Lamont Library, Harvard University (Cambridge, Massachusetts) 68, 69, 78n24
Lansky, Meyer 39
L'Architecture d'Aujourd'hui 19, 20, 107
Last, Clifford 196n37
Latour, Bruno 5–6
Laurens, Claude 24; Air terminus building (Kinshasa) 24, *25*; Hôtel Aviamar (Kinshasa) 24; Sabena residential tower (Kinshasa) 24
Lazlo, Paul 89
Leclerc, Albert 58
Le Corbusier 19, 143; architecture: (Ministry of Education and Health Building [Rio de Janeiro] 139; Unité d'Habitation [Marseilles] 105); art in Australian Square 183; furniture 55 (Basculant sling chair 141, 190; Chandigarh [with Pierre Jeanneret] 28, 32n61; Grand confort sofa 141); furniture and art trade 28, 32n61; rue de Sévres office (Paris) 101; *see also* Charlotte Perriand; Pierre Jeanneret
Lees-Maffei, Grace 6
Legrand, Roger 79n43, 103, 104, 115n17; connection to Jorge Ferrari-Hardoy 115n17; design of *Sens de l'espace et de la couleur* 106, *plates 5–6*; work for Knoll Planning Unit (Paris) 104, 79n43, 115n17
Lemesre, Eric 23
Le Monde 112
Leopold II (Belgian king) 62, 65, 75
Leopold III (Belgian king) *see* Royal Question
Le Printemps (Paris): exhibitions: *Sens de l'espace et de la couleur* 7, 104–6,

115n27, 115n28, *plate 5*, *plate 6*; in-house decorating department 115n23; Knoll concession 116n33
l'Equipement de l'Union française exhibition (Paris) 21
Lesage, Jean 58
Librije van Bourgondië see Royal Library (Brussels): collections
Liebaers, Herman 67–70, 73, 76; director of Royal Library (Brussels) 67; influence on architecture and design of Royal Library (Brussels) 67–70, 73, 76; study trips to US 68
Life 20
Lipton, Seymour 170
Loeffler, Jane 5, 152–3, 155, 184
L'Œil: establishment by Georges and Rosamond Bernier 108; KI France advertisements in 109, *plate 7*; "L'Œil du décorateur" 109; York Castle in 109
Loewy, Raymond 5
Loja Oca 141, 142
LOOK 110–11, *110*
Lotz, Peter 114n8
Louchheim, Aline B. 35, 161, 176n33; *see also* Aline B. Saarinen
Lowen, Fred 180
Lundquist, Oliver 159

McAndrew, John 96n11
McCandless, Stanley 169
Machine Art see Museum of Modern Art (New York): exhibitions; Philip Johnson
Mackenzie, Alexander Marshall & Son 179
Mccormick, James 180, *plate 14*
McCutcheon, Osborn 184, 186; *see also* Bates, Smart & McCutcheon
McDonald, Gay 5
McKenzie, Bruce 190
McLaughlin, Donal 159
McMahon, William 179, 187
McMillen, Eleanor *see* Brown, Eleanor McMillen
Maebashi Prison 130
Magis 76
Maison & Jardin 107; KI France advertisements *103*, 107
Makeig, Peter 182; manufacture of unlicensed copies of Knoll and Herman Miller furniture 182–3; see also Descon Laminates
Mallet-Stevens, Robert 52
Malraux, André 143
Manufactures des Gobelins, de Beauvais et de la Savonnerie *see* Mobilier national
Mao Zedong 188
Marshall Fields (Chicago) 33
Marshall Plan 71

Marx, Karl 140
Matheson, Anne 191, 193
Mathsson, Bruno 181
Matta, Roberto 98
Matter, Herbert: advertisements for Knoll 3, 104, 108, 109; display techniques *plate 5*
Meadmore, Clement 180
Melville, Robert 163–4
Menzies, Robert 179, 186
Merchandise Mart (Chicago) 9n4, 87, 93–4; Herman Miller showroom 87, 88; *see also* Good Design *exhibition program*
Metcalf, Keyes 68
Metropolitan Museum of Art (New York) 96n18, 173
Michel, Jacques 112
Michel, Paul-Amaury: Hall d'honneur de la Belgique, Kisangani/Stanleyville Commercial Fair 22, 22
Mies van der Rohe, Ludwig 55, 71, 98, 112, 143, 183; architecture (Seagram Building [New York] 113); furniture 55, 71, 98, 112, 143, 183 (Barcelona chair 99, 141; Barcelona couch 141; Barcelona ottoman 1, 112; Barcelona table 177n58; Brno chair 190, MR chair 112); Knoll acquisition of manufacture and distribution rights to produce furniture 73
Miller Company *see* Tremaine, Burton G.; Tremaine Emily Hall
Ministry of Education and Health (Rio de Janeiro) 136, 138, 139–40
Ministry of Foreign Affairs (Brasília) *see* Itamaraty Palace (Brasília)
Ministry of Justice (Brasília) *see* Oscar Niemeyer
Miranda, Carmen 150n11
Mitsukoshi department store (Tokyo) 123
Mobilier International 115n16
Mobilier national 1; Atelier de recherche et de creation 1; Manufactures des Gobelins, de Beauvais et de la Savonnerie 1
For Modern Living exhibition *see* Detroit Institute of Fine Arts: *An Exhibition for Modern Living*; Girard, Alexander
Moholy–Nagy, Sibyl 143
Mole armchair *see* Rodrigues, Sérgio
Molleman, Marcel 22; Hall d'honneur de la Belgique, Kisangani/Stanleyville Commercial Fair 22, 22
Möller, Anita 177n56
Mondrian, Piet 181
Mont des Arts (Brussels): site of Royal Library 62–3, 63, 65, 66, 67
Moore, David 192, 192, 194, *plate 16*
Morrison, Andrew *see* Morrison & Hannah
Morrison & Hannah 114n3, 190
Morrow, Charles 114n4

Mosan 131n5
Moscoso, Teodoro *see* Puerto Rico Industrial Development Company
Moulin des Corbeaux (Saint-Maurice, Marne): interior design by Charles Sévigny 109; Knoll International events held at 109; stage set for Knoll advertisements 109–10, *plate 9*
Movement for the Improvement of Living 123
M. Singer & Sons Furniture 92
Mumford, Lewis 158, 161, 170, 172, 173
Munsing, Stephen P. 177n65
Murtinho, Wladimir 144–6
Musée des Arts Décoratifs (Paris): *Knoll au Louvre/Knoll au Musée* 98–100, 99, 100, 111–12, 191; designers included in 114n3; presentation of company history and sound environment in 98, 114n4; reception of 99, 112–13
Musée des Beaux-Arts (Rouen): *Art 1955* 115–16n29
Musée des Maîtres et artisans du Québec (Montréal) 59
Musée national d'art moderne (Paris): *50 Years of American Art* 5, 115n21
Museum of Modern Art (New York) 5, 19, 54, 72, 84, 91, 92–4, 106, 139–40, 163, 172, 176n36, 181: design competition (*Organic Design in Home Furnishings* [1940] 54, 86); exhibitions (*Brazil Builds: Architecture New and Old 1652–1942* 139–40; *50 Years of American Art* [1955] 5, 115n21; *Good Design* [1950–5] 7, 91, 92–5; *Machine Art* [1934] 84, 85, 85, 91, 94; *The New American Painting* 163; *Useful Objects* [1938] 85–6, 93, 94); USIS exhibitions 163 (*American Design for Home and Decorative Use* 72)
Museum of Modern Art (São Paulo) 145

Nagoya Prison 122
Nash, John 156
Nassau Chapel (Brussels) 67, 72
National Alliance of Art and Industry (New York) 84
National Artistic Heritage Service (Brazil) 140, 150n18, 150n18
National Capital Development Commission (Canberra) 187
National Congress (Brasília) 135, 136, 143, 144; *see also* Oscar Niemeyer
National Industrial Design Council of Canada: presentation at 1954 Triennale di Milano 56
National Prison Industry Exhibition *see* Japanese Ministry of Law and specific fairs

210 *Index*

Neerman, Philippe 72; agency (Industrial Design Planning Office Philippe Neerman & co 79n45); furniture and interiors (Belgian Royal Library [Brussels] 72, 73, 75, 76; Philips chair 74, *plate 4*; Philips headquarters [Eindhoven] 74); training 72; work for TVR-Contract Jobs (De Coene) 72

Nelson, George: criticism of American furniture industry 88; design direction of Herman Miller Furniture Co. 88, 90; design of Herman Miller room, *An Exhibition For Modern Living* 92; furniture collection for Herman Miller 89; Herman Miller showrooms designed by (Grand Rapids 89; Merchandise Mart [Chicago] 89; New York 89)

Nervi, Pier Luigi 180; Australian Embassy (Paris) 188, 192; Australian Square (Sydney) 186, 188; MLC Tower (Sydney) 188; UNESCO headquarters (Paris) 73

Neutra, Richard 143

Newby, Frank 160

"New Look" as coined by Carmel Snow 101, 107

New Yorker 96n5, 108; Knoll Associates advertisements 108

New York Public Library (New York) 68

New York Times 35, 84, 111, 161, 164

New York World's Fair (1939): Australian Pavilion 180; *Futurama* exhibition 159

Niedringhaus, Charles 102, 116n45

Niemeyer, Oscar 149n2; architecture (Alvorada [Presidential] Palace [Brasília] 138, 141, 156; Itamaraty Palace [Brasília] 8, 135, *136*, *137*, *138*, 141, *141*, 143–4, *146*, *148*, *plate 10*, *plate 11*; Ministry of Justice [Brasília] 144; National Congress [Brasília] 143; Planalto Palace [Brasília] 138, 141, 143; Supreme Court of Justice [Brasília] 143); tapestries and furniture for the Ministry of Education and Health (Rio de Janeiro) 139

Nixon, Richard 4, 172, 188

Noguchi, Isamu 89, *103*, 170

Nolan, Sidney 196n37

Nordiska Kompaniet 2

Noterman, André: model house for Belgian Congo "white colonizers," Expo 58, *21*

Noyes, Eliot: *Organic Design in Home Furnishings* competition 54; *Useful Objects* 96n11; wartime director of the Museum of Modern Art's Department of Industrial Design 86, 87, 94

Nye, Joseph 4, 33; *see also* soft power

oil shocks 4, 127

Okayama Prison: manufacture of steel office furniture 122

Oldenziel, Ruth and Karin Zachmann 4

Ollman, Wallace O. 93

Olympio, José 150n5

Operation Bootstrap *see* Puerto Rico

Organic Design in Home Furnishings competition *see* Museum of Modern Art (New York)

Oro *see* Guys, Raoul

Osaka Prison: *karaki* production 128, *129*; teaching method 128

OSS *see* US Office of Strategic Services

Overall, John 187

Palais de l'Industrie (Brussels) 64

Palmer, Alexandra 5

Paragon chair 19

Paris (city): Académie de la Grande Chaumière 53; design galleries on Left Bank 101; fashion industry 107; Faubourg Saint-Antoine furniture manufacture district 49, 101, 105; French home furnishings market and taste 104, 105; *grands magasins*: Galeries Lafayette 49; Le Bon Marché 49; metal furniture manufacturers 101; *see also* Le Printemps (Paris)

Paris Match 1, 112

Paris World's Fair (1937): Australian Pavilion 180; Belgian Congo pavilion 22, 23

Parizeau, Marcel: architecture: École du Meuble extension (Montréal) 52–3; furniture: coffee table 52, *52*; influence of Robert Mallet-Stevens and René Herbst on 52

Parker Knoll 177n58

Parkin, John B. 55

Partido Popular Democrático (PPD) 34

Parvin, Alvin *see* Parvin-Dohrman Company (Los Angeles)

Parvin-Dohrman Company (Los Angeles) 40

Pas Toe 23

Paulin, Pierre: design of private presidential apartments, Elysée Palace 1, 112; influence of Eero Saarinen on 1, 113

Paulsen, Glen 176n49

Pearson, Max: Knoll furniture 114n3, 183, 190

Pedrosa, Mário 143

Pei, Ieoh Ming 190

Perceval, John 196n37

Perriand, Charlotte 6, 27; furniture and interiors (Air France residence [Brazzaville] [with Jean Prouvé and Raoul Guys] 27; Basculant sling chair [with Le Corbusier and Pierre Jeanneret] 141; Cité Universitaire [Antony] [with Jean Prouvé and Raoul Guys] 27; Basculant sling chair [with Le Corbusier and Pierre Jeanneret] 141;

Index 211

Cité Universitaire [Antony] [with Jean Prouvé and Raoul Guys] 27; Grand confort sofa [with Le Corbusier and Pierre Jeanneret] 141; Maison de Brésil, Cité Universitaire [Paris] [with Jean Prouvé] 27; Maison de Turquie, Cité Universitaire [Paris] [with Jean Prouvé] 27)

Perrigault, Pierre 103

Peter, John 110

Petit, Eugène *see* Claudius-Petit, Eugène

Petit, Fernand: Belgian Congo pavilion, Paris World's Fair (1937) 22, 23

Pevsner, Nikolaus 155

Philips headquarters (Eindhoven) 74; *see also* Neerman, Philippe

Planalto Palace (Brasília) *see* Oscar Niemeyer

Platner, Warren 114n3

Plaza of the Three Powers (Brasília) 143, 144

Plyform chair *see* Eames, Charles

Point Four Program *see* US State Department

Polevitzky, Igor 39

Polevitzky, Johnson & Associates: Havana Riviera hotel 39, *40*, *plate 3*; Miami based office 39

Polk, Benjamin 195n4

Pollock, Charles 114n3; Knoll chairs 183, 185, 190

Pollock, Jackson 162, 163; British reception of 163, 164; London exhibitions (US Embassy 172; ICA 164); works: *Black and White No. 15* 172

Pompidou, Claude: interior decoration of private apartments in Elysée Palace (Paris) 1, 112, 113, *plate 1*

Pompidou, Georges: private apartments in Elysée Palace (Paris) 1, 112, 113, *plate 1*; request for Saarinen dining table and chairs for presidential vacation home, Fort de Brégançon 117n59

Pope, John Russell 155

Portinari, Cândido 150n9; paintings in Itamaraty Palace (Brasília): *Os Gaúchos*; *Os Jangadeiros* 148; tile panels of the Ministry of Education and Health (Rio de Janeiro) 139

Praz, Mario: *La Casa Della Vita* 8, 9

presidential palace (Brasília) *see* Alvorado (Presidential) Palace; Oscar Niemeyer

prêt-à-porter: connections to furniture design 105

Primois, Jacques 99, *plate 8*

Prisona *see* Sachiyo Yoshida

Progressive Architecture 143

Prouvé, Jean 6, 27–8; architecture (*Maison Tropique à Portique* 17, 20, 21; Maison tropique prototypes [Niamey and Brazzaville] 20, 27, 28); art trade 27–8; furniture and interiors (Air France

residence [Brazzaville] [with Charlotte Perriand and Raoul Guys] 27, 28; *Chaise Cafétéria no.300/Cafétéria chair* [1950] 20; Cité Universitaire [Antony] [with Charlotte Perriand and Raoul Guys] 27; *Fauteuil Colonial FC 10* [1949] 20; Maison de Brésil, Cité Universitaire [Paris] [with Charlotte Perriand] 27; Maison de Turquie, Cité Universitaire [Paris] [with Charlotte Perriand] 27)

Provost, Pol 71, 72, 79n33

Puerto Rico: Committee on the Design of Public Works 38; Operation Bootstrap and post-war economic development 34, 35, 39; status as unincorporated territory 33, 44n2; tourism economy 34

Puerto Rico Industrial Development Company (PRIDCO) 35

Québec (province): aluminum industry 58; British, Anglo-Canadian and American influence/pressure 47; *Commission Parent*, educational reform and design 58; French historical legacy 47; French influence on Québec design 49, 50, 51; furniture design education in 7, 48, 49, 53, 58, 59; furniture production in 48, 55, 57, 60; identity shift from French Canadian to Québecois 48; local craftsmanship 48, 49, 59, 60; local wood production 49; *see also* Jean Lesage; Maurice Duplessis

Quiet Revolution 47–8, 58, 60; and *Le Refus Global* 50; and rise of Québec national identity 7, 48

Rae, Christine 114n8; on Knoll's US marketing strategy 117n50; *see also Knoll Design* book project

Rapson, Ralph 181

Rasmussen, Jorgen 114n3

Reader's Digest 20

Reif, Rita 111

Renouf, Alan 187, 188

Retailing 87

Rexroth, Kenneth 163

Revillon frères: joint advertisement with KI France 109, *plate 9*

Rimanque, Charles 72

Risom, Jens 181; furniture: chairs in Caribe Hilton 37, 38; furniture produced under licence in Australia 183; *see also* Jens Risom Design

Robin, Ron 152–3

Roche, Kevin 162, *162*

Rodrigues, Sérgio 142; criticism of Brazil's military dictatorship 147; furniture (Eleh side table/bench *138*; Mole armchair 142; table *plate 10*); *see also* Loja Oca

212   *Index*

Rohde, Gilbert: appointment as design director for Herman Miller 87, 92; criticism of American furniture industry 87, 88; death 88; furniture for Herman Miller 96n17; Herman Miller showrooms (Merchandise Mart [Chicago] 87, *88*; New York 87)

Romberg & Boyd *186*

Roosevelt, Franklin D. 150n11, 155

Roszak, Theodore 164; works (bell tower, MIT Chapel [Cambridge, Massachusetts] 164, *165*; eagle sculpture for US Embassy [London] 152, *153*, 164–5, *166*, *167*, 170; studies for lamps for US Embassy [London] 164, *166*; *Flight* [1959] 176n38; *Golden Hawk* [1961] 176n38; Monument to the *Unknown Political Prisoner* [1952] 176n36; *Night Flight* [1962] 176n38)

Rousseau, Jean-Jacques 140

Royal Library (Brussels) 7, 62, *63*, *64*, *66*, *68*, *69*, *74*, *75*, *plate 4*; collections 62, 64, 68; competition for 65; construction delay 66–7; furnishings (Knoll 70 series chairs; Knoll executive chairs 73, 76); interior design 71, 72, 73, 75, 76; location 62; state-of-the-art technology in 74, *74*; *see also* Albert I (Belgian king)

Royal Question (Belgium) 63, 66

Rudolph, Paul 94

Saarinen, Aline B. 161–2, *162*; press relations for Eero Saarinen & Associates 161; *Proud Possessors* 176n39; *see also* Aline B. Louchheim

Saarinen, Eero 5, 54, 58, 71, 73, 98, 104, *162*; architecture (IBM Manufacturing and Training Facility [Rochester, Minnesota] 162, *162*; IBM Thomas J. Watson Research Center [Yorktown Heights, New York] 176n52; Miller House [Columbus, Indiana] 117n57; MIT Chapel, Massachusetts Institute of Technology [Cambridge, Massachusetts] 164, *165*; TWA Terminal (New York) 113; unrealized project for addition to US Embassy [Helsinki] 154, 157; US Embassy [London] 8, 152–61, *153*, *154*, *157*, *158*, *160*, 163–73, *168*, *171*, *plates 12–13*; US Embassy [Oslo] 154, 157, 160); early work for Norman Bel Geddes 159; furniture (custom furniture for US Embassy [London] 171–2, *173*; Grasshopper chair, Australian copies of 182; Pedestal series chair and table 1, *105*, 109, 110, 111, 112, 113, 159, 172, 190, *cover*, *plate 1*, *plate 8*, *plate 9*); popularity of furniture in France 105; 70 series

chairs 63–4, *64*, 73, *103*, 109, *plate 7*; Womb chair [1946–8] 36, 99, *103*, 104, 109–10, *110*, 141, 181, 182, *plate 2*, *plate 5*, *plate 6*, *plate 9*); marriage to Aline B. Louchheim 161; member of *Good Design* selection committee 94; OSS wartime work 159; psychoanalysis 156

Saarinen, Eliel 159

Sabena: Hôtel Aviamar (Kinshasa) 24

Saint-Jacques, Alphonse 51

Saint-Laurent, Yves 106

St. Peter of the Clerics (Rio de Janeiro): angels reinstalled in Itamaraty Palace (Brasília) 148, *plate 11*

Samuely, Felix J. and Partners 174n2

Sarfetti, Gino: Arteluce lamp *103*, *plate 6*

Sato, Kunio 130

Scandinavian influence: on Australian furniture 181; on Canadian designers 52, 57, *57*

Scarpa, Tobia 114n3

Schulmann, Michael and Théo 115n16

Schultz, Richard 114n3

Second World War 34, 43, 77n9, 97n39, 119, 121, 123

Seidler, Harry 181; architecture (Australia Square [Sydney] 183, 186; Australian Embassy [Paris] 179, 181, 187–94, *189*, *191*, *192*, *plates 16–17*; Harry and Penelope Seidler House [Killara] 190–1; MLC Tower [Sydney] 188; Seidler House [Wahroonga]) 181, 182; Trade Group Offices (Barton, Canberra) 188; Waks House [Northbridge] 182); art collection 193, 195n18; emigration to Australia 181; furniture (bookcase and cabinet, background pieces 181, 182); influence of De Stijl on 181; internationalist views of 182, 192; marriage to Penelope Evatt Seidler 187; studies at GSD, Harvard and Black Mountain College 181; use of art in architecture 181, 183, 193, 194; use of Knoll furniture 181, 182, 183, 190, 191, 193, 194; work for and with Marcel Breuer 181, 188, 190, 196n44; work with Descon Laminates 182–3; writings ("Aesthetics in Modern Architecture" 195n15; *Houses, Interiors, Projects* 182; "Painting Toward Architecture" 181)

Seidler, Penelope Evatt 181, 187

Seikatsu Kaizen Doumei-kai 123; *see also* better living; good design

Sens de l'espace et de la couleur see Le Printemps (Paris)

Sévigny, Charles 100–1, 110; art collection 110, 116n39, *plate 9*; design approach 100–1, 106, 107, 109–10, 111, 112, 113,

117n48; design of Knoll Paris showrooms (9, rue du Faubourg-Saint-Honoré 112; 13, rue de l'Abbaye 102, *103*); early years in Paris 106; friendship with Christian Dior 106; furniture (Knoll adjustable table 106); interior design (apartment of Hubert de Givenchy 107; contributions to Australian Embassy [Paris] 190; Moulin des Corbeaux [Saint Maurice] 109–10, *plate 9*; US embassy residences 106; York Castle [Tangier] 109, 110–11, *110*, *cover*, *plate 8*); life with Yves Vidal 106, 107, 116n39; origins and education at Parsons School of Design 106; use of Knoll furniture 100–1, 107, 109, 111, 112, 113, 117n48; wartime experience 106; work for the US State Department 106, 190
Shepley, Henry R. 78n26, 156
Shimane Prison 132n26
Siegel, Amie: *Provenance* (2013) 32n61
Silva, Artur da Costa e *146*
Silva, Iolanda Barbosa Costa e *146*
Simonis 73
Sir John Soane's Museum (London) 170
Skidmore, Owings & Merrill 183–4; AMP Square/St James Building (Melbourne) 183; Banque Lambert (Brussels) 73
Slater, Norman 55
Smithson, Peter 164
Snelling, Douglas 180
Snow, Carmel 107
Société Générale de Belgique 72
soft power 4, 5, 33–4, 72, 95, 155, 161, 170, 172, 173
So-yo-cho 121
special relationship *see* US-UK relations
Stam, Mart 180
Steelcase (furniture company): swivel lounge chair 185, *185*
Stein, Joseph Allen 195n4
Stephens, William (Bill): Landscape furniture system for Knoll 98, 190
Stone, Edward Durell 46n28; architecture (competition project for US Embassy [London] 157–8, 171; US Embassy [New Delhi] 157–8, 171); *see also* US Embassy (New Delhi)
Strachan, Harold 183
Strub, Henri 59
Sun-Lite *see* Sigmund Werner
Superflex 28
Supreme Court of Justice (Brasília) *see* Oscar Niemeyer

Tafuri, Manfredo 147, 149
Takahama, Kazuhide 98
Taliesin Fellowship 38

Talking chairs *see* Grant Featherston
Tendo Mokko 119–20, *120*, 122; *see also* Sori Yanagi
Tenreiro, Joaquim 140, 141–2
"Three Sacred Treasures" of modern Japanese home 132n19
Tippett, Bruce 114n3
Toro, Ferrer and Torregrosa: Caribe Hilton (San Juan) 35, 37, *plate 2*
Toro, Osvaldo 45n10
Toro-Ferrer: La Concha Hotel (San Juan) 44
Torregrosa, Luis 45n10
Touchaleaume, Eric 27–8
Toyoguchi, Kappei 122
Tremaine, Burton G. 181
Tremaine, Emily Hall 181
Triennale di Milano (1954) 56
Tripolina chair 19
tropical modernism (concept of) 6, 17, 27, 36–9
Truex, Van Day 106
Tsuzuki, Kyoichi 131
Tucker, Albert 196n37
TVR-Contract Jobs: influence of Knoll Planning Unit on 72; takeover by Société Générale de Belgique 72; *see also* Kortrijkse Kunstwerkstede Gebroeders De Coene: interiors; Royal Library (Brussels): interior design

Uchida, Shigeru 119, 131n2
UFC *see Union des Femmes Coloniales*
UK Chancery (Washington, DC) 156
Umeda, Masanori 127
UNESCO headquarters (Paris) 80n49, 188, 194; furnishings: conference desks by De Coene 73; *see also* Marcel Breuer
Unimark International *plate 8*
Union des Femmes Coloniales (UFC) 23
Union of Life Improvement *see* Seikatsu Kaizen Doumei-kai
United Nations (New York) 105; library 68
United Nations Asian Conference (Tokyo) 125
United Nations San Francisco Conference 159
Uren, Tom 188
US-Cuban relations 33, 34, 39, 40, 42, 44, 46n24
Useful Objects (1938) *see* Edgar Kaufmann Jr.; Museum of Modern Art (New York): exhibitions
US Embassy (Brussels) 177n55
US Embassy (Helsinki) *see* Eero Saarinen: architecture

214 *Index*

US Embassy (London): architecture 152–5, 156–8, 159–61, 163–6; art collection (portraits 173); competition for 155–8; decommissioning and redevelopment of 152; departments (consular services 156–7, 167, 169, 171; employee and ambassador's dining room 172; lobby *154*, 169, 170; USIS auditorium *168*, 169; USIS exhibition space 156, 169, 172; USIS library 156, *168*, 169, 170, 172; visa and passport services 156, 167, 170, 173, *plates 12–13*); engineer of 160; English Heritage designation of 152, 167; exhibitions (inaugural exhibition 172; *Jasper Johns Lithographs* 177–8n65; *Rauschenberg: Illustrations for Dante's Inferno* 177–8n65; *Vanguard American Painting* 177–8n65); furnishing (Dunbar Furniture Co. 171, *171*, 173; Eero Saarinen *168*, 171–2, 173, *plates 12–13*; Herman Miller 172); Great Seal 157, 169, 170; interior architecture 167–70; materials of *154*, 155, 157, 160, 161; planning 159–60; reception of 152, 158, 161, 167, 170, 172–3; response to Georgian architecture 157; urban planning 154–6; use of art in 152, 162–6, 170; *see also* Abstract Expressionism; individual ambassadors; Theodore Roszak; Winfield House
US Embassy (London): new embassy Nine Elms, South Bank: 152
US Embassy (New Delhi) 157–8, 171; Dunbar furniture 171
US Embassy (Oslo) 154, 157, 160
US Embassy (The Hague) 171; Dunbar furniture 171
USIA *see* US Information Agency
US Information Agency: exhibitions (*American Design for Home and Decorative Use* 72; *American National Exhibition* [Moscow] 172; *Salute to France* 115n21); *see also* Museum of Modern Art (New York): USIS exhibitions
US Information Service 169, 176n43, 176n44; libraries, exhibition spaces, information centers 156, 170, 176n49, 177n65
USIS *see* US Information Service
US Occupation Army (Japan): furniture commissions for American Dependent Houses 122; influence on furniture styles 119
US Office of Strategic Services 156, 159; *see also* Donal McLaughlin; Eero Saarinen: OSS wartime service; Oliver Lundquist
US-Puerto Rican relations 33, 34–5, 44
USSR Embassy (London): Kensington Palace Gardens 156; espionage activities connected to 156

USSR Embassy (New Delhi) 156
US State Department 71, 101, 106, 152, 153, 158, 159, 161, 163, 171, 190; cultural propaganda efforts 104, 163, 170; "Good Neighbor" policy 150n11; Latin American foreign policy 150n1; Point Four Program for economic aid to developing countries 35
US State Department Office of Foreign Buildings Operations 71, 190; appointment of architects 155, 157; Architectural Advisory Committee 153, 157, 158, 160, 175n23; architectural policy of 156, 165; interior design department 116n41, 171, 172; shift to "buy American" policy 171
US-UK relations: Special relationship 152–3, 155–6

Vacherot Park (Brussels) 67
Valentim, Rubem 138, 149n2
Vanden Berghe, Anatole 20
Vanderheyden, Jan Frans 62
Van Doosselaere, Jean: model house for Belgian Congo "white colonizers," Expo 58 *21*
Van Hoof, Guido 67
Van Nueten, Charles 15, 17, 23
Vargas, Getúlio 139, 140, 150n18
Vasarely, Victor 183; carpet in Pompidou apartments, Élysée Palace *plate 1*; mural in KI France showroom 104
Venice Biennale 28
Viau, Guy 57, *57*
Vidal, Yves 98, 100–1, *110*; art collection 109–10, 116n39, *plate 9*; connections to the fashion world 106; direction of and early work for KI France 98, 100–1, 103, 104, 105, 106–11, 112, 113, 190; dismissal as director of KI France 112; early experience 106; homes (Moulin des Corbeaux and York Castle) 109–11; life with Charles Sévigny 106, 107; origins and education 106
Vieira, Mary 149n4; *Ponto de encontro/ Meeting Point* (sculpture) 136, *137*
Vietnam War 179, 188
Vignelli, Lella 98, *99*, *100*, 111–12, 113, 191; *see also* Musée des Arts Décoratifs: *Knoll au Louvre/Knoll au Musée*
Vignelli, Massimo 98, *99*, *100*, 111–12, 113, 114n8, 191; and "Knoll look" 113; *see also Knoll Design* book project; Musée des Arts Décoratifs: *Knoll au Louvre/Knoll au Musée*
Vignelli Associates 98, *99*, *100*, 111–12, 113
Villa Caldogna (Italy) 113
Volpi, Alfredo 138, 149n2
Voorhees, Walker, Foley & Smith 78n26

Index 215

Wabbes, Jules 171, 177n56
Wadsworth Atheneum (Hartford, Connecticut): exhibition: *Painting Toward Architecture* 181
Waldheim, Jack and Bartolucci, Edgar: BARWA lounge chair 181, 195n13
Walker, Ralph 153; *see also* Voorhees, Walker, Foley & Smith
Walt Disney Studios 150n11
Ward, Fred 180
Ward, Susan 2
Wegner, Hans 98, 181; Knoll acquisition of distribution rights 114n2
Werner, Sigmund 55; Sun-Lite, aluminum furniture company (Montréal) 54, 55, 55, 56
Wery Brothers 23
West, Laurie 183; *see also* West's Furniture Showroom (Brisbane)
West's Furniture Showroom (Brisbane) 183
White, Kenneth B. 101, 117n61
Whitlam, Gough 187–8, 193, 194
Whitlam, Margaret 194
Widdicomb Furniture Company 92
William Bedford Company (Melbourne) 195n7
William Latchford & Sons (Melbourne): Australian license to manufacture Knoll International and Herman Miller furniture 183

Winfield House, US Ambassador's Residence (London) 173
Wolfe, Elsie de 106
Womb chair *see* Eero Saarinen: furniture
World's Fair, Brussels, 1958 *see* Expo 58, Brussels (1958)
World War I *see* First World War
World War II *see* Second World War
Wormley, Edward J. 171; *see also* Dunbar Furniture Co.
Wright, Russel 182
Wurman, Richard Saul *see* *Knoll Design* book project

Yanagi, Sori 120, 127; Butterfly stool 119–20, *120*
York Castle (Tangier) 109–11, *110*, *cover*, *plate 8*; architectural renovation 109; *L'Œil* feature 117n53; *LOOK* feature 110–11, *110*; stage set for Knoll advertisements 109–11; *see also* Charles Sévigny: interior design
Yorke, Rosenberg and Mardall 174n2
Yoshida, Sachiyo 130

Zadkine, Ossip 53
Zalszupin, Jorge 142
Zapf, Otto: Knoll office chairs 190
Zehrfuss, Bernard 73
Zevi, Bruno 143